D•N•ANGEL

BY YUKIRU SUGISAKI

VOLUME 4

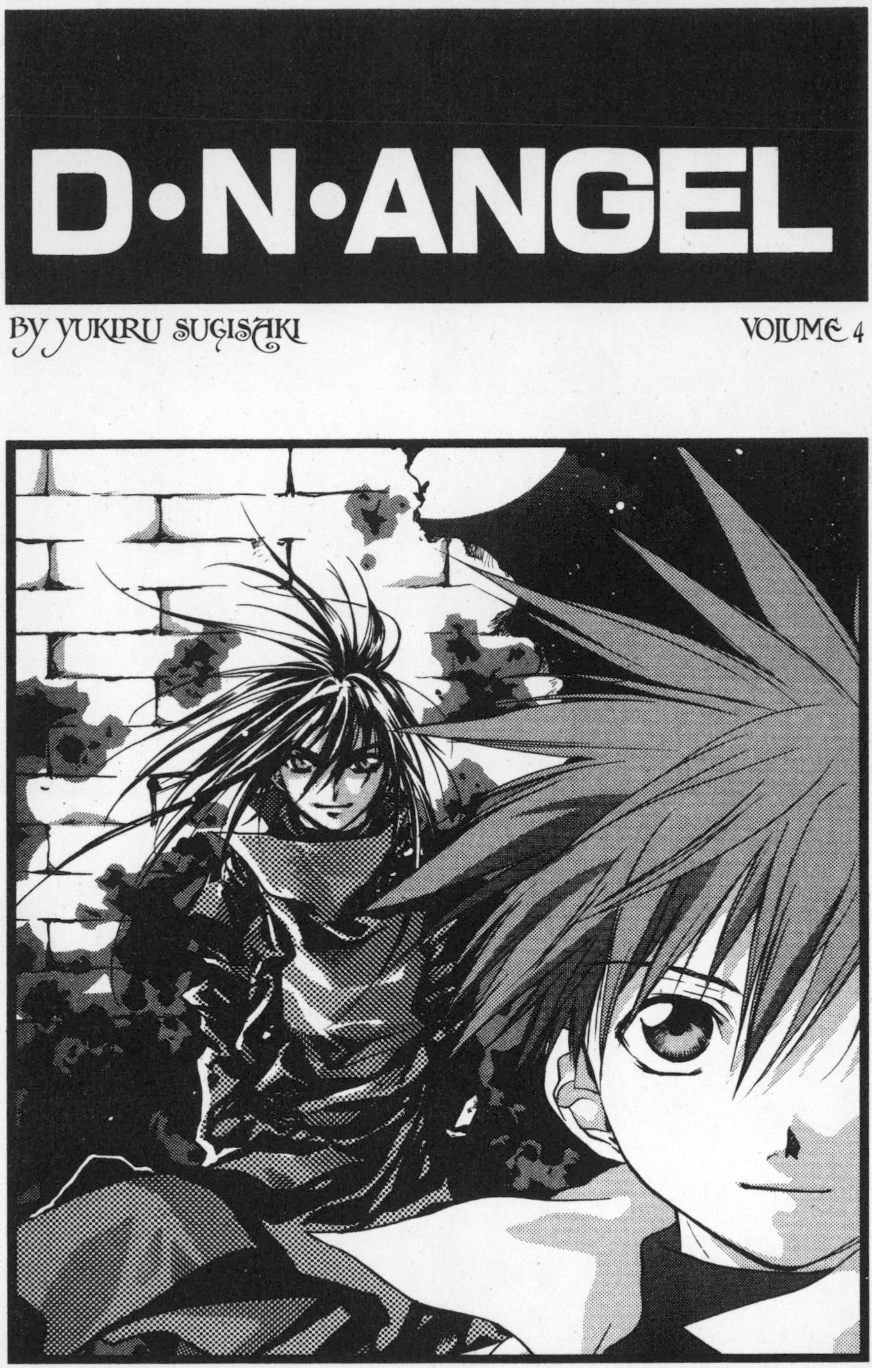

CHARACTERS & STORY

WHENEVER DAISUKE NIWA HAS STRONG ROMANTIC FEELINGS, HIS DNA CAUSES HIM TO TRANSFORM INTO THE LEGENDARY PHANTOM THIEF DARK. THE FIRST GIRL HE LIKED, RISA HARADA, REJECTED HIM. BUT HE THEN BEGAN TO LIKE HER OLDER SISTER RIKU ...AND WHEN HE CONFESSED HIS FEELINGS TO RIKU, SHE RESPONDED. DAISUKE THOUGHT THAT GETTING THE GIRL HE LOVED TO LOVE HIM BACK WOULD CURE HIS CONDITION, BUT DARK CONTINUES TO APPEAR. AND TO COMPLICATE THINGS FURTHER, A MYSTERY IS DEEPENING ABOUT THE CONNECTION BETWEEN THE HIKARU AND NIWA FAMILIES...

WIZ

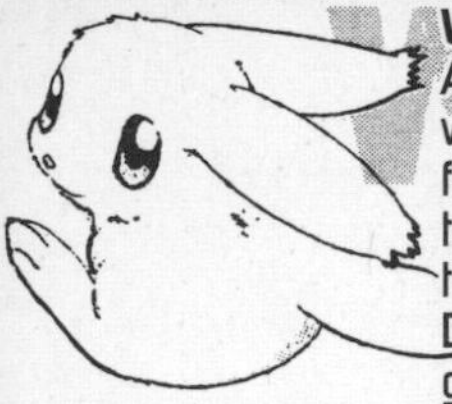

Wiz
A mysterious animal who acts as Dark's familiar and who can transform into many things. He's been with Daisuke's family for generations.
And he hates water.

DAISUKE NIWA

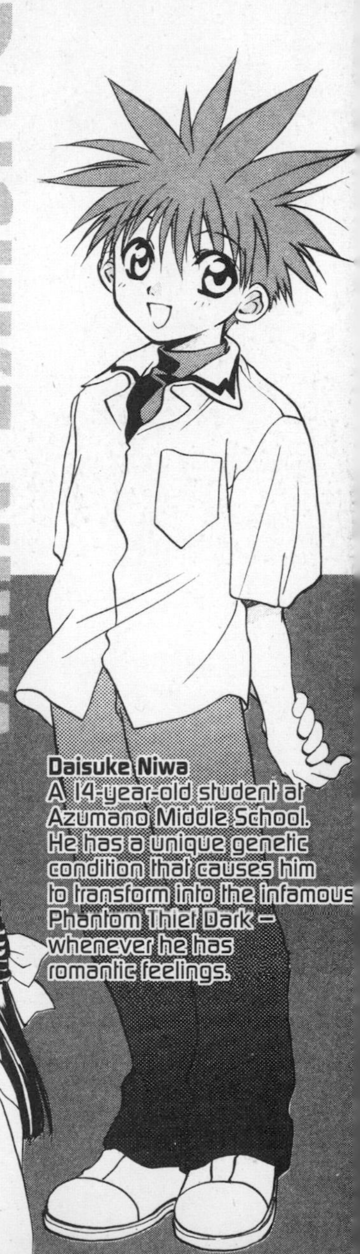

Daisuke Niwa
A 14-year-old student at Azumano Middle School. He has a unique genetic condition that causes him to transform into the infamous Phantom Thief Dark – whenever he has romantic feelings.

RISA HARADA

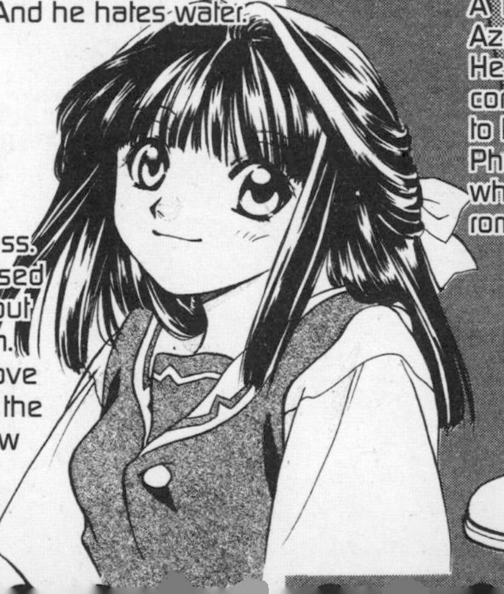

Risa Harada
In Daisuke's class. Daisuke confessed his love to her but she rejected him. She's been in love with Dark since the first time she saw him on TV.

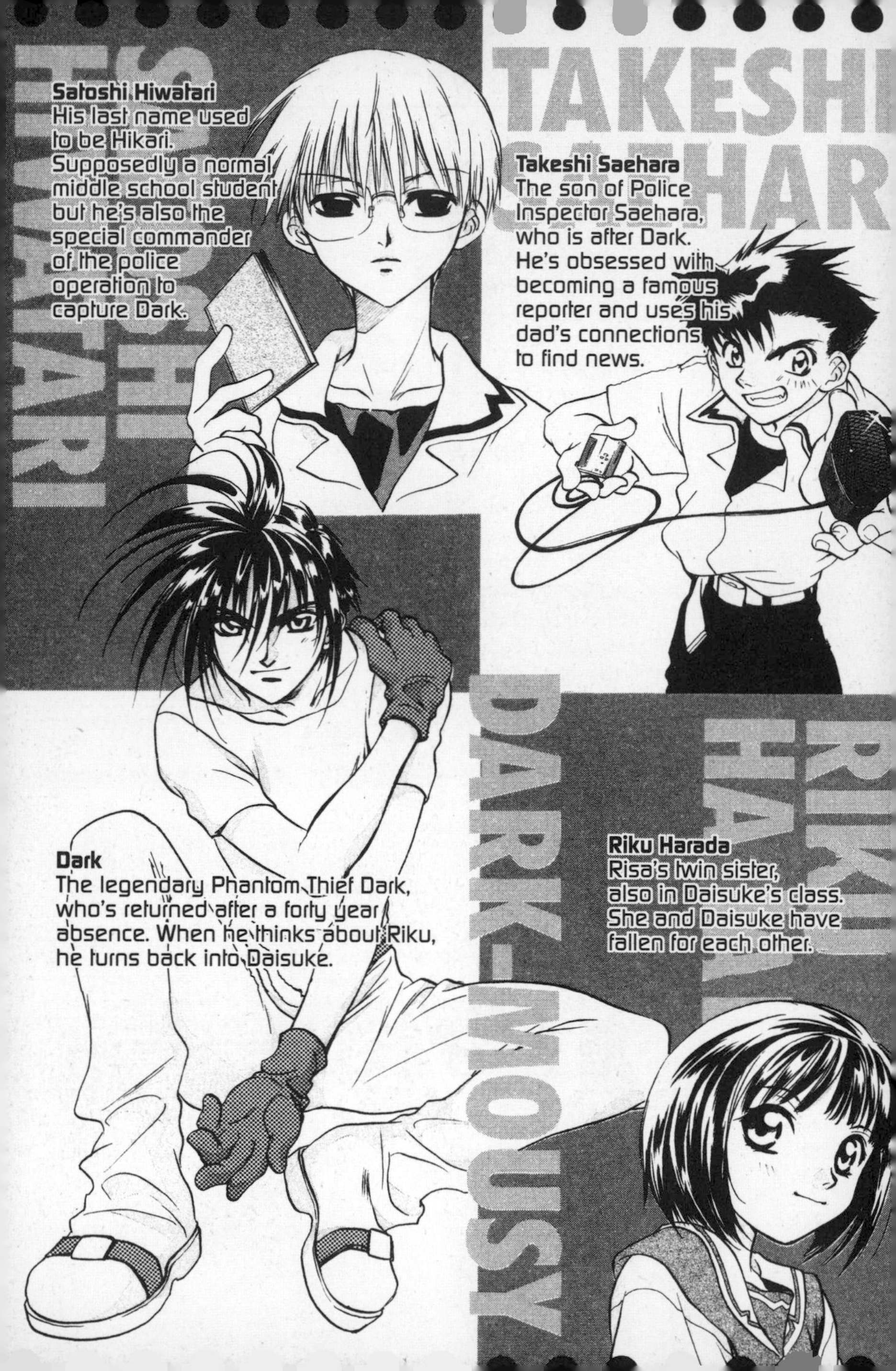
Takeshi Saehara
The son of Police Inspector Saehara, who is after Dark. He's obsessed with becoming a famous reporter and uses his dad's connections to find news.
Satoshi Hiwatari
His last name used to be Hikari. Supposedly a normal middle school student but he's also the special commander of the police operation to capture Dark.
Riku Harada
Risa's twin sister, also in Daisuke's class. She and Daisuke have fallen for each other.
Dark
The legendary Phantom Thief Dark, who's returned after a forty year absence. When he thinks about Riku, he turns back into Daisuke.

D•N•ANGEL Vol. 4
Created by Yukiru Sugisaki

Translation - Alethea Nibley
English Adaptation - Sarah Dyer
Copy Editors - Troy Lewter, Hope Donovan
Retouch and Lettering - Paul Tanck
Production Artist - Yoohae Yang
Cover Layout - Gary Shum

Editor - Bryce P. Coleman
Digital Imaging Manager - Chris Buford
Pre-Press Manager - Antonio DePietro
Production Managers - Jennifer Miller and Mutsumi Miyazaki
Art Director - Matt Alford
Managing Editor - Jill Freshney
VP of Production - Ron Klamert
President and C.O.O. - John Parker
Publisher and C.E.O. - Stuart Levy

A  Manga

TOKYOPOP Inc.
5900 Wilshire Blvd. Suite 2000
Los Angeles, CA 90036

E-mail: info@TOKYOPOP.com
Come visit us online at www.TOKYOPOP.com

ISBN: 1-59182-802-3

First TOKYOPOP printing: October 2004
10 9 8 7
Printed in the USA

D•N•ANGEL

Volume 4

By

Yukiru Sugisaki

TOKYOPOP

HAMBURG // LONDON // LOS ANGELES // TOKYO

CONTENTS

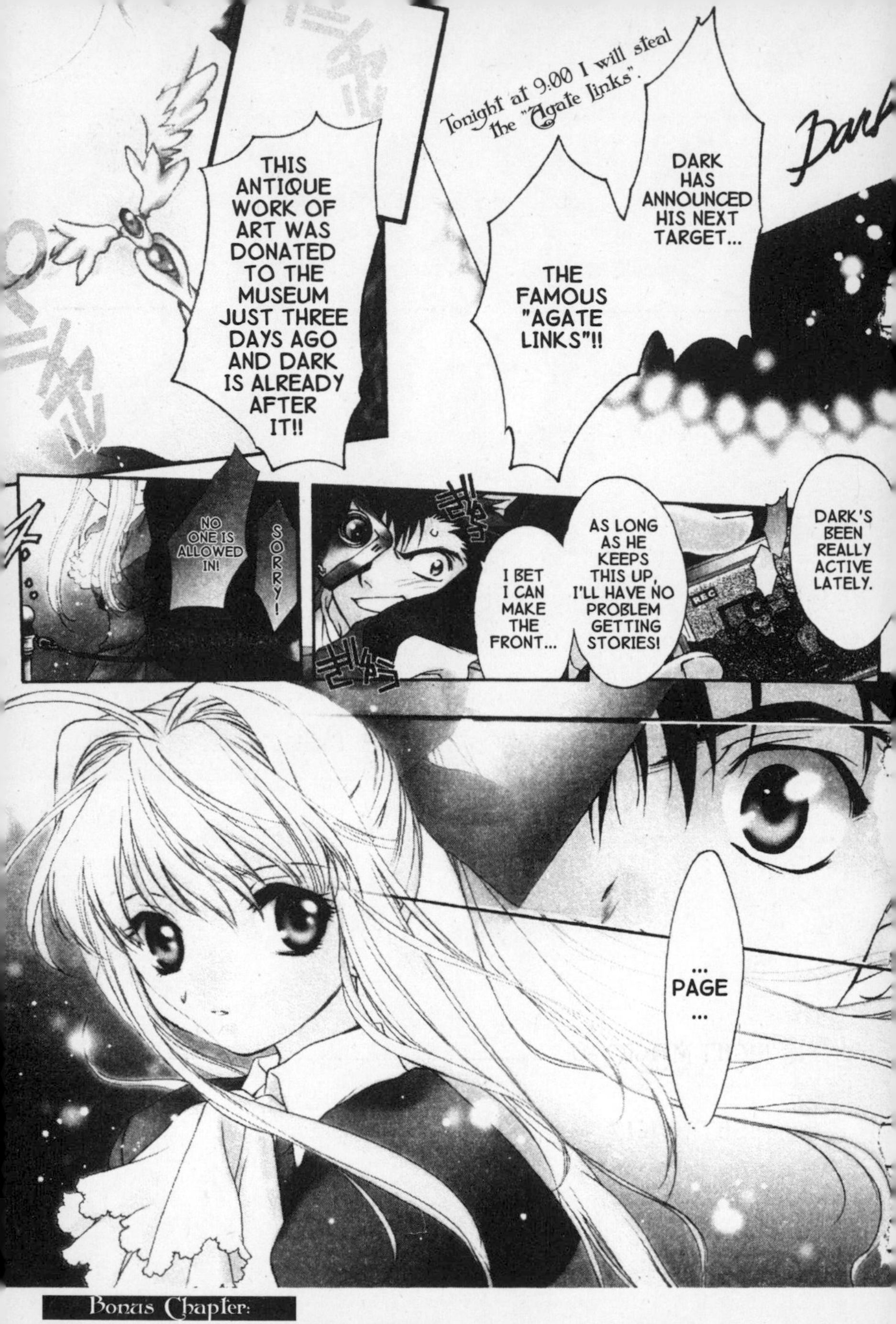
Dark
Tonight at 9:00 I will steal the "Agate Links".
DARK HAS ANNOUNCED HIS NEXT TARGET...
THE FAMOUS "AGATE LINKS"!!
THIS ANTIQUE WORK OF ART WAS DONATED TO THE MUSEUM JUST THREE DAYS AGO AND DARK IS ALREADY AFTER IT!!
REC
DARK'S BEEN REALLY ACTIVE LATELY.
AS LONG AS HE KEEPS THIS UP, I'LL HAVE NO PROBLEM GETTING STORIES!
I BET I CAN MAKE THE FRONT...
SORRY!
NO ONE IS ALLOWED IN!
... PAGE ...

Bonus Chapter:
WARNING ABOUT GLASS (AND MENOU)

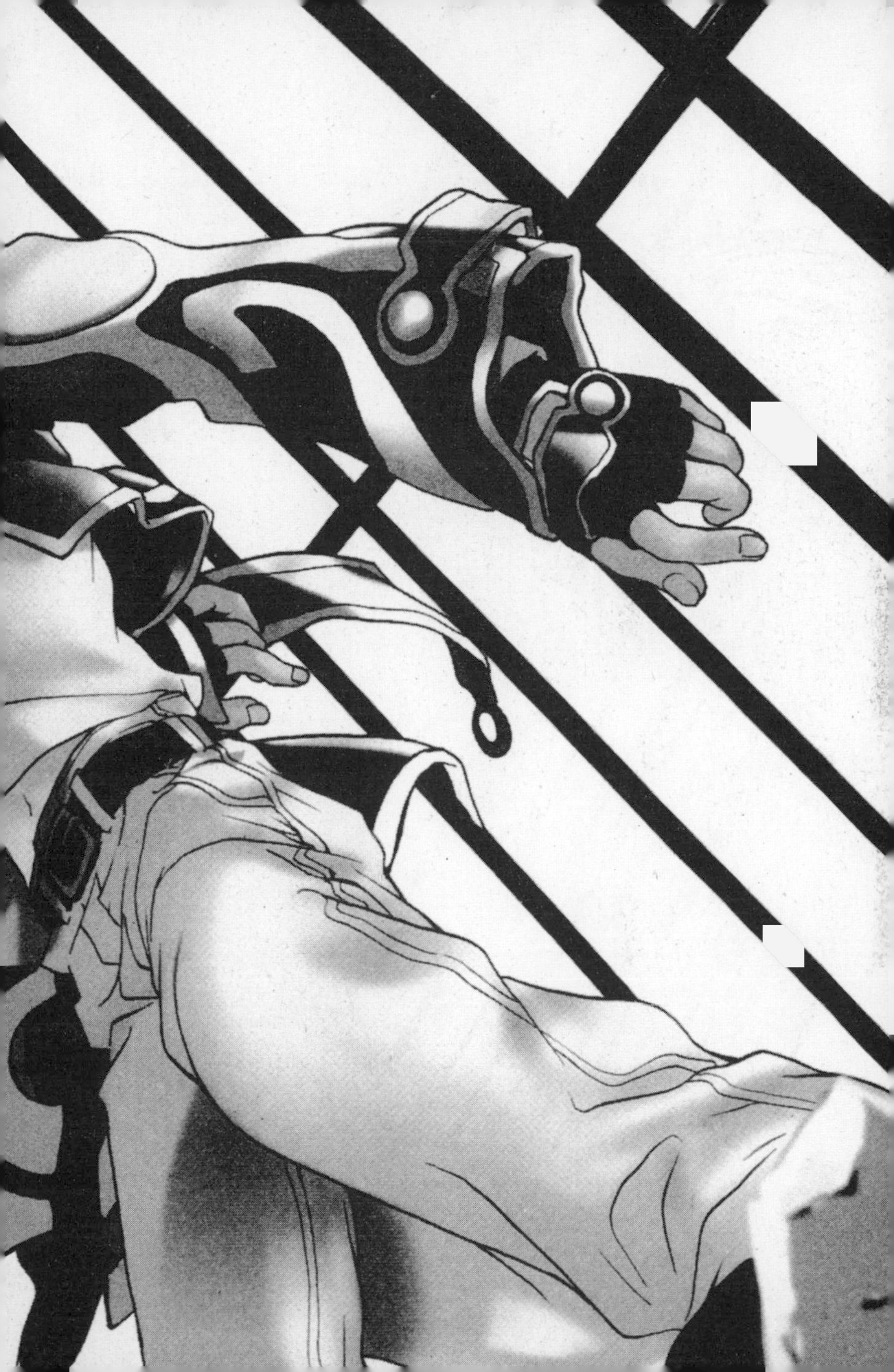

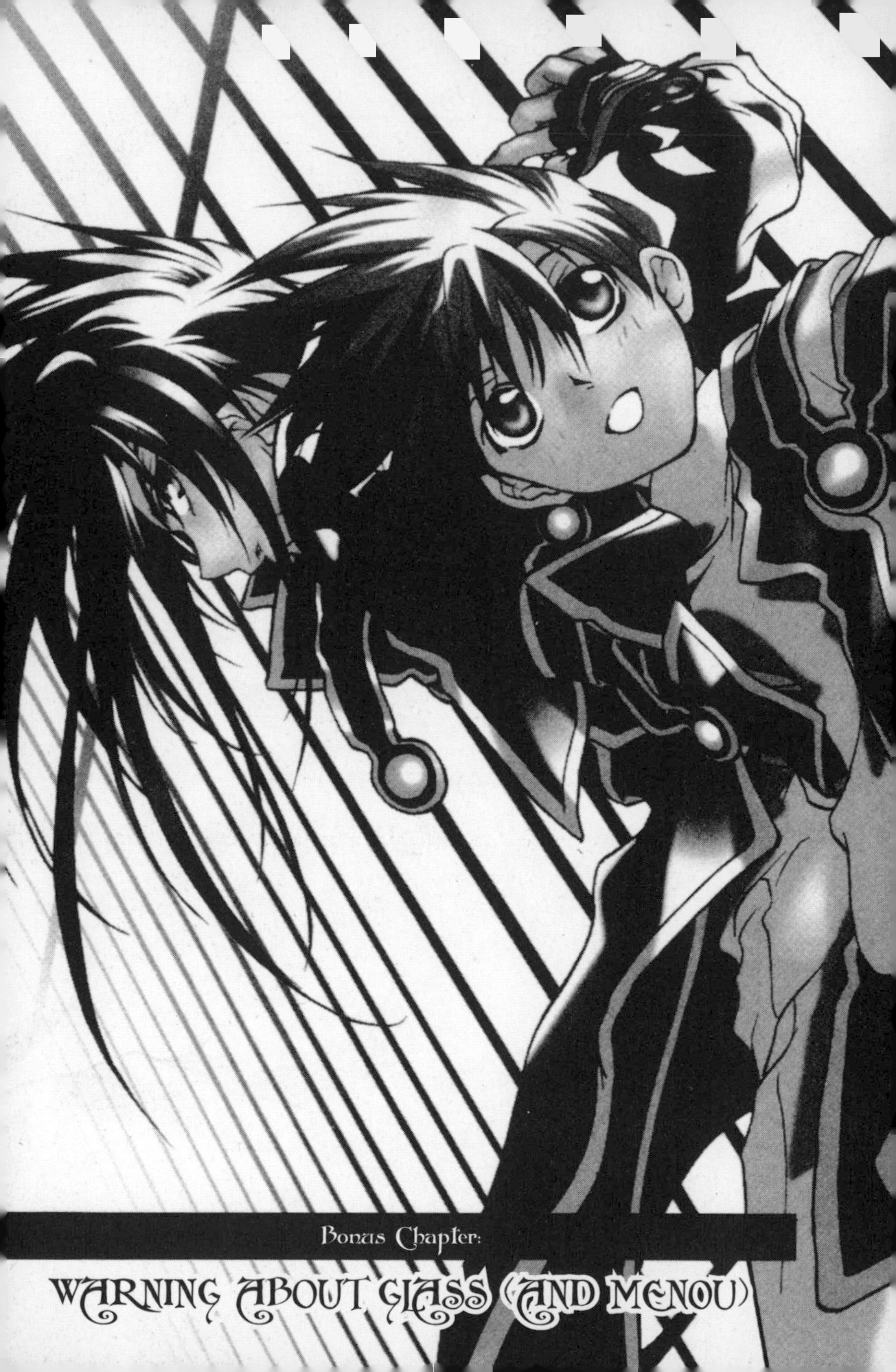

Bonus Chapter:

WARNING ABOUT GLASS (AND MENOU)

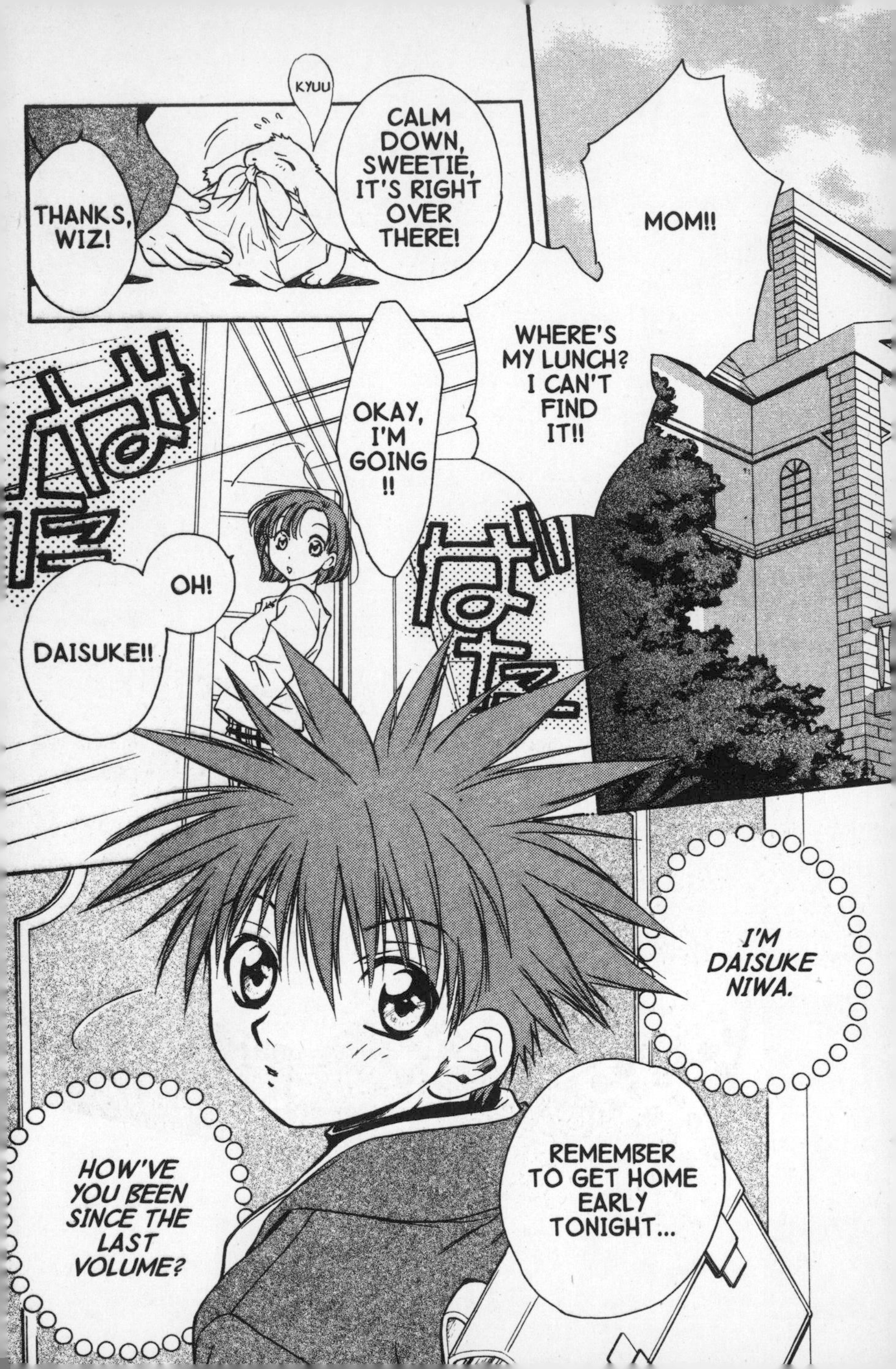
MOM!!
WHERE'S MY LUNCH? I CAN'T FIND IT!!
CALM DOWN, SWEETIE, IT'S RIGHT OVER THERE!
KYUU
THANKS, WIZ!
OKAY, I'M GOING!!
OH!
DAISUKE!!
I'M DAISUKE NIWA.
REMEMBER TO GET HOME EARLY TONIGHT...
HOW'VE YOU BEEN SINCE THE LAST VOLUME?

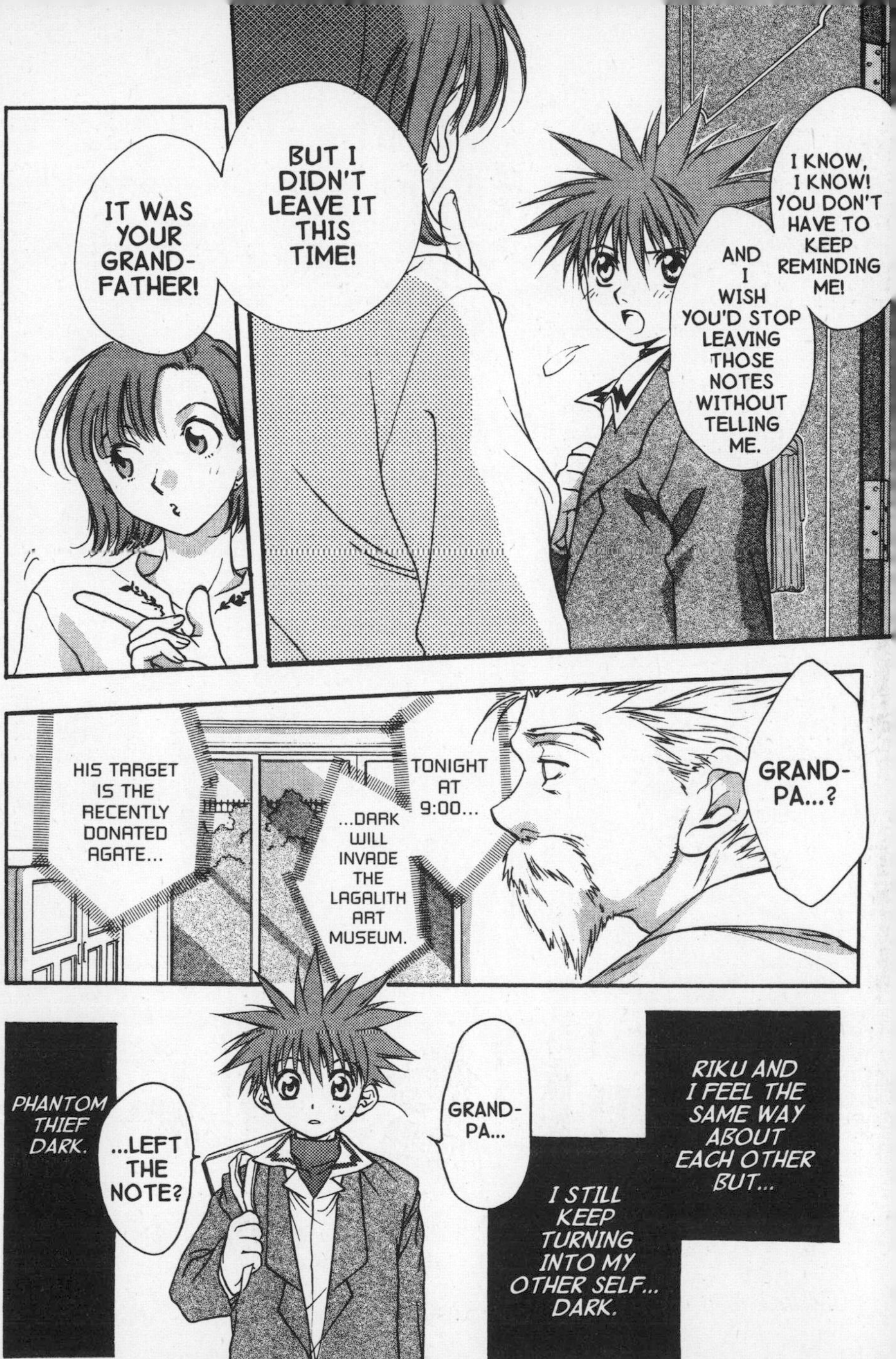
I KNOW, I KNOW! YOU DON'T HAVE TO KEEP REMINDING ME!
AND I WISH YOU'D STOP LEAVING THOSE NOTES WITHOUT TELLING ME.
BUT I DIDN'T LEAVE IT THIS TIME!
IT WAS YOUR GRAND-FATHER!
GRAND-PA...?
TONIGHT AT 9:00...
...DARK WILL INVADE THE LAGALITH ART MUSEUM.
HIS TARGET IS THE RECENTLY DONATED AGATE...
RIKU AND I FEEL THE SAME WAY ABOUT EACH OTHER BUT...
I STILL KEEP TURNING INTO MY OTHER SELF... DARK.
GRAND-PA...
...LEFT THE NOTE?
PHANTOM THIEF DARK.

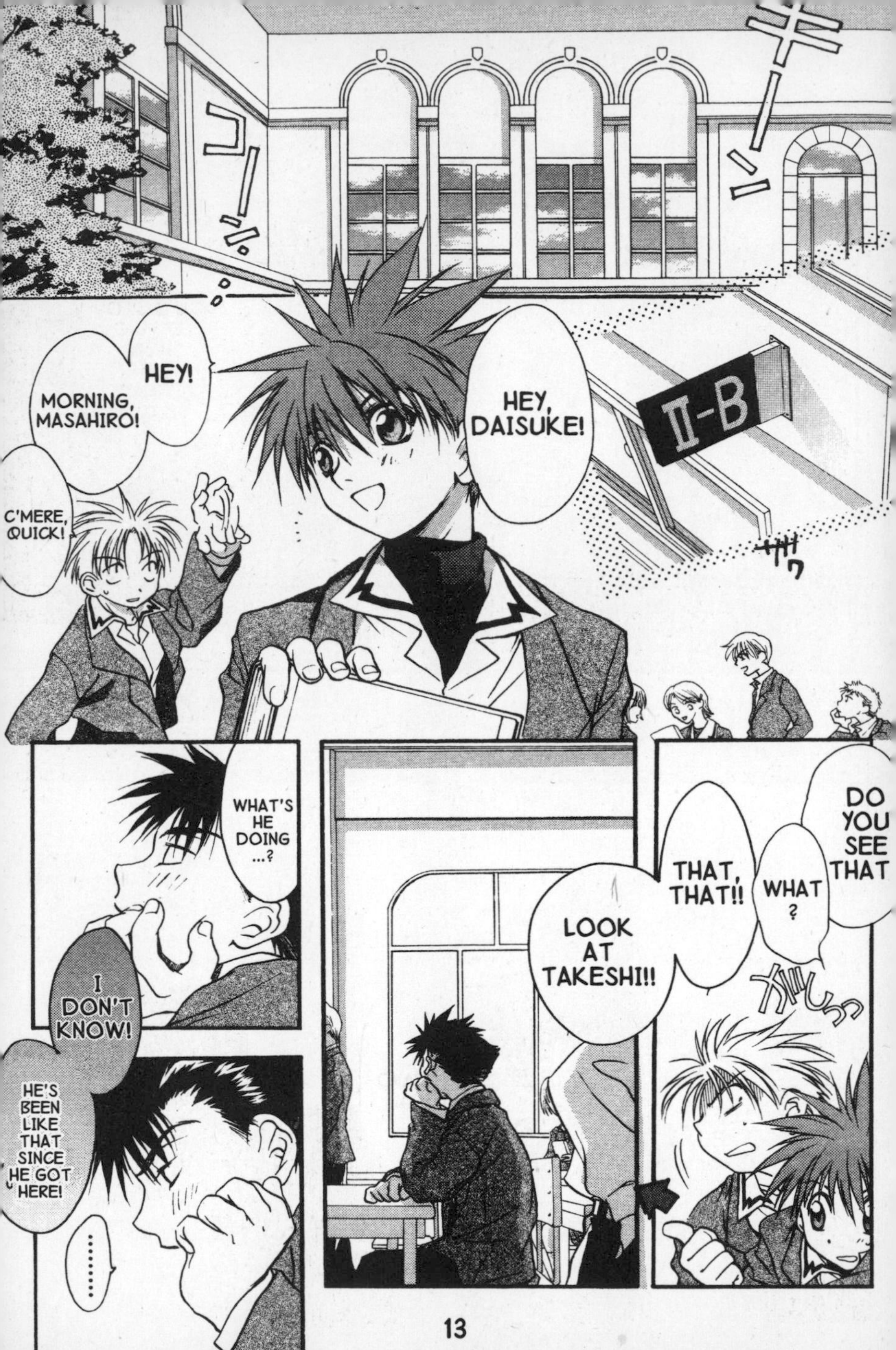
HEY, DAISUKE!
HEY!
MORNING, MASAHIRO!
C'MERE, QUICK!
DO YOU SEE THAT
WHAT?
THAT, THAT!!
LOOK AT TAKESHI!!
WHAT'S HE DOING ...?
I DON'T KNOW!
HE'S BEEN LIKE THAT SINCE HE GOT HERE!
......

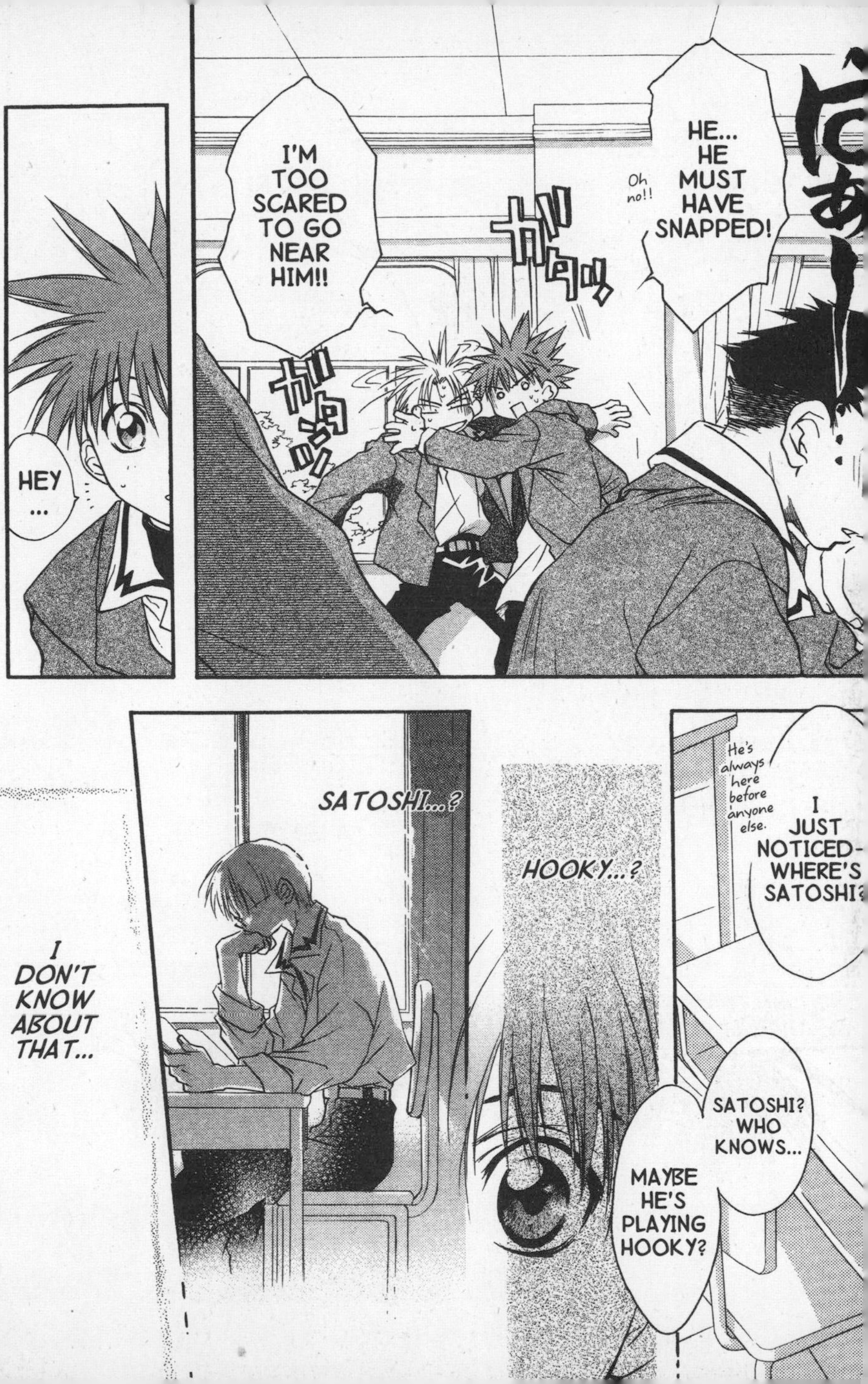
HE... HE MUST HAVE SNAPPED!
Oh no!!
I'M TOO SCARED TO GO NEAR HIM!!
HEY ...
He's always here before anyone else.
I JUST NOTICED-WHERE'S SATOSHI?
SATOSHI? WHO KNOWS...
MAYBE HE'S PLAYING HOOKY?
HOOKY...?
SATOSHI...?
I DON'T KNOW ABOUT THAT...

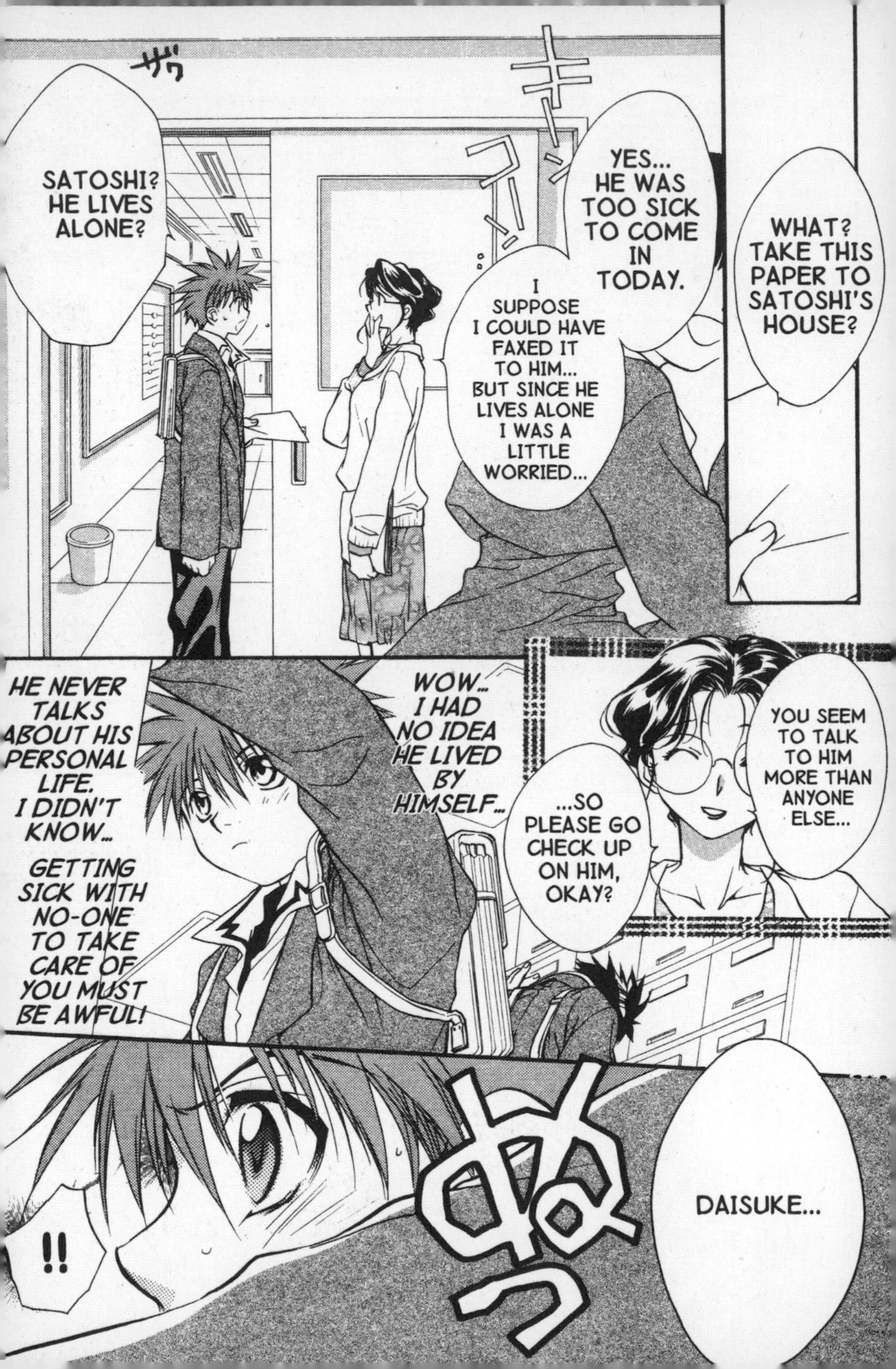
WHAT? TAKE THIS PAPER TO SATOSHI'S HOUSE?
YES... HE WAS TOO SICK TO COME IN TODAY.
I SUPPOSE I COULD HAVE FAXED IT TO HIM... BUT SINCE HE LIVES ALONE I WAS A LITTLE WORRIED...
SATOSHI? HE LIVES ALONE?
YOU SEEM TO TALK TO HIM MORE THAN ANYONE ELSE...
...SO PLEASE GO CHECK UP ON HIM, OKAY?
WOW... I HAD NO IDEA HE LIVED BY HIMSELF...
HE NEVER TALKS ABOUT HIS PERSONAL LIFE. I DIDN'T KNOW...
GETTING SICK WITH NO-ONE TO TAKE CARE OF YOU MUST BE AWFUL!
DAISUKE...
!!

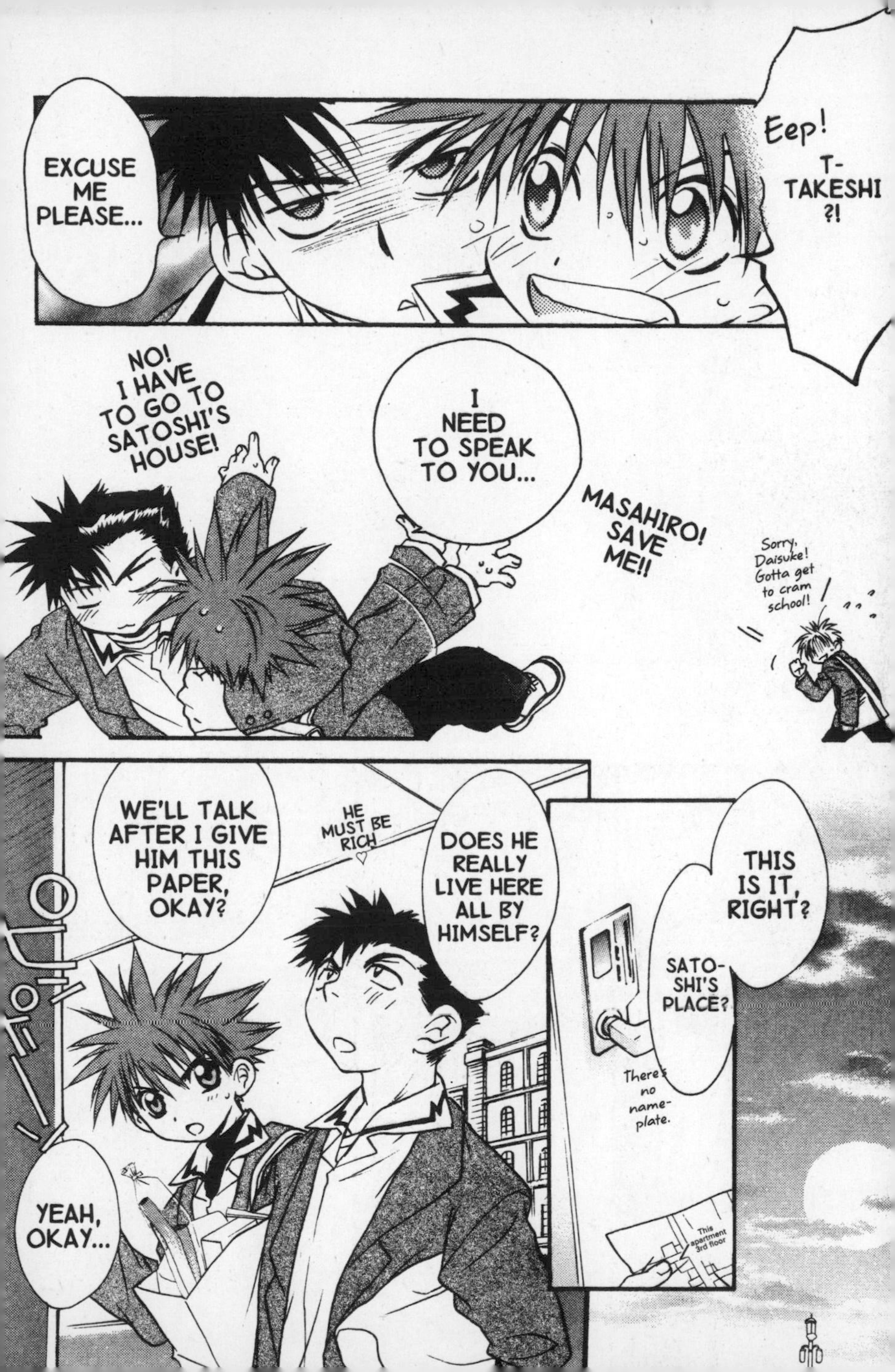
Eep!
T-TAKESHI?!
EXCUSE ME PLEASE...
Sorry, Daisuke! Gotta get to cram school!
MASAHIRO! SAVE ME!!
I NEED TO SPEAK TO YOU...
NO! I HAVE TO GO TO SATOSHI'S HOUSE!
THIS IS IT, RIGHT?
SATOSHI'S PLACE?
There's no name-plate.
This apartment 3rd floor
DOES HE REALLY LIVE HERE ALL BY HIMSELF?
HE MUST BE RICH ♡
WE'LL TALK AFTER I GIVE HIM THIS PAPER, OKAY?
YEAH, OKAY...

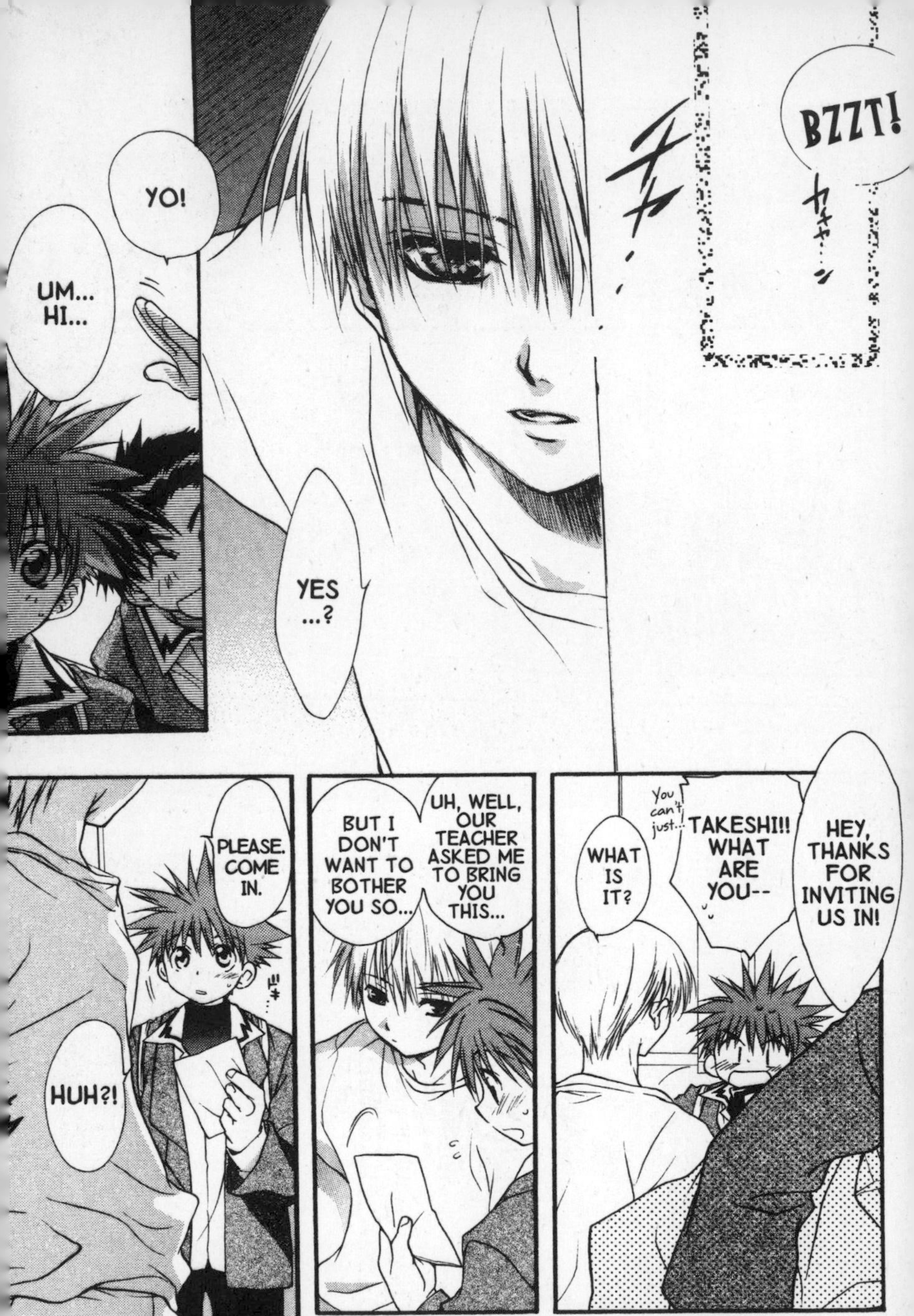
BZZT!
カチャーン
YES ...?
YO!
UM... HI...
HEY, THANKS FOR INVITING US IN!
TAKESHI!! WHAT ARE YOU--
You can't just...
WHAT IS IT?
UH, WELL, OUR TEACHER ASKED ME TO BRING YOU THIS...
BUT I DON'T WANT TO BOTHER YOU SO...
PLEASE. COME IN.
ドキ
HUH?!

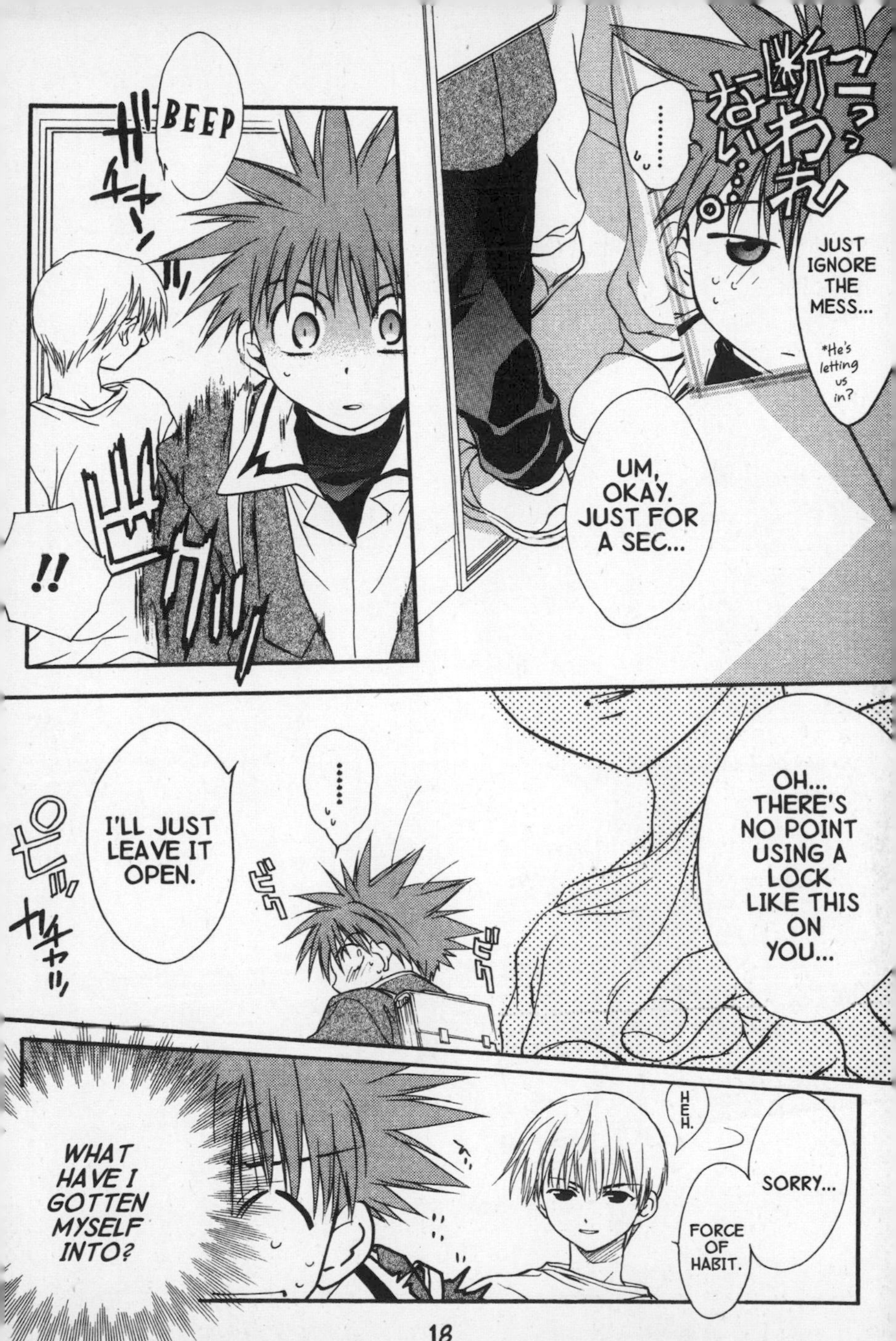
......
JUST IGNORE THE MESS...
*He's letting us in?
UM, OKAY. JUST FOR A SEC...
BEEP
!!
OH... THERE'S NO POINT USING A LOCK LIKE THIS ON YOU...
......
I'LL JUST LEAVE IT OPEN.
HEH.
SORRY...
FORCE OF HABIT.
WHAT HAVE I GOTTEN MYSELF INTO?

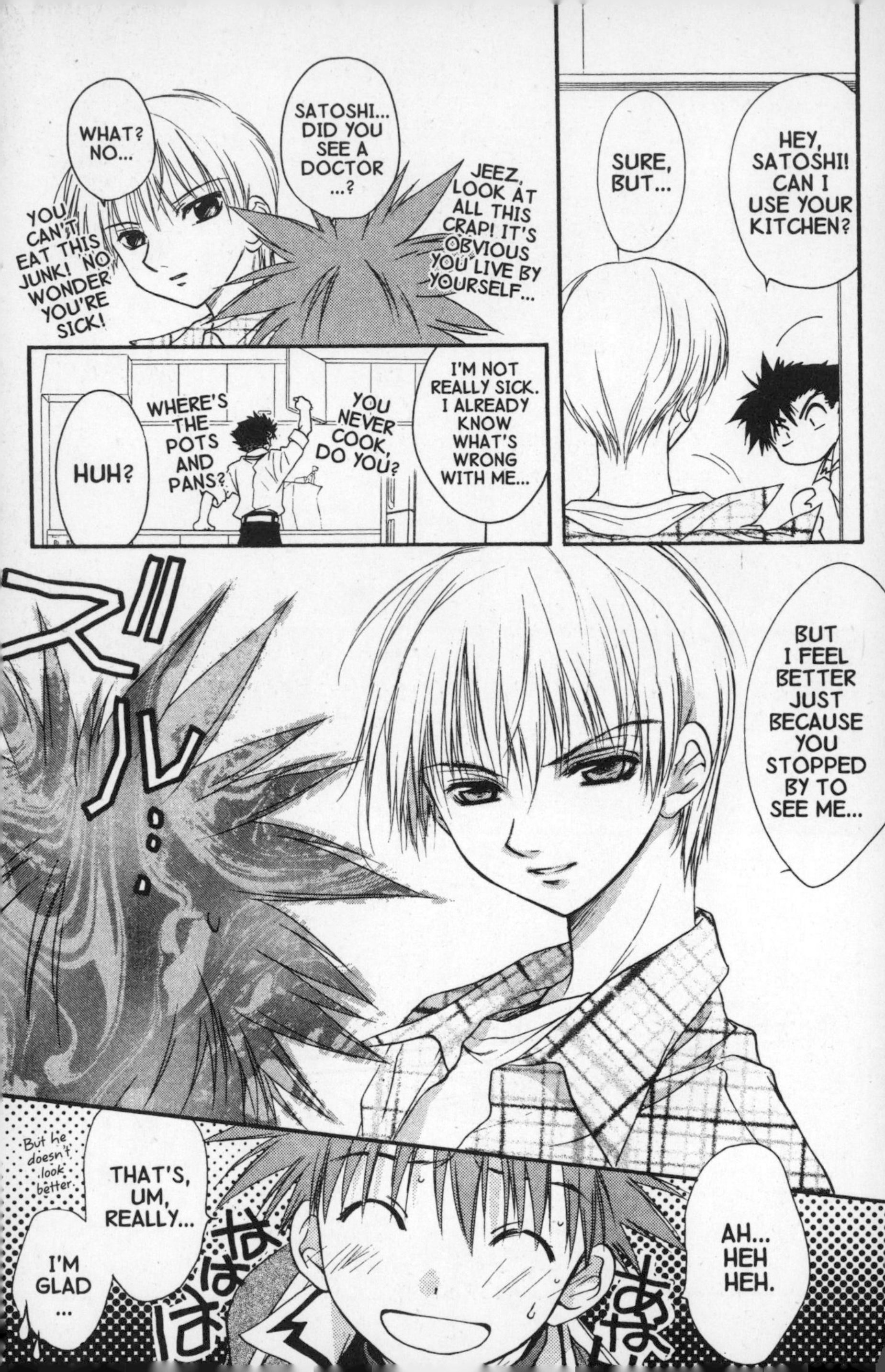
HEY, SATOSHI! CAN I USE YOUR KITCHEN?
SURE, BUT...
JEEZ, LOOK AT ALL THIS CRAP! IT'S OBVIOUS YOU LIVE BY YOURSELF...
SATOSHI... DID YOU SEE A DOCTOR ...?
WHAT? NO...
YOU CAN'T EAT THIS JUNK! NO WONDER YOU'RE SICK!
I'M NOT REALLY SICK. I ALREADY KNOW WHAT'S WRONG WITH ME...
YOU NEVER COOK, DO YOU?
WHERE'S THE POTS AND PANS?
HUH?
BUT I FEEL BETTER JUST BECAUSE YOU STOPPED BY TO SEE ME...
ズル
AH... HEH HEH.
THAT'S, UM, REALLY...
I'M GLAD ...
But he doesn't look better.
はは

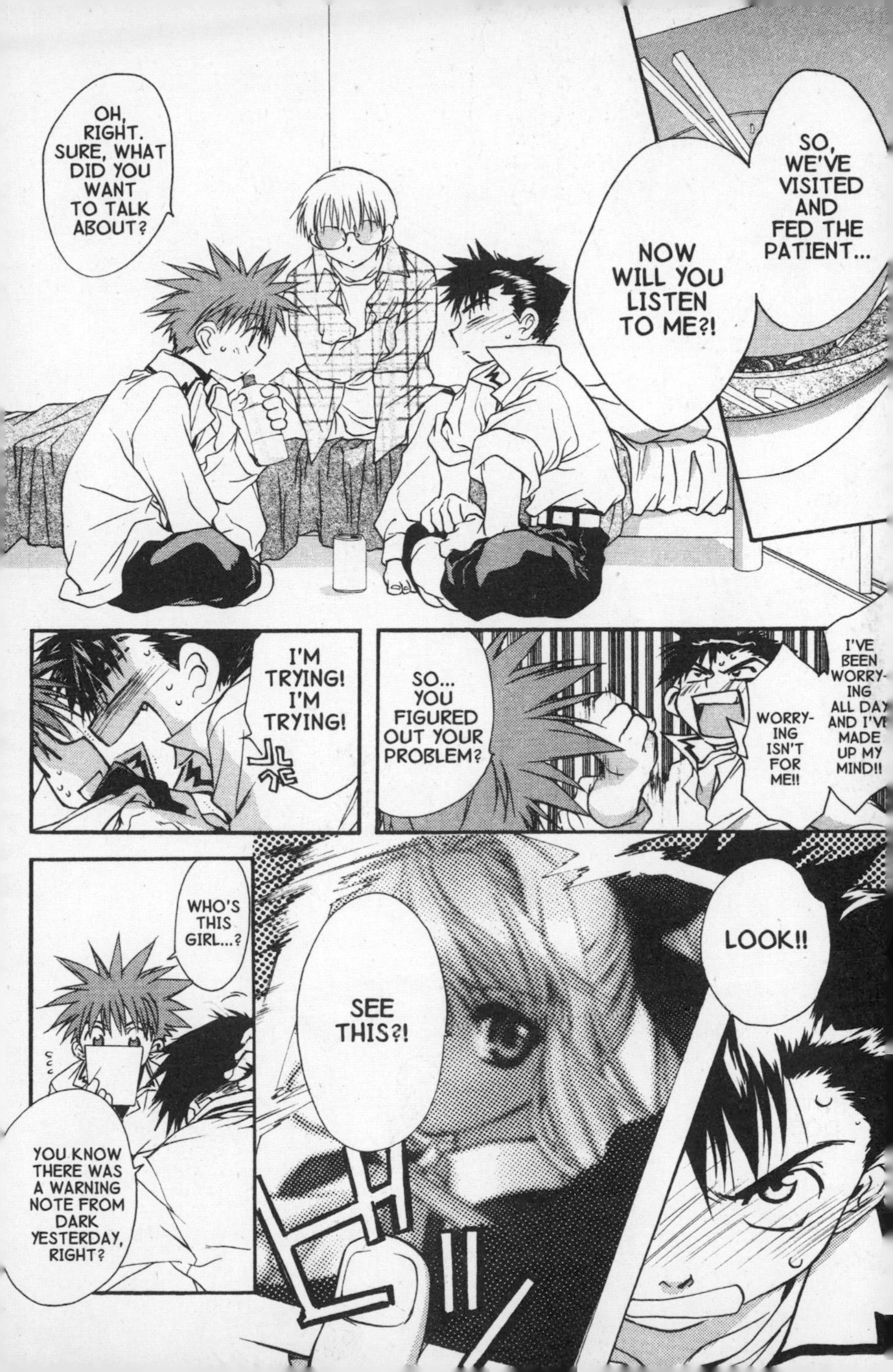
SO, WE'VE VISITED AND FED THE PATIENT...
NOW WILL YOU LISTEN TO ME?!
OH, RIGHT. SURE, WHAT DID YOU WANT TO TALK ABOUT?
I'VE BEEN WORRY-ING ALL DAY AND I'VE MADE UP MY MIND!!
WORRY-ING ISN'T FOR ME!!
SO... YOU FIGURED OUT YOUR PROBLEM?
I'M TRYING! I'M TRYING!
LOOK!!
SEE THIS?!
WHO'S THIS GIRL...?
YOU KNOW THERE WAS A WARNING NOTE FROM DARK YESTERDAY, RIGHT?

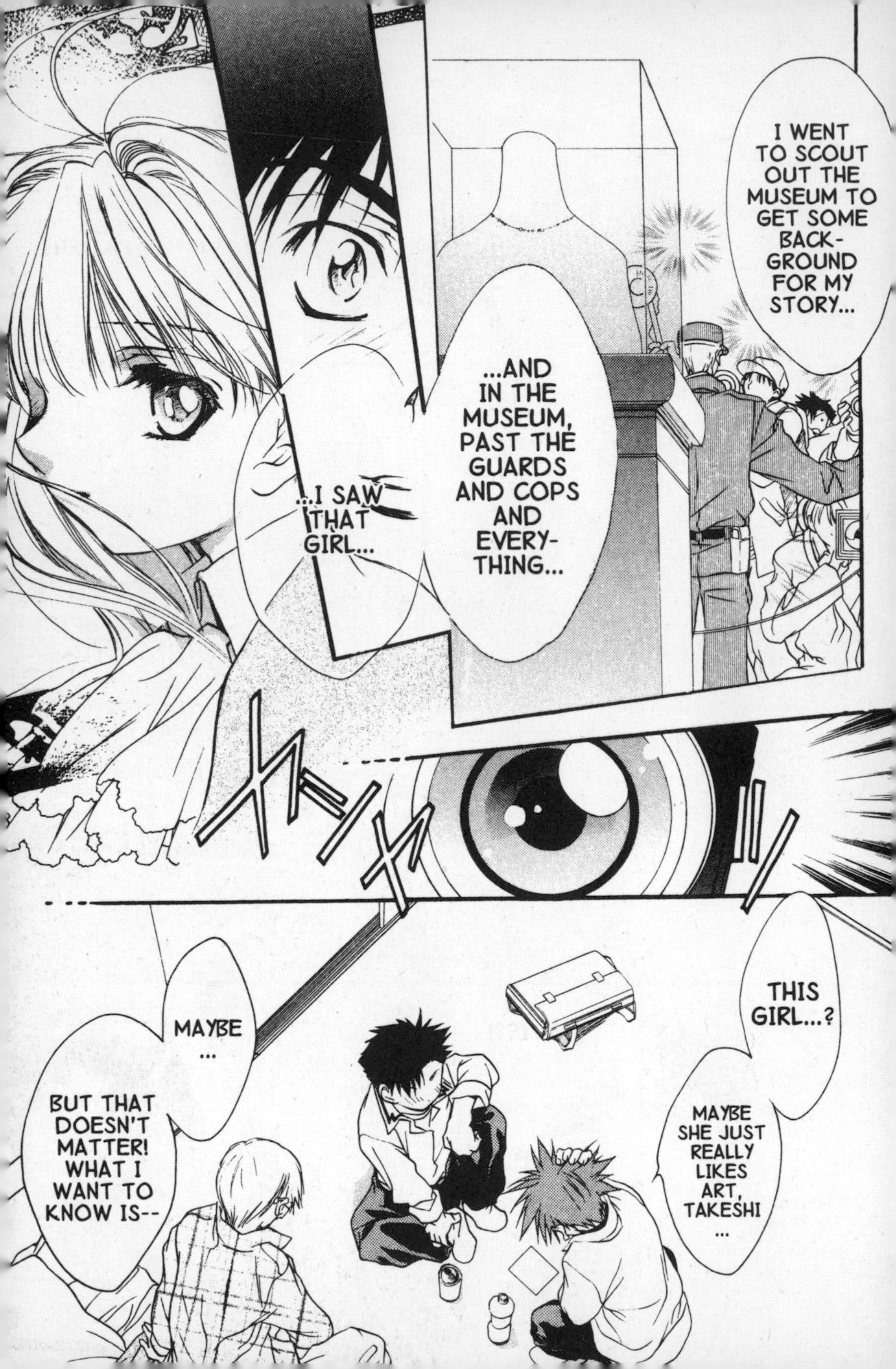

I WENT TO SCOUT OUT THE MUSEUM TO GET SOME BACK-GROUND FOR MY STORY...
...AND IN THE MUSEUM, PAST THE GUARDS AND COPS AND EVERY-THING...
...I SAW THAT GIRL...
THIS GIRL...?
MAYBE SHE JUST REALLY LIKES ART, TAKESHI ...
MAYBE ...
BUT THAT DOESN'T MATTER! WHAT I WANT TO KNOW IS--

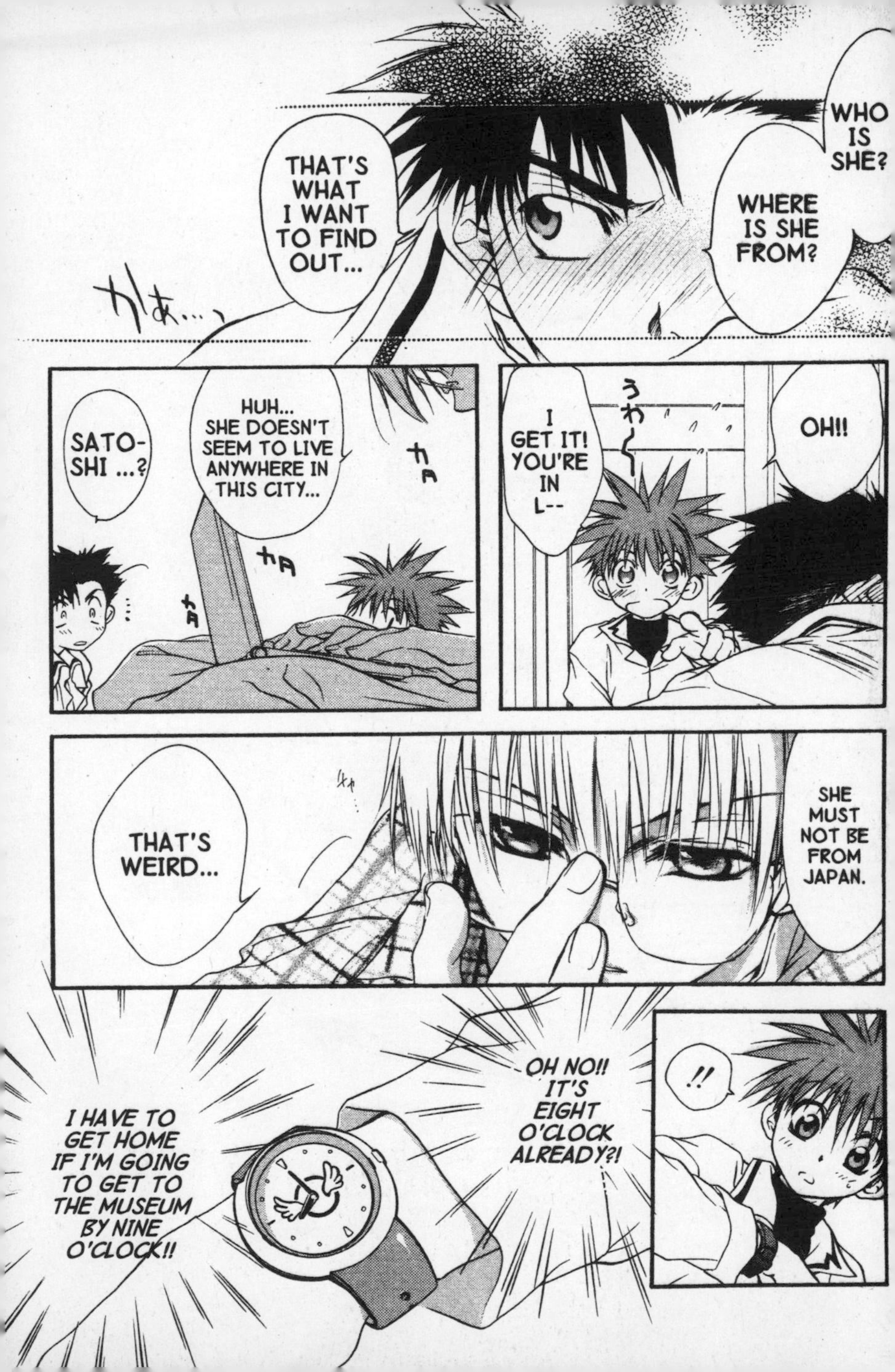
WHO IS SHE?
WHERE IS SHE FROM?
THAT'S WHAT I WANT TO FIND OUT...
OH!!
I GET IT! YOU'RE IN L--
HUH... SHE DOESN'T SEEM TO LIVE ANYWHERE IN THIS CITY...
SATO-SHI ...?
SHE MUST NOT BE FROM JAPAN.
THAT'S WEIRD...
!!
OH NO!! IT'S EIGHT O'CLOCK ALREADY?!
I HAVE TO GET HOME IF I'M GOING TO GET TO THE MUSEUM BY NINE O'CLOCK!!

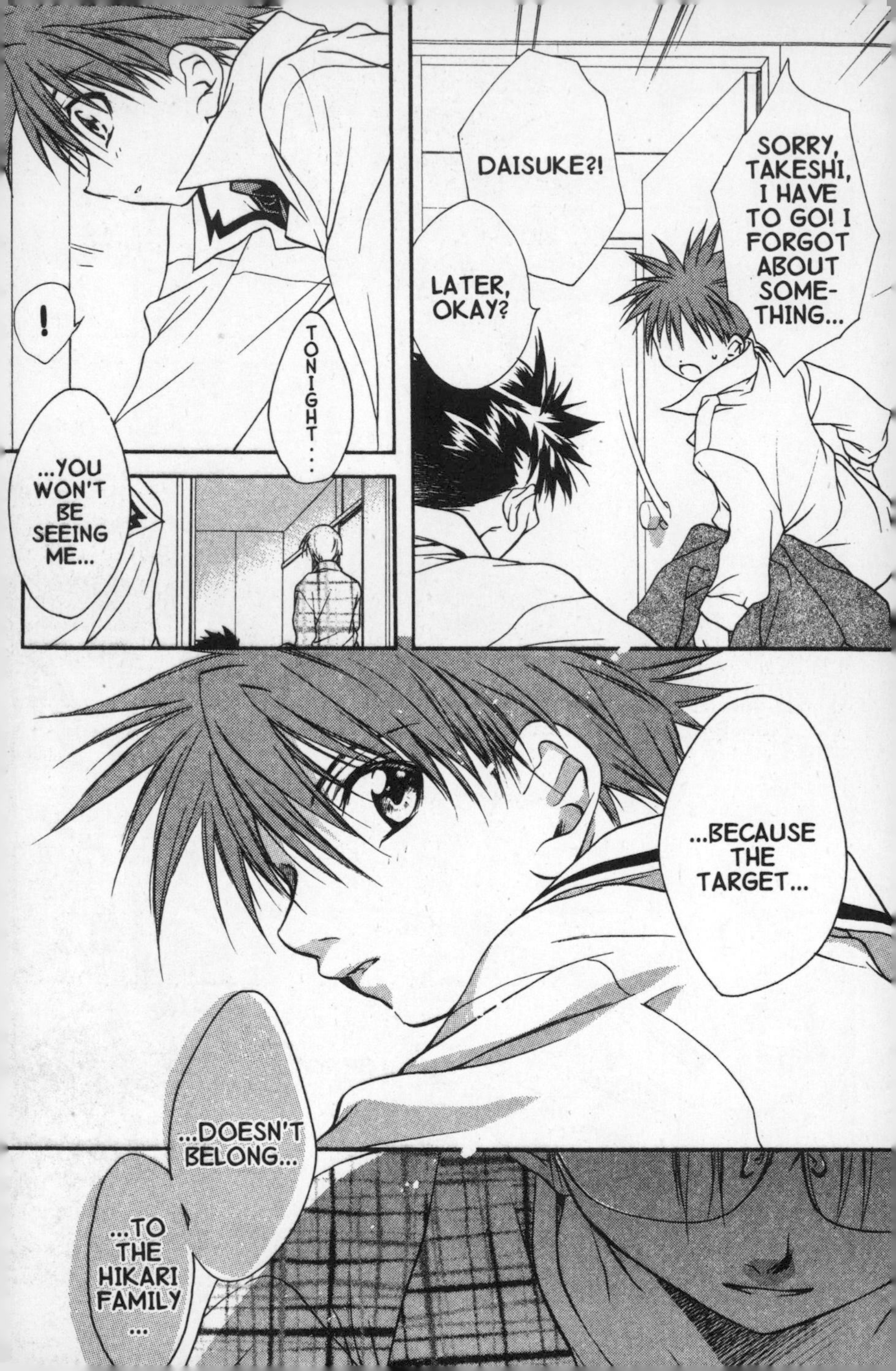
SORRY, TAKESHI, I HAVE TO GO! I FORGOT ABOUT SOME-THING...
DAISUKE?!
LATER, OKAY?
TONIGHT...
!
...YOU WON'T BE SEEING ME...
...BECAUSE THE TARGET...
...DOESN'T BELONG...
...TO THE HIKARI FAMILY ...

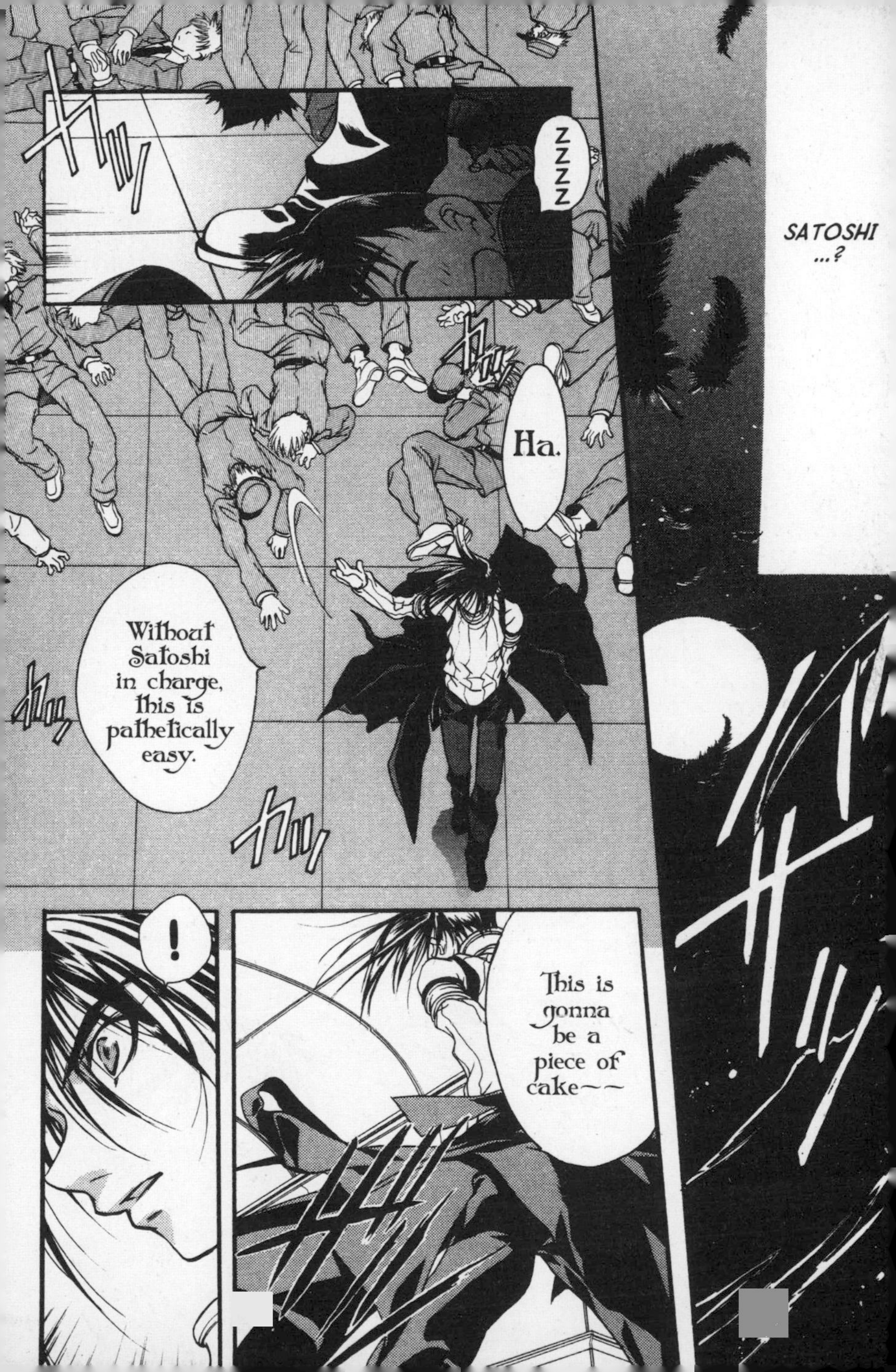
SATOSHI ...?
ZZZZ
Ha.
Without Satoshi in charge, this is pathetically easy.
This is gonna be a piece of cake~~
!

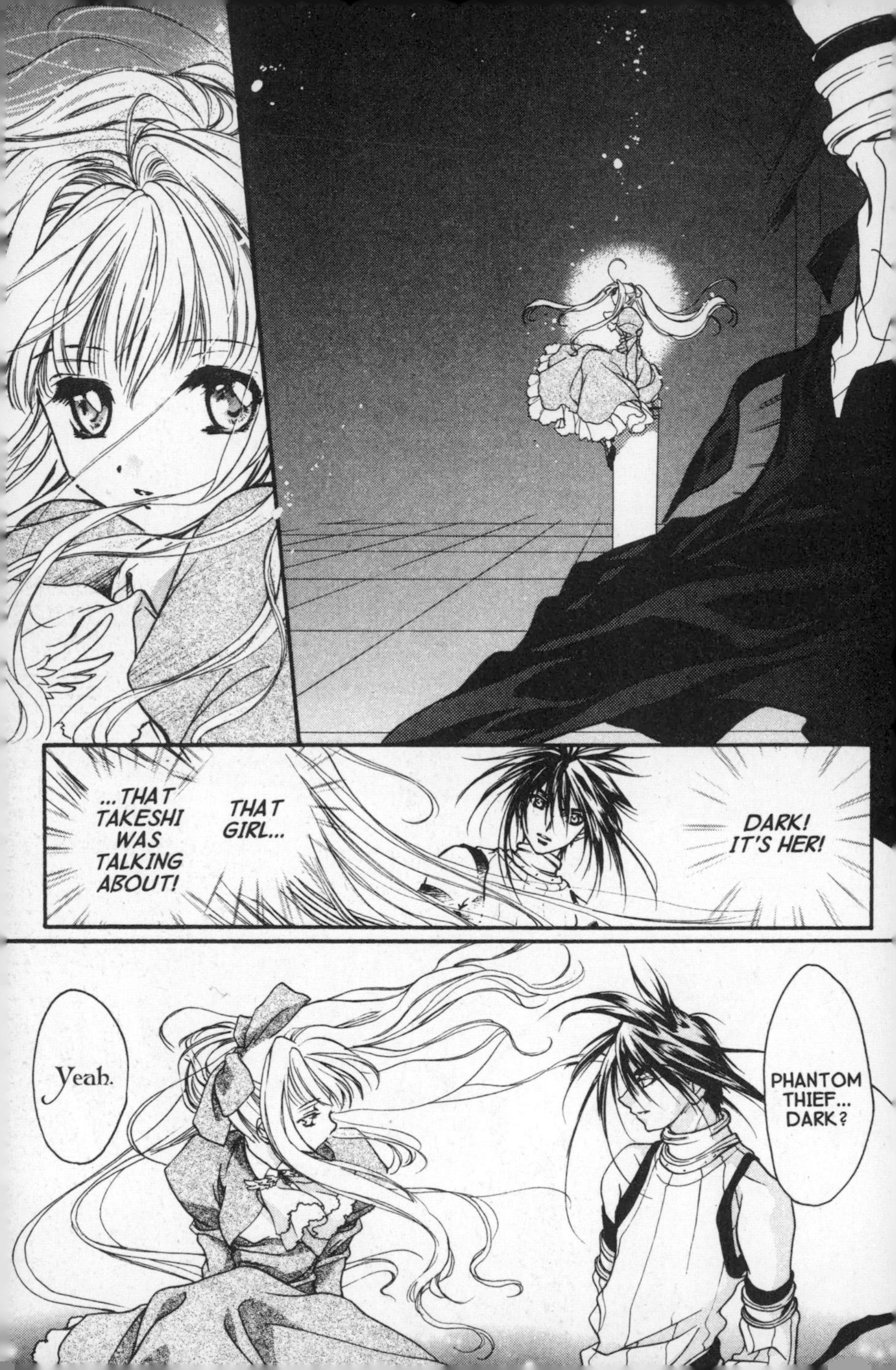
DARK! IT'S HER!
THAT GIRL...
...THAT TAKESHI WAS TALKING ABOUT!
PHANTOM THIEF... DARK?
Yeah.

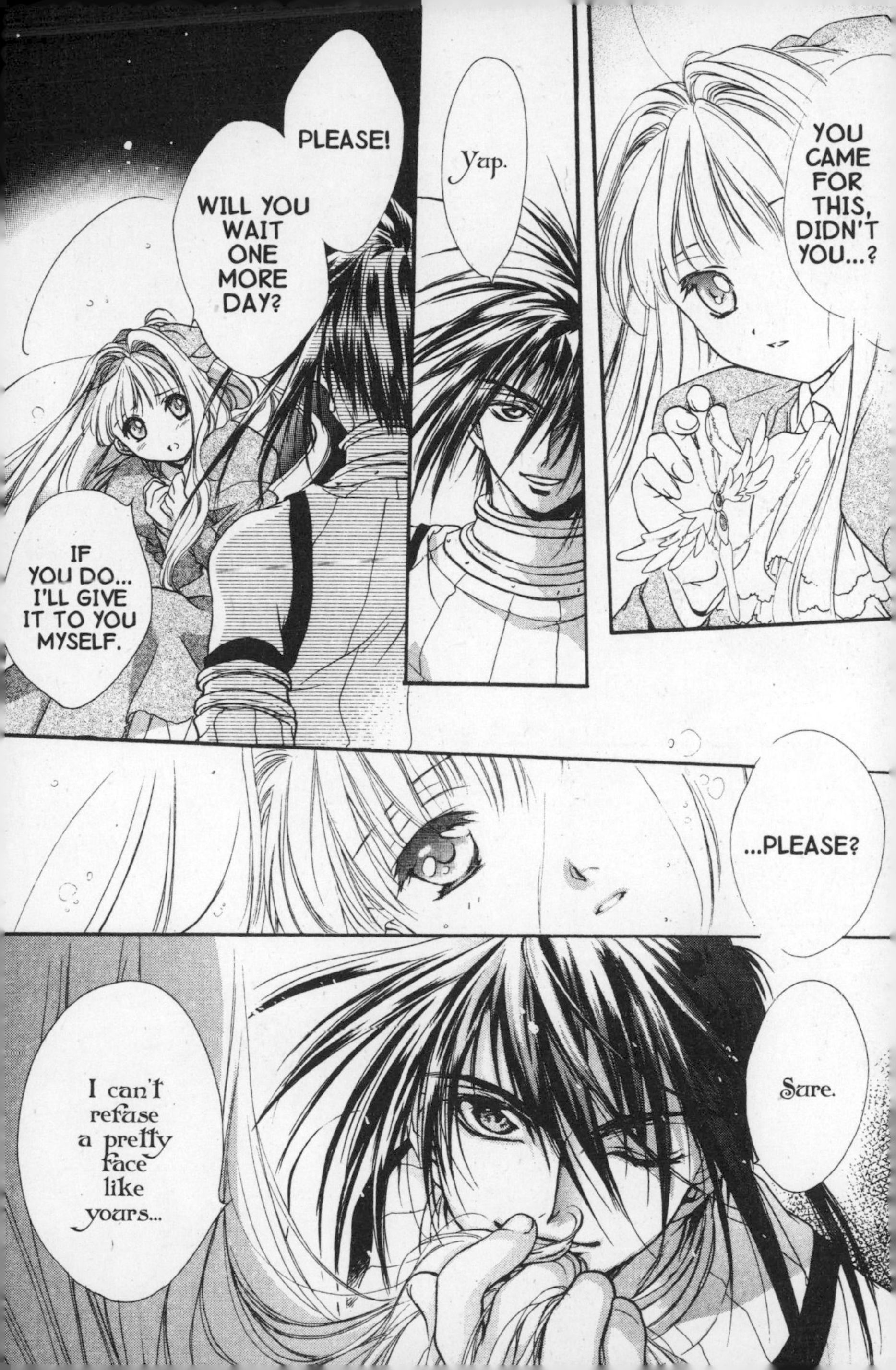
YOU CAME FOR THIS, DIDN'T YOU...?
Yup.
PLEASE!
WILL YOU WAIT ONE MORE DAY?
IF YOU DO... I'LL GIVE IT TO YOU MYSELF.
...PLEASE?
Sure.
I can't refuse a pretty face like yours...

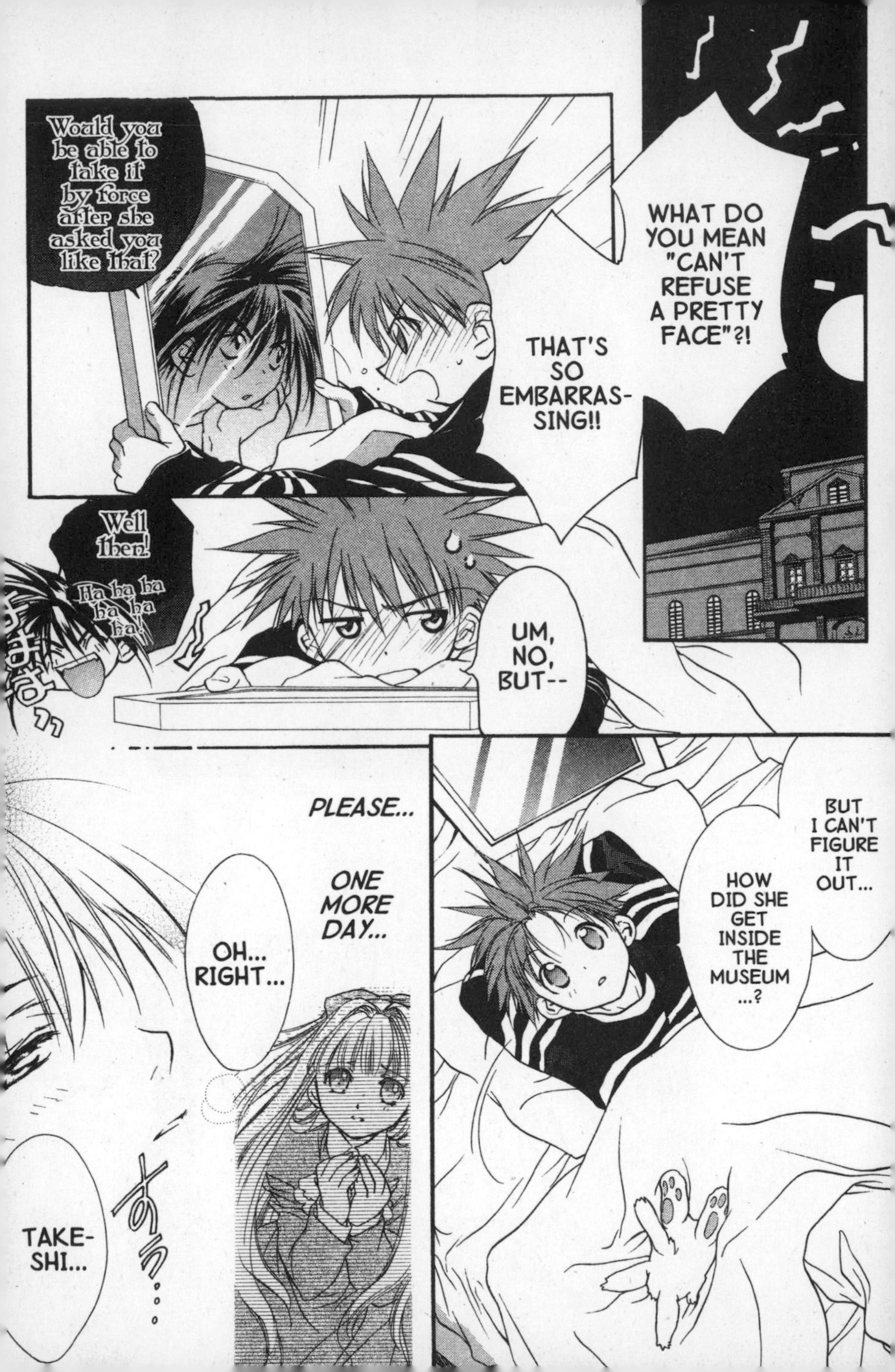
WHAT DO YOU MEAN "CAN'T REFUSE A PRETTY FACE"?!
THAT'S SO EMBARRAS-SING!!
Would you be able to take it by force after she asked you like that?
UM, NO, BUT--
Well then!
Ha ha ha ha ha ha!
BUT I CAN'T FIGURE IT OUT...
HOW DID SHE GET INSIDE THE MUSEUM ...?
PLEASE...
ONE MORE DAY...
OH... RIGHT...
TAKE-SHI...

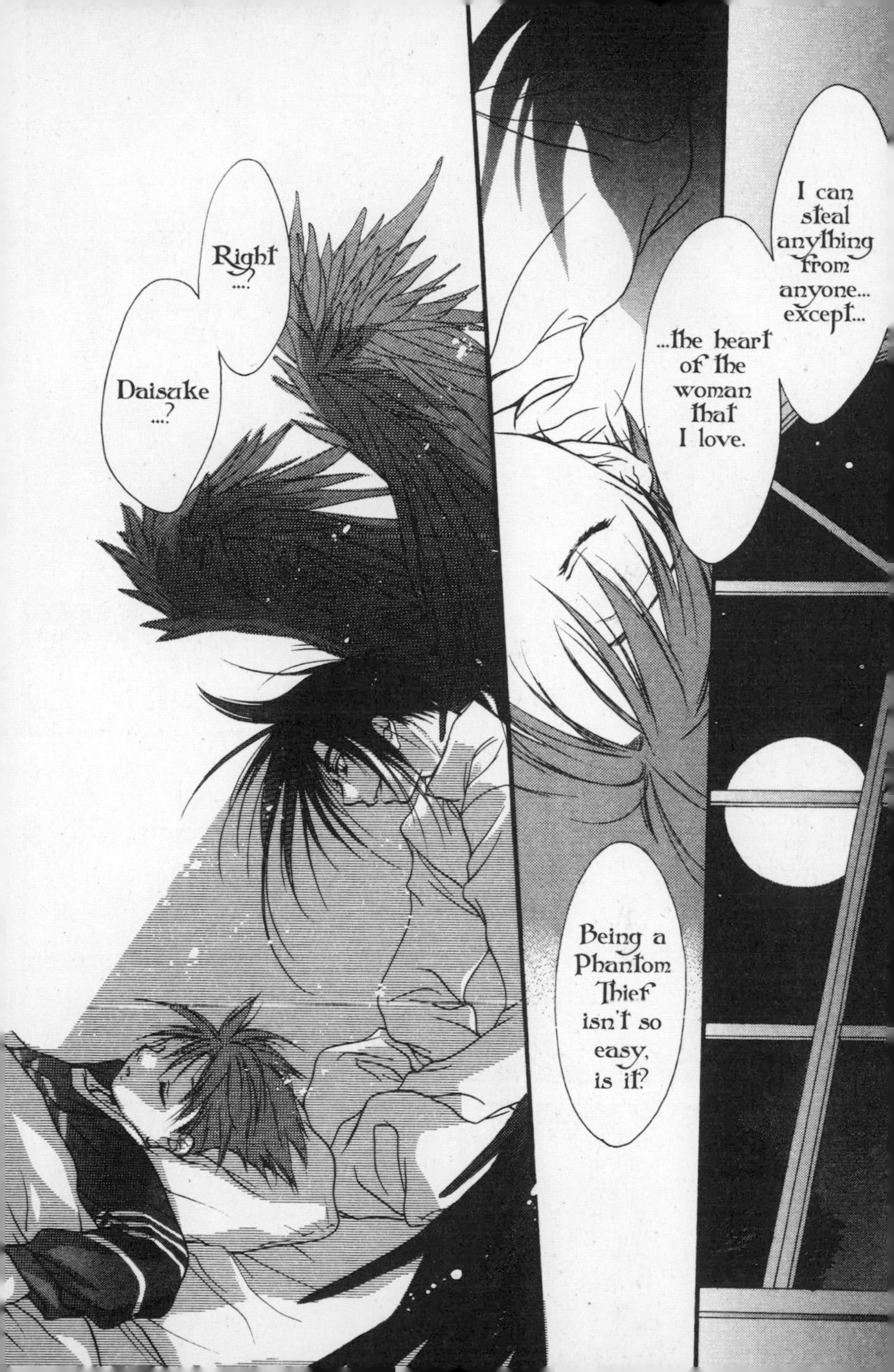
I can steal anything from anyone... except...
...the heart of the woman that I love.
Being a Phantom Thief isn't so easy, is it?
Right ....?
Daisuke ....?

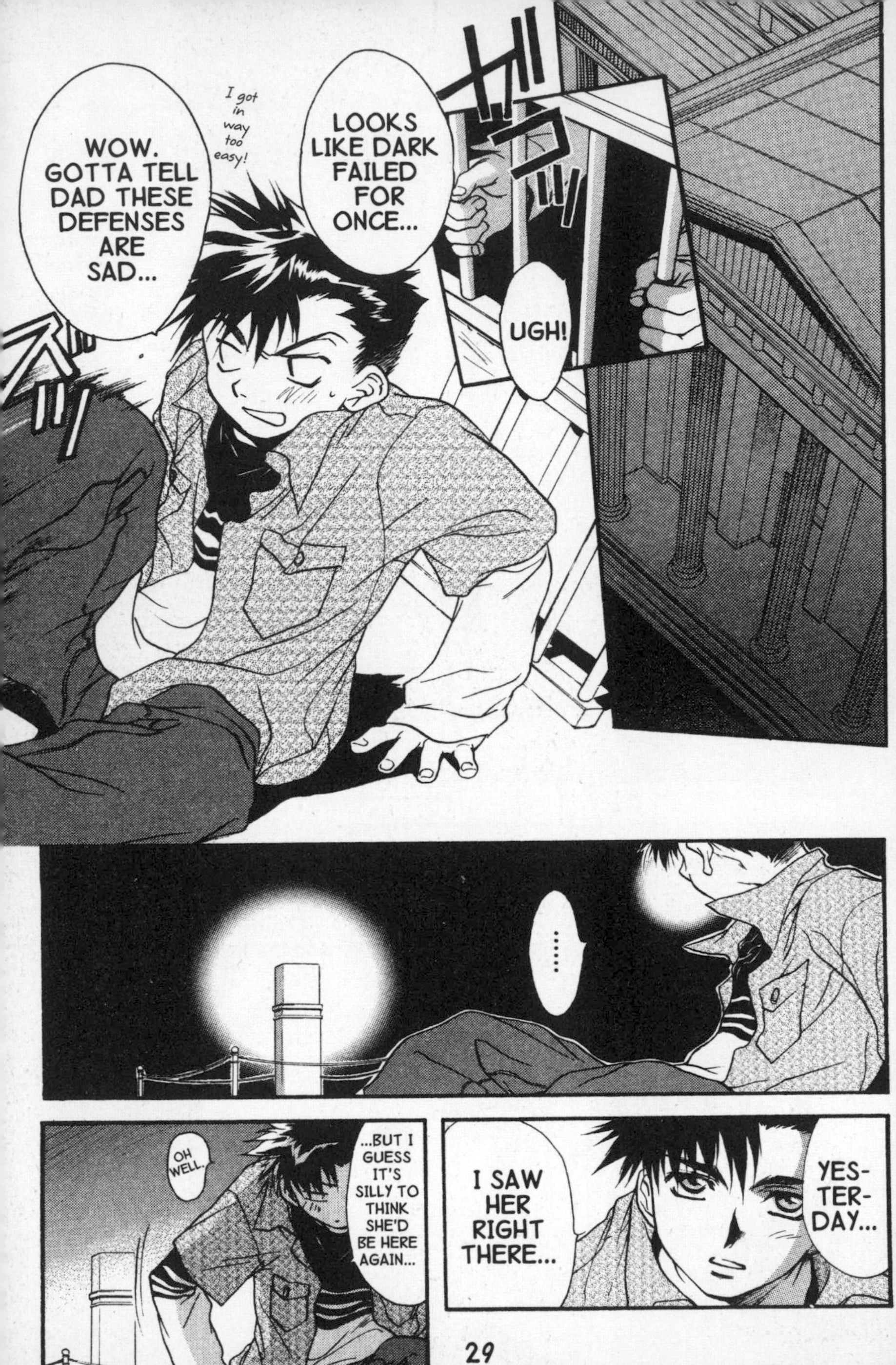
UGH!
LOOKS LIKE DARK FAILED FOR ONCE...
I got in way too easy!
WOW. GOTTA TELL DAD THESE DEFENSES ARE SAD...
......
YES-TER-DAY...
I SAW HER RIGHT THERE...
...BUT I GUESS IT'S SILLY TO THINK SHE'D BE HERE AGAIN...
OH WELL.

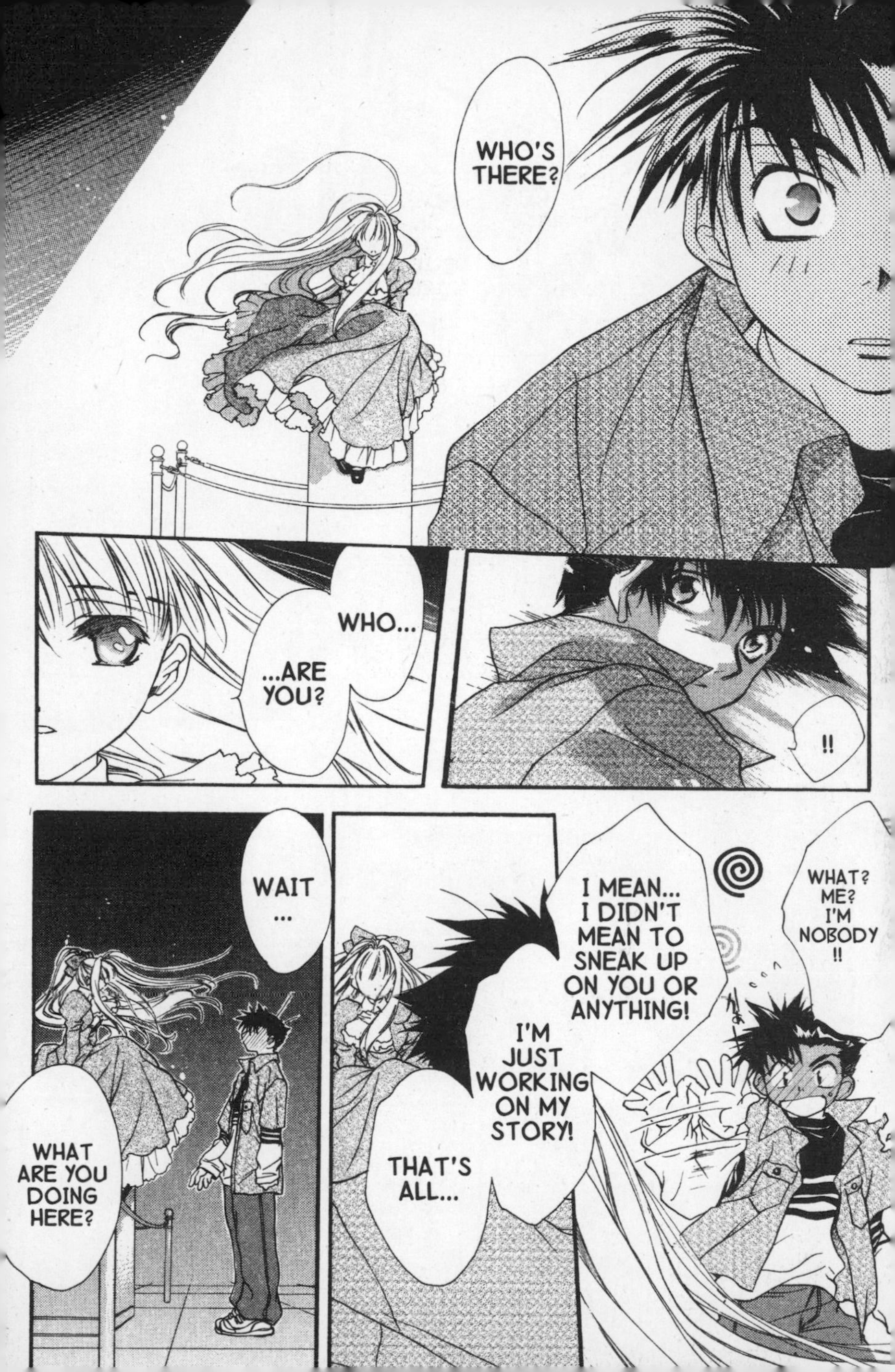
WHO'S THERE?
!!
WHO...
...ARE YOU?
WHAT? ME? I'M NOBODY !!
I MEAN... I DIDN'T MEAN TO SNEAK UP ON YOU OR ANYTHING!
I'M JUST WORKING ON MY STORY!
THAT'S ALL...
WAIT ...
WHAT ARE YOU DOING HERE?

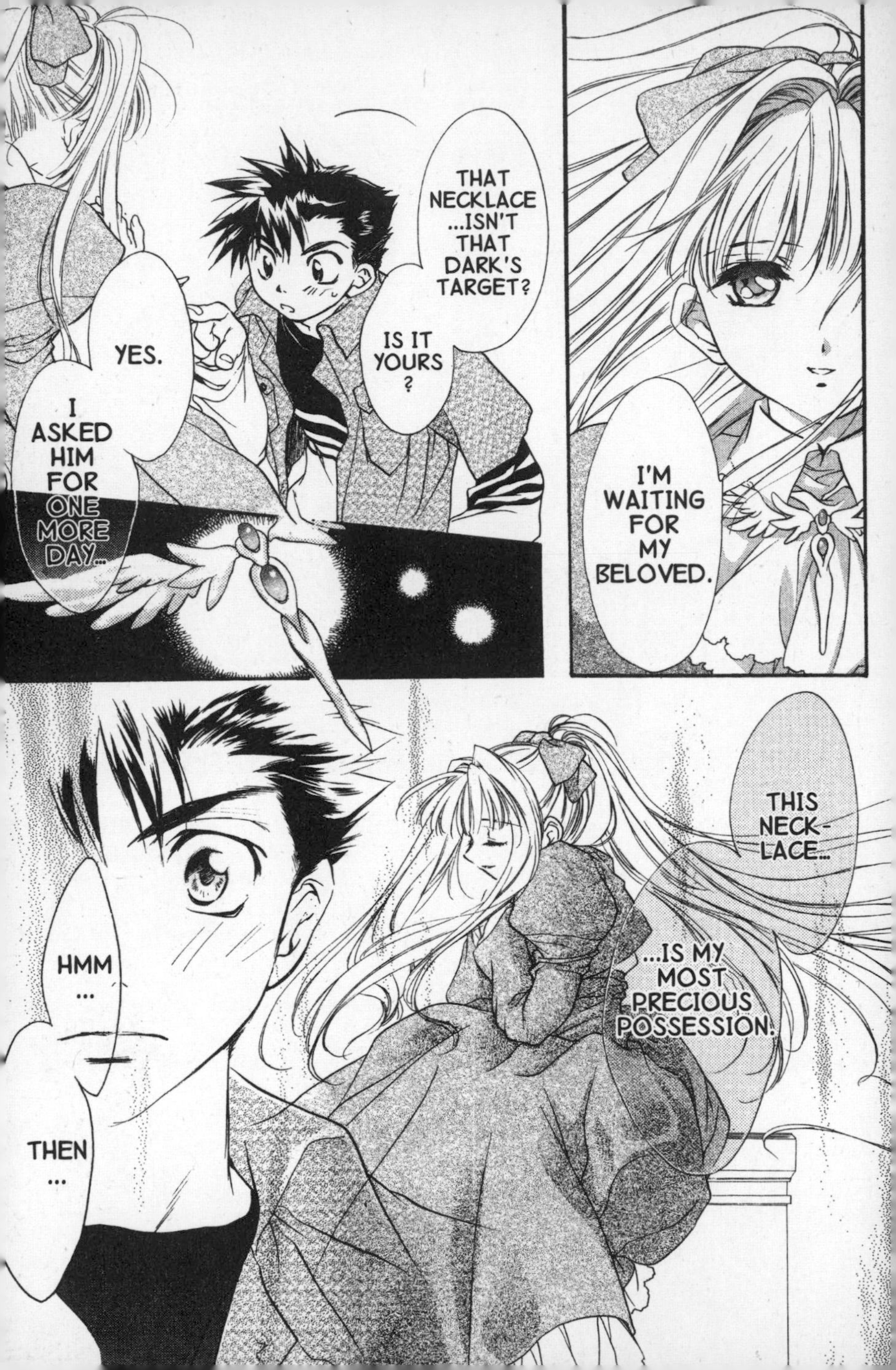
I'M WAITING FOR MY BELOVED.
THAT NECKLACE ...ISN'T THAT DARK'S TARGET?
IS IT YOURS?
YES.
I ASKED HIM FOR ONE MORE DAY...
THIS NECKLACE...
...IS MY MOST PRECIOUS POSSESSION.
HMM...
THEN...

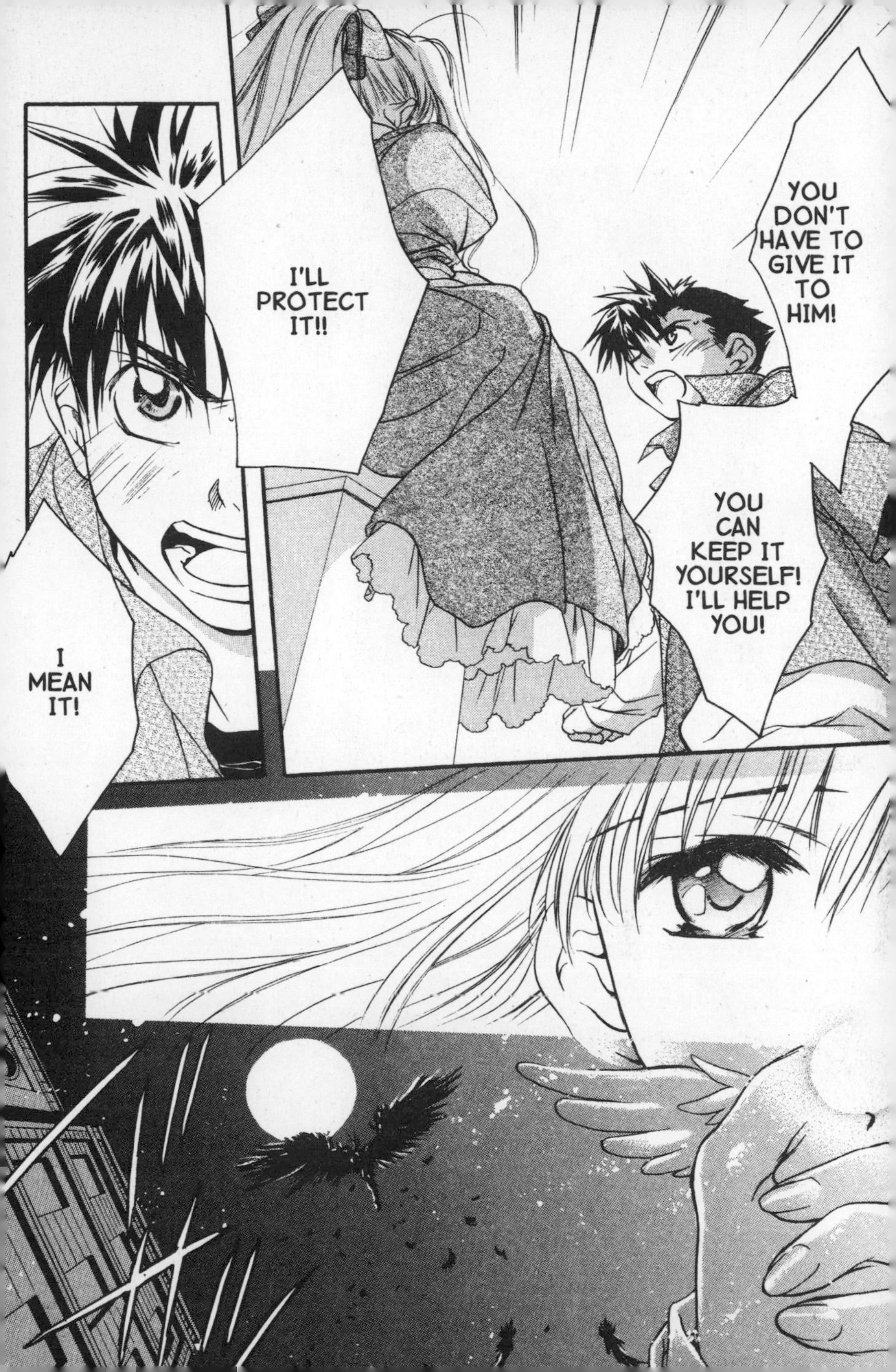
YOU DON'T HAVE TO GIVE IT TO HIM!
YOU CAN KEEP IT YOURSELF! I'LL HELP YOU!
I'LL PROTECT IT!!
I MEAN IT!

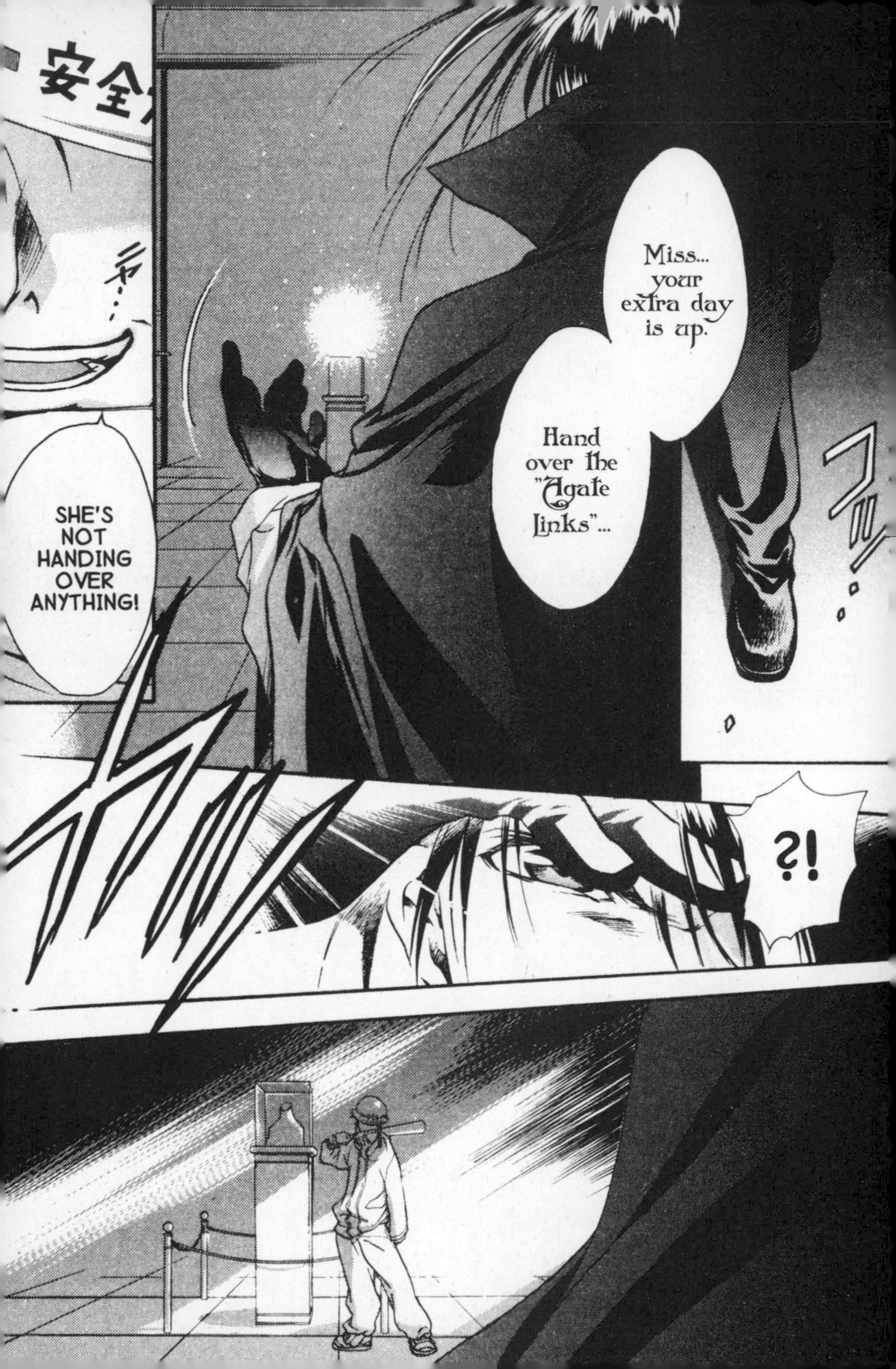
Miss... your extra day is up.
Hand over the "Agate Links"...
安全
SHE'S NOT HANDING OVER ANYTHING!
?!

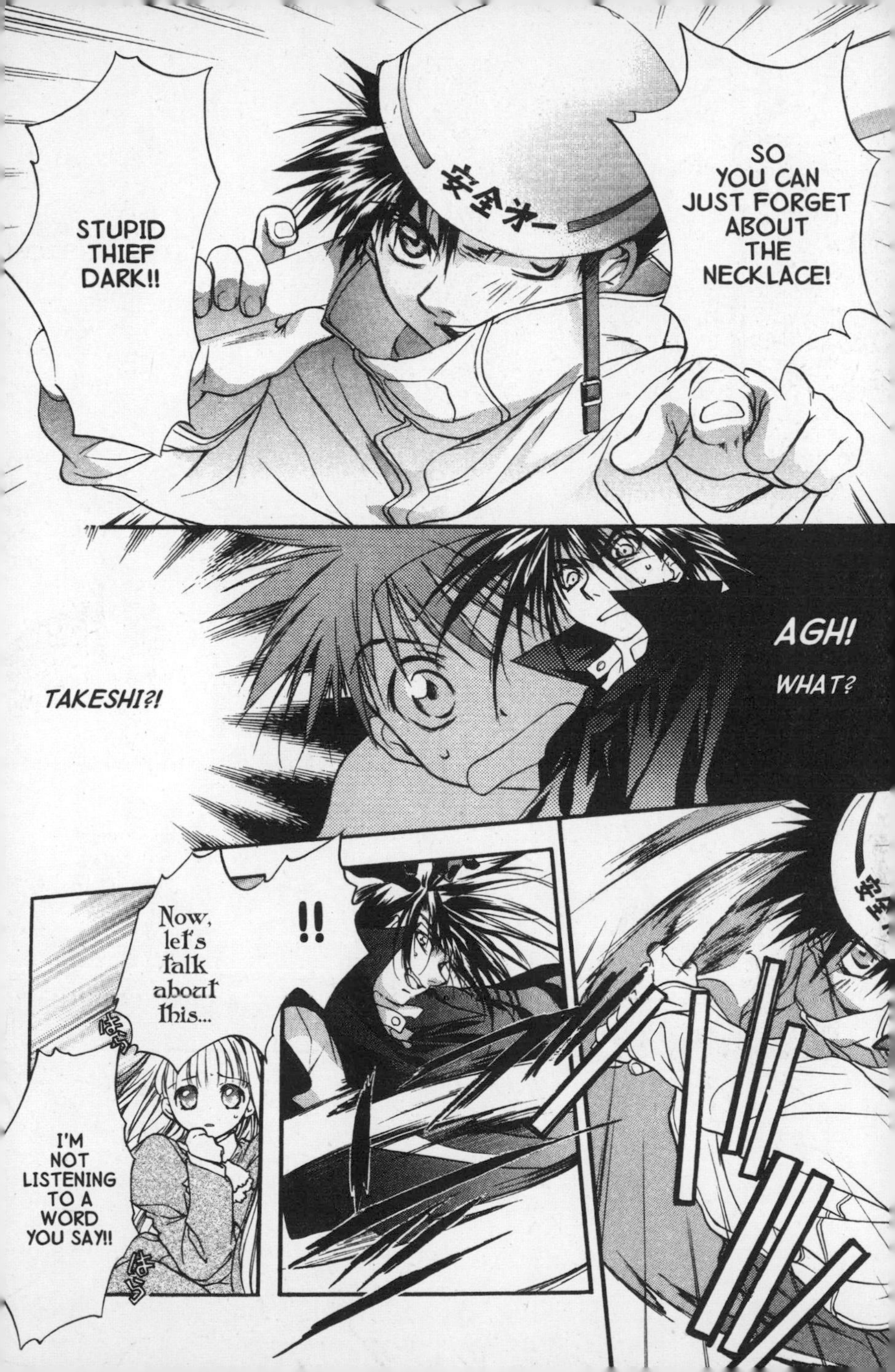
SO YOU CAN JUST FORGET ABOUT THE NECKLACE!
STUPID THIEF DARK!!
AGH!
WHAT?
TAKESHI?!
!!
Now, let's talk about this...
I'M NOT LISTENING TO A WORD YOU SAY!!

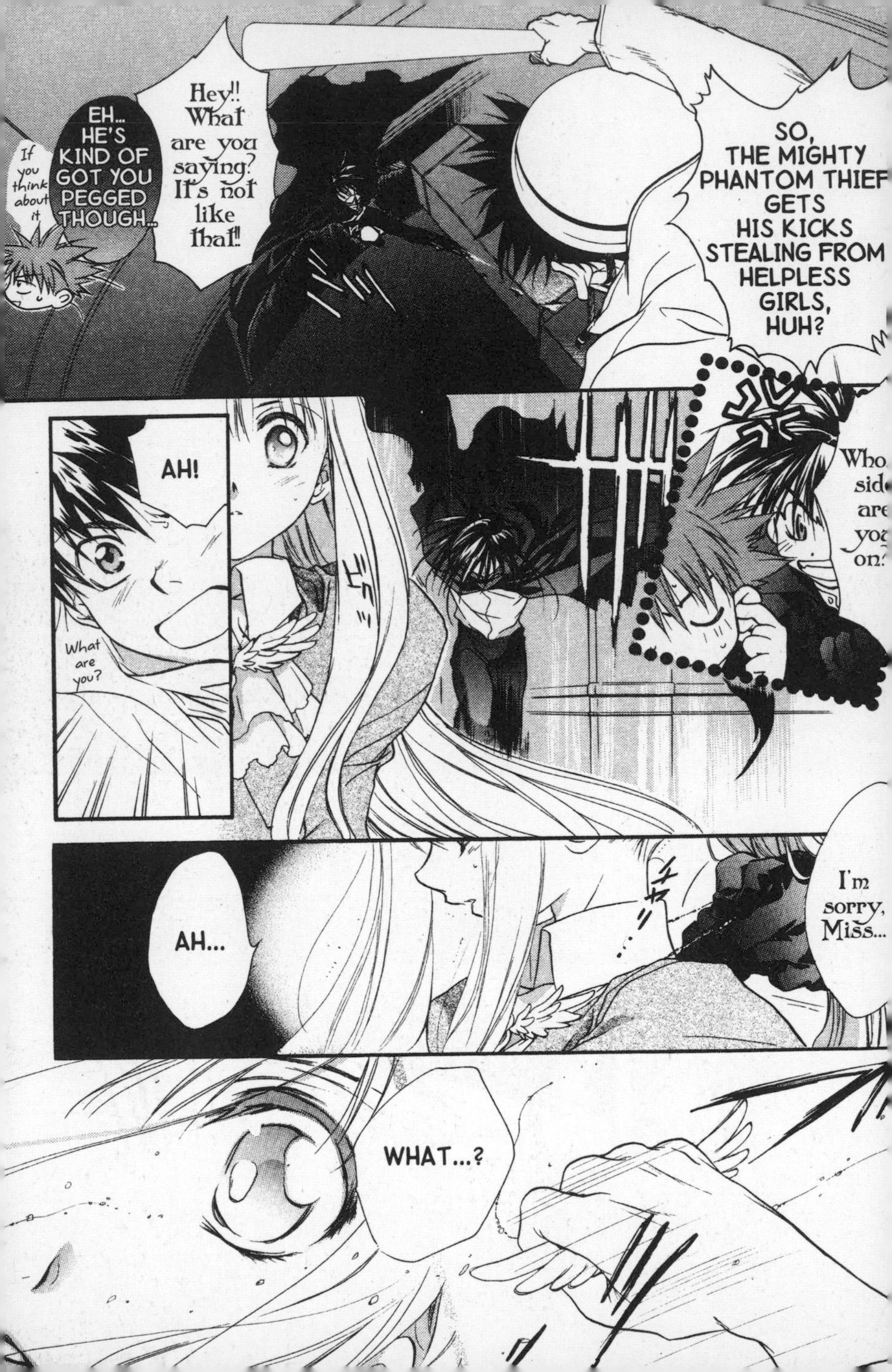
SO, THE MIGHTY PHANTOM THIEF GETS HIS KICKS STEALING FROM HELPLESS GIRLS, HUH?
Hey!! What are you saying? It's not like that!!
EH... HE'S KIND OF GOT YOU PEGGED THOUGH...
If you think about it
Who sid are yo on?
AH!
What are you?
I'm sorry, Miss...
AH...
WHAT...?

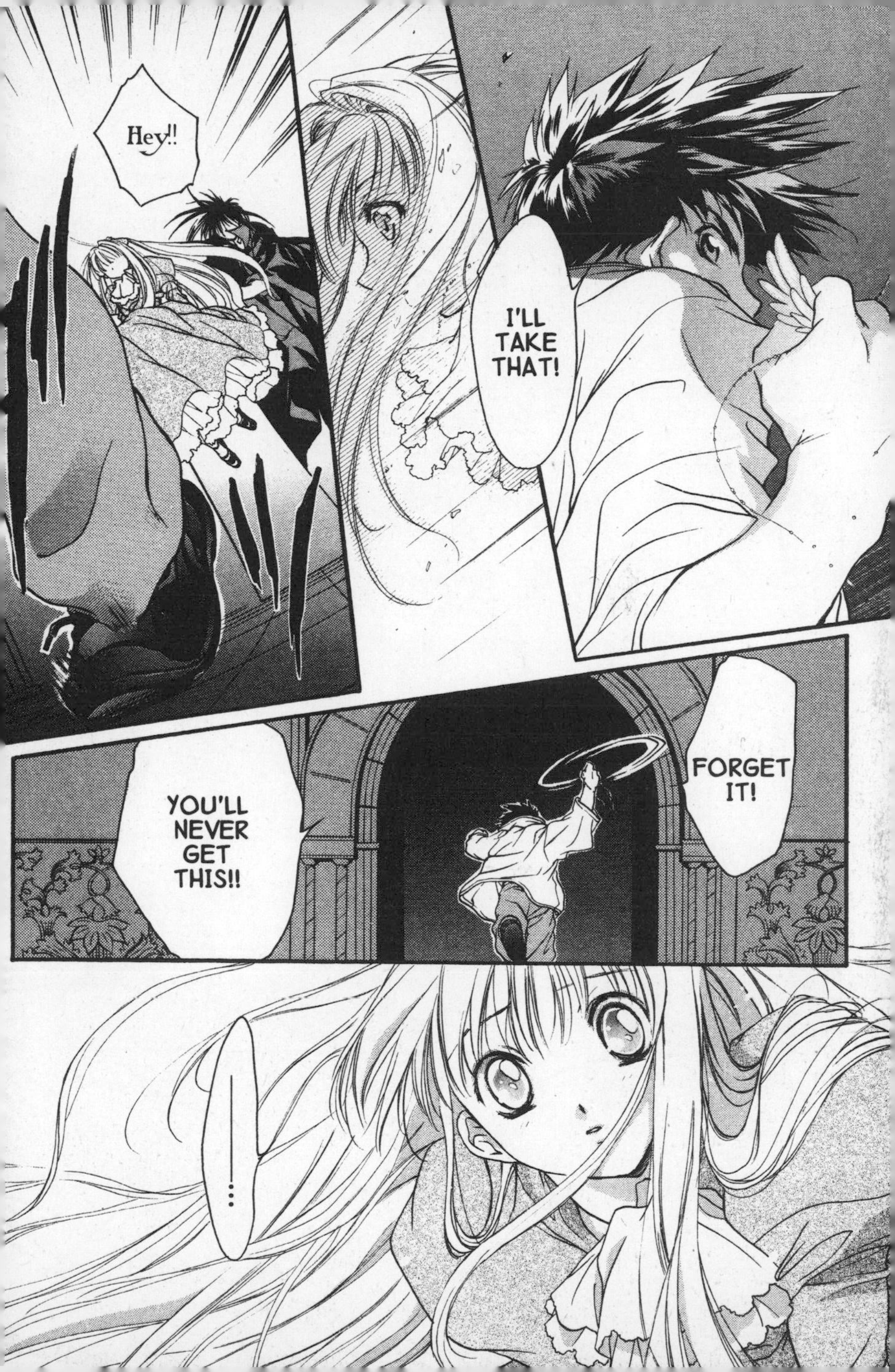
I'LL TAKE THAT!
Hey!!
FORGET IT!
YOU'LL NEVER GET THIS!!
……

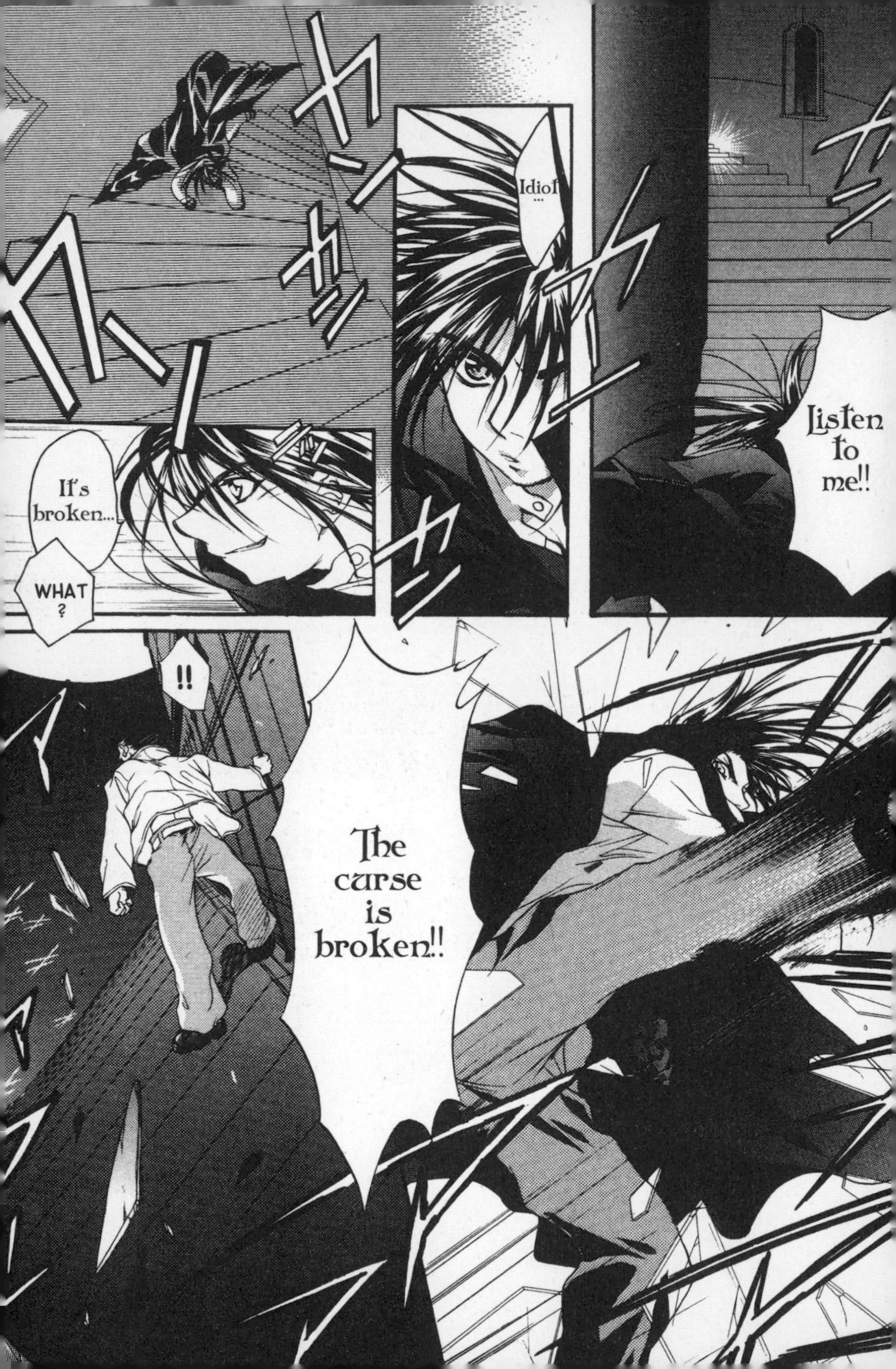
Listen to me!!
Idiot...
It's broken...
WHAT?
The curse is broken!!
!!

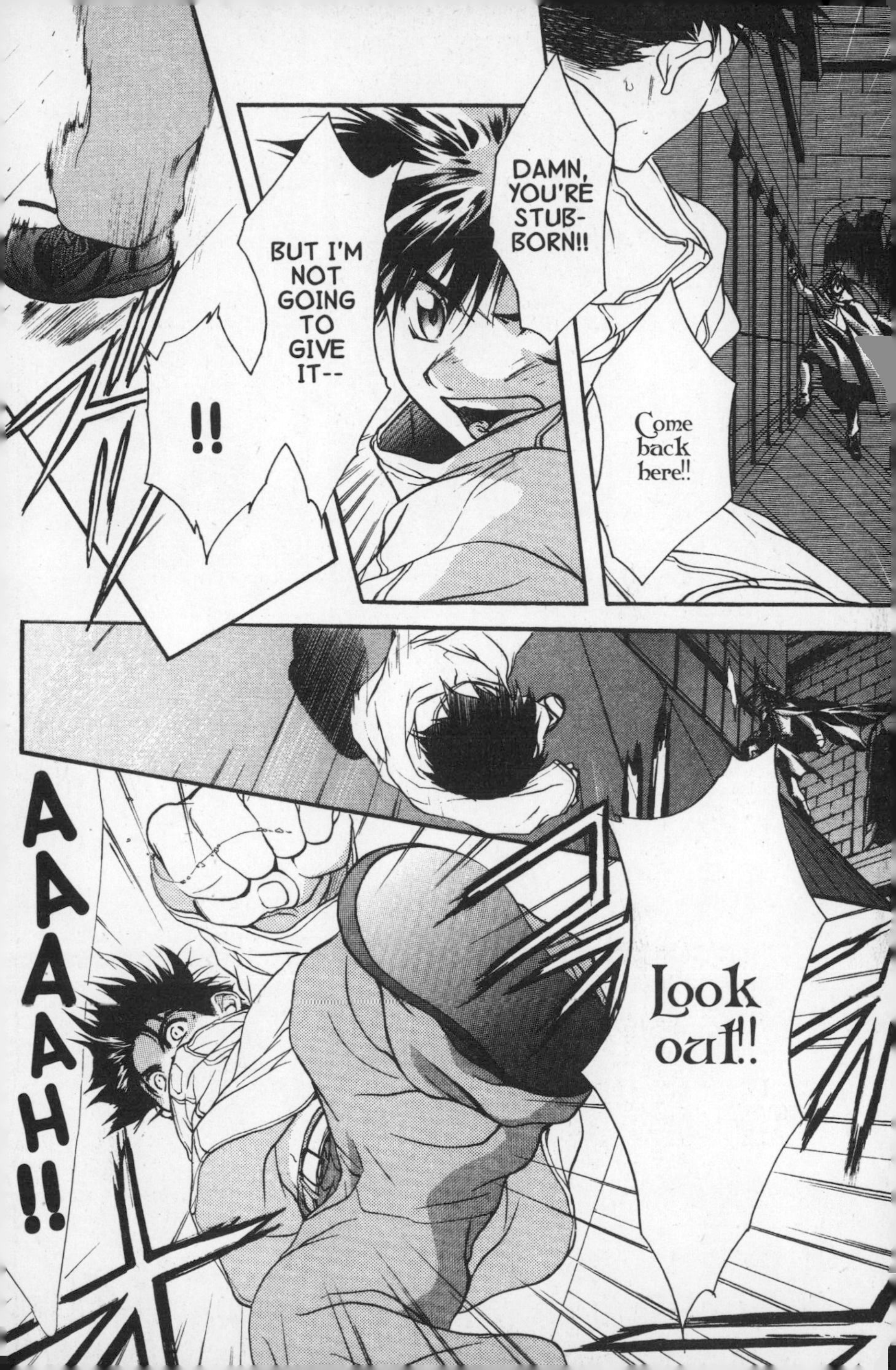
Come back here!!
DAMN, YOU'RE STUBBORN!!
BUT I'M NOT GOING TO GIVE IT--
!!
Look out!!
AAAAH!!

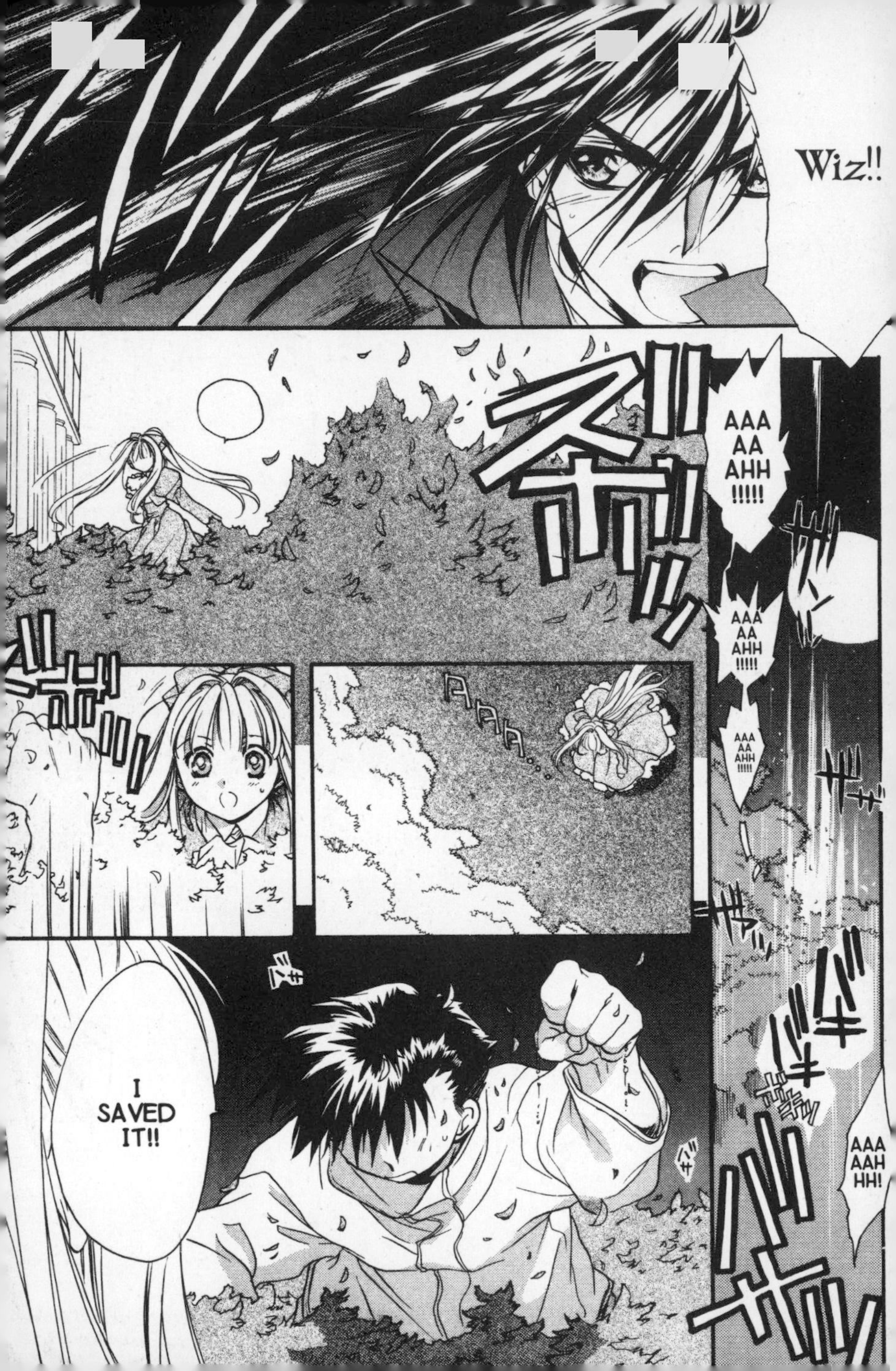
Wiz!!
AAA AA AHH !!!!!
AAA AA AHH !!!!!
AAA AA AHH !!!!!
AAA AAH HH!
AAAA...
I SAVED IT!!

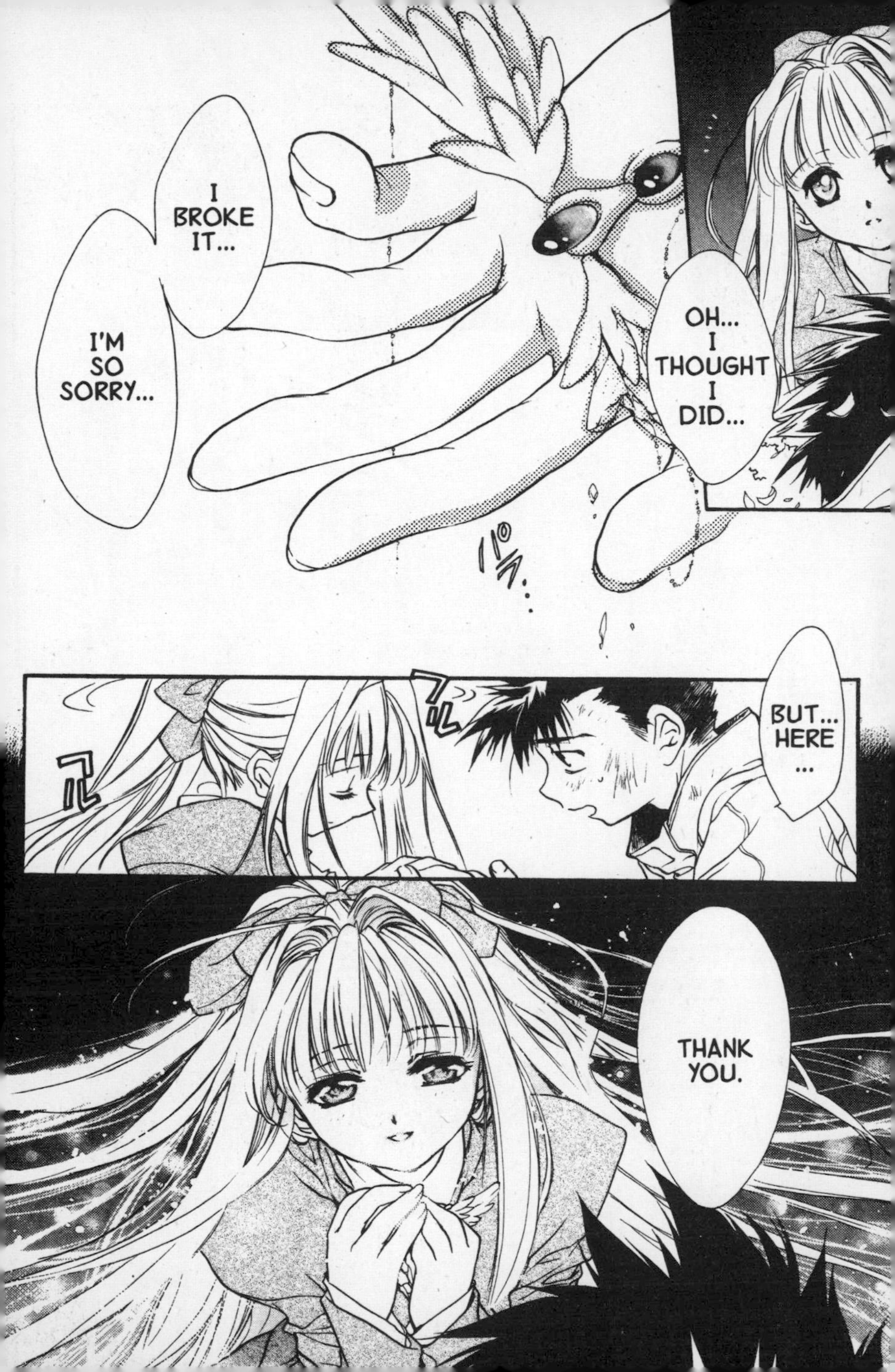

I BROKE IT...
I'M SO SORRY...
OH... I THOUGHT I DID...
BUT... HERE ...
THANK YOU.

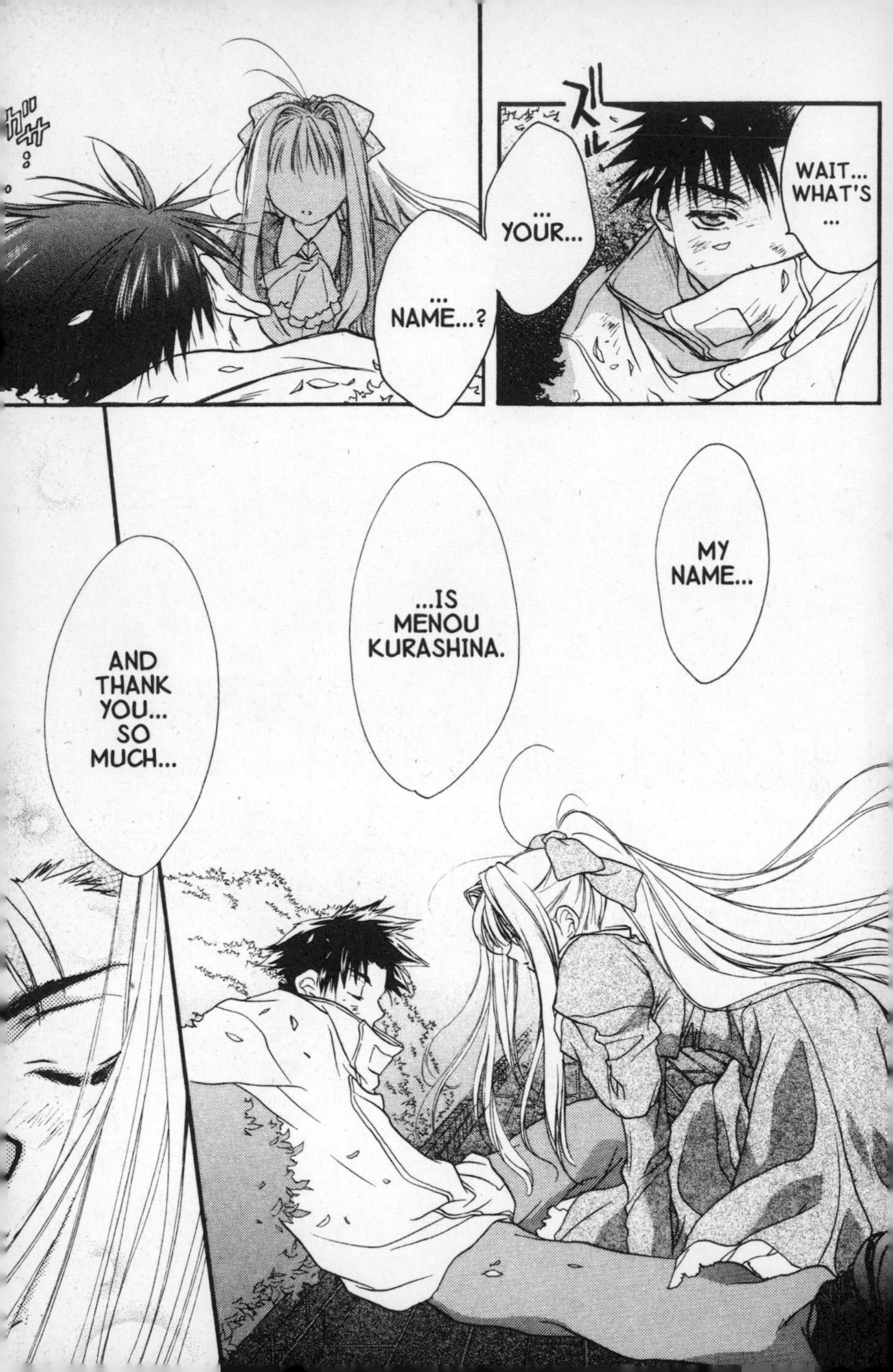
ズル
WAIT... WHAT'S ...
... YOUR...
... NAME...?
ガサ
MY NAME...
...IS MENOU KURASHINA.
AND THANK YOU... SO MUCH...

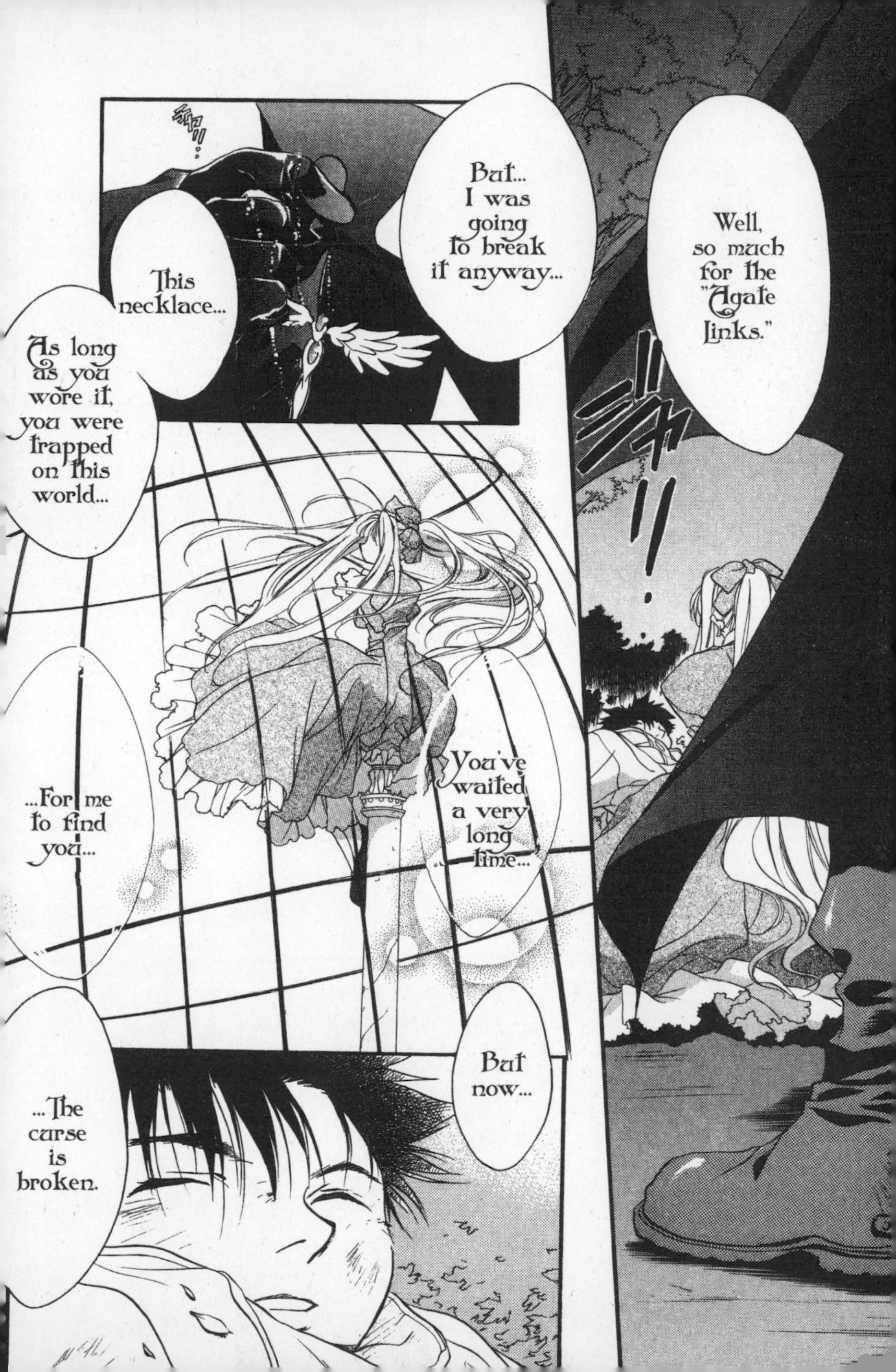

Well, so much for the "Agate Links."
ジャリ!
But... I was going to break it anyway...
This necklace...
As long as you wore it, you were trapped on this world...
You've waited a very long time...
...For me to find you...
But now...
...The curse is broken.

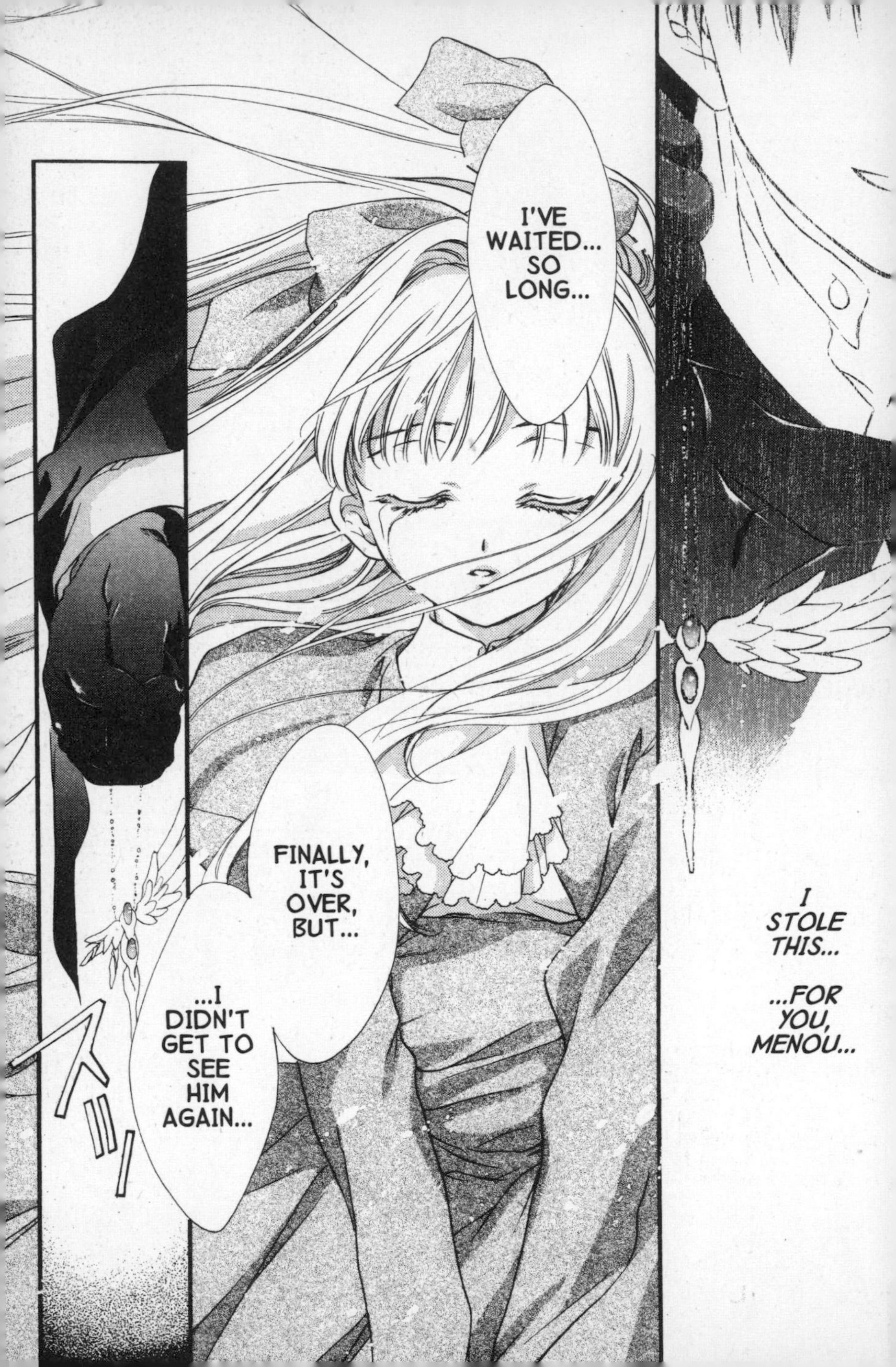
I STOLE THIS...
...FOR YOU, MENOU...
I'VE WAITED... SO LONG...
FINALLY, IT'S OVER, BUT...
...I DIDN'T GET TO SEE HIM AGAIN...

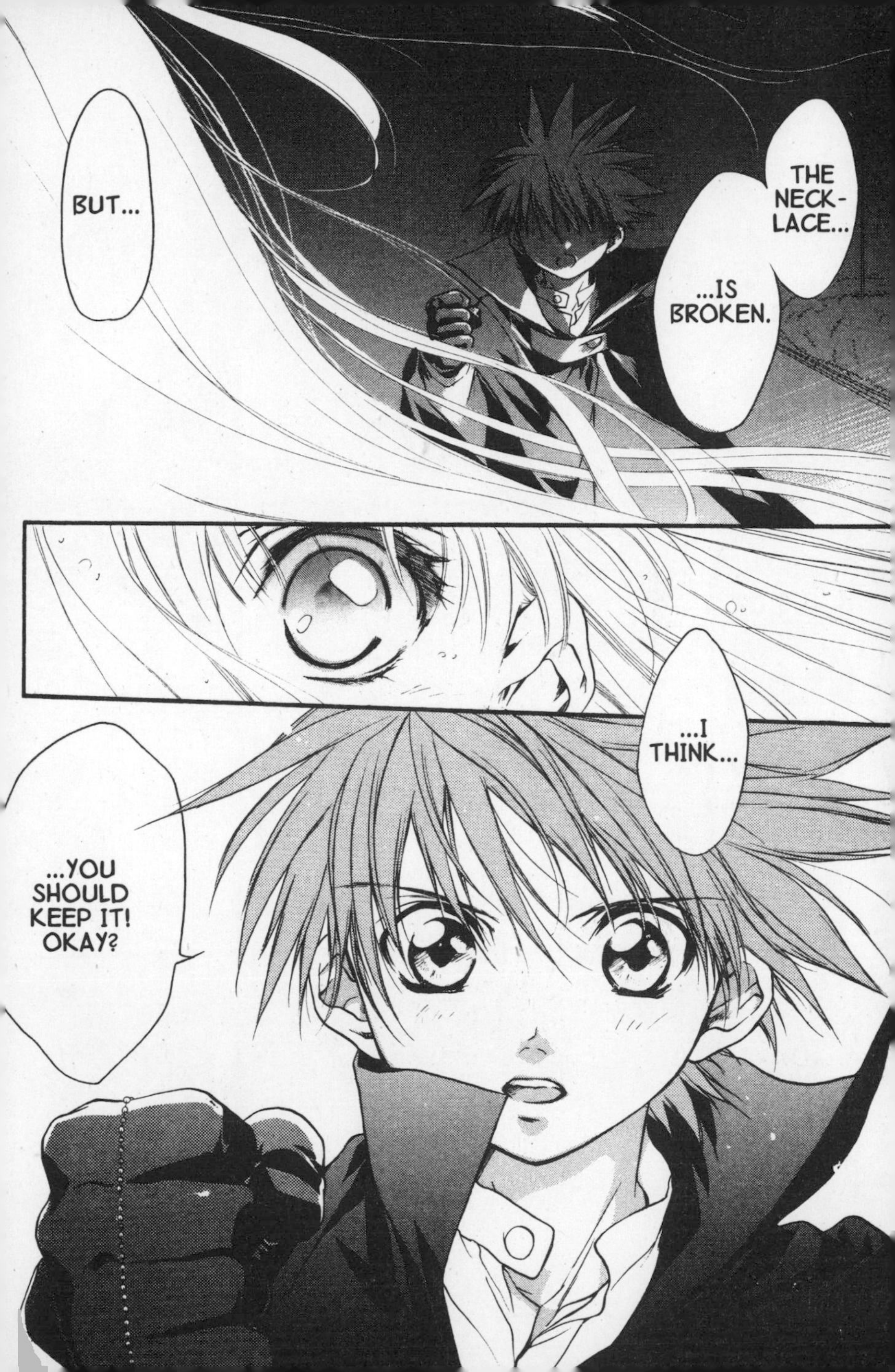
THE NECK-LACE...
...IS BROKEN.
BUT...
...I THINK...
...YOU SHOULD KEEP IT! OKAY?

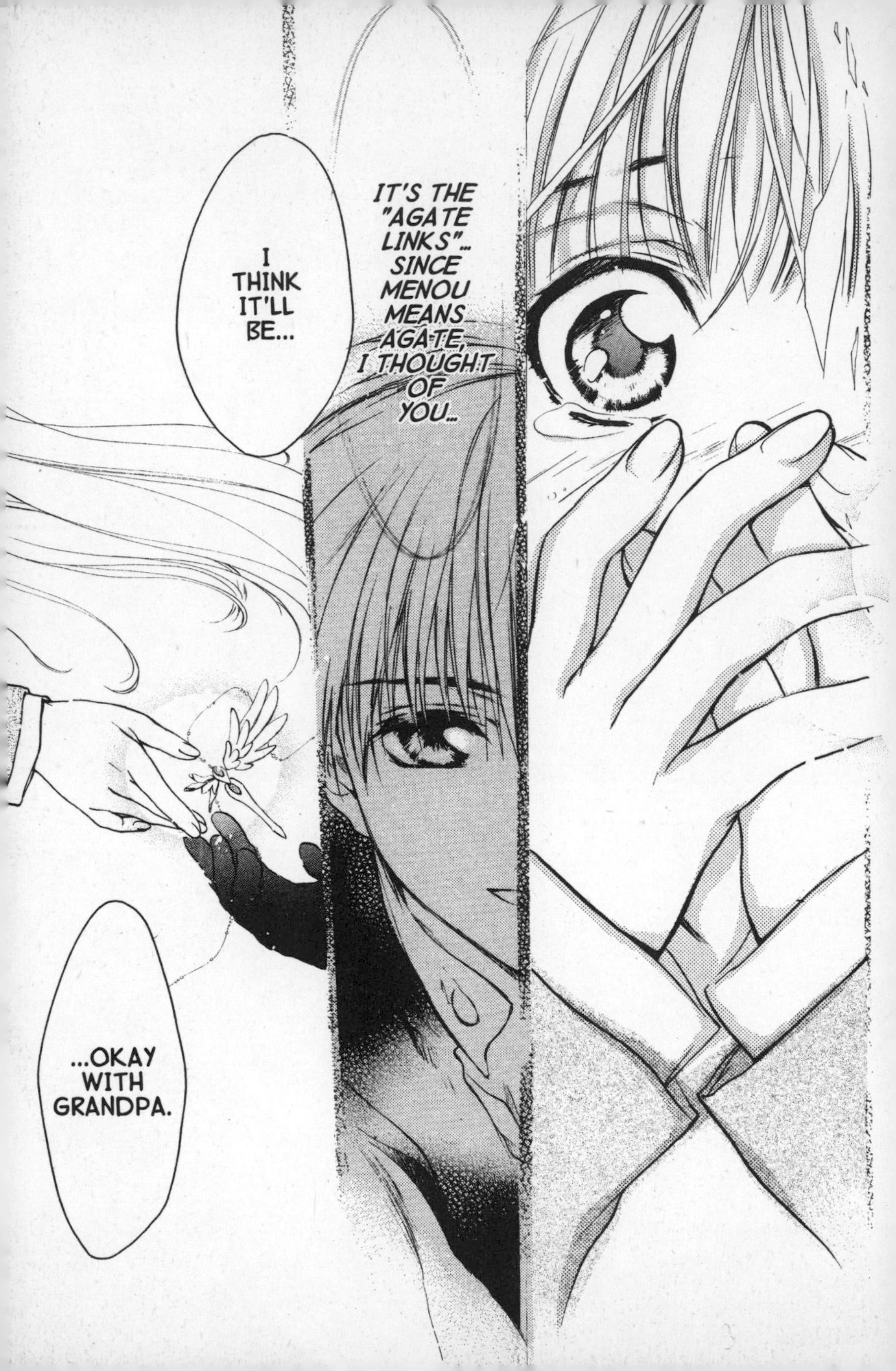
IT'S THE "AGATE LINKS"... SINCE MENOU MEANS AGATE, I THOUGHT OF YOU...
I THINK IT'LL BE...
...OKAY WITH GRANDPA.

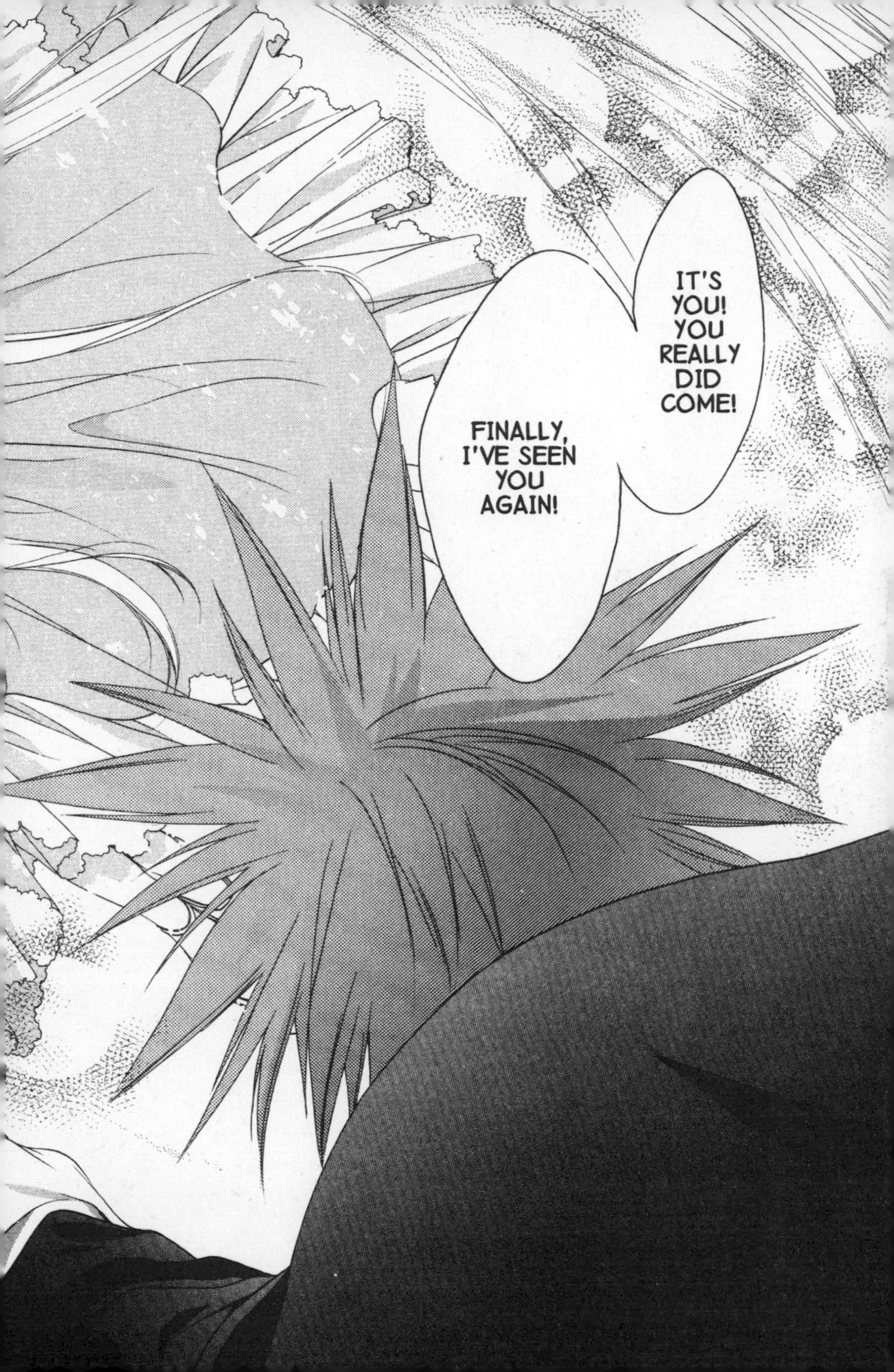
IT'S YOU! YOU REALLY DID COME!
FINALLY, I'VE SEEN YOU AGAIN!

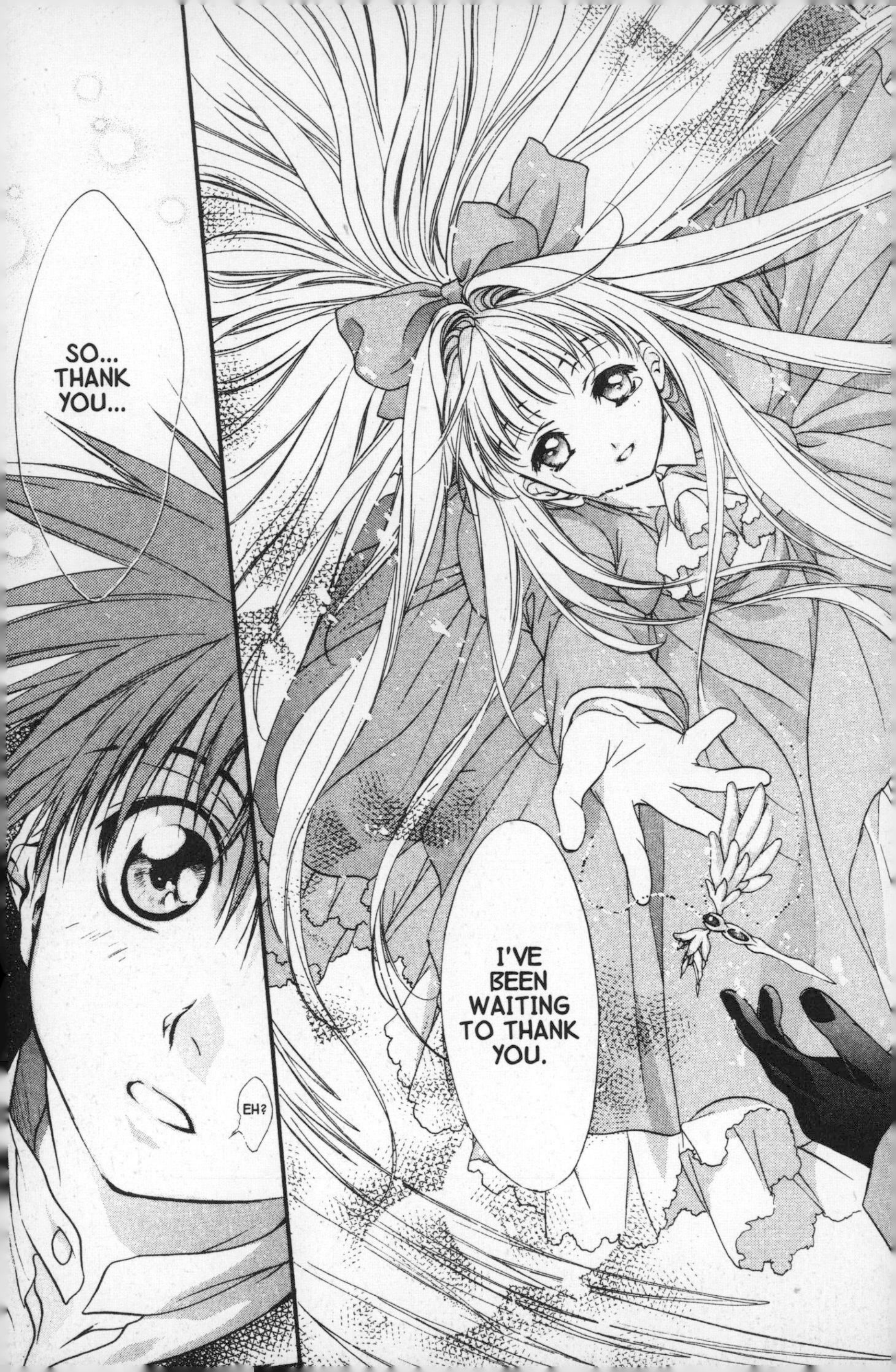
I'VE BEEN WAITING TO THANK YOU.
SO... THANK YOU...
EH?

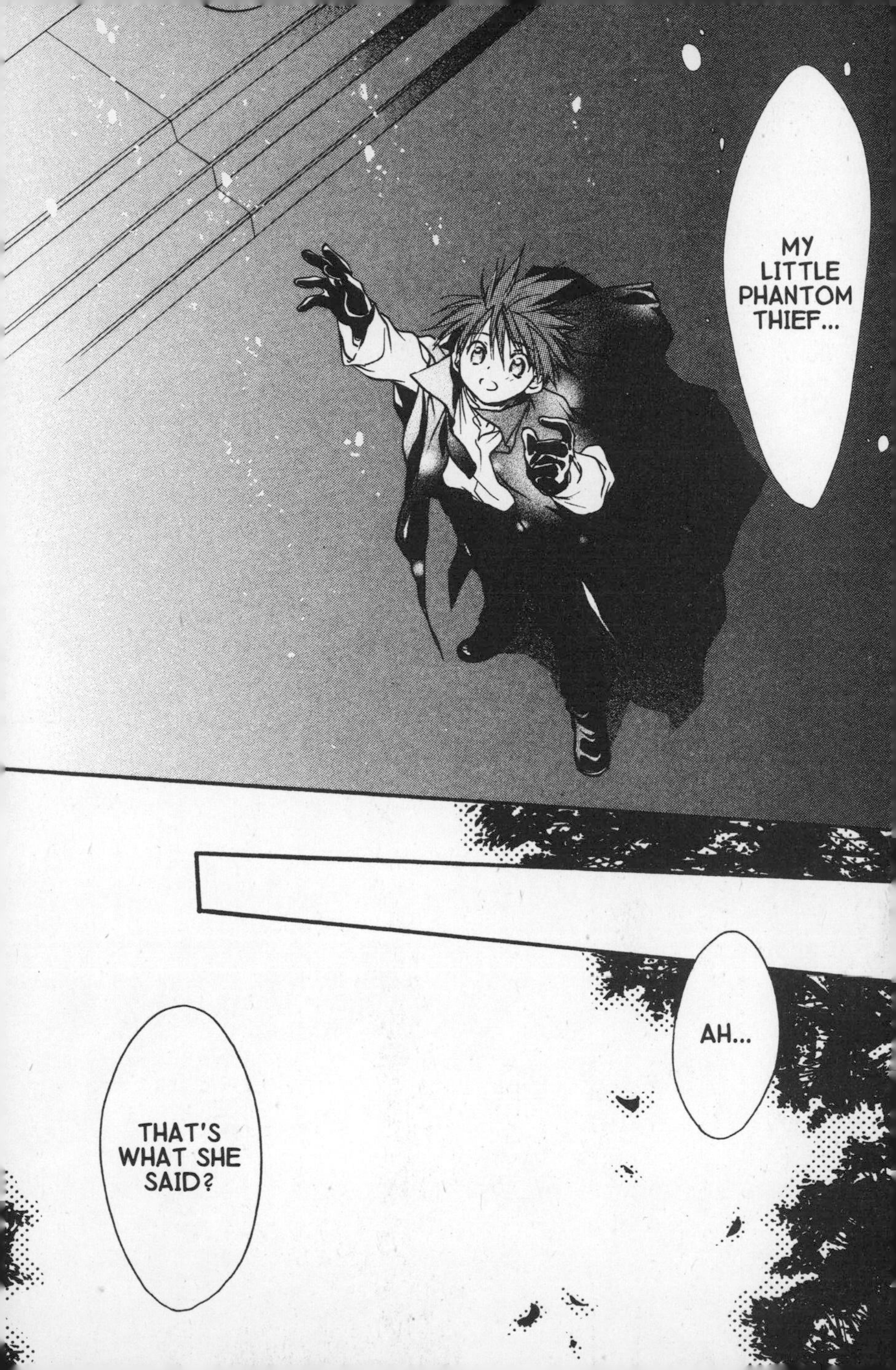
MY LITTLE PHANTOM THIEF...
AH...
THAT'S WHAT SHE SAID?

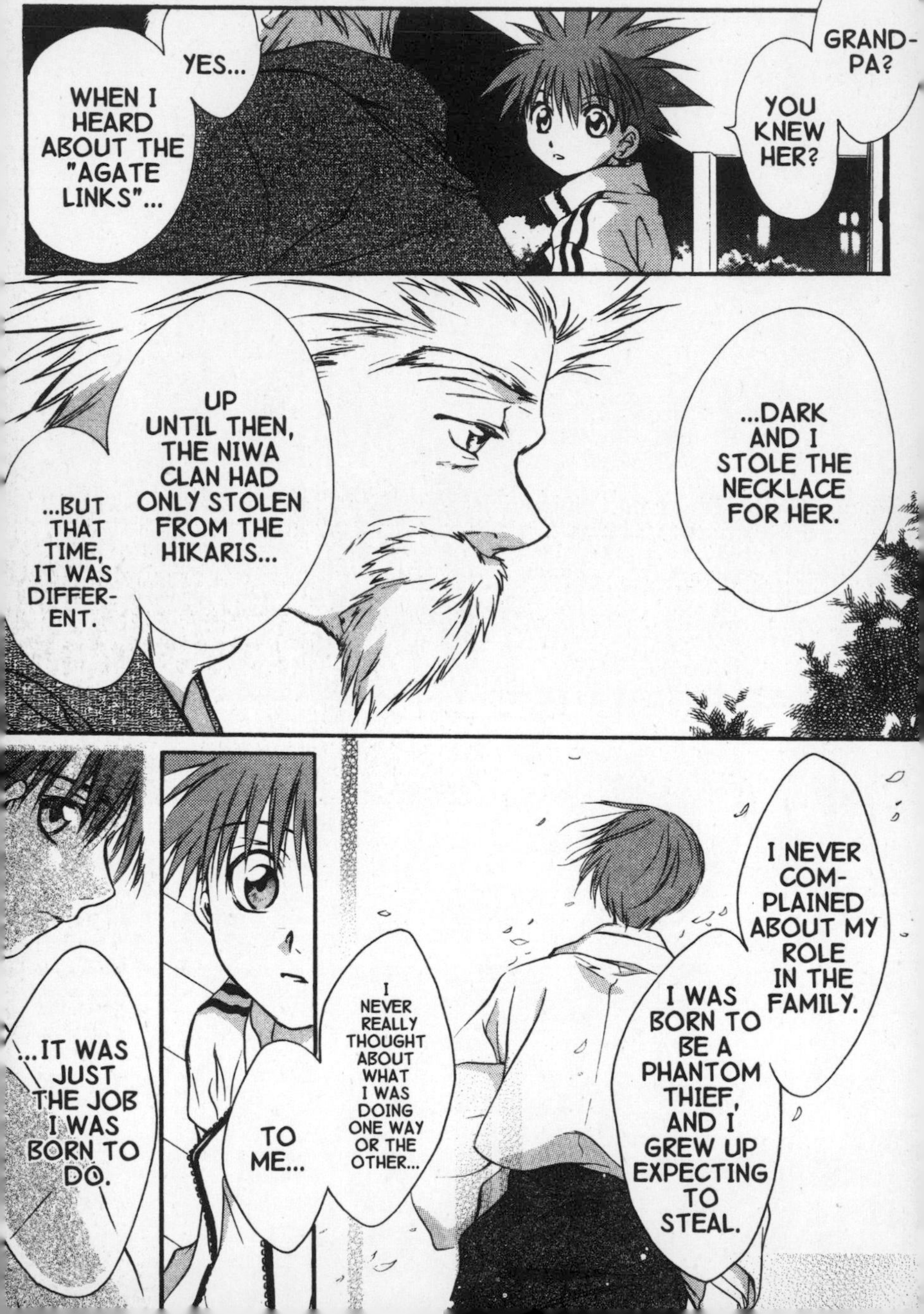
GRAND-PA?
YOU KNEW HER?
YES...
WHEN I HEARD ABOUT THE "AGATE LINKS"...
...DARK AND I STOLE THE NECKLACE FOR HER.
UP UNTIL THEN, THE NIWA CLAN HAD ONLY STOLEN FROM THE HIKARIS...
...BUT THAT TIME, IT WAS DIFFER-ENT.
I NEVER COM-PLAINED ABOUT MY ROLE IN THE FAMILY.
I WAS BORN TO BE A PHANTOM THIEF, AND I GREW UP EXPECTING TO STEAL.
I NEVER REALLY THOUGHT ABOUT WHAT I WAS DOING ONE WAY OR THE OTHER...
TO ME...
...IT WAS JUST THE JOB I WAS BORN TO DO.

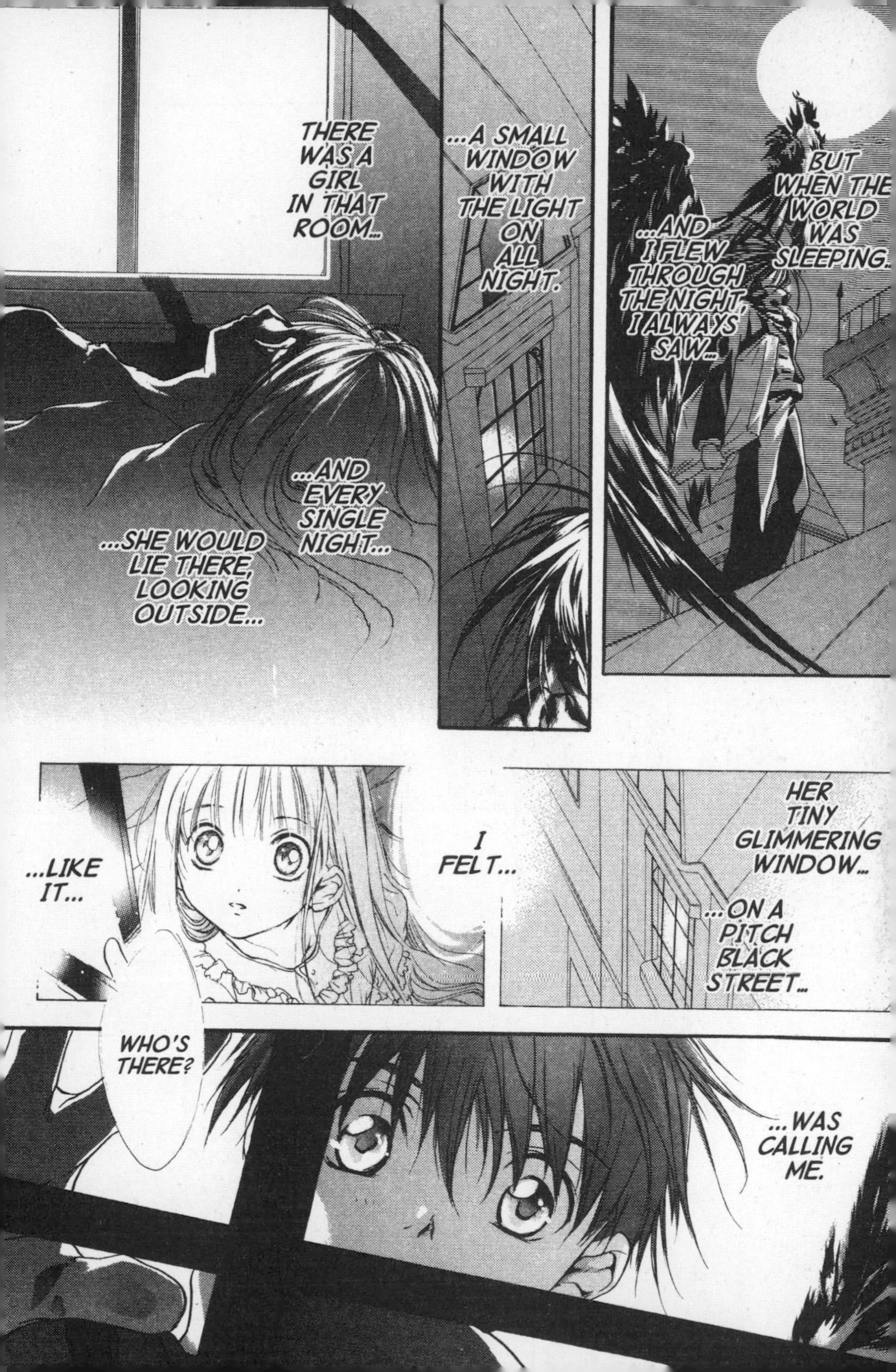
BUT WHEN THE WORLD WAS SLEEPING...
...AND I FLEW THROUGH THE NIGHT, I ALWAYS SAW...
...A SMALL WINDOW WITH THE LIGHT ON ALL NIGHT.
THERE WAS A GIRL IN THAT ROOM...
...AND EVERY SINGLE NIGHT...
...SHE WOULD LIE THERE, LOOKING OUTSIDE...
HER TINY GLIMMERING WINDOW...
...ON A PITCH BLACK STREET...
I FELT...
...LIKE IT...
...WAS CALLING ME.
WHO'S THERE?

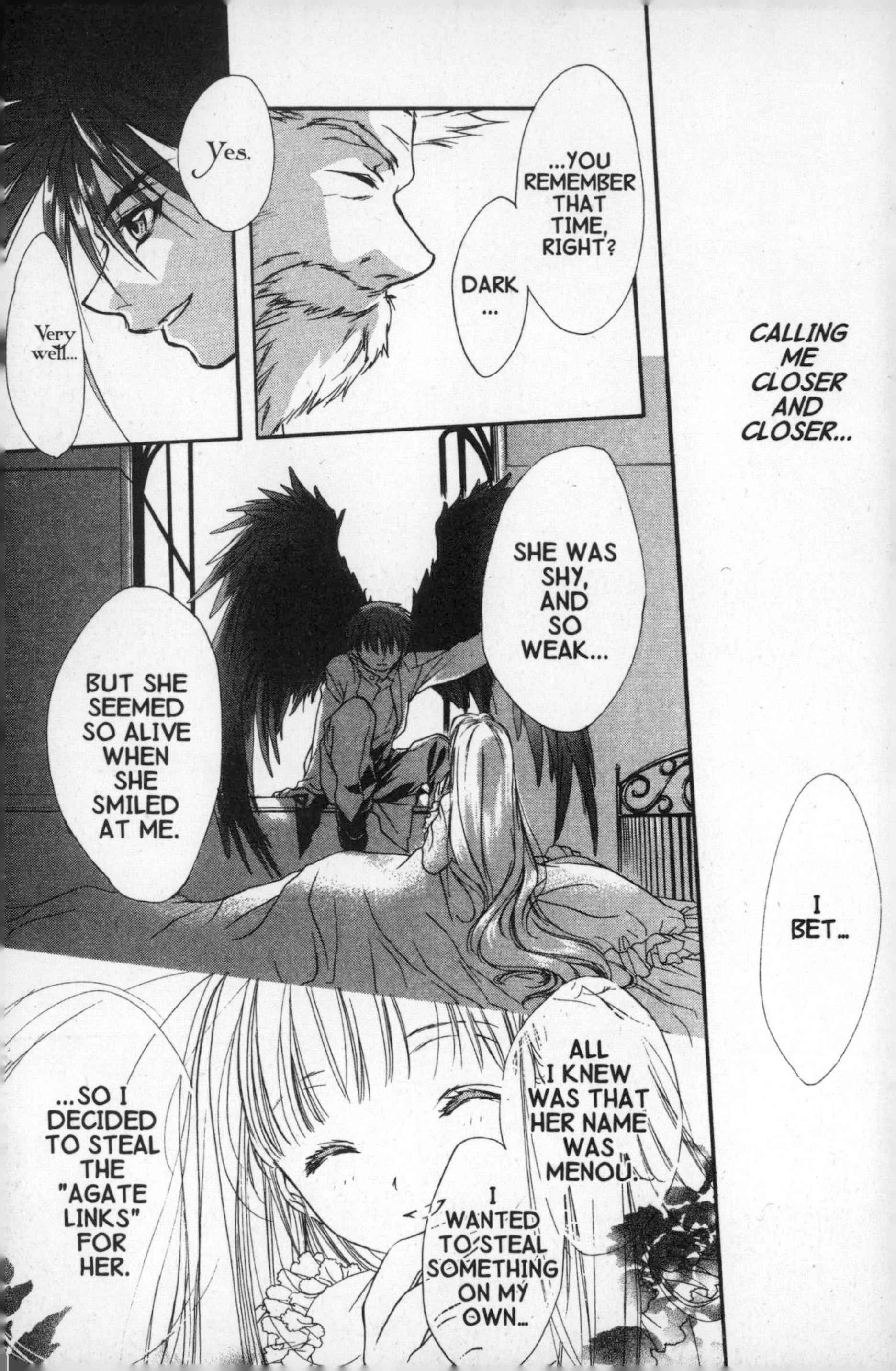
CALLING ME CLOSER AND CLOSER...
I BET...
...YOU REMEMBER THAT TIME, RIGHT?
DARK...
Yes.
Very well...
SHE WAS SHY, AND SO WEAK...
BUT SHE SEEMED SO ALIVE WHEN SHE SMILED AT ME.
ALL I KNEW WAS THAT HER NAME WAS MENOU.
I WANTED TO STEAL SOMETHING ON MY OWN...
...SO I DECIDED TO STEAL THE "AGATE LINKS" FOR HER.

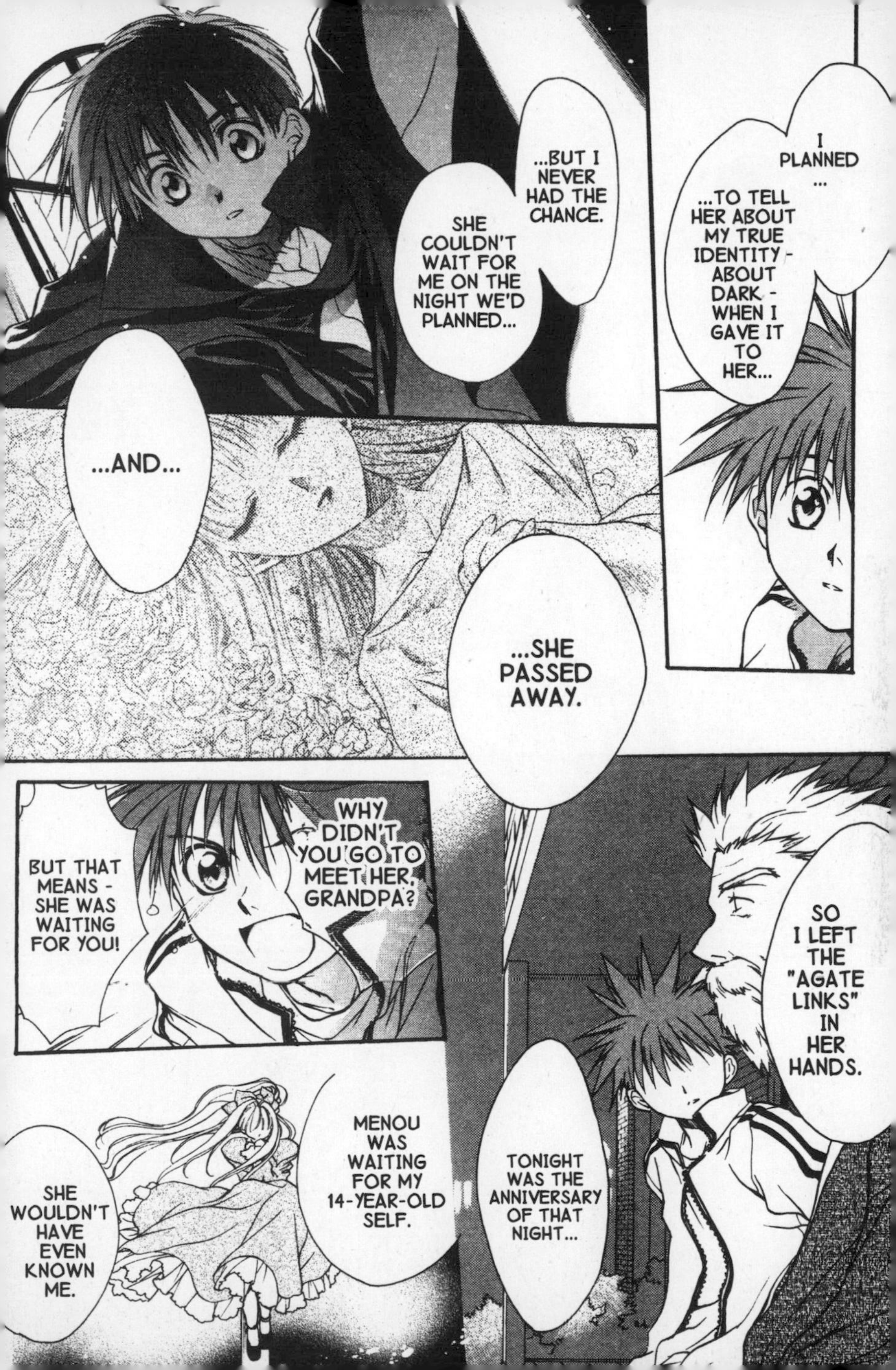
I PLANNED...
...TO TELL HER ABOUT MY TRUE IDENTITY - ABOUT DARK - WHEN I GAVE IT TO HER...
...BUT I NEVER HAD THE CHANCE.
SHE COULDN'T WAIT FOR ME ON THE NIGHT WE'D PLANNED...
...AND...
...SHE PASSED AWAY.
SO I LEFT THE "AGATE LINKS" IN HER HANDS.
TONIGHT WAS THE ANNIVERSARY OF THAT NIGHT...
WHY DIDN'T YOU GO TO MEET HER, GRANDPA?
BUT THAT MEANS - SHE WAS WAITING FOR YOU!
MENOU WAS WAITING FOR MY 14-YEAR-OLD SELF.
SHE WOULDN'T HAVE EVEN KNOWN ME.

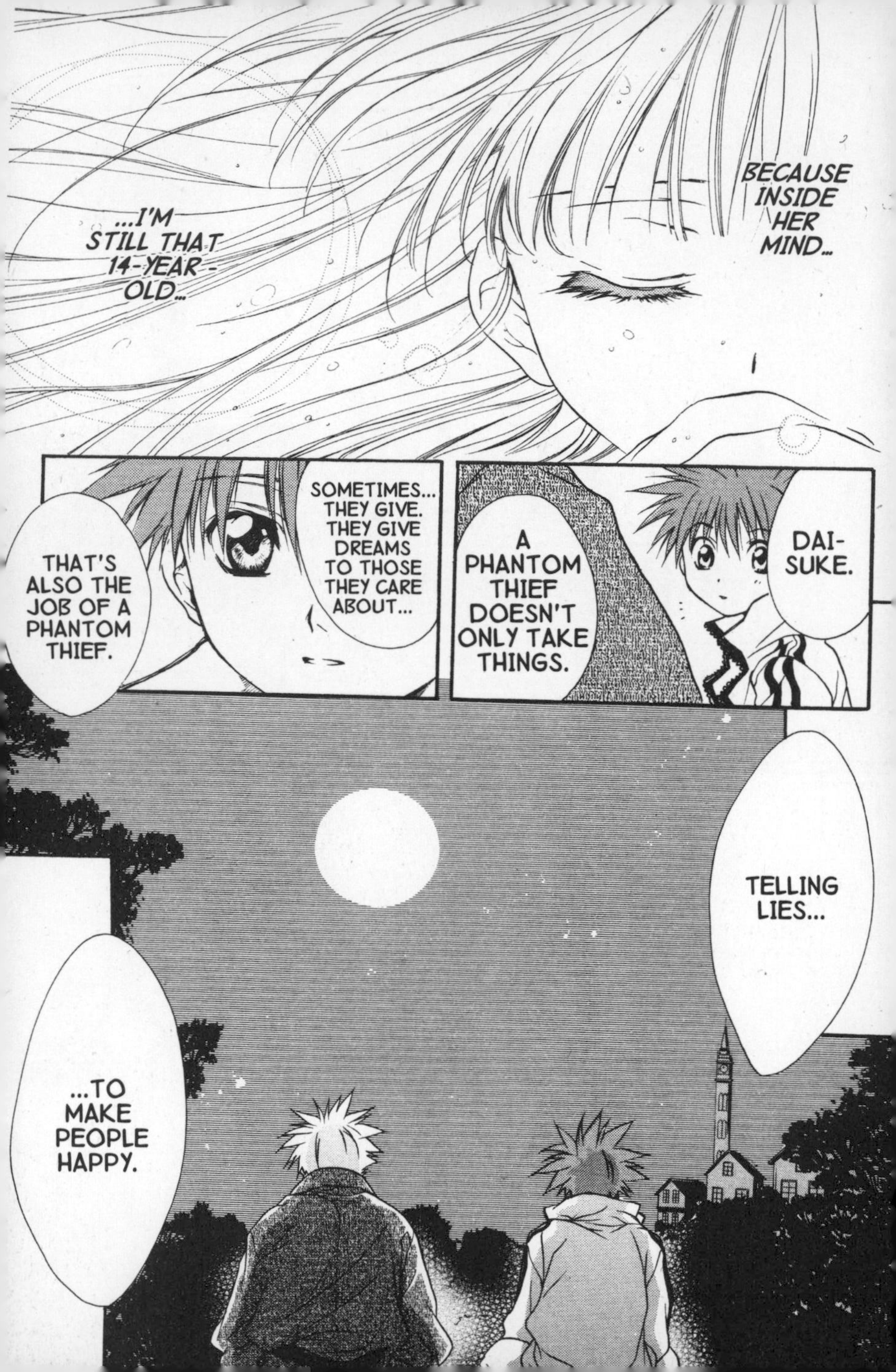
BECAUSE INSIDE HER MIND...
...I'M STILL THAT 14-YEAR-OLD...
DAI-SUKE.
A PHANTOM THIEF DOESN'T ONLY TAKE THINGS.
SOMETIMES... THEY GIVE. THEY GIVE DREAMS TO THOSE THEY CARE ABOUT...
THAT'S ALSO THE JOB OF A PHANTOM THIEF.
TELLING LIES...
...TO MAKE PEOPLE HAPPY.

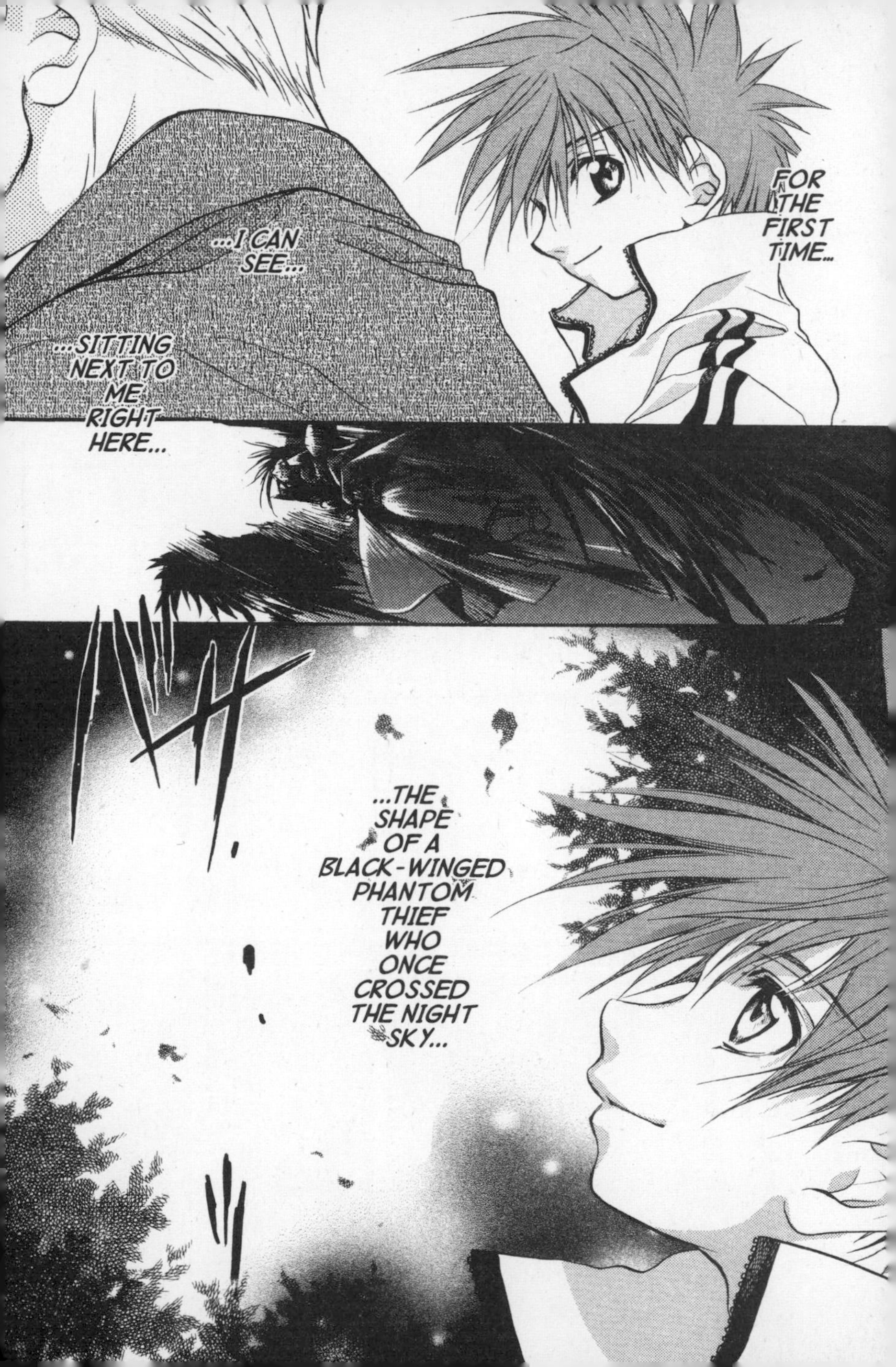
FOR THE FIRST TIME...
...I CAN SEE...
...SITTING NEXT TO ME RIGHT HERE...
...THE SHAPE OF A BLACK-WINGED PHANTOM THIEF WHO ONCE CROSSED THE NIGHT SKY...

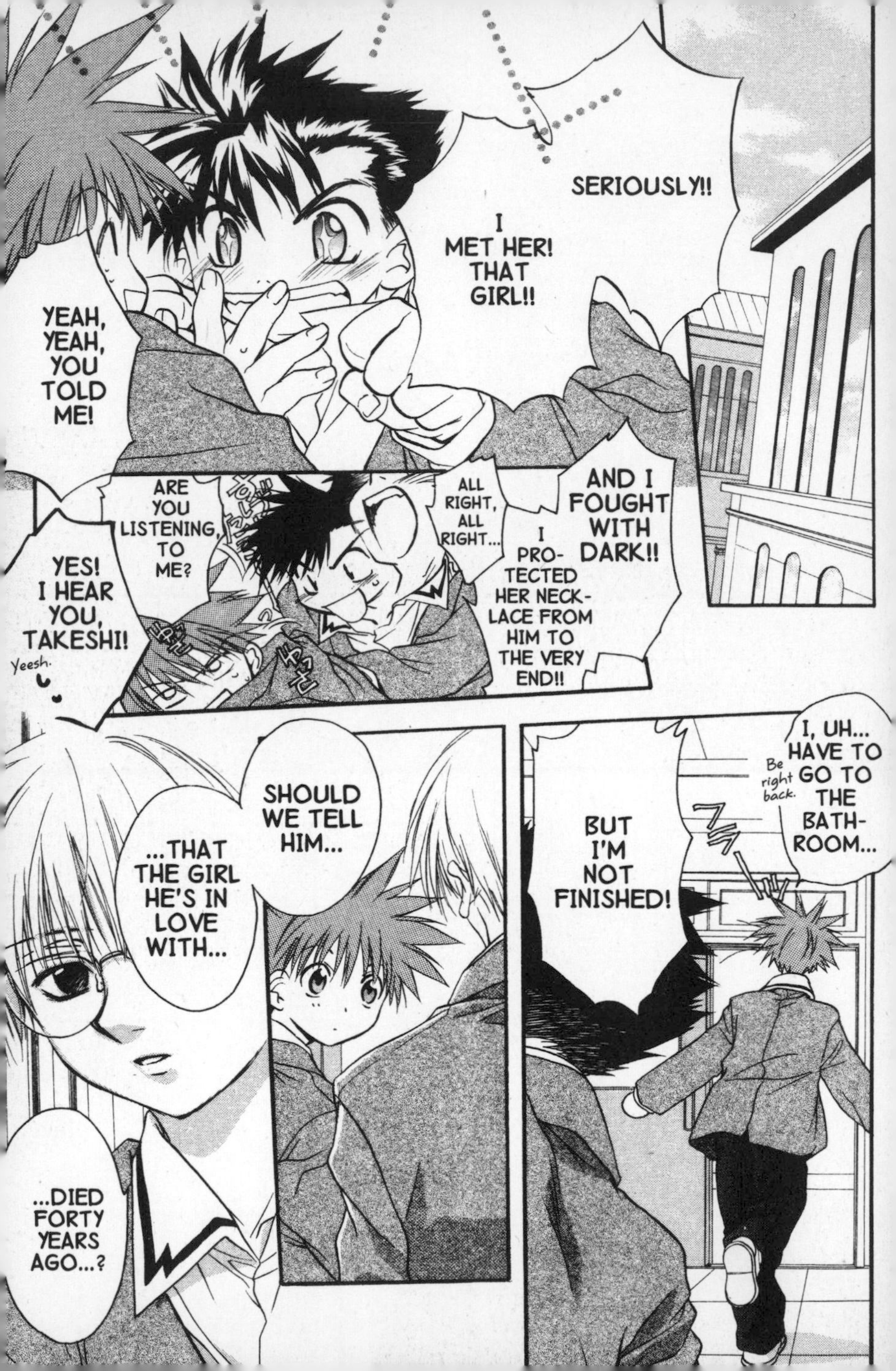
SERIOUSLY!!
I MET HER! THAT GIRL!!
YEAH, YEAH, YOU TOLD ME!
AND I FOUGHT WITH DARK!!
I PROTECTED HER NECKLACE FROM HIM TO THE VERY END!!
ALL RIGHT, ALL RIGHT...
ARE YOU LISTENING, TO ME?
YES! I HEAR YOU, TAKESHI!
Yeesh.
I, UH... HAVE TO GO TO THE BATHROOM...
Be right back.
BUT I'M NOT FINISHED!
SHOULD WE TELL HIM...
...THAT THE GIRL HE'S IN LOVE WITH...
...DIED FORTY YEARS AGO...?

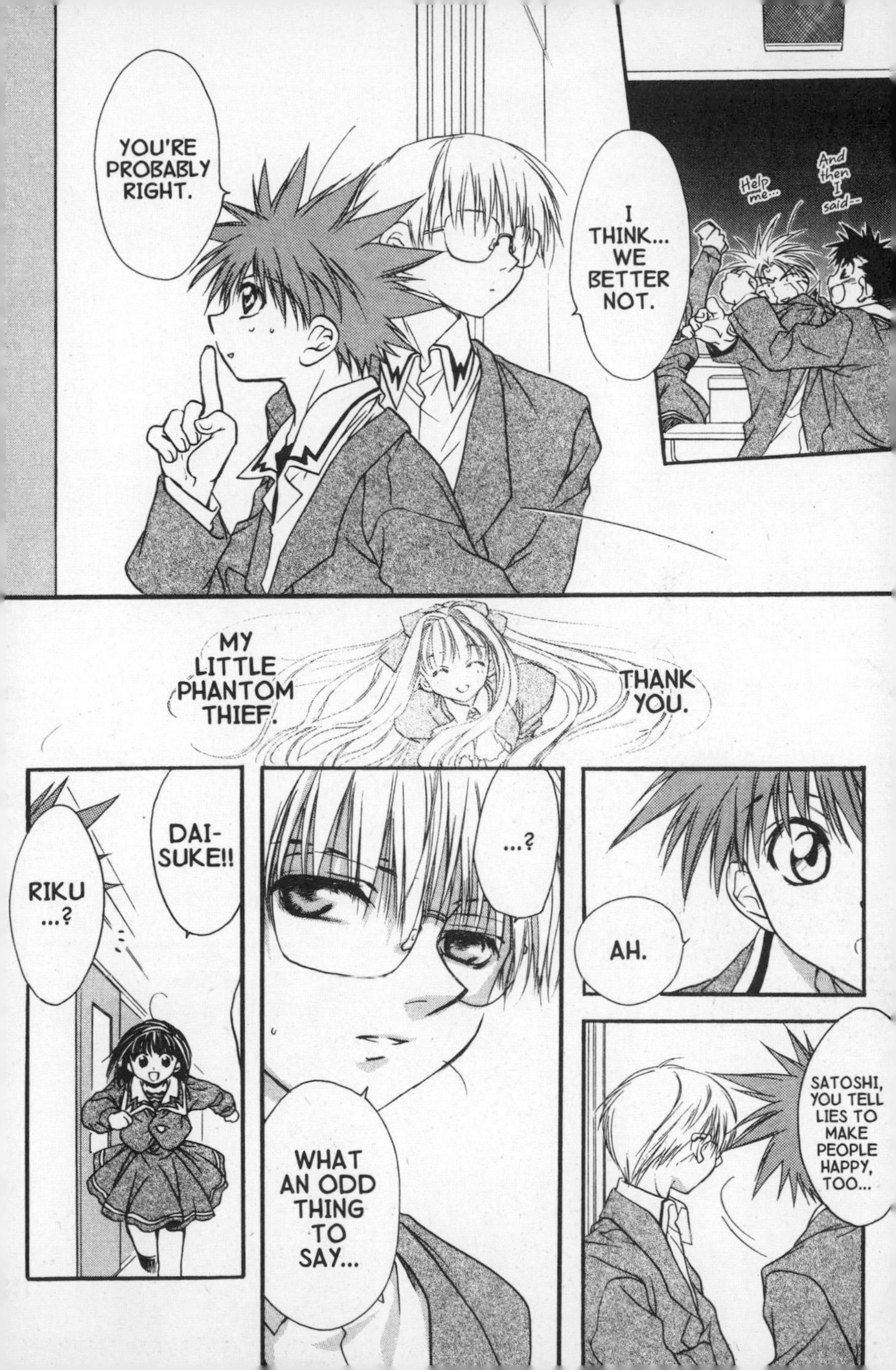
And then I said--
Help me...
I THINK... WE BETTER NOT.
YOU'RE PROBABLY RIGHT.
THANK YOU.
MY LITTLE PHANTOM THIEF.
AH.
SATOSHI, YOU TELL LIES TO MAKE PEOPLE HAPPY, TOO...
...?
WHAT AN ODD THING TO SAY...
DAI-SUKE!!
RIKU ...?

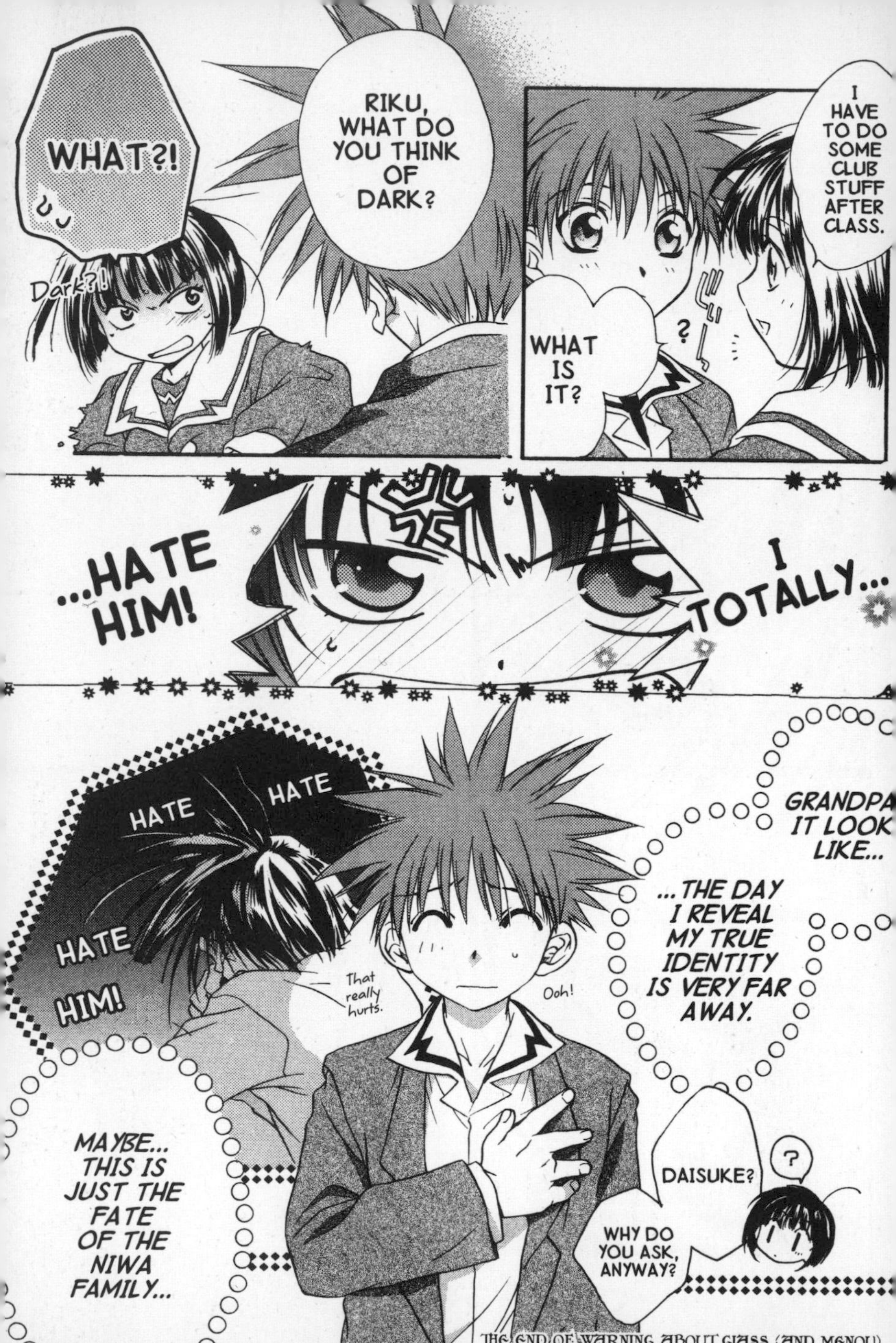
I HAVE TO DO SOME CLUB STUFF AFTER CLASS.
?
WHAT IS IT?
RIKU, WHAT DO YOU THINK OF DARK?
WHAT?!
Dark?!
I TOTALLY...
...HATE HIM!
GRANDPA IT LOOK LIKE...
...THE DAY I REVEAL MY TRUE IDENTITY IS VERY FAR AWAY.
HATE HATE
HATE
HIM!
That really hurts.
Ooh!
MAYBE... THIS IS JUST THE FATE OF THE NIWA FAMILY...
DAISUKE?
?
WHY DO YOU ASK, ANYWAY?

THE END OF WARNING ABOUT GLASS (AND MENOU)

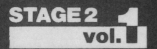

THE LEGENDARY PHANTOM THIEF,
CAUSING TROUBLE
THROUGHOUT THE WORLD...

DARK

NO ONE KNOWS HIS TRUE IDENTITY.

SOMETIMES I THINK I DON'T, EITHER...

DARK?

WHO ARE YOU?
WHAT ARE YOU?

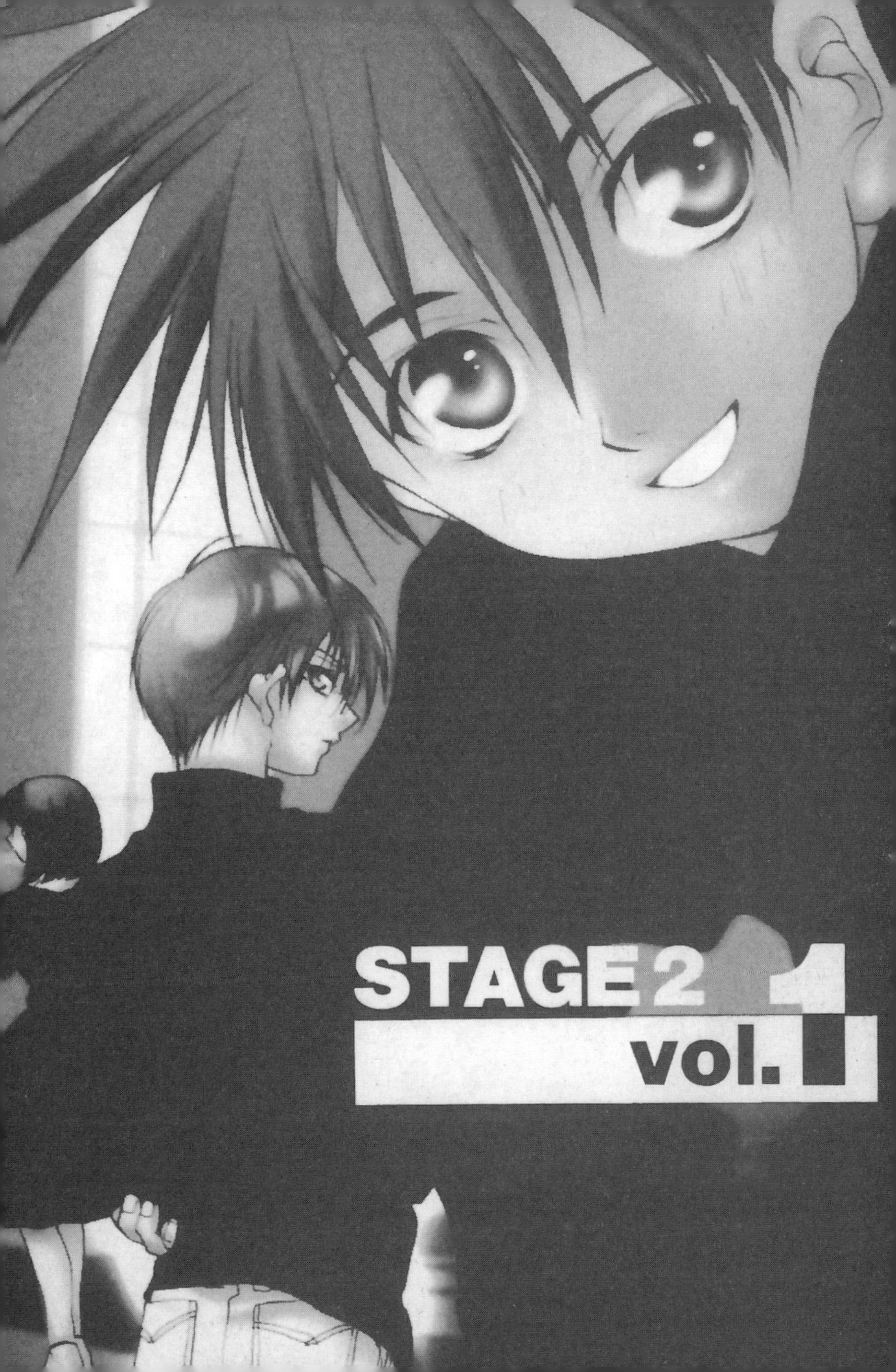
STAGE 2
vol. 1

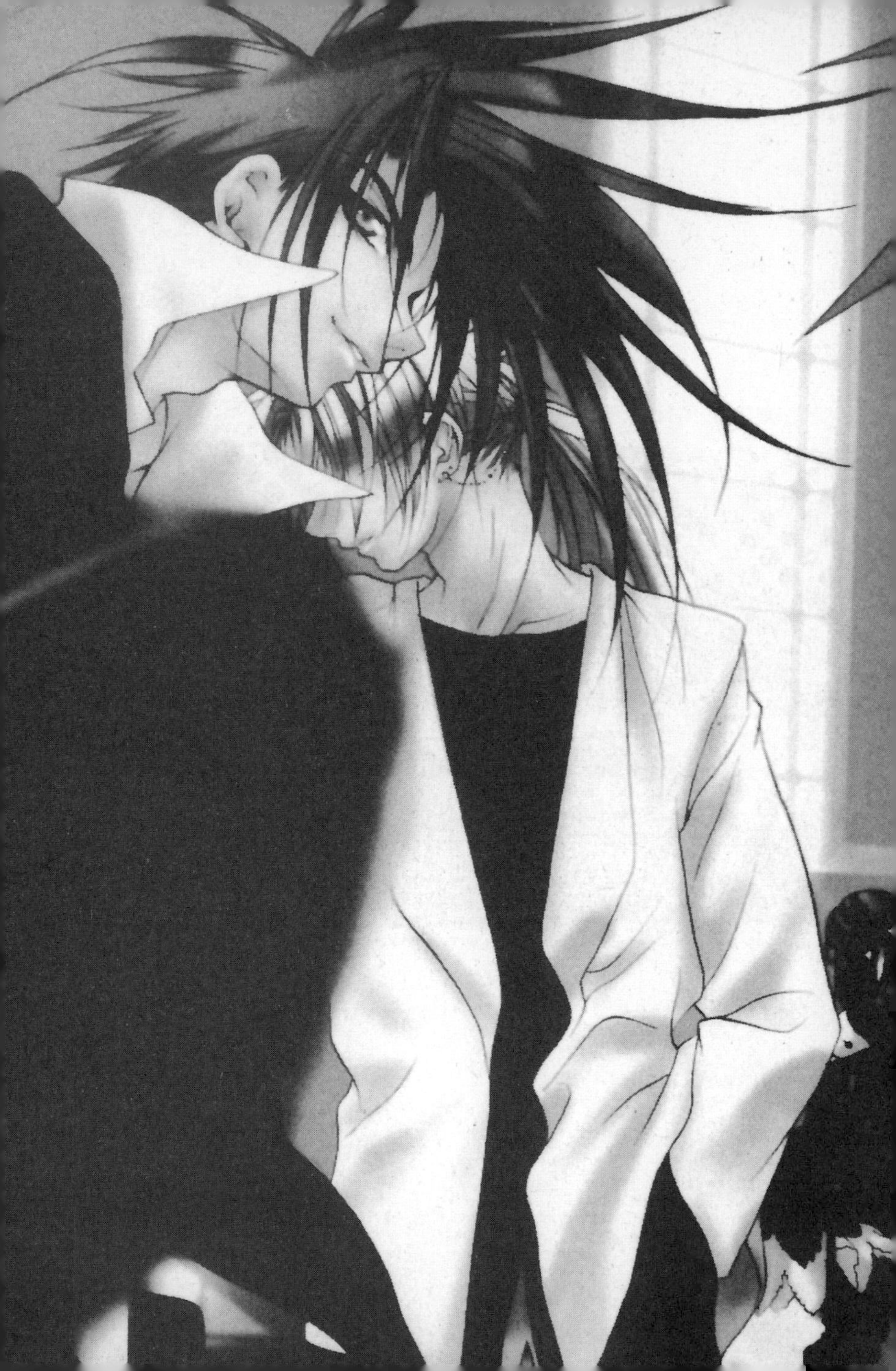

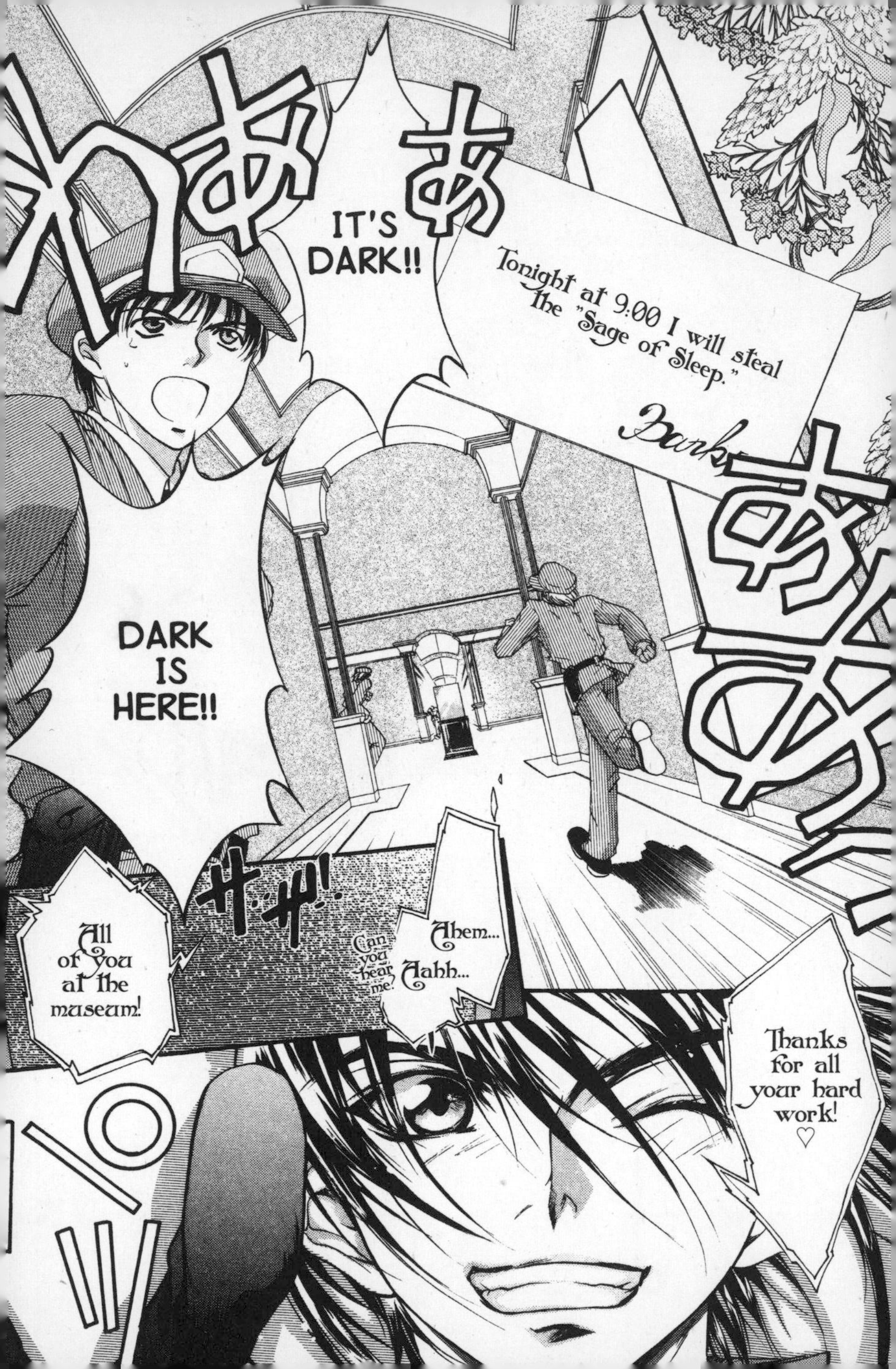
Tonight at 9:00 I will steal the "Sage of Sleep."
Dark
IT'S DARK!!
DARK IS HERE!!
ザ…ザ!
Ahem... Aahh...
Can you hear me?
All of you at the museum!
Thanks for all your hard work! ♡

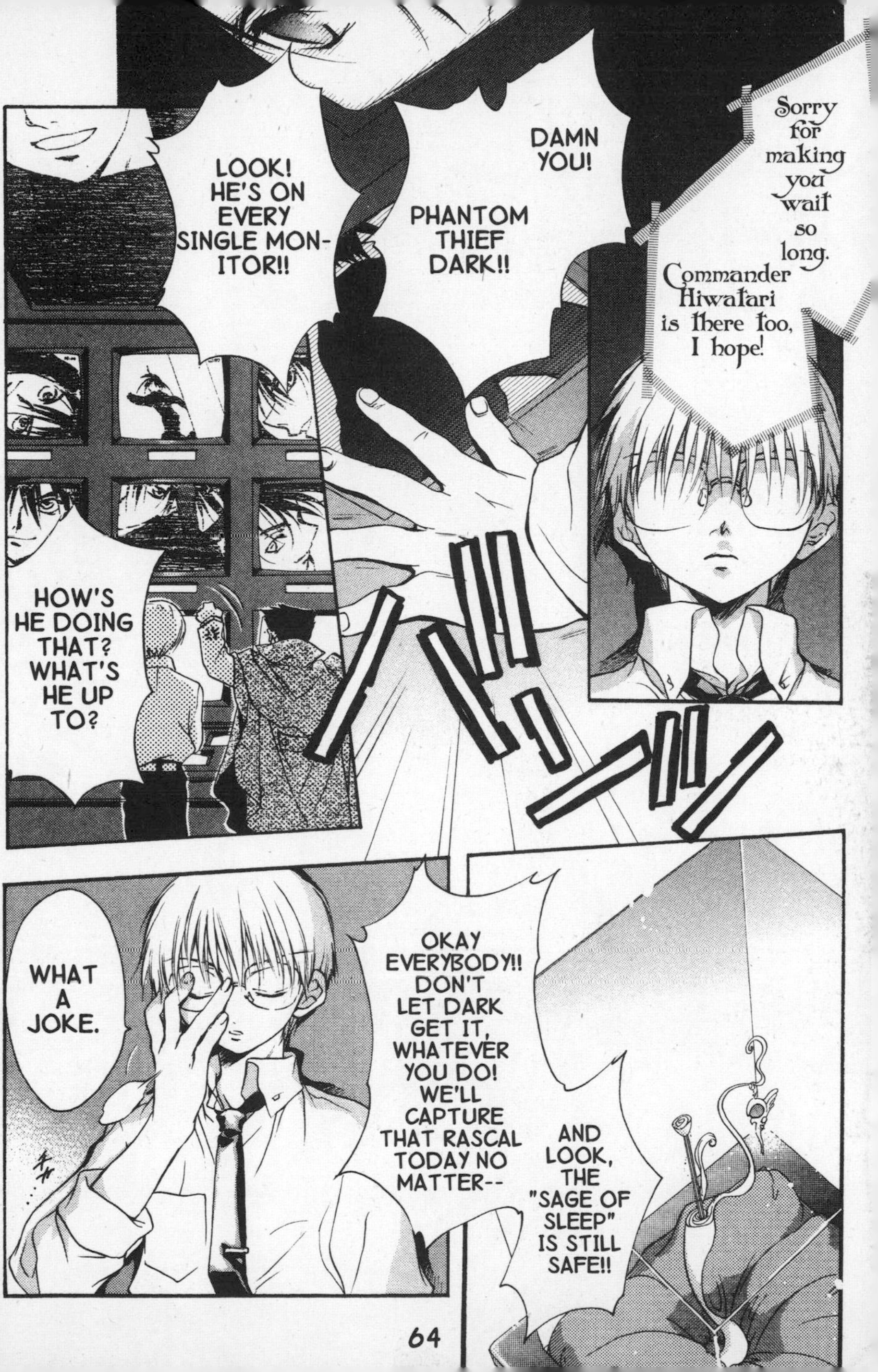
Sorry for making you wait so long. Commander Hiwatari is there too, I hope!
DAMN YOU!
PHANTOM THIEF DARK!!
LOOK! HE'S ON EVERY SINGLE MON-ITOR!!
HOW'S HE DOING THAT? WHAT'S HE UP TO?
OKAY EVERYBODY!! DON'T LET DARK GET IT, WHATEVER YOU DO! WE'LL CAPTURE THAT RASCAL TODAY NO MATTER--
AND LOOK, THE "SAGE OF SLEEP" IS STILL SAFE!!
WHAT A JOKE.

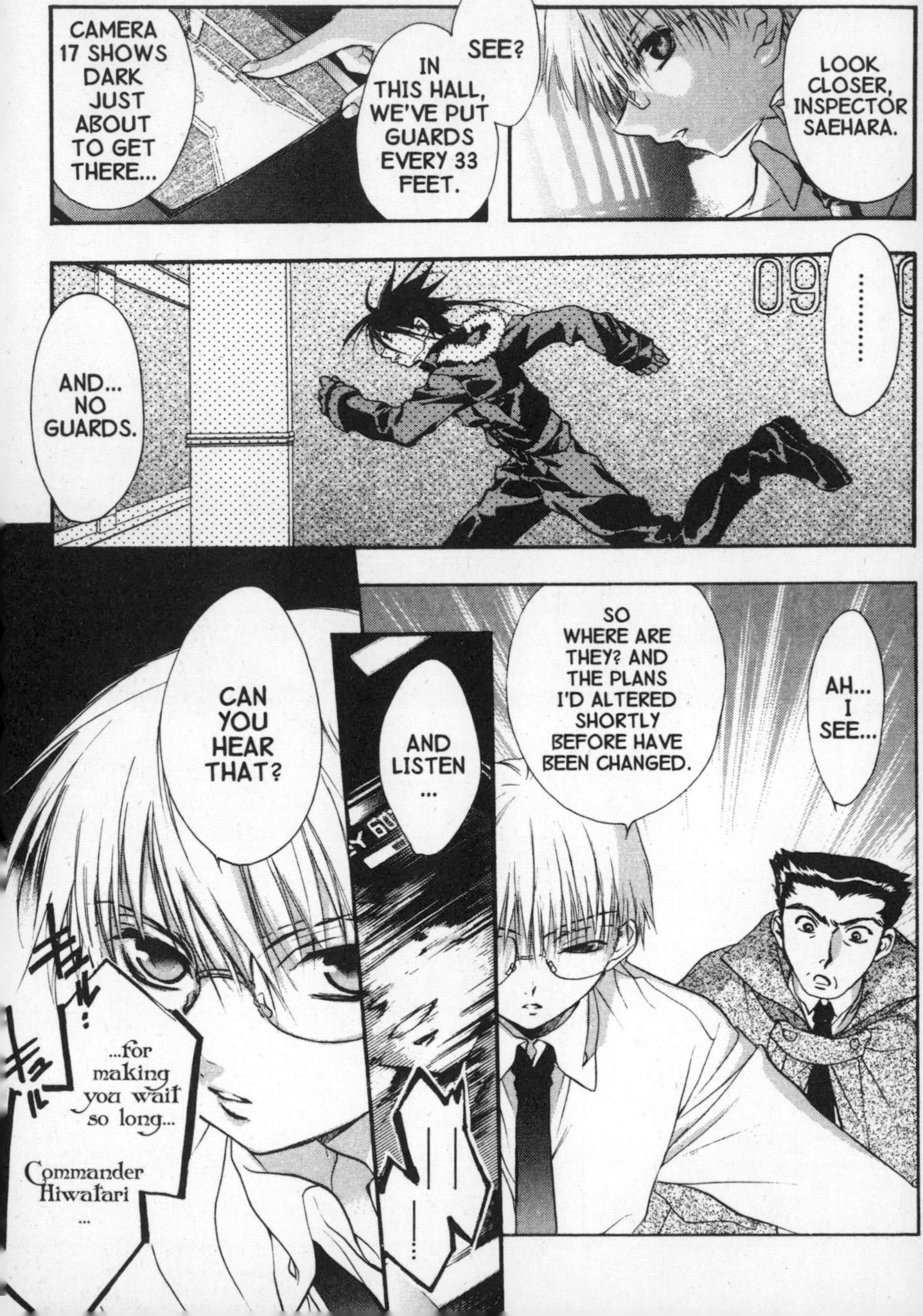
LOOK CLOSER, INSPECTOR SAEHARA.
SEE?
IN THIS HALL, WE'VE PUT GUARDS EVERY 33 FEET.
CAMERA 17 SHOWS DARK JUST ABOUT TO GET THERE...
......
AND... NO GUARDS.
AH... I SEE...
SO WHERE ARE THEY? AND THE PLANS I'D ALTERED SHORTLY BEFORE HAVE BEEN CHANGED.
AND LISTEN ...
CAN YOU HEAR THAT?
...for making you wait so long...
Commander Hiwatari ...

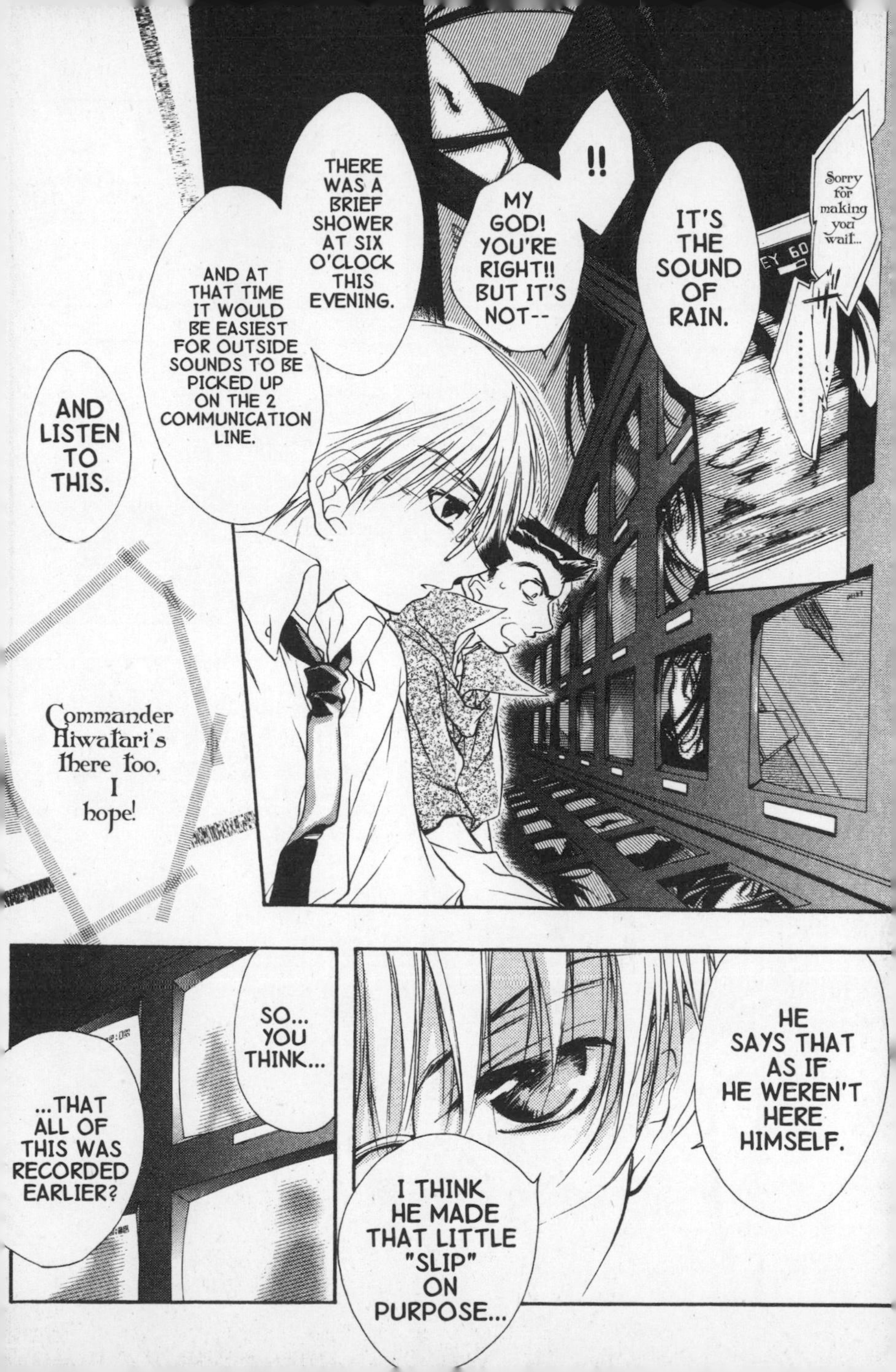
Sorry for making you wait...
......
IT'S THE SOUND OF RAIN.
!!
MY GOD! YOU'RE RIGHT!! BUT IT'S NOT--
THERE WAS A BRIEF SHOWER AT SIX O'CLOCK THIS EVENING.
AND AT THAT TIME IT WOULD BE EASIEST FOR OUTSIDE SOUNDS TO BE PICKED UP ON THE 2 COMMUNICATION LINE.
AND LISTEN TO THIS.
Commander Hiwatari's there too, I hope!
HE SAYS THAT AS IF HE WEREN'T HERE HIMSELF.
I THINK HE MADE THAT LITTLE "SLIP" ON PURPOSE...
SO... YOU THINK...
...THAT ALL OF THIS WAS RECORDED EARLIER?

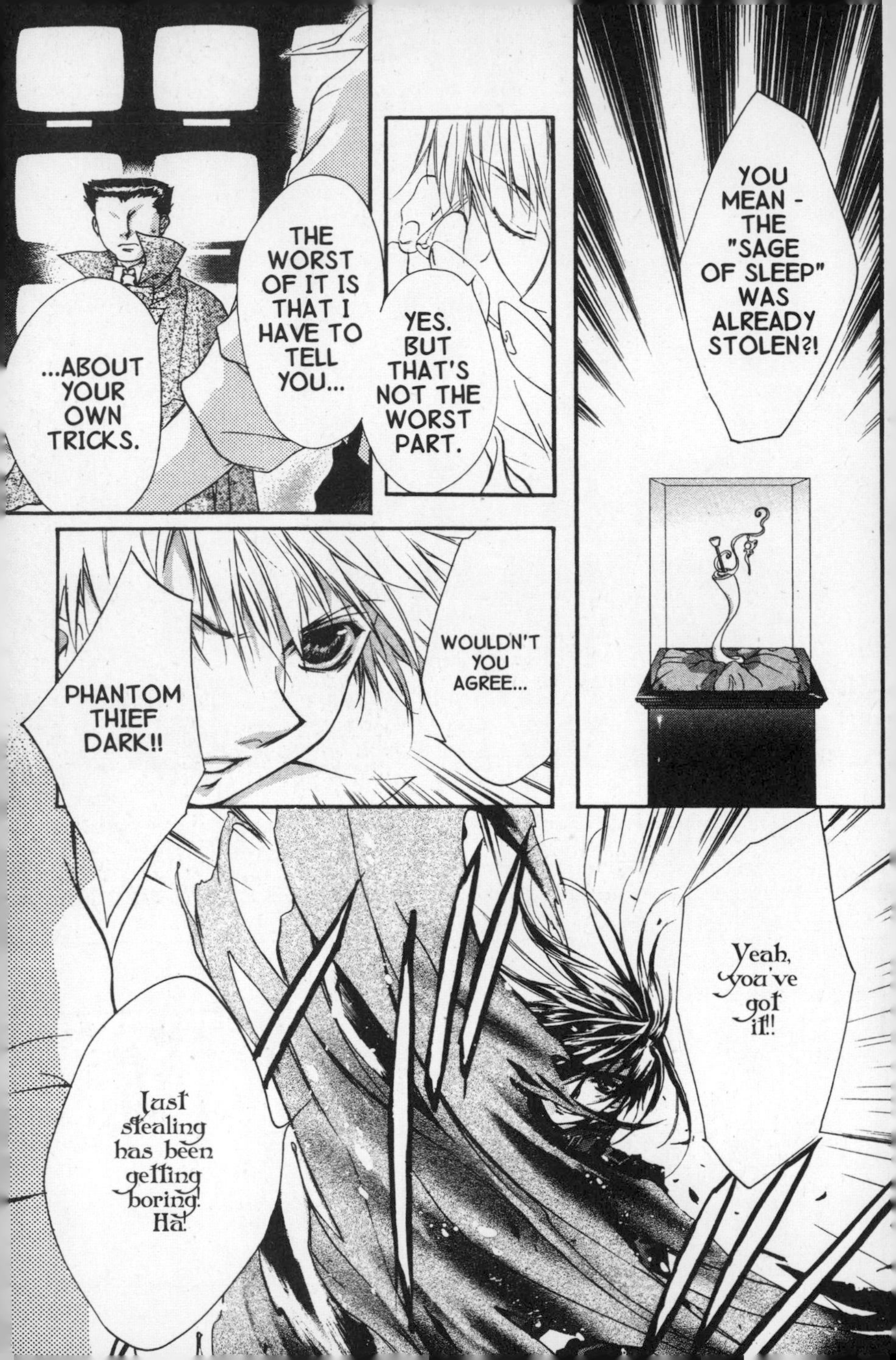
YOU MEAN - THE "SAGE OF SLEEP" WAS ALREADY STOLEN?!
YES. BUT THAT'S NOT THE WORST PART.
THE WORST OF IT IS THAT I HAVE TO TELL YOU...
...ABOUT YOUR OWN TRICKS.
WOULDN'T YOU AGREE...
PHANTOM THIEF DARK!!
Yeah, you've got it!!
Just stealing has been getting boring! Ha!

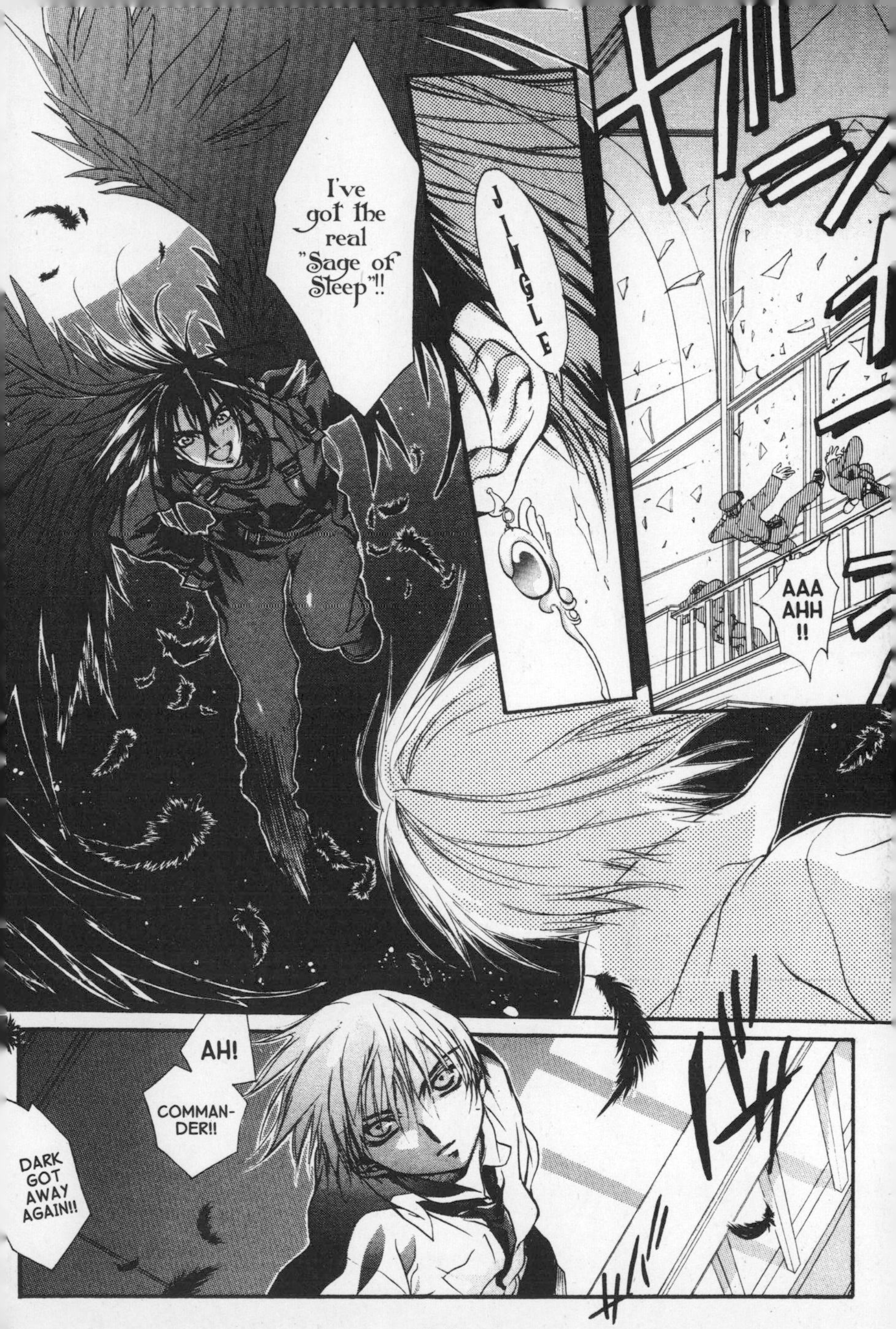
AAA AHH!!
JINGLE
I've got the real "Sage of Sleep"!!
AH!
COMMANDER!!
DARK GOT AWAY AGAIN!!

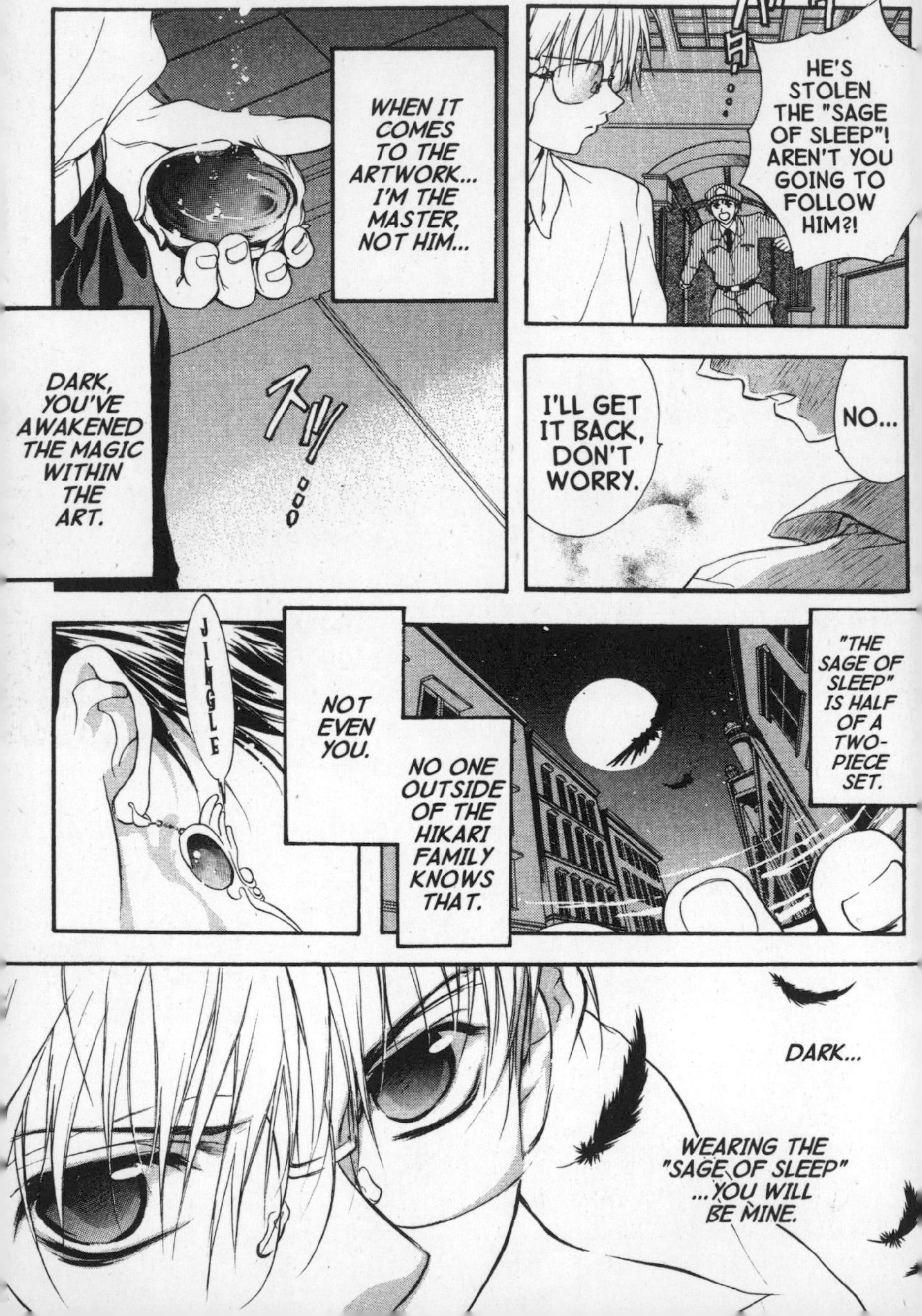
HE'S STOLEN THE "SAGE OF SLEEP"! AREN'T YOU GOING TO FOLLOW HIM?!
NO...
I'LL GET IT BACK, DON'T WORRY.
WHEN IT COMES TO THE ARTWORK... I'M THE MASTER, NOT HIM...
DARK, YOU'VE AWAKENED THE MAGIC WITHIN THE ART.
"THE SAGE OF SLEEP" IS HALF OF A TWO-PIECE SET.
NO ONE OUTSIDE OF THE HIKARI FAMILY KNOWS THAT.
NOT EVEN YOU.
JINGLE
DARK...
WEARING THE "SAGE OF SLEEP" ...YOU WILL BE MINE.

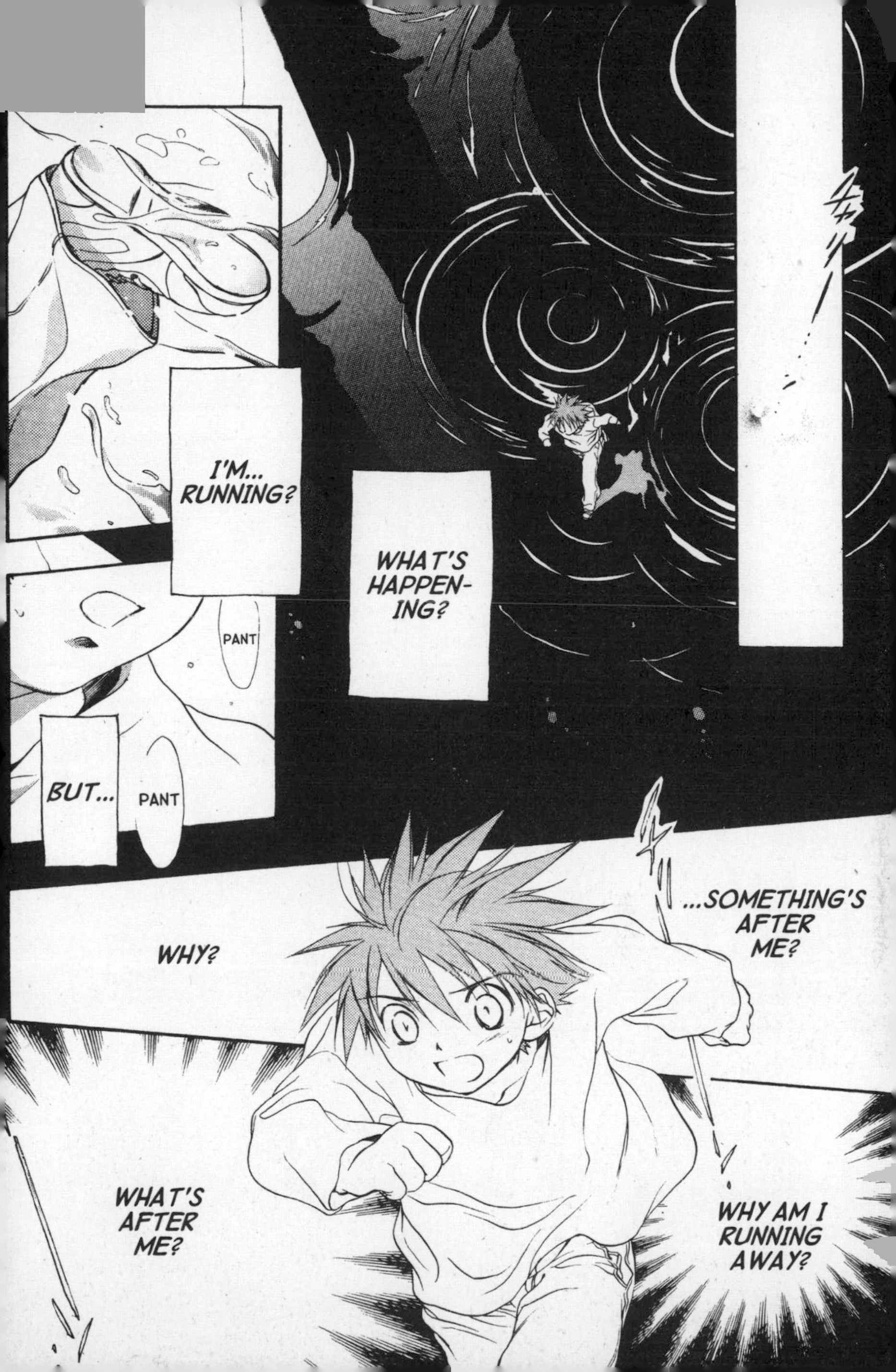
WHAT'S HAPPENING?
I'M... RUNNING?
PANT
BUT...
PANT
...SOMETHING'S AFTER ME?
WHY?
WHY AM I RUNNING AWAY?
WHAT'S AFTER ME?

vol. 1

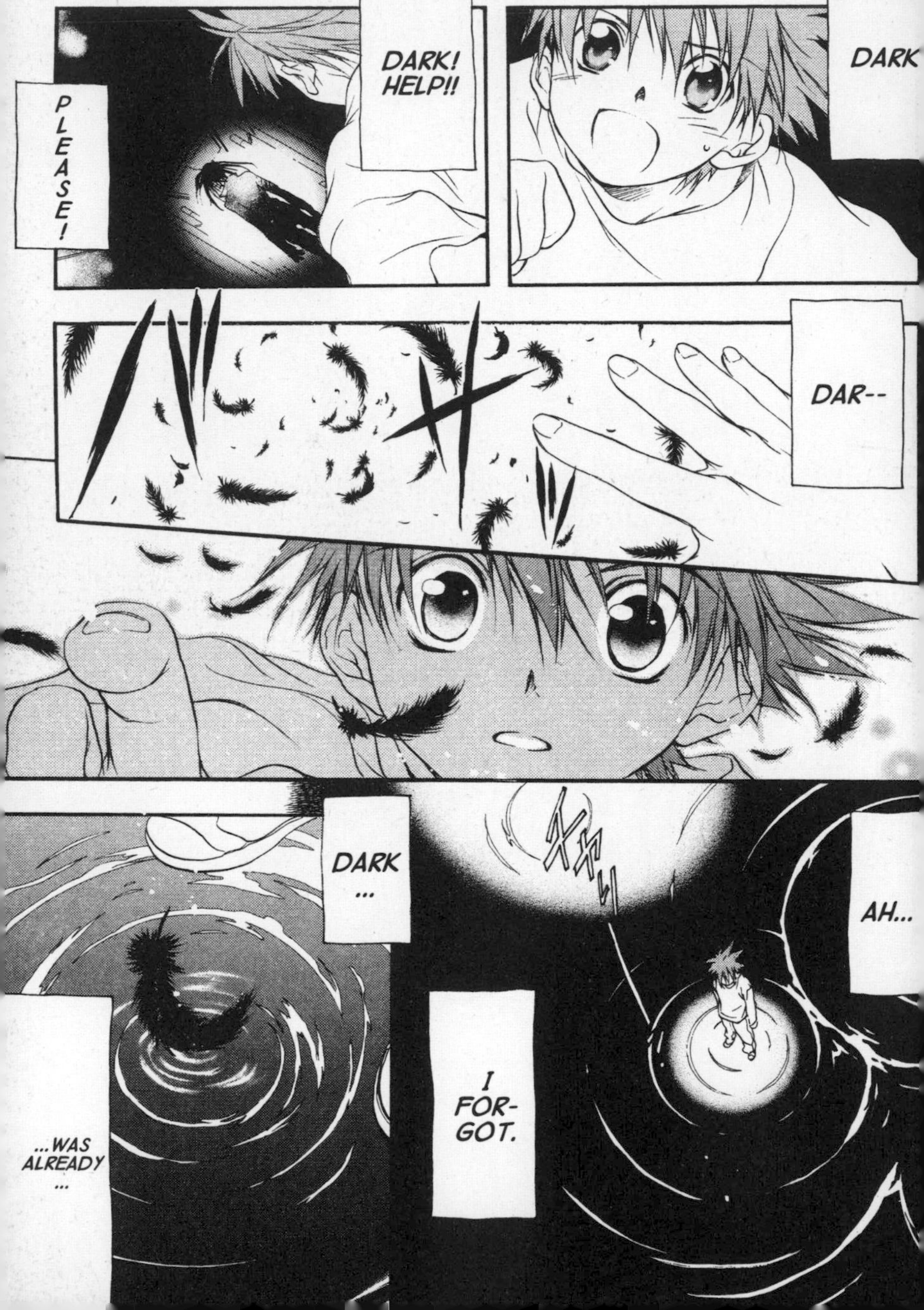

DARK
DARK! HELP!!
PLEASE!
DAR--
AH...
I FOR-GOT.
DARK ...
...WAS ALREADY ...

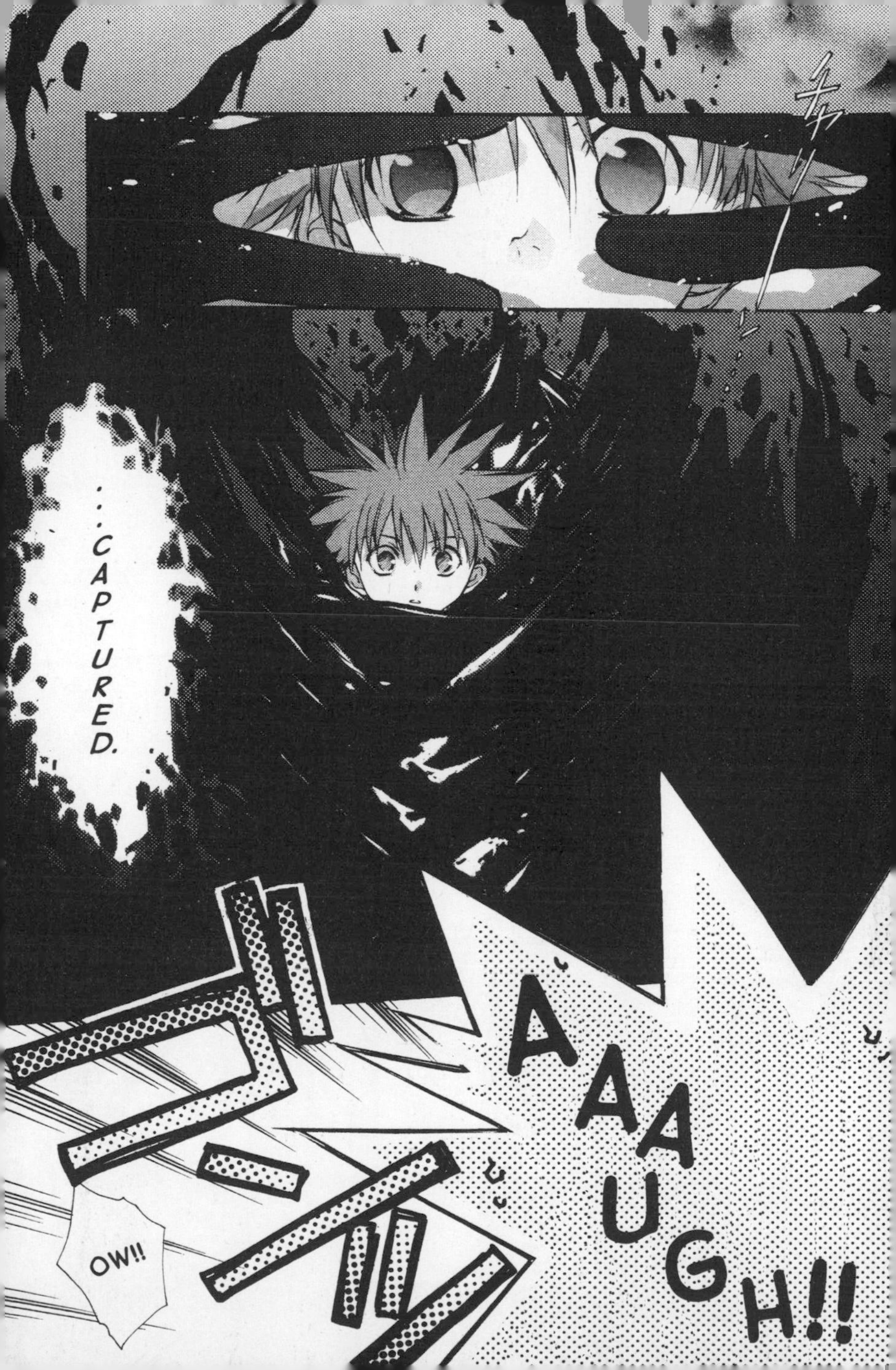
...CAPTURED.
AAAUGH!!
OW!!

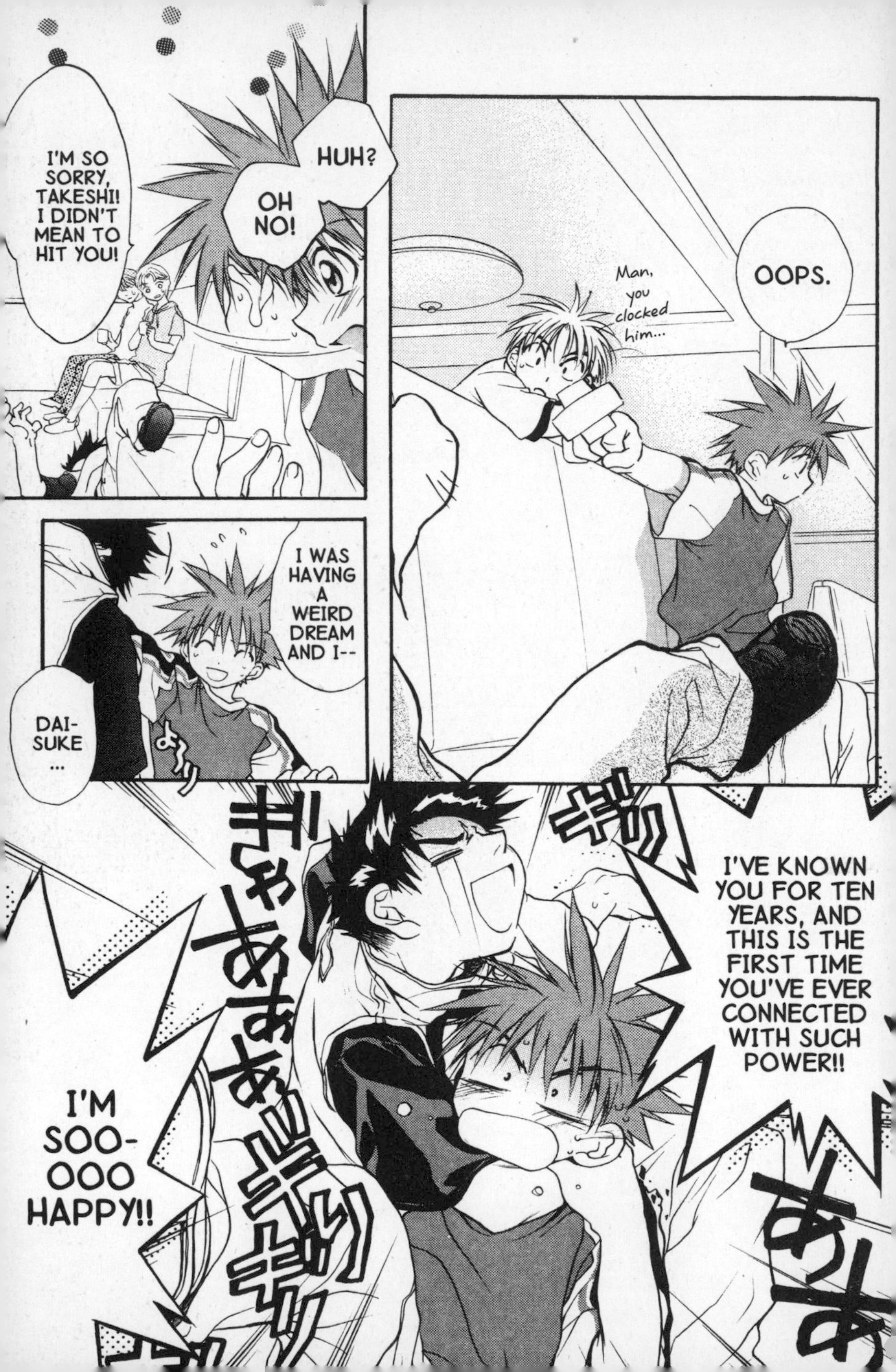
OOPS.
Man, you clocked him...
HUH?
OH NO!
I'M SO SORRY, TAKESHI! I DIDN'T MEAN TO HIT YOU!
I WAS HAVING A WEIRD DREAM AND I--
DAI-SUKE ...
ぎゅ
I'VE KNOWN YOU FOR TEN YEARS, AND THIS IS THE FIRST TIME YOU'VE EVER CONNECTED WITH SUCH POWER!!
ああ
ぎゃあああ
I'M SOO-OOO HAPPY!!

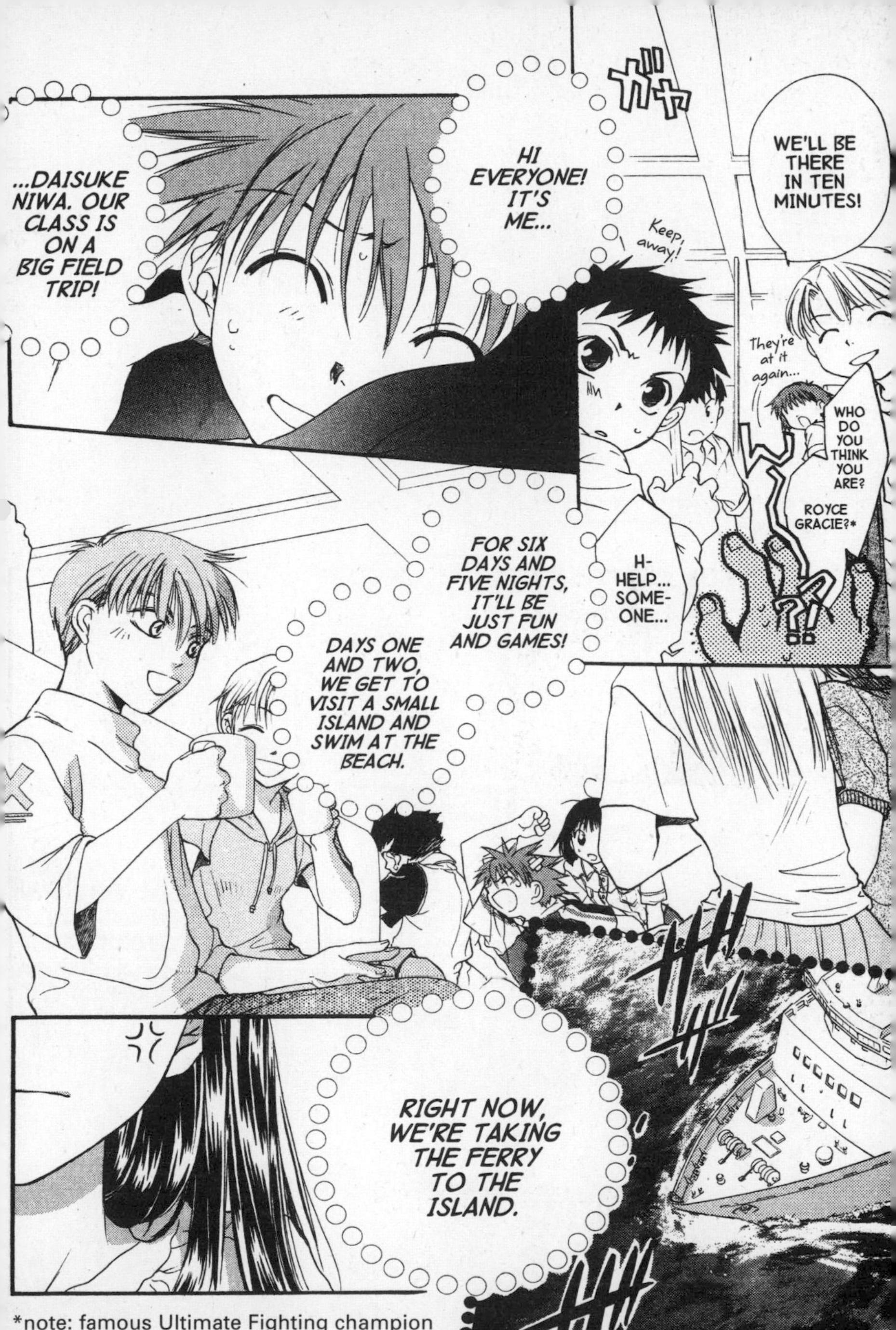
ガヤ
WE'LL BE THERE IN TEN MINUTES!
They're at it again...
WHO DO YOU THINK YOU ARE? ROYCE GRACIE?*
Keep away!
H-HELP... SOME-ONE...
HI EVERYONE! IT'S ME...
...DAISUKE NIWA. OUR CLASS IS ON A BIG FIELD TRIP!
FOR SIX DAYS AND FIVE NIGHTS, IT'LL BE JUST FUN AND GAMES!
DAYS ONE AND TWO, WE GET TO VISIT A SMALL ISLAND AND SWIM AT THE BEACH.
RIGHT NOW, WE'RE TAKING THE FERRY TO THE ISLAND.

*note: famous Ultimate Fighting champion

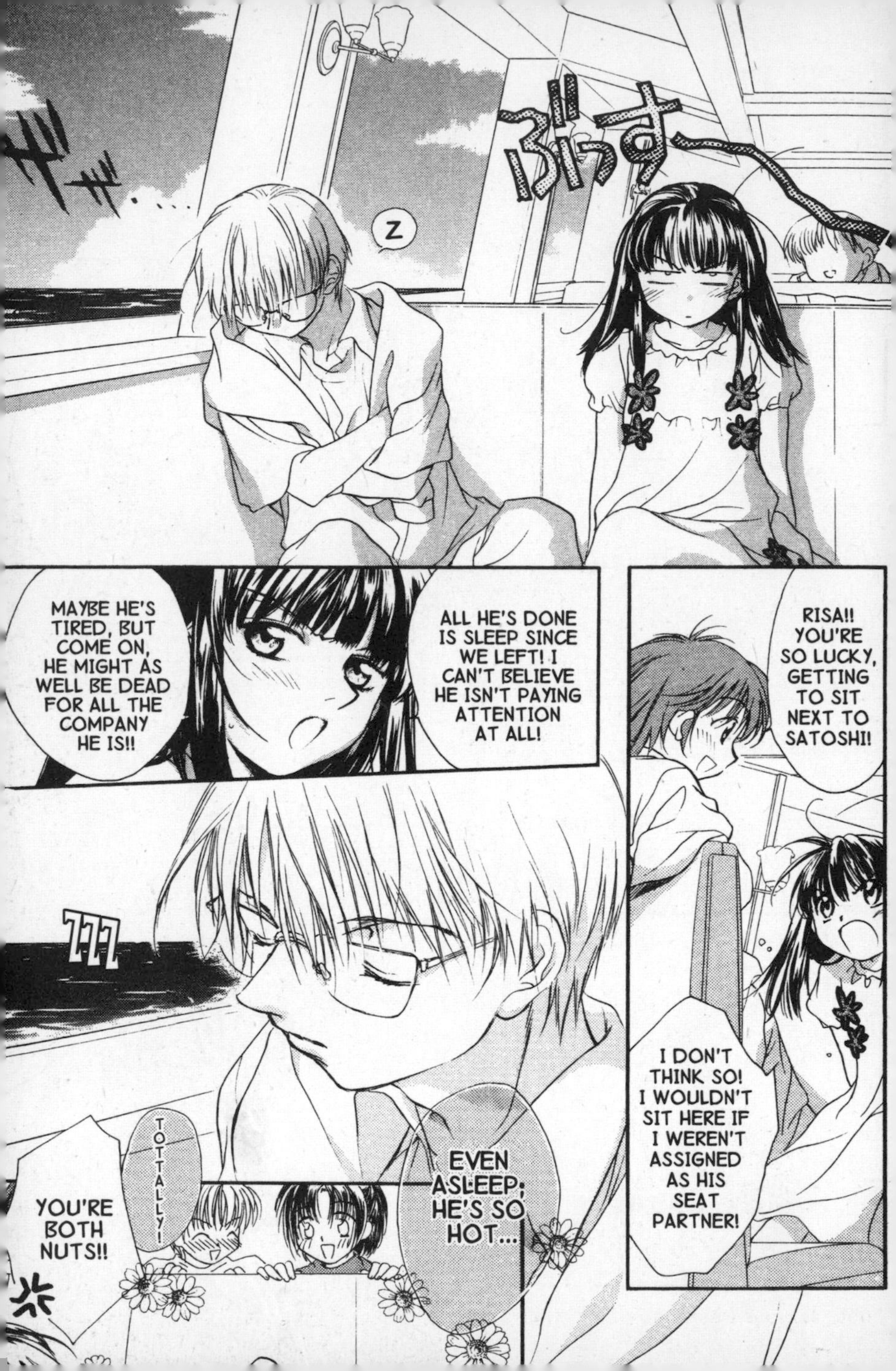
ぶっす
Z
ギ ギ・・・
RISA!! YOU'RE SO LUCKY, GETTING TO SIT NEXT TO SATOSHI!
I DON'T THINK SO! I WOULDN'T SIT HERE IF I WEREN'T ASSIGNED AS HIS SEAT PARTNER!
ALL HE'S DONE IS SLEEP SINCE WE LEFT! I CAN'T BELIEVE HE ISN'T PAYING ATTENTION AT ALL!
MAYBE HE'S TIRED, BUT COME ON, HE MIGHT AS WELL BE DEAD FOR ALL THE COMPANY HE IS!!
ZZZ
EVEN ASLEEP, HE'S SO HOT...
TOTTALLY!
YOU'RE BOTH NUTS!!

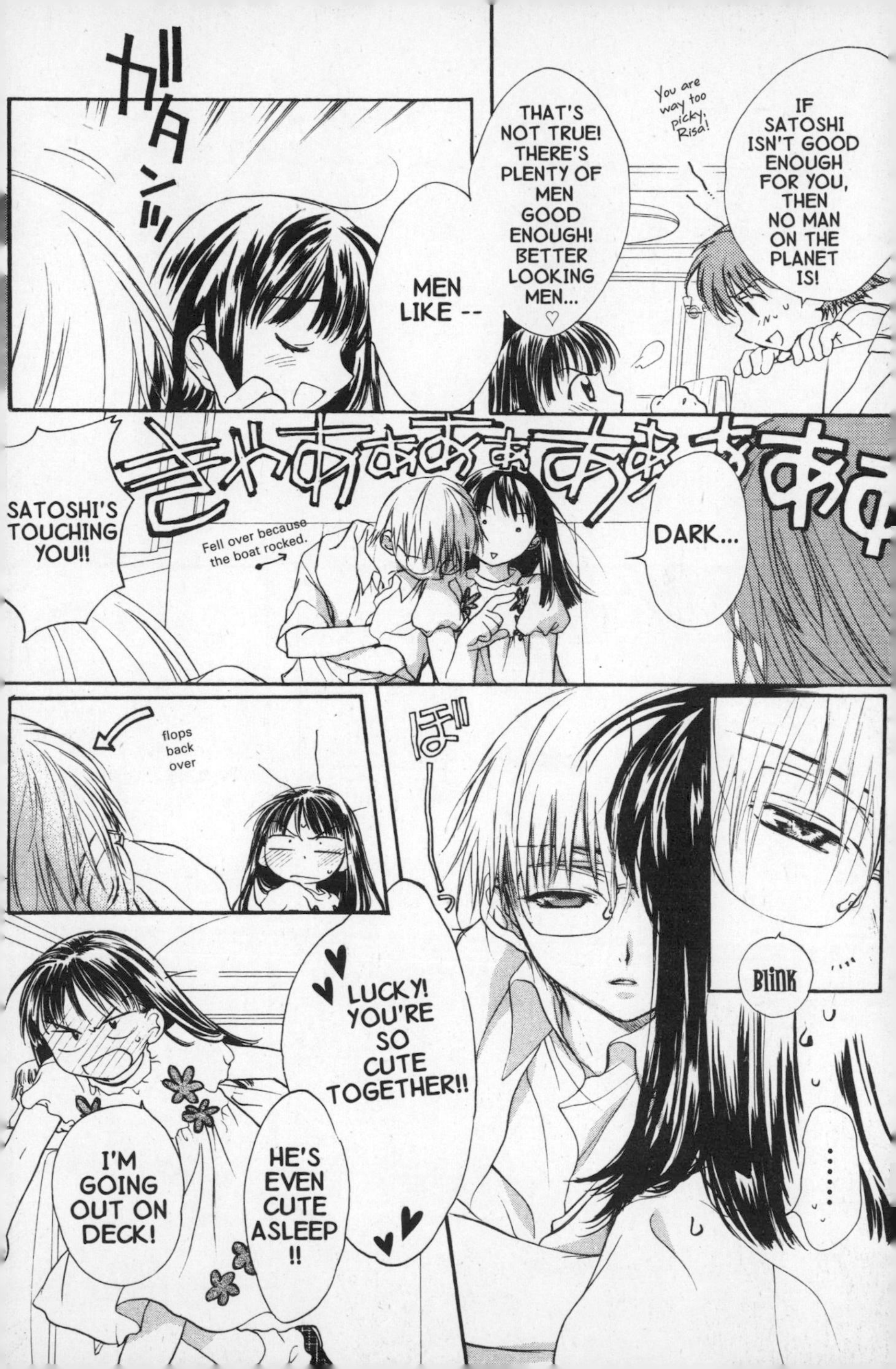

IF SATOSHI ISN'T GOOD ENOUGH FOR YOU, THEN NO MAN ON THE PLANET IS!
You are way too picky, Risa!
THAT'S NOT TRUE! THERE'S PLENTY OF MEN GOOD ENOUGH! BETTER LOOKING MEN... ♡
MEN LIKE --
ガタンッ
きゃああああああああ
DARK...
Fell over because the boat rocked.
SATOSHI'S TOUCHING YOU!!
Blink
......
flops back over
ぼしっ
LUCKY! YOU'RE SO CUTE TOGETHER!!
HE'S EVEN CUTE ASLEEP!!
I'M GOING OUT ON DECK!

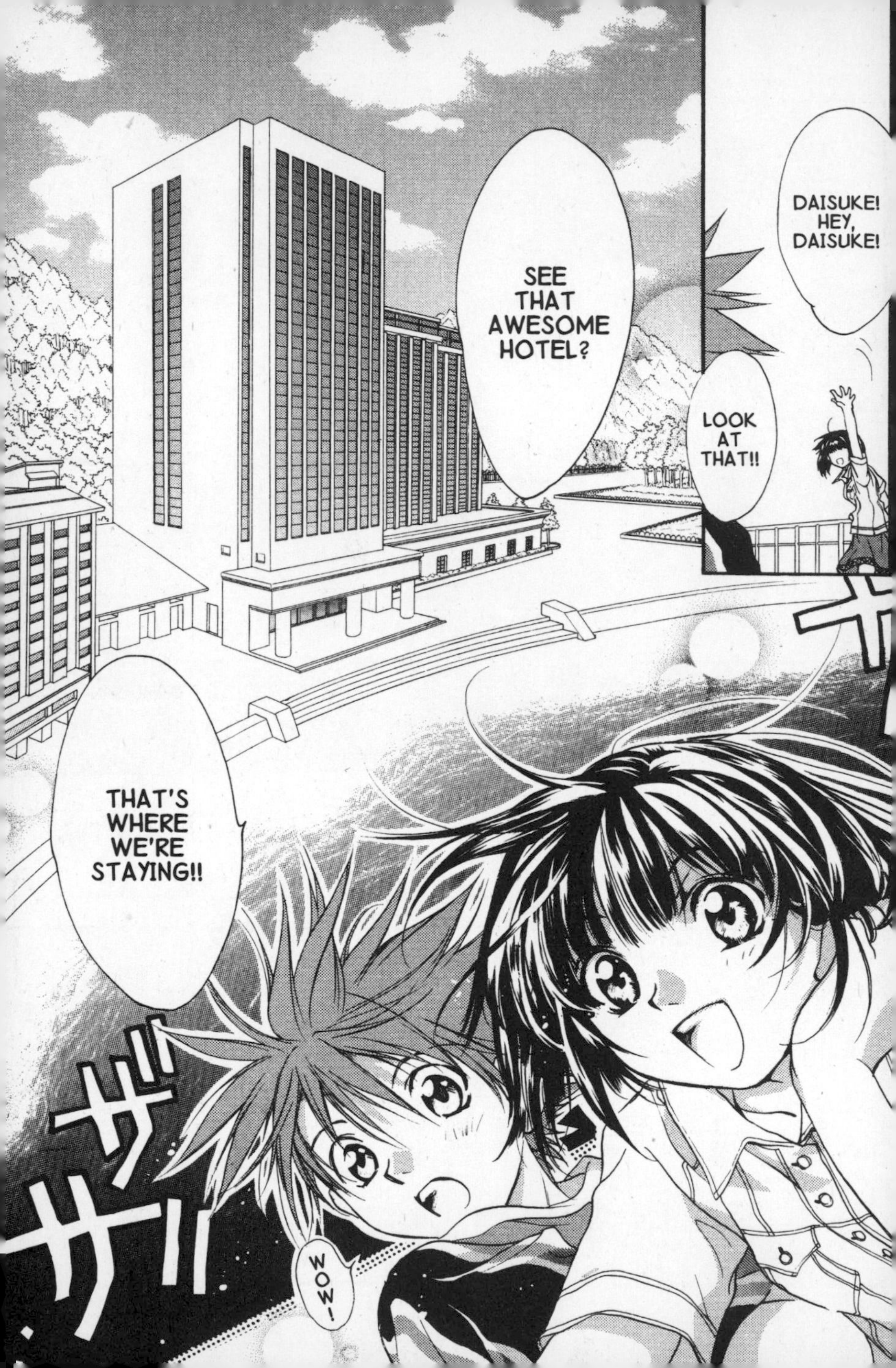
DAISUKE! HEY, DAISUKE!
LOOK AT THAT!!
SEE THAT AWESOME HOTEL?
THAT'S WHERE WE'RE STAYING!!
WOW!

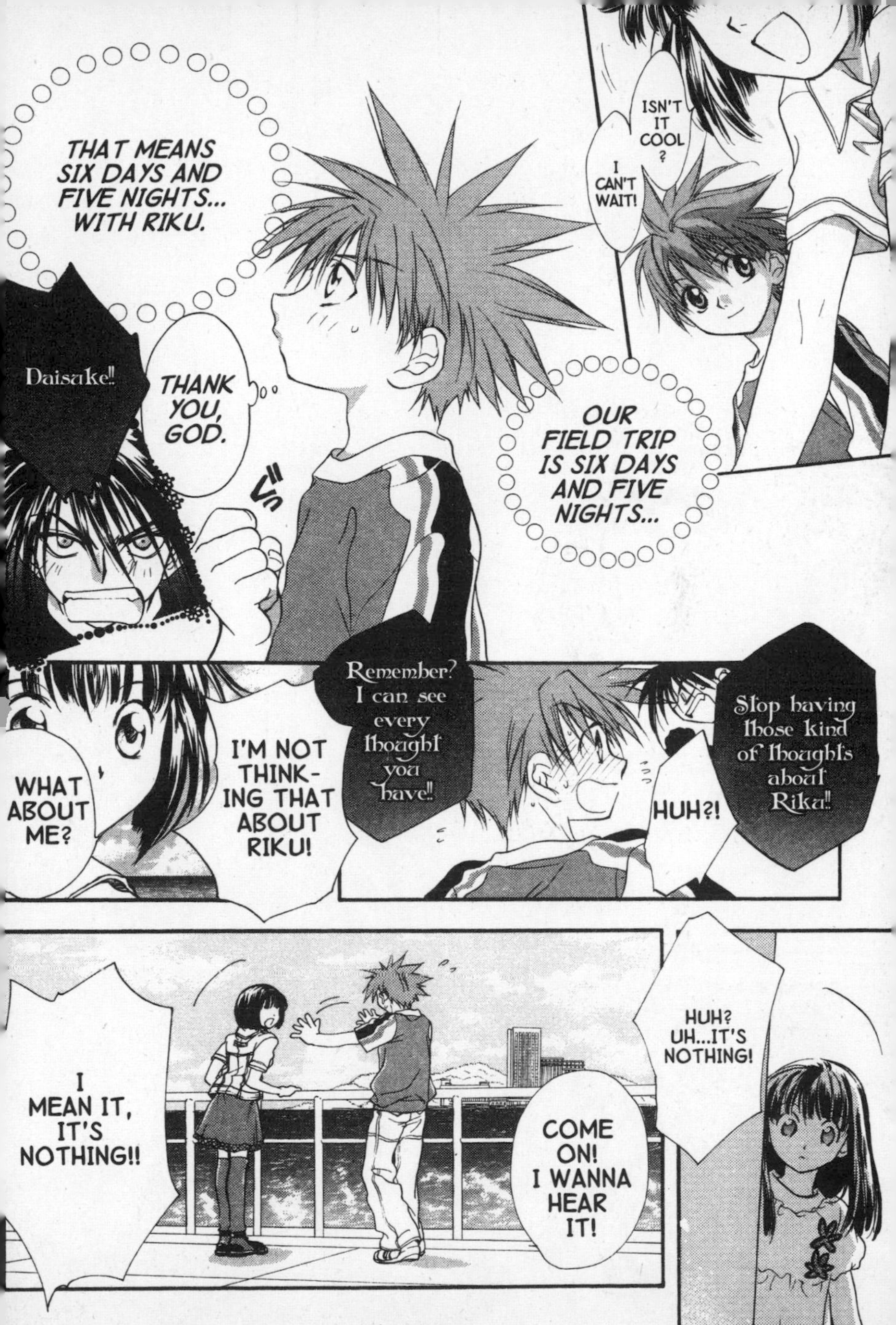
ISN'T IT COOL?
I CAN'T WAIT!
OUR FIELD TRIP IS SIX DAYS AND FIVE NIGHTS...
THAT MEANS SIX DAYS AND FIVE NIGHTS... WITH RIKU.
THANK YOU, GOD.
Daisuke!!
Stop having those kind of thoughts about Riku!!
HUH?!
Remember? I can see every thought you have!!
I'M NOT THINKING THAT ABOUT RIKU!
WHAT ABOUT ME?
HUH? UH...IT'S NOTHING!
COME ON! I WANNA HEAR IT!
I MEAN IT, IT'S NOTHING!!

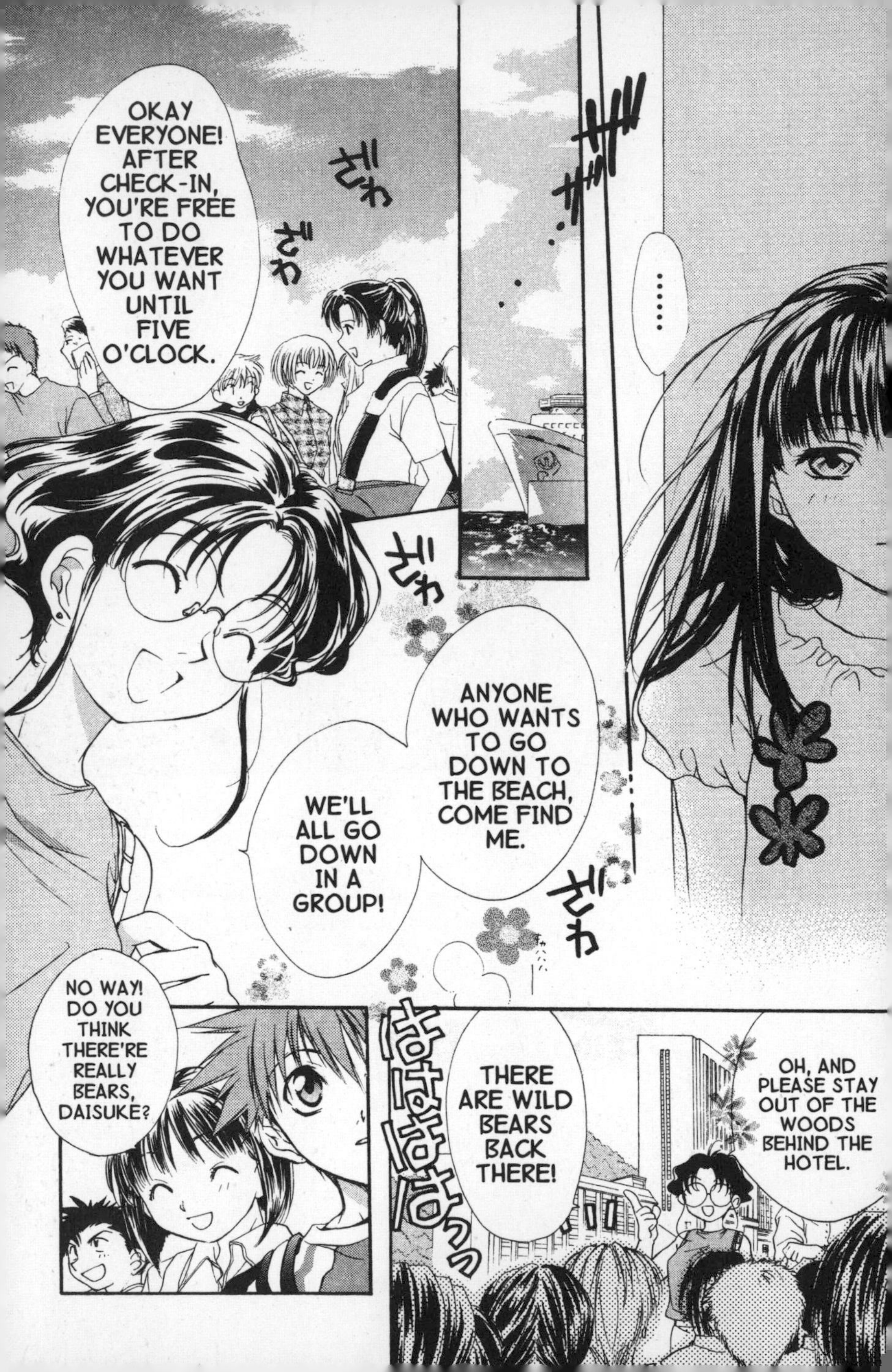

......
OKAY EVERYONE! AFTER CHECK-IN, YOU'RE FREE TO DO WHATEVER YOU WANT UNTIL FIVE O'CLOCK.
ざわ
ざわ
ざわ
ANYONE WHO WANTS TO GO DOWN TO THE BEACH, COME FIND ME.
WE'LL ALL GO DOWN IN A GROUP!
ざわ
OH, AND PLEASE STAY OUT OF THE WOODS BEHIND THE HOTEL.
THERE ARE WILD BEARS BACK THERE!
はははは
NO WAY! DO YOU THINK THERE'RE REALLY BEARS, DAISUKE?

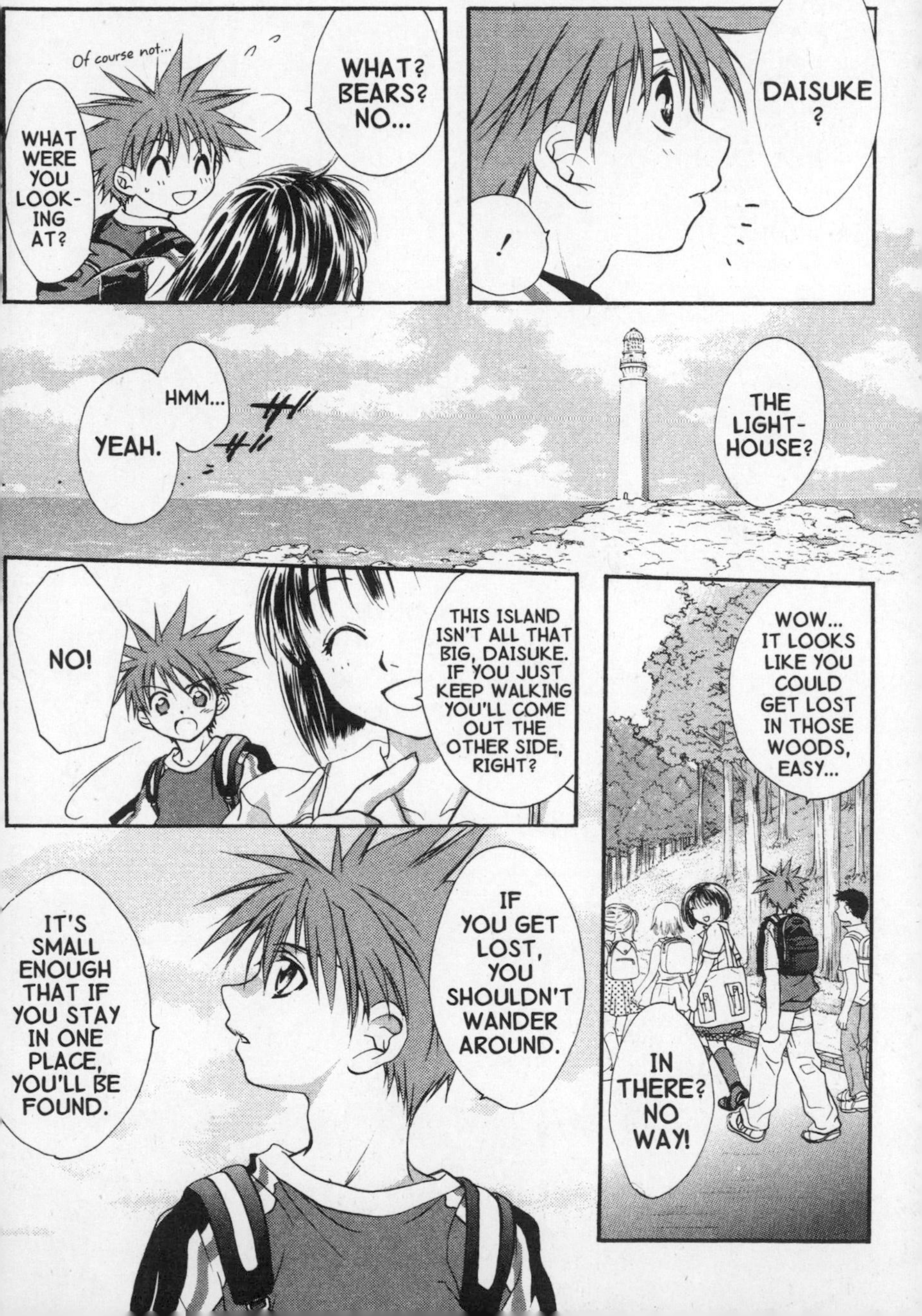
DAISUKE ?
!
WHAT? BEARS? NO...
Of course not...
WHAT WERE YOU LOOK-ING AT?
THE LIGHT-HOUSE?
HMM... YEAH.
WOW... IT LOOKS LIKE YOU COULD GET LOST IN THOSE WOODS, EASY...
IN THERE? NO WAY!
THIS ISLAND ISN'T ALL THAT BIG, DAISUKE. IF YOU JUST KEEP WALKING YOU'LL COME OUT THE OTHER SIDE, RIGHT?
NO!
IF YOU GET LOST, YOU SHOULDN'T WANDER AROUND.
IT'S SMALL ENOUGH THAT IF YOU STAY IN ONE PLACE, YOU'LL BE FOUND.

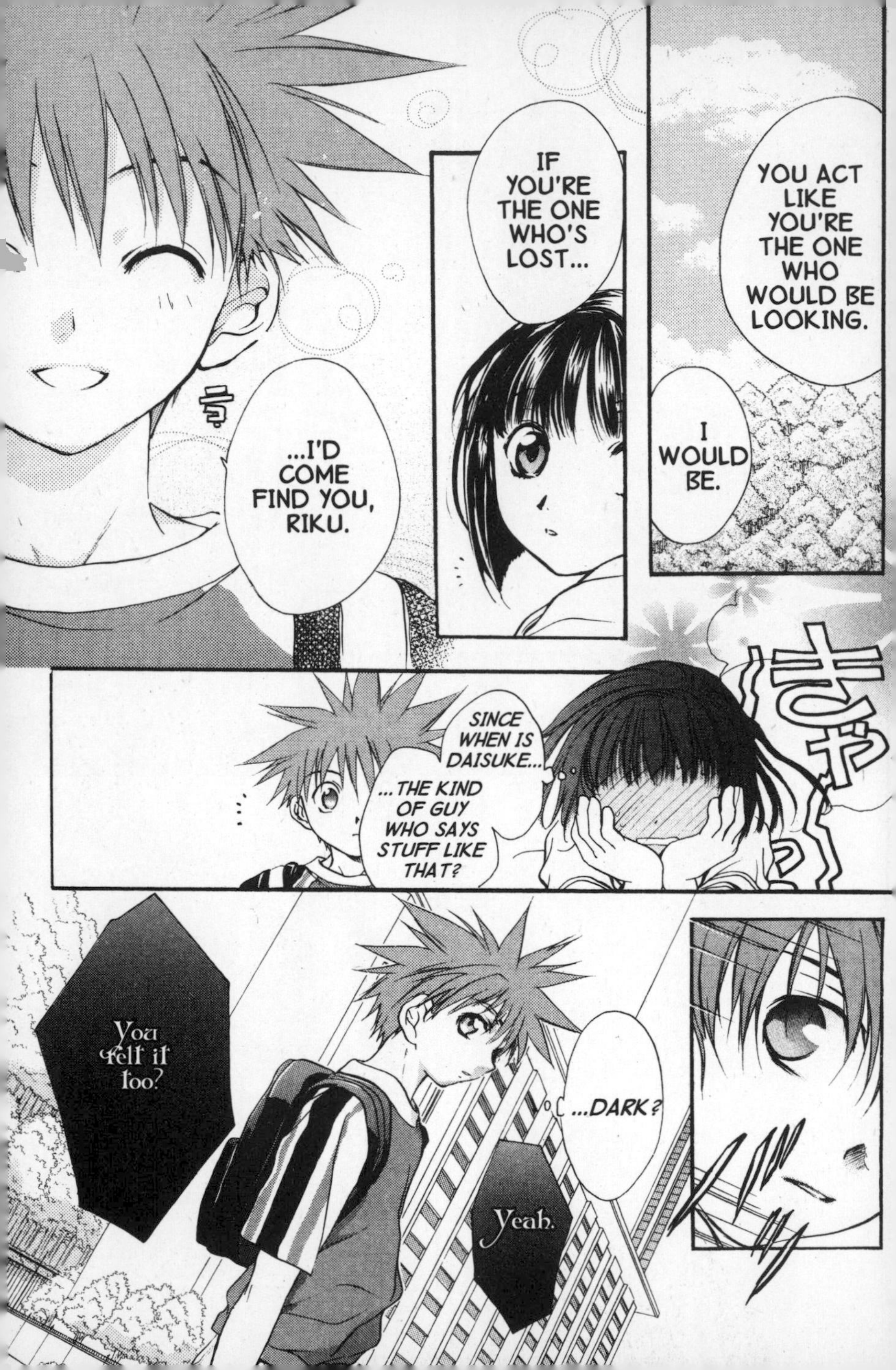
YOU ACT LIKE YOU'RE THE ONE WHO WOULD BE LOOKING.
I WOULD BE.
IF YOU'RE THE ONE WHO'S LOST...
...I'D COME FIND YOU, RIKU.
きゃっ
SINCE WHEN IS DAISUKE...
...THE KIND OF GUY WHO SAYS STUFF LIKE THAT?
...DARK?
You felt it too?
Yeah.

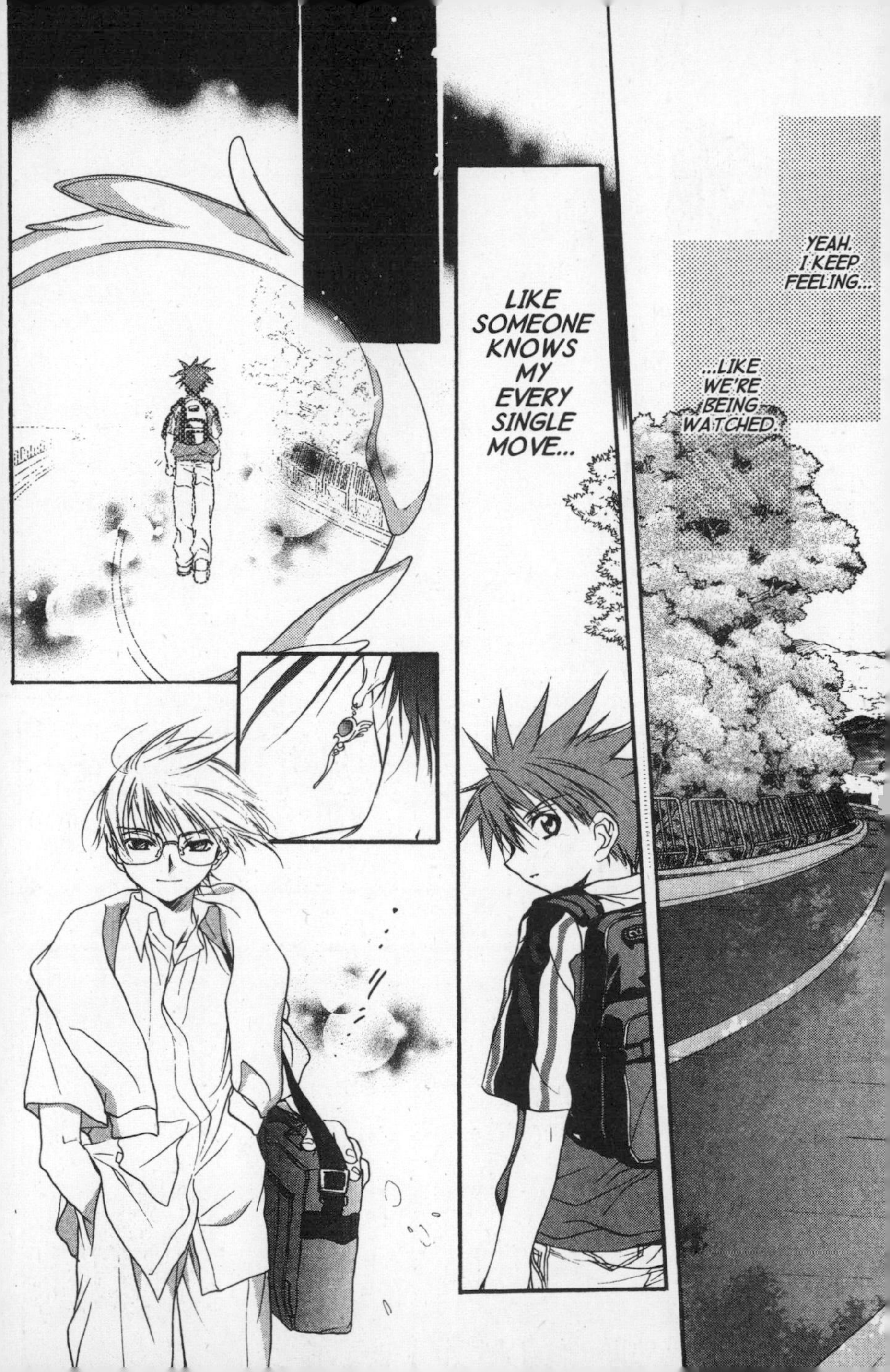
YEAH. I KEEP FEELING...
...LIKE WE'RE BEING WATCHED.
LIKE SOMEONE KNOWS MY EVERY SINGLE MOVE...

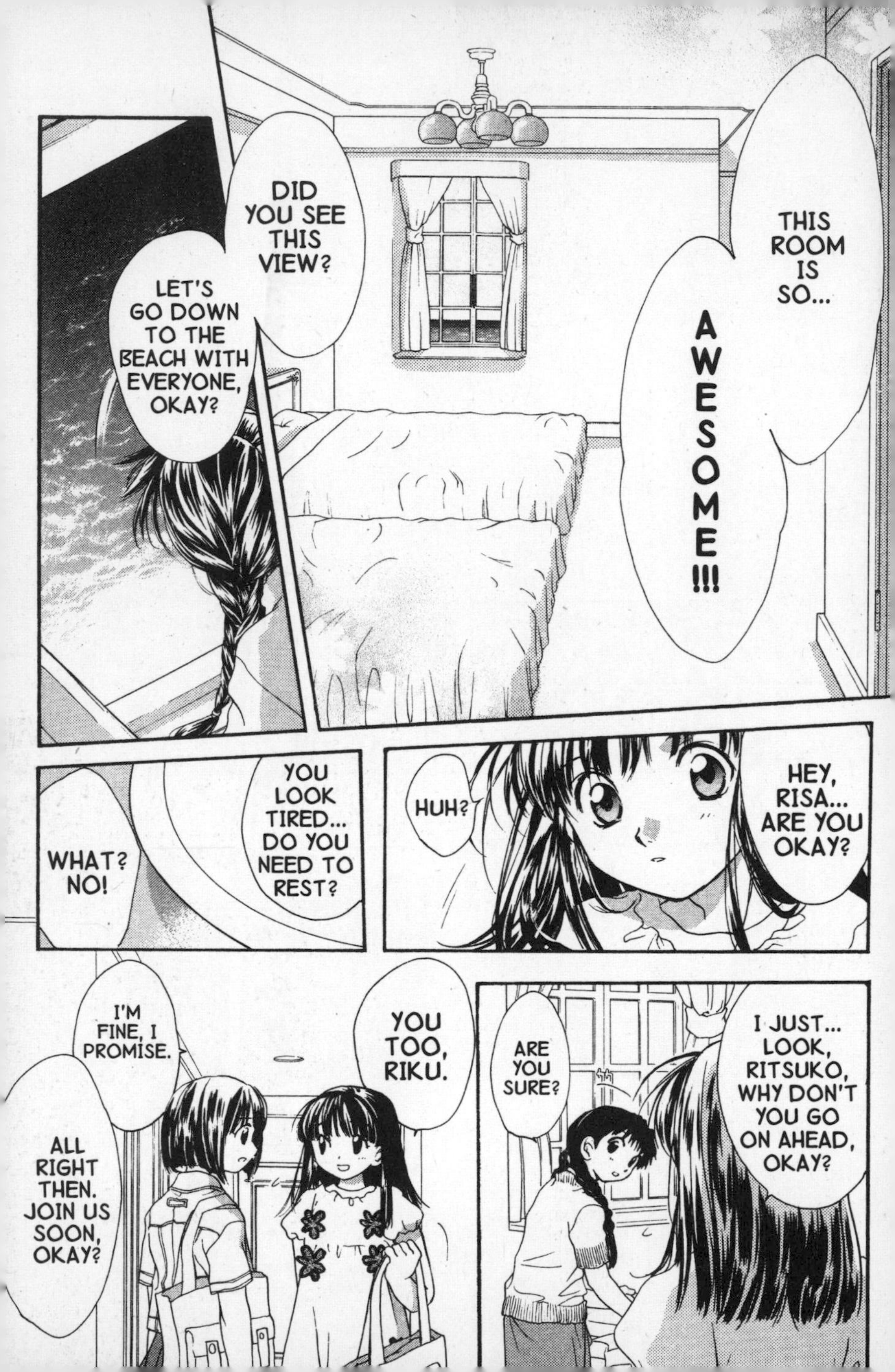
THIS ROOM IS SO...
AWESOME!!!
DID YOU SEE THIS VIEW?
LET'S GO DOWN TO THE BEACH WITH EVERYONE, OKAY?
HEY, RISA... ARE YOU OKAY?
HUH?
YOU LOOK TIRED... DO YOU NEED TO REST?
WHAT? NO!
I JUST... LOOK, RITSUKO, WHY DON'T YOU GO ON AHEAD, OKAY?
ARE YOU SURE?
YOU TOO, RIKU.
I'M FINE, I PROMISE.
ALL RIGHT THEN. JOIN US SOON, OKAY?

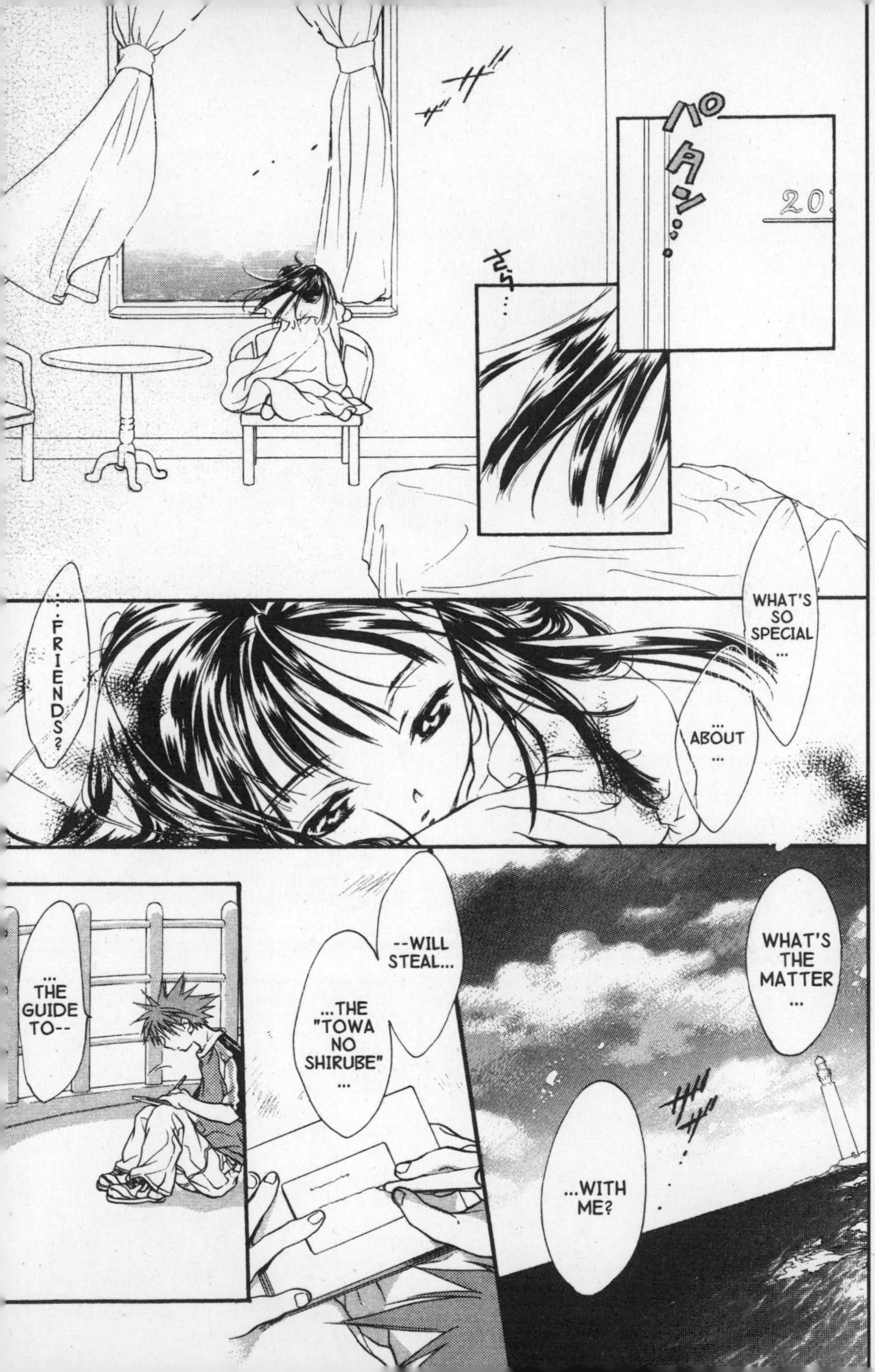
パタン・・・
WHAT'S SO SPECIAL ...
... ABOUT ...
...FRIENDS?
WHAT'S THE MATTER ...
...WITH ME?
--WILL STEAL...
...THE "TOWA NO SHIRUBE" ...
... THE GUIDE TO--

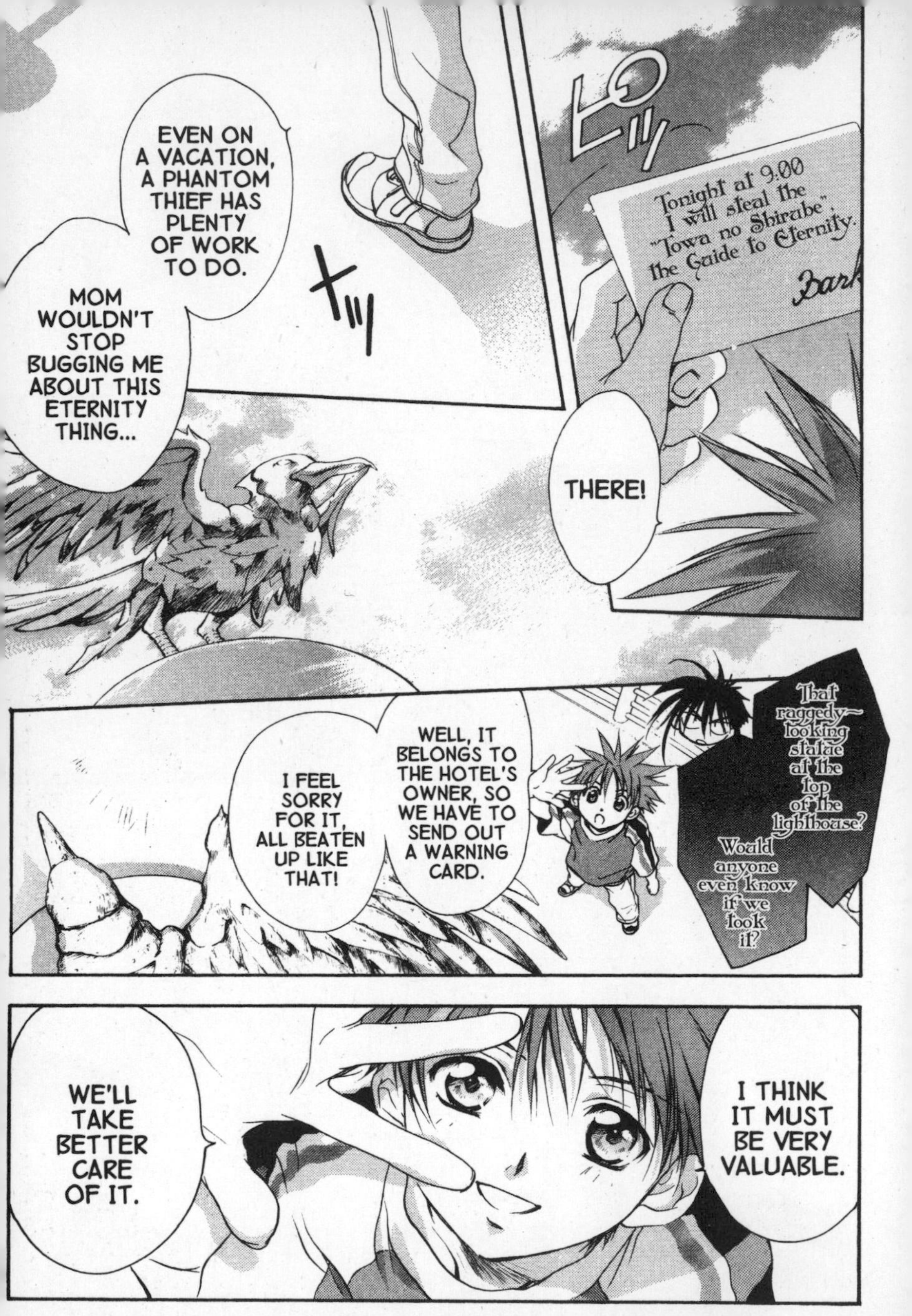

Tonight at 9.00 I will steal the "Towa no Shirube", the Guide to Eternity.
Dark
THERE!
EVEN ON A VACATION, A PHANTOM THIEF HAS PLENTY OF WORK TO DO.
MOM WOULDN'T STOP BUGGING ME ABOUT THIS ETERNITY THING...
That raggedy-looking statue at the top of the lighthouse?
Would anyone even know if we took it?
WELL, IT BELONGS TO THE HOTEL'S OWNER, SO WE HAVE TO SEND OUT A WARNING CARD.
I FEEL SORRY FOR IT, ALL BEATEN UP LIKE THAT!
I THINK IT MUST BE VERY VALUABLE.
WE'LL TAKE BETTER CARE OF IT.

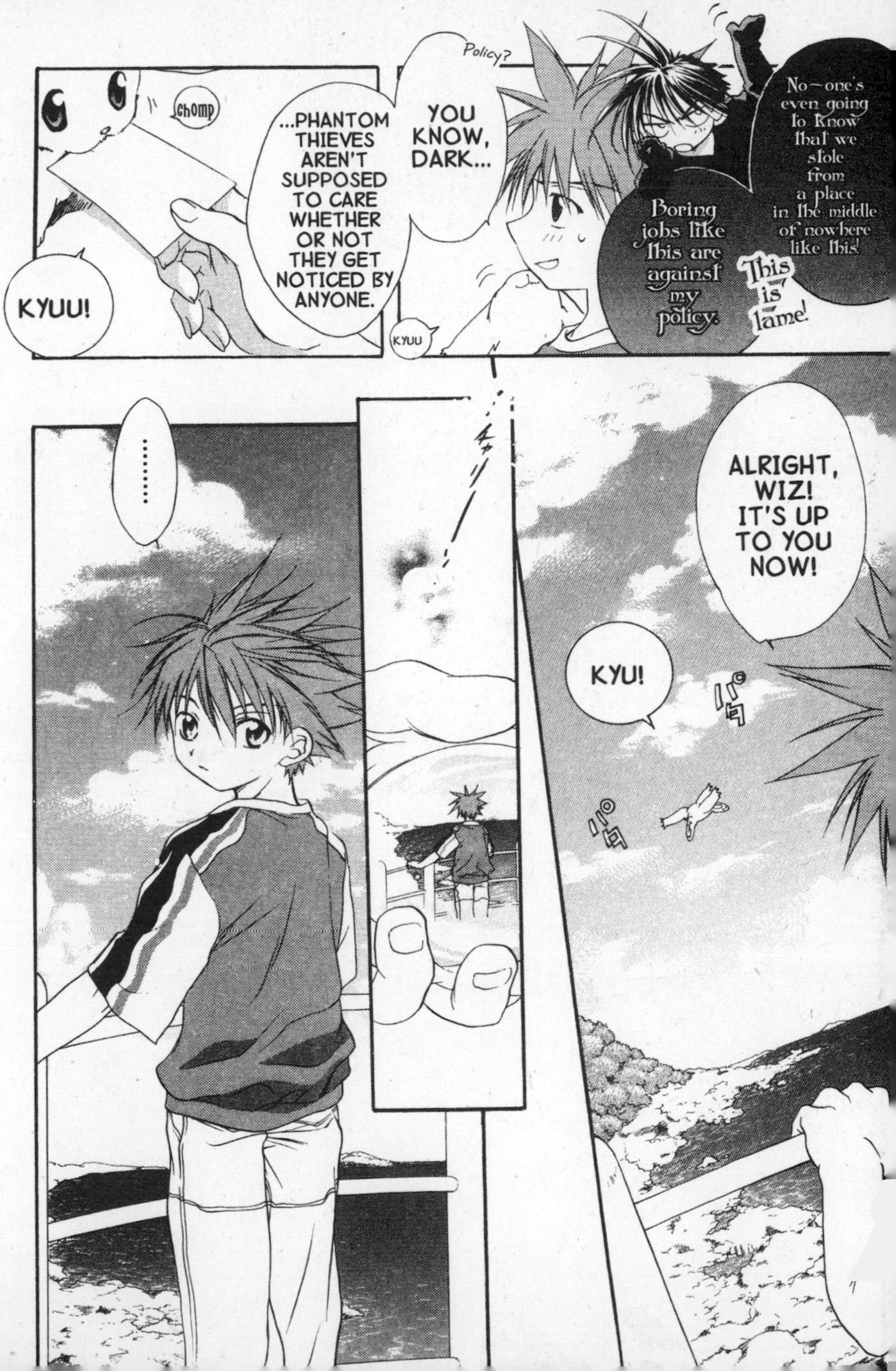

No-one's even going to know that we stole from a place in the middle of nowhere like this!
This is lame!
Boring jobs like this are against my policy.
Policy?
YOU KNOW, DARK...
...PHANTOM THIEVES AREN'T SUPPOSED TO CARE WHETHER OR NOT THEY GET NOTICED BY ANYONE.
KYUU
chomp
KYUU!
ALRIGHT, WIZ! IT'S UP TO YOU NOW!
KYU!
パタ
パタ
......

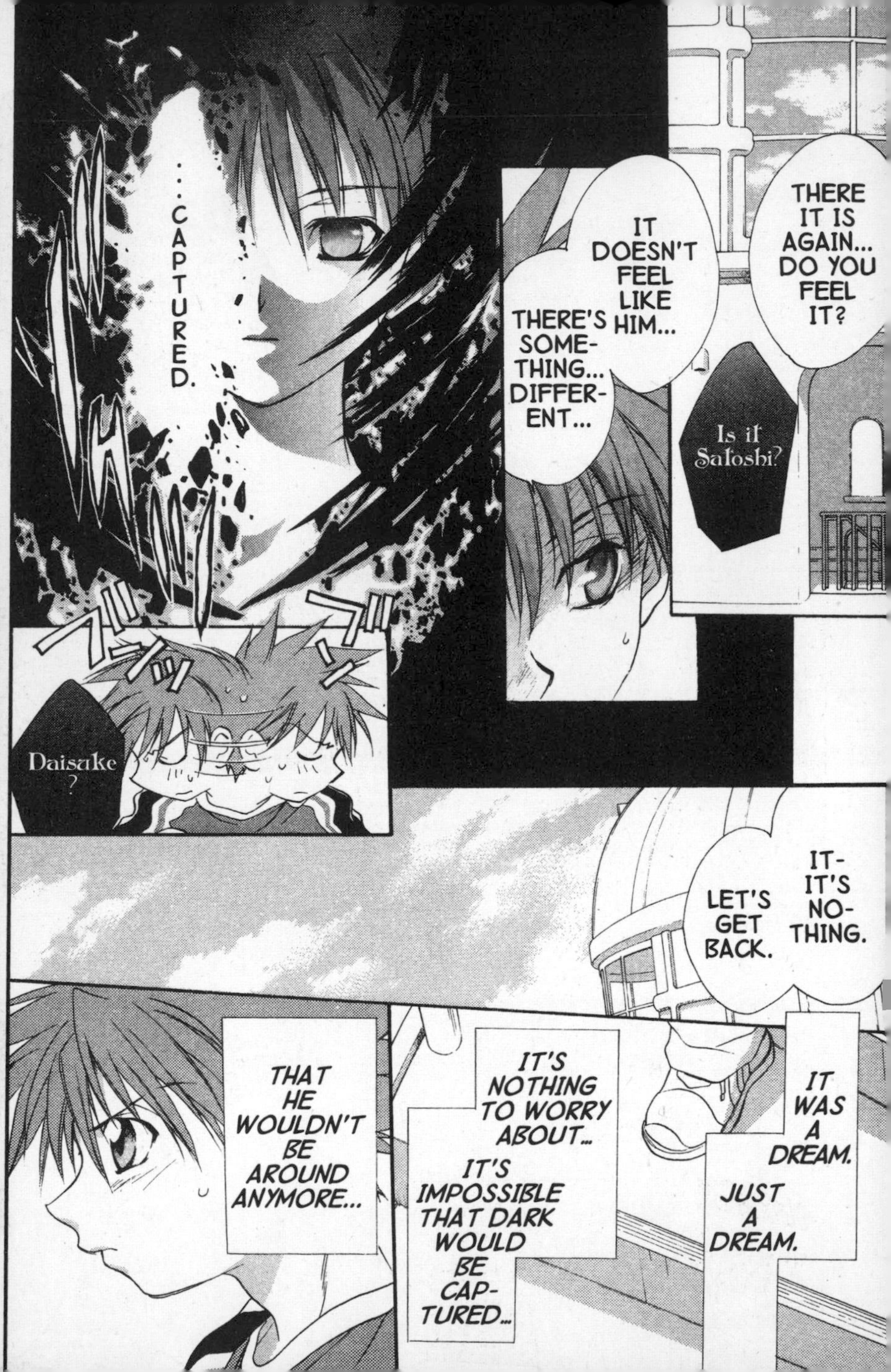
THERE IT IS AGAIN... DO YOU FEEL IT?
Is it Satoshi?
IT DOESN'T FEEL LIKE HIM...
THERE'S SOMETHING... DIFFERENT...
...CAPTURED.
Daisuke ?
IT- IT'S NOTHING.
LET'S GET BACK.
IT WAS A DREAM.
JUST A DREAM.
IT'S NOTHING TO WORRY ABOUT...
IT'S IMPOSSIBLE THAT DARK WOULD BE CAPTURED...
THAT HE WOULDN'T BE AROUND ANYMORE...

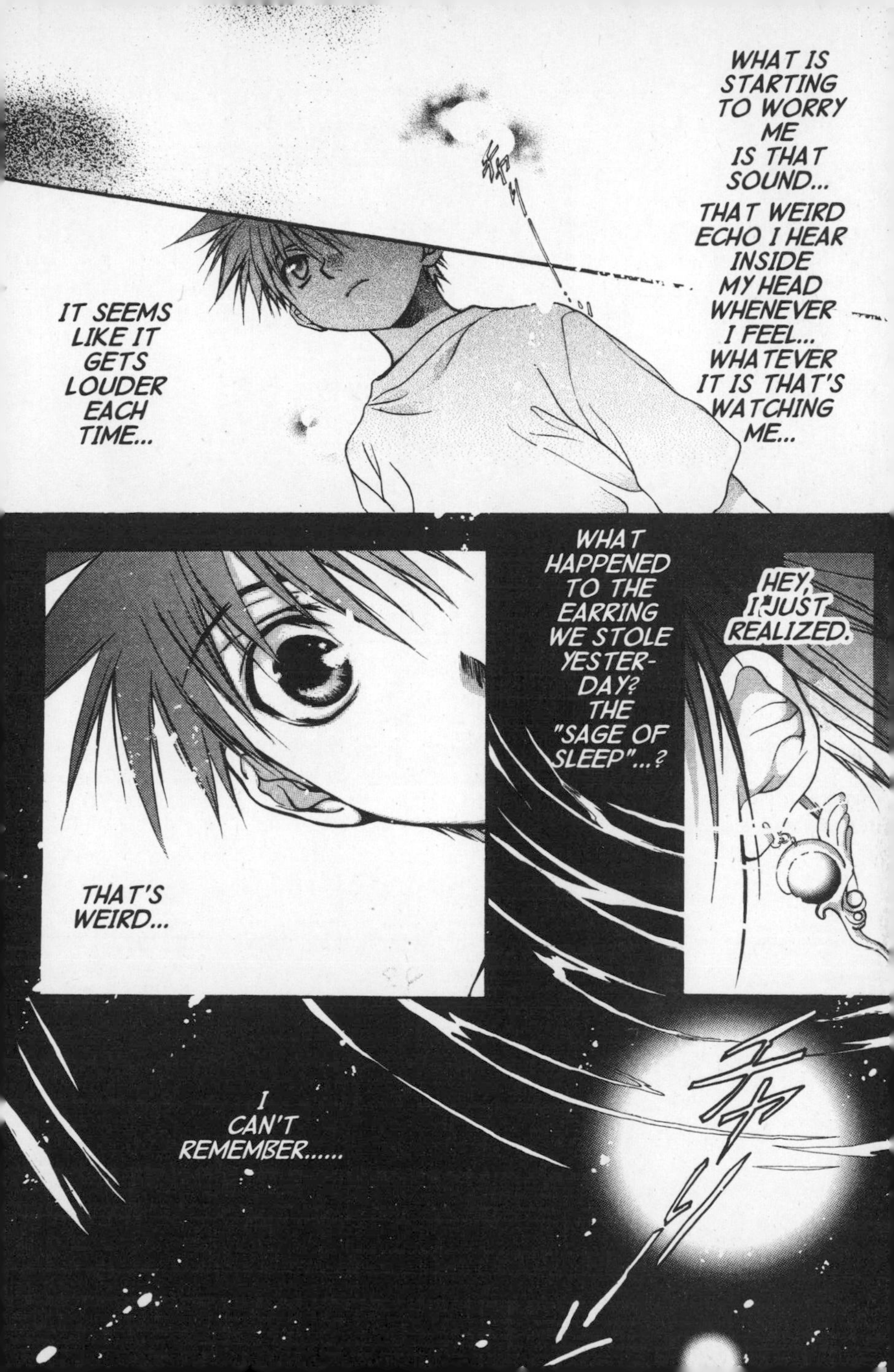
WHAT IS STARTING TO WORRY ME IS THAT SOUND...
THAT WEIRD ECHO I HEAR INSIDE MY HEAD WHENEVER I FEEL... WHATEVER IT IS THAT'S WATCHING ME...
IT SEEMS LIKE IT GETS LOUDER EACH TIME...
HEY, I JUST REALIZED.
WHAT HAPPENED TO THE EARRING WE STOLE YESTER-DAY? THE "SAGE OF SLEEP"...?
THAT'S WEIRD...
I CAN'T REMEMBER......

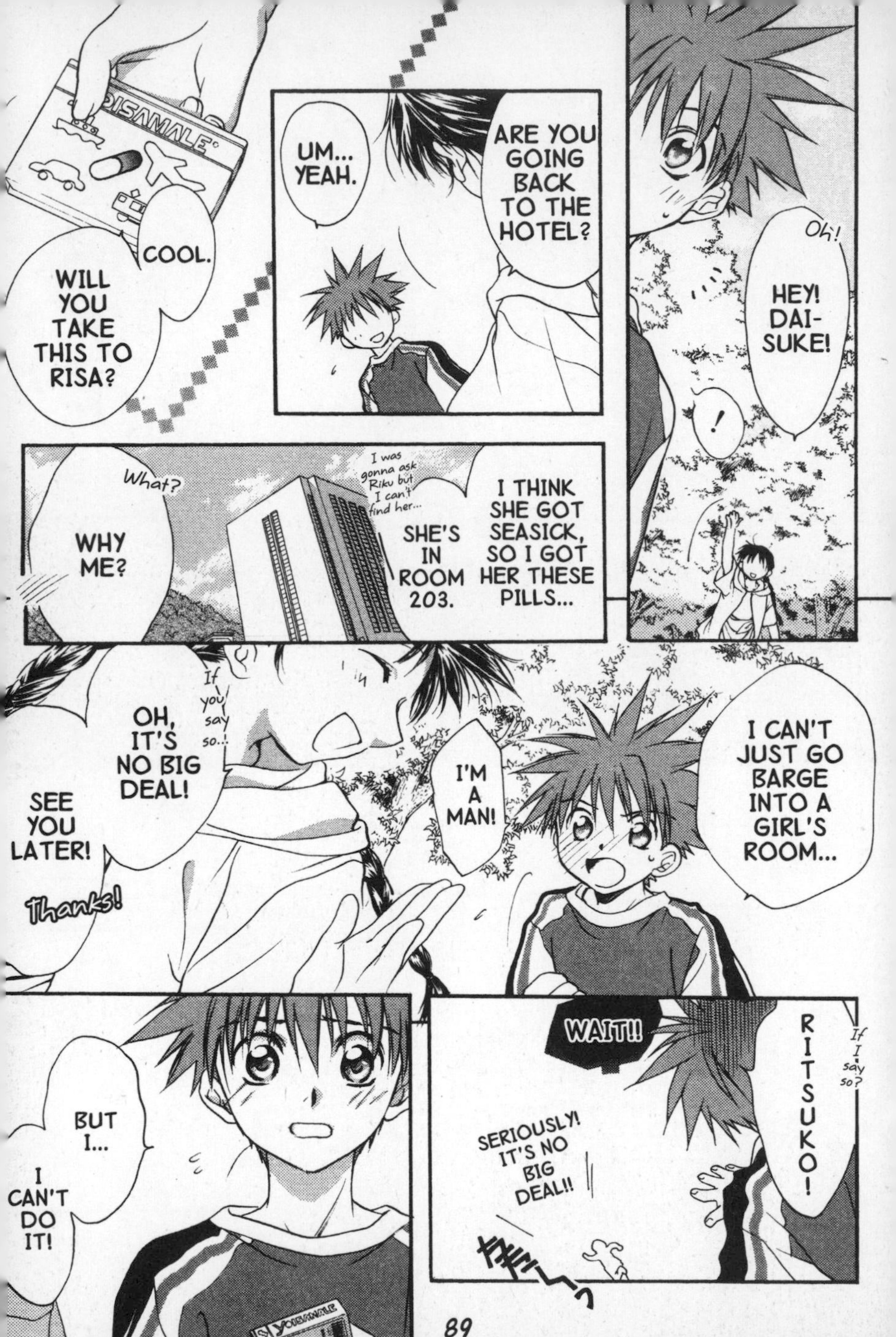
Oh!
HEY! DAI-SUKE!
!
ARE YOU GOING BACK TO THE HOTEL?
UM... YEAH.
COOL.
WILL YOU TAKE THIS TO RISA?
I THINK SHE GOT SEASICK, SO I GOT HER THESE PILLS...
SHE'S IN ROOM 203.
I was gonna ask Riku but I can't find her...
What?
WHY ME?
I CAN'T JUST GO BARGE INTO A GIRL'S ROOM...
I'M A MAN!
If you say so...!
OH, IT'S NO BIG DEAL!
SEE YOU LATER!
Thanks!
WAIT!!
RITSUKO!
If I say so?
SERIOUSLY! IT'S NO BIG DEAL!!
BUT I...
I CAN'T DO IT!

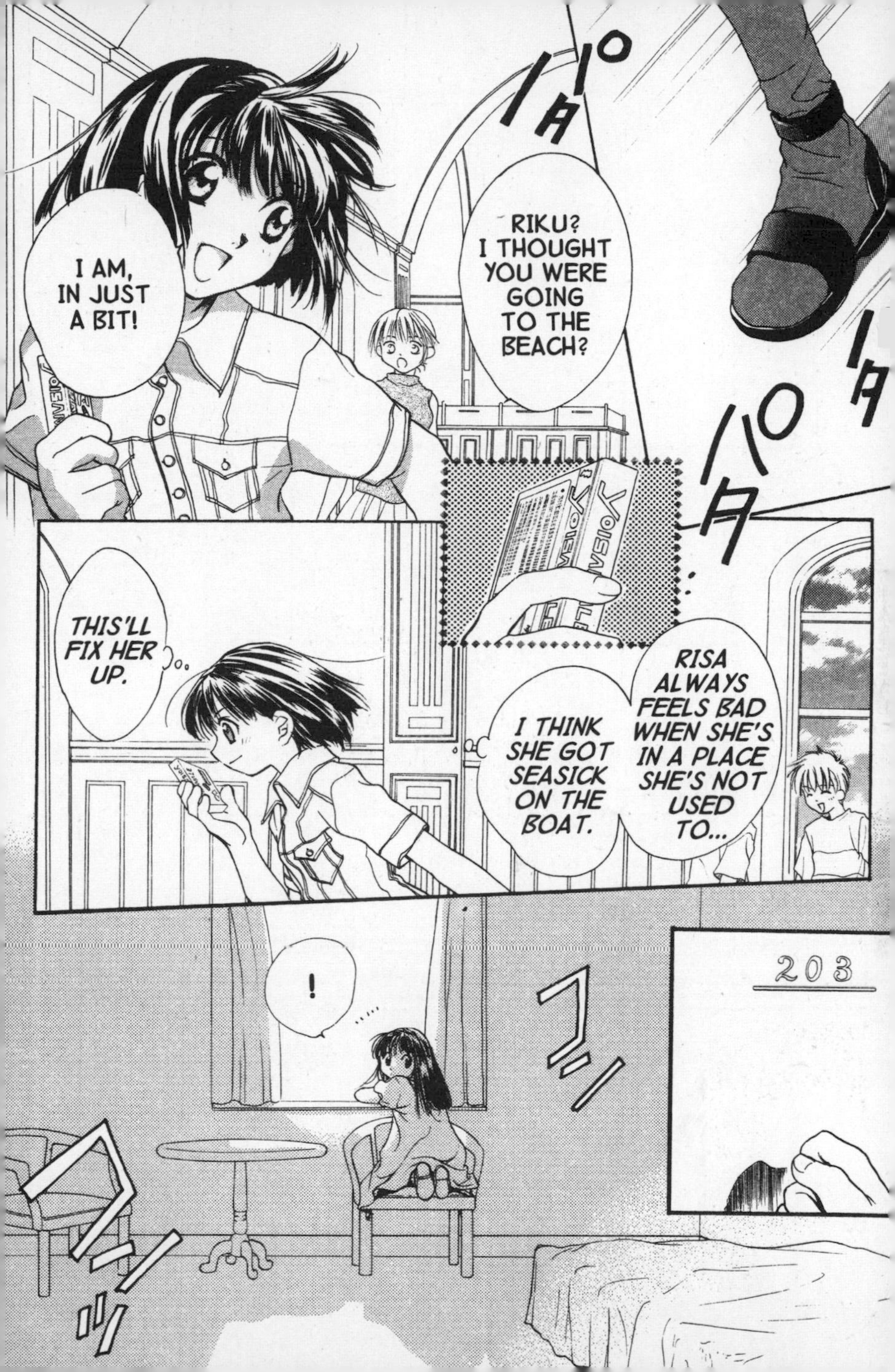
パタ
パタ
RIKU? I THOUGHT YOU WERE GOING TO THE BEACH?
I AM, IN JUST A BIT!
RISA ALWAYS FEELS BAD WHEN SHE'S IN A PLACE SHE'S NOT USED TO...
I THINK SHE GOT SEASICK ON THE BOAT.
THIS'LL FIX HER UP.
203
!

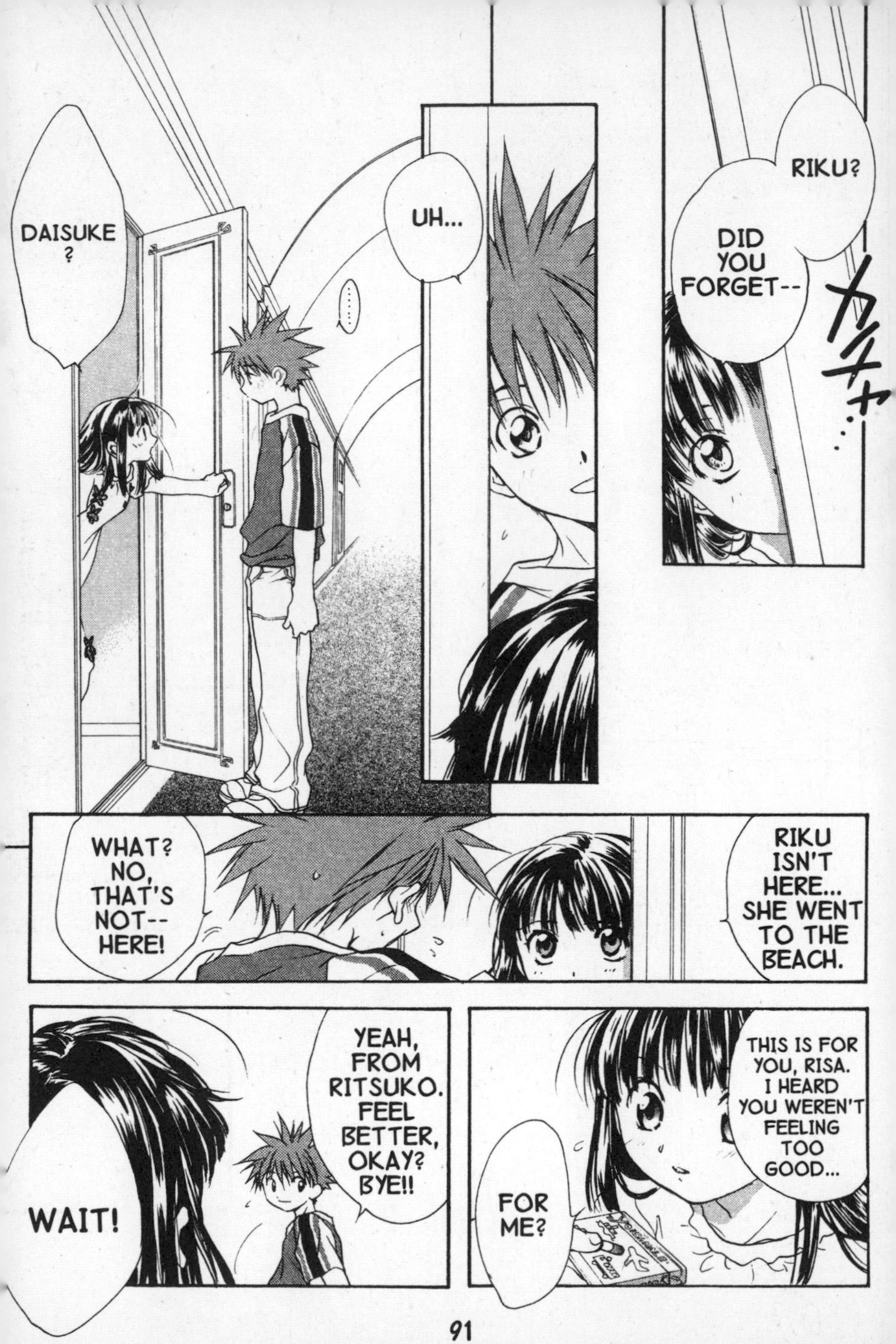
RIKU?
DID YOU FORGET--
カチャ...
UH...
DAISUKE?
......
RIKU ISN'T HERE... SHE WENT TO THE BEACH.
WHAT? NO, THAT'S NOT-- HERE!
THIS IS FOR YOU, RISA. I HEARD YOU WEREN'T FEELING TOO GOOD...
FOR ME?
YEAH, FROM RITSUKO. FEEL BETTER, OKAY? BYE!!
WAIT!

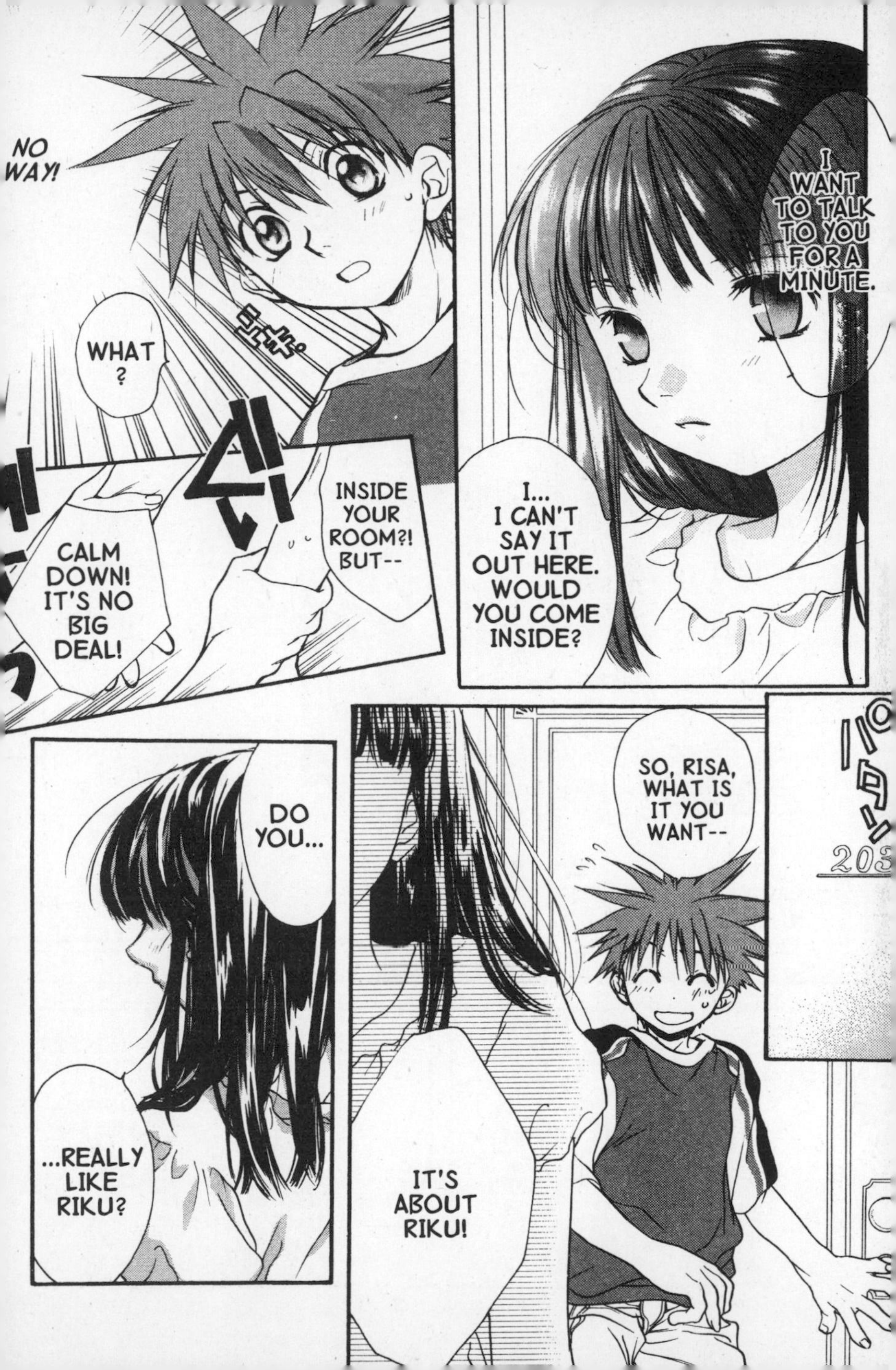

I WANT TO TALK TO YOU FOR A MINUTE.
I... I CAN'T SAY IT OUT HERE. WOULD YOU COME INSIDE?
NO WAY!
WHAT?
INSIDE YOUR ROOM?! BUT--
CALM DOWN! IT'S NO BIG DEAL!
203
SO, RISA, WHAT IS IT YOU WANT--
IT'S ABOUT RIKU!
DO YOU...
...REALLY LIKE RIKU?

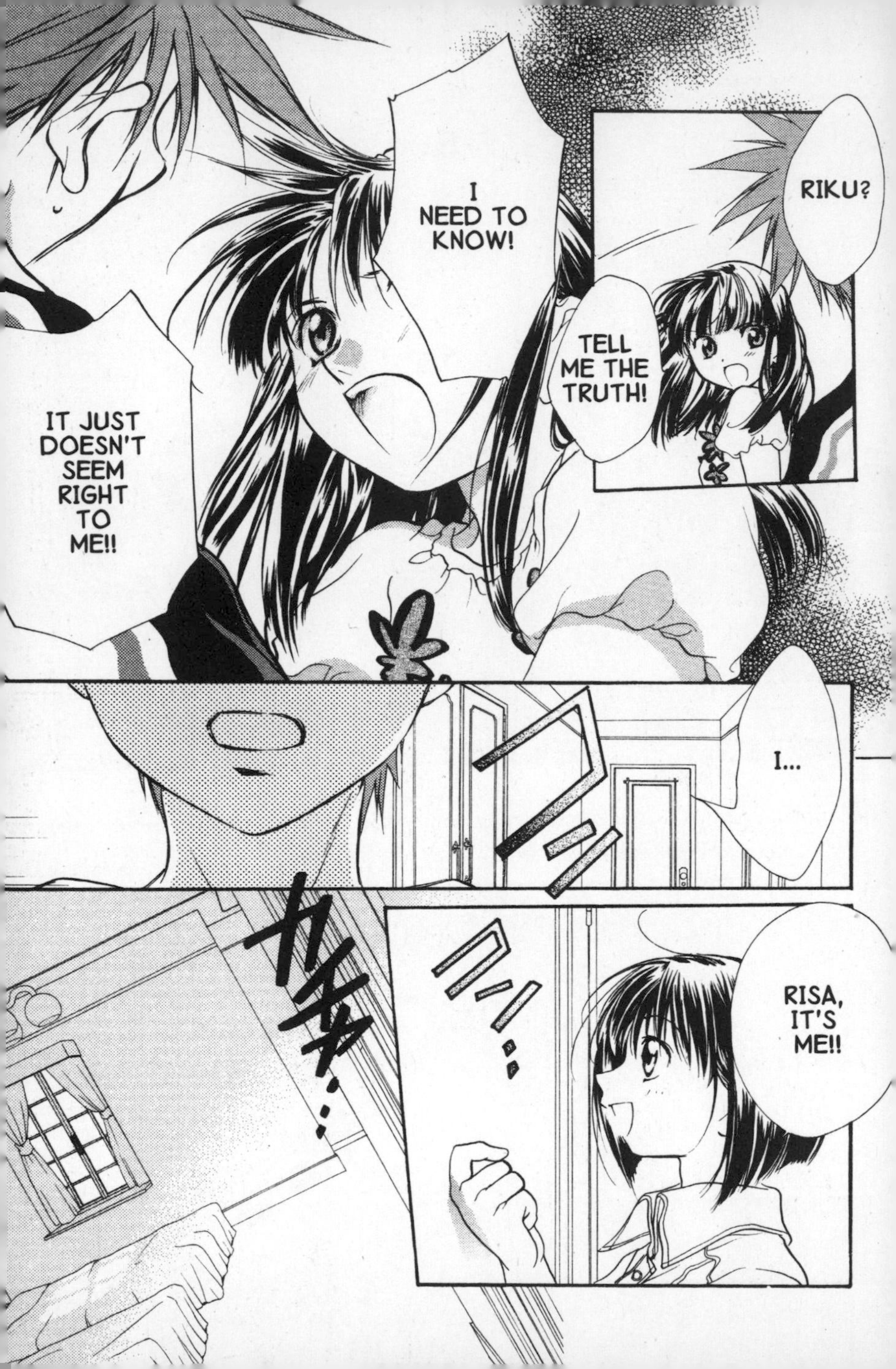
RIKU?
TELL ME THE TRUTH!
I NEED TO KNOW!
IT JUST DOESN'T SEEM RIGHT TO ME!!
I...
RISA, IT'S ME!!

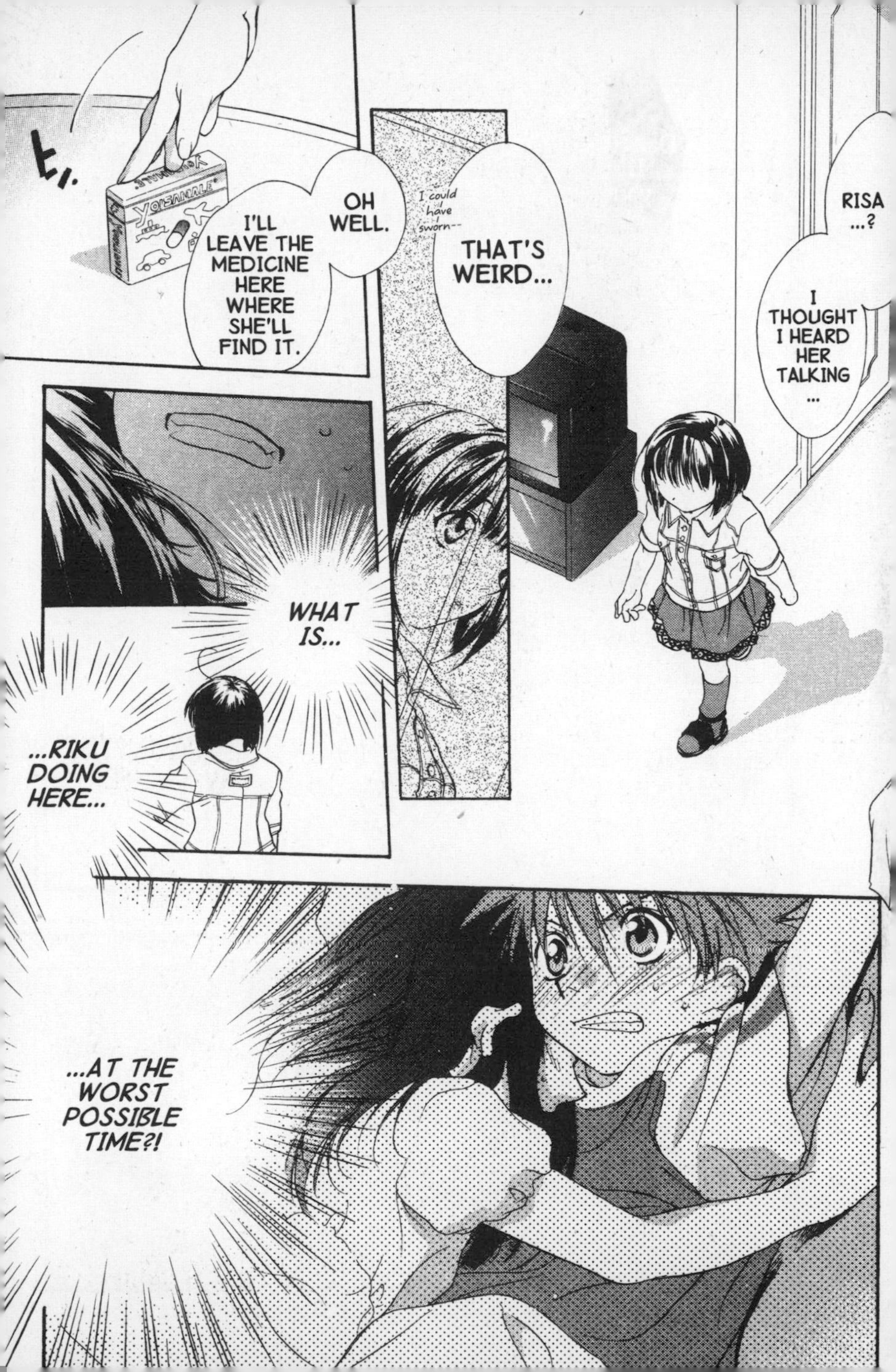
RISA ...?
I THOUGHT I HEARD HER TALKING ...
THAT'S WEIRD...
I could have sworn--
OH WELL.
I'LL LEAVE THE MEDICINE HERE WHERE SHE'LL FIND IT.
WHAT IS...
...RIKU DOING HERE...
...AT THE WORST POSSIBLE TIME?!

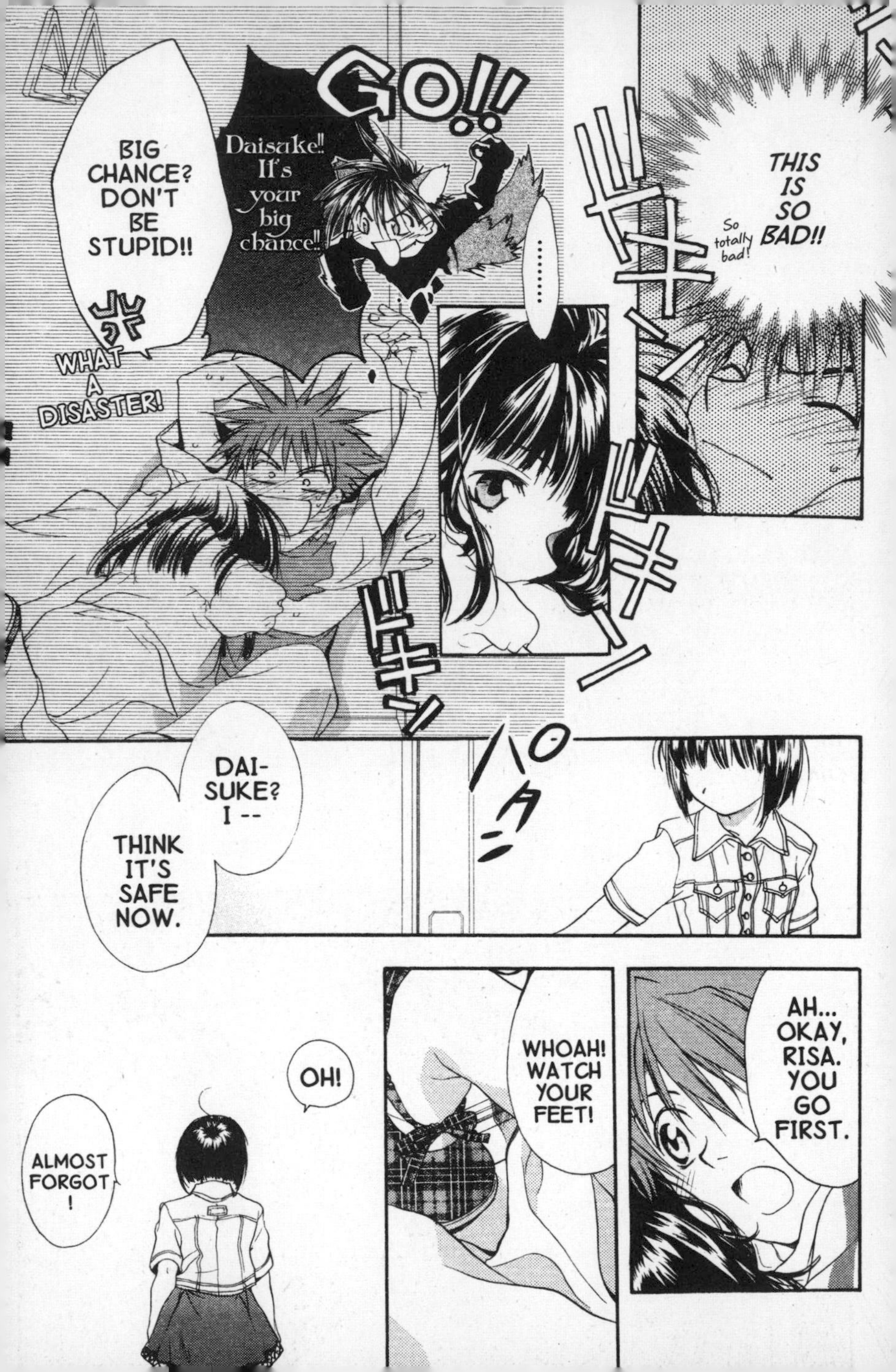
THIS IS SO BAD!!
So totally bad!
......
GO!!
Daisuke!! It's your big chance!!
BIG CHANCE? DON'T BE STUPID!!
WHAT A DISASTER!
DAI-SUKE? I --
THINK IT'S SAFE NOW.
AH... OKAY, RISA. YOU GO FIRST.
WHOAH! WATCH YOUR FEET!
OH!
ALMOST FORGOT!

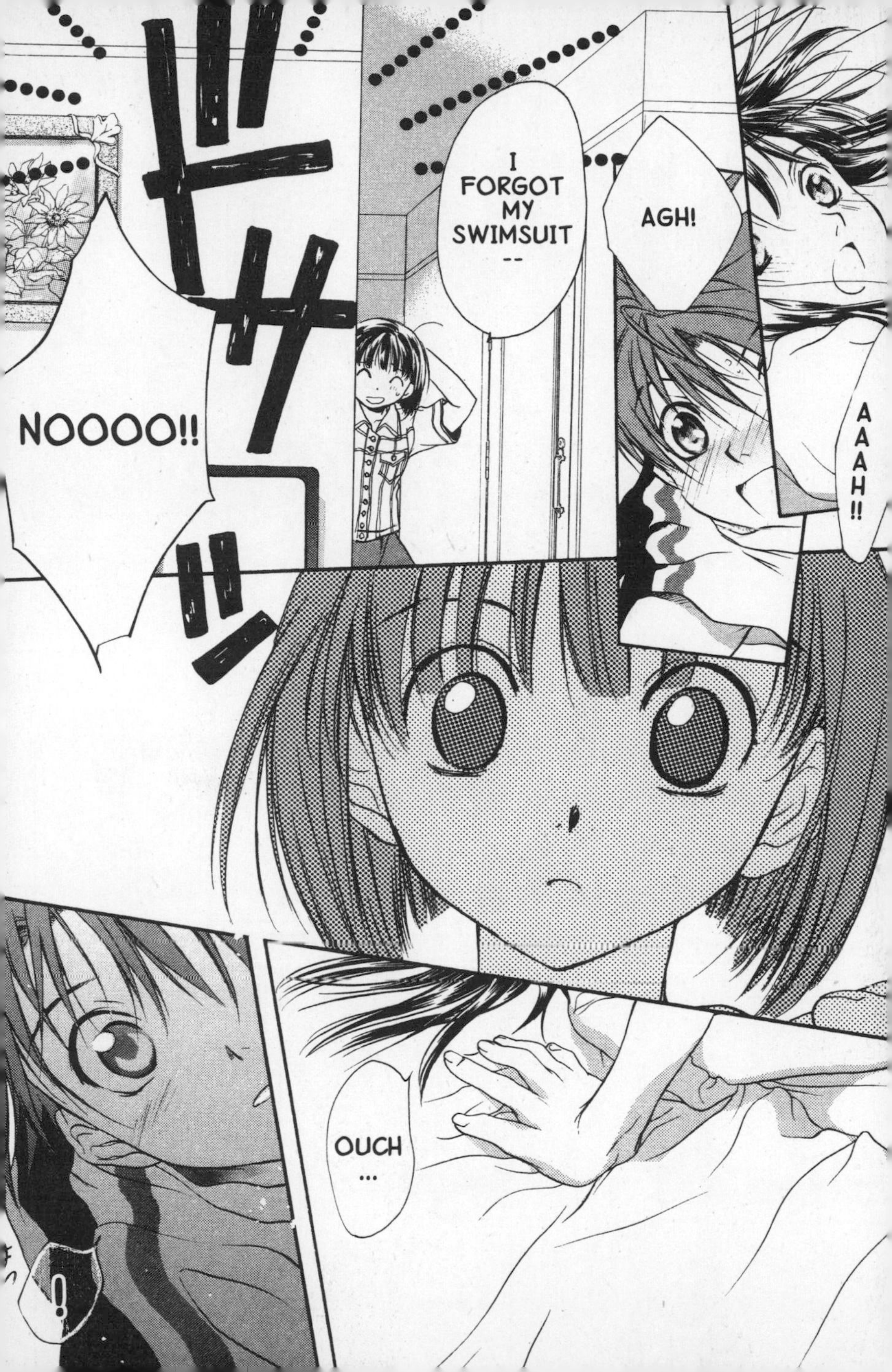
AAAH!!
AGH!
I FORGOT MY SWIMSUIT --
NOOOO!!
OUCH ...
!

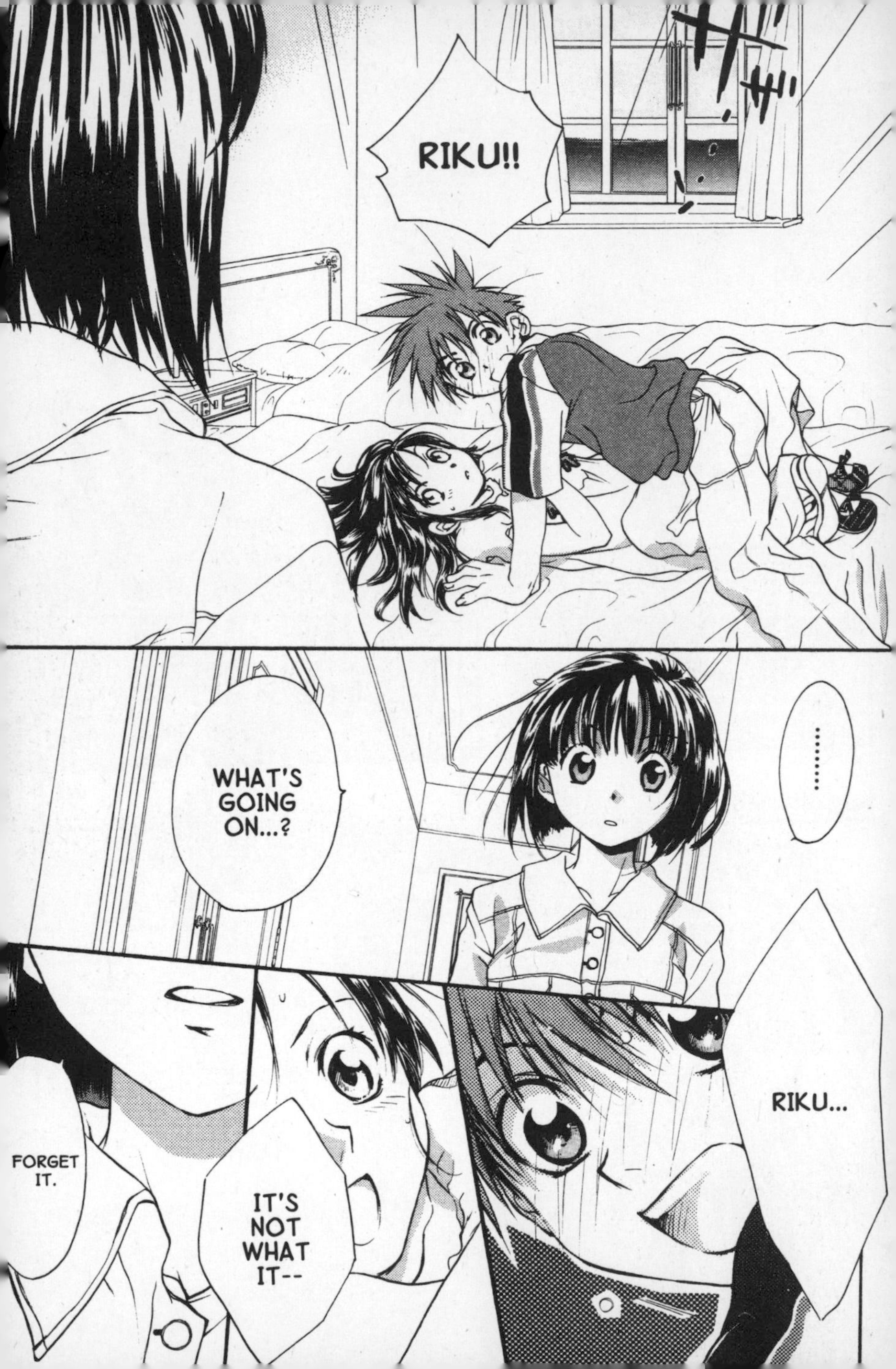

RIKU!!
......
WHAT'S GOING ON...?
RIKU...
IT'S NOT WHAT IT--
FORGET IT.

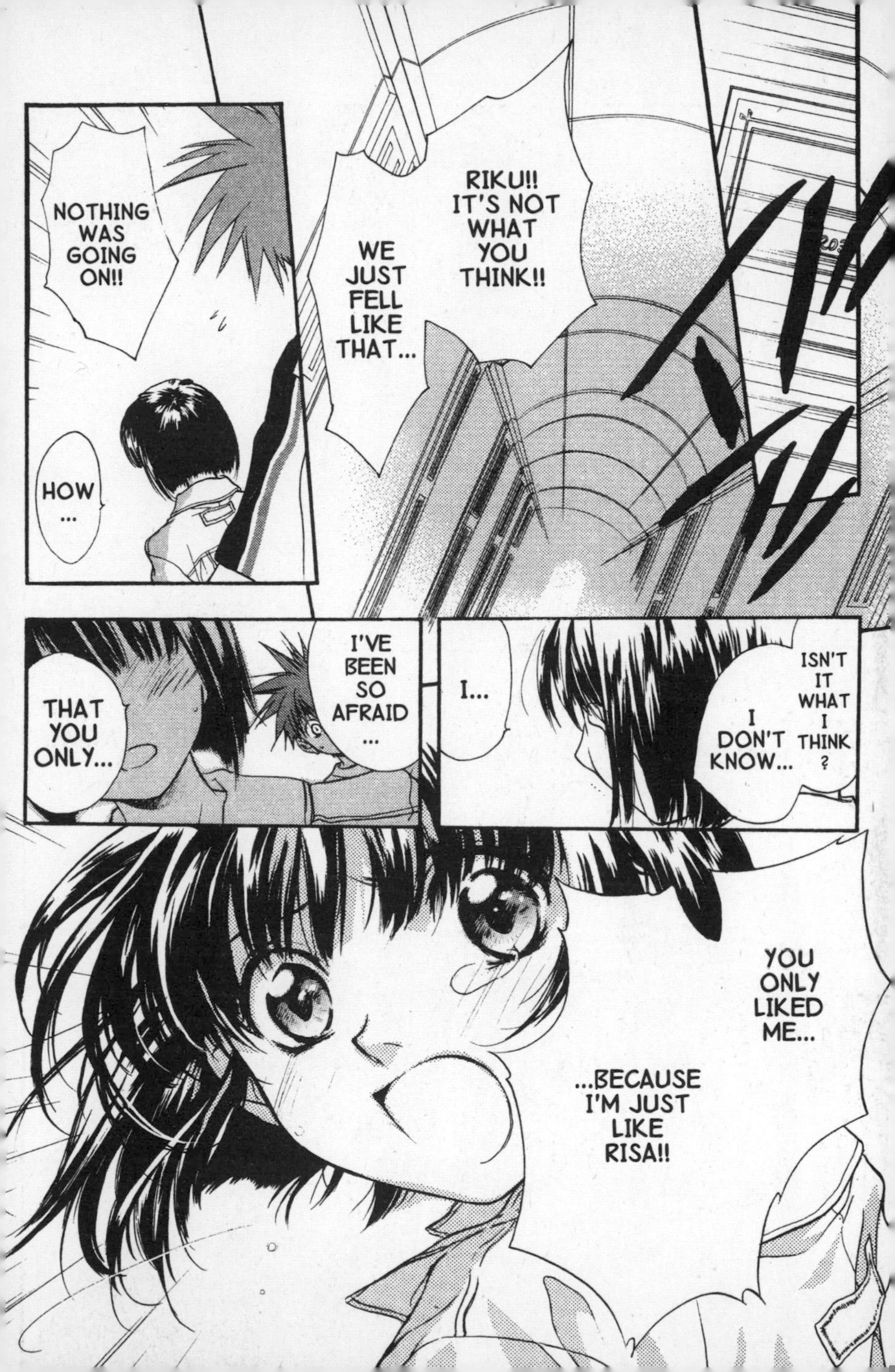
RIKU!! IT'S NOT WHAT YOU THINK!!
WE JUST FELL LIKE THAT...
NOTHING WAS GOING ON!!
HOW ...
ISN'T IT WHAT I THINK?
I DON'T KNOW...
I...
I'VE BEEN SO AFRAID ...
THAT YOU ONLY...
YOU ONLY LIKED ME...
...BECAUSE I'M JUST LIKE RISA!!

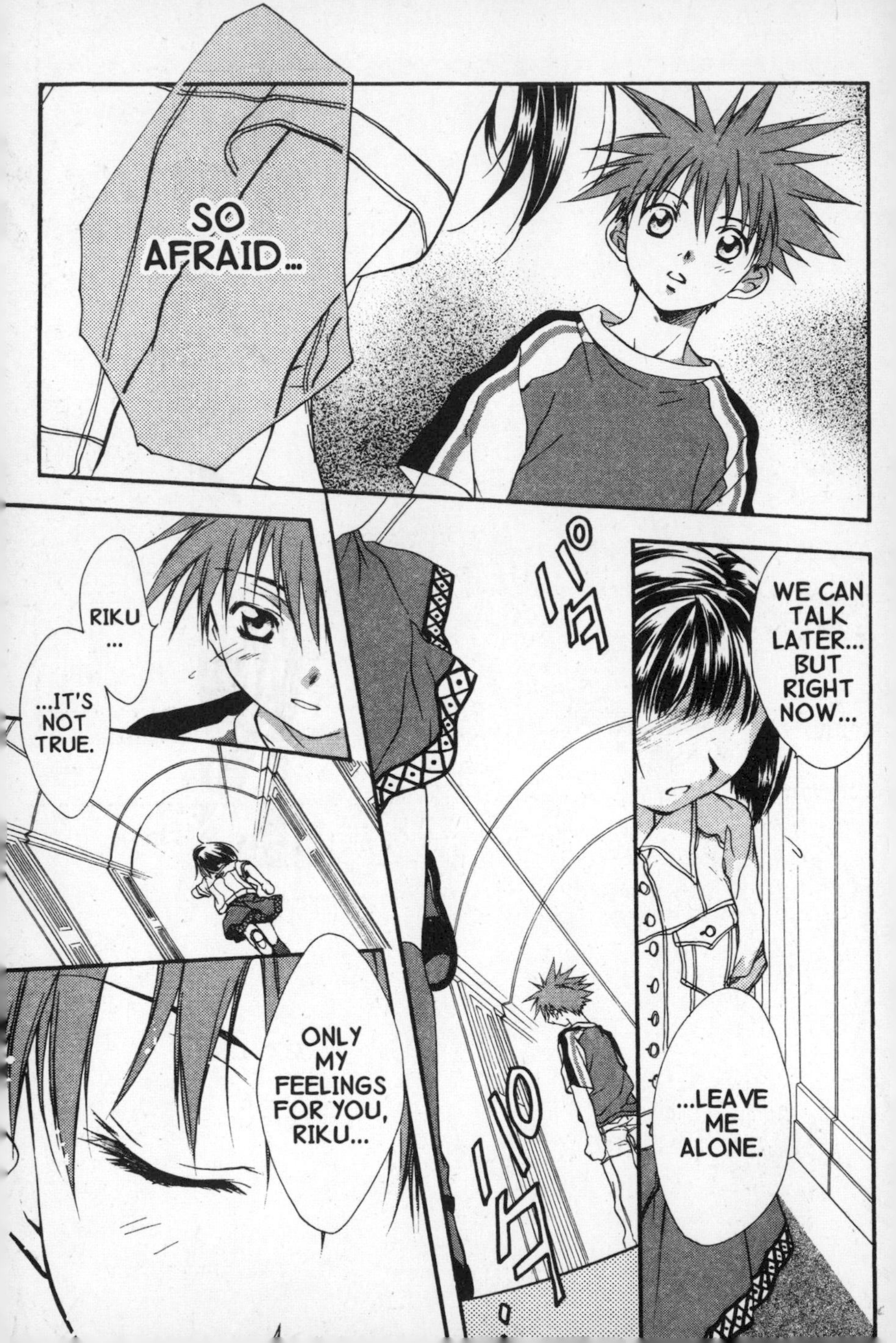
SO AFRAID...
WE CAN TALK LATER... BUT RIGHT NOW...
...LEAVE ME ALONE.
RIKU ...
...IT'S NOT TRUE.
ONLY MY FEELINGS FOR YOU, RIKU...

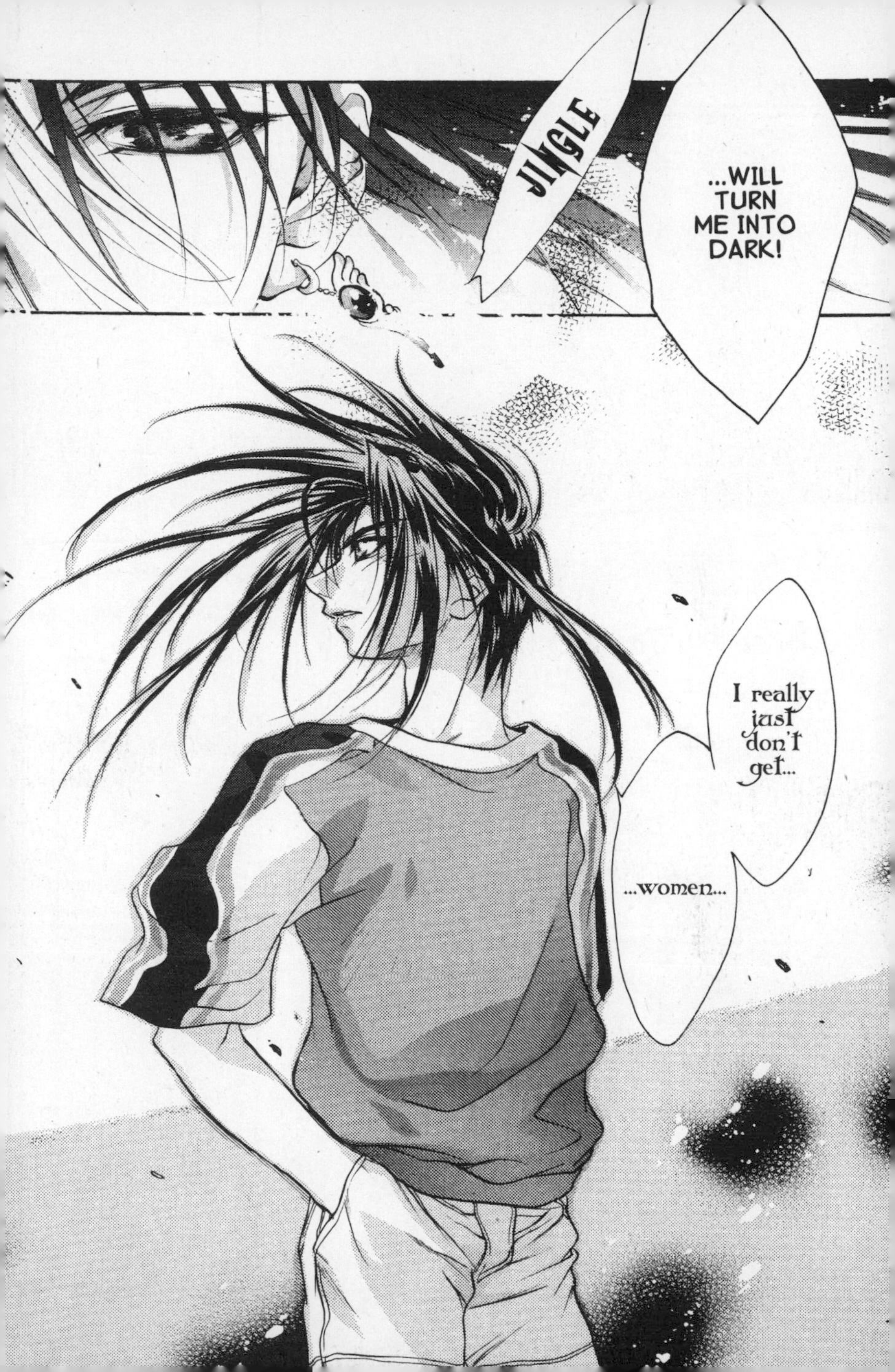
...WILL TURN ME INTO DARK!
JINGLE
I really just don't get...
...women...

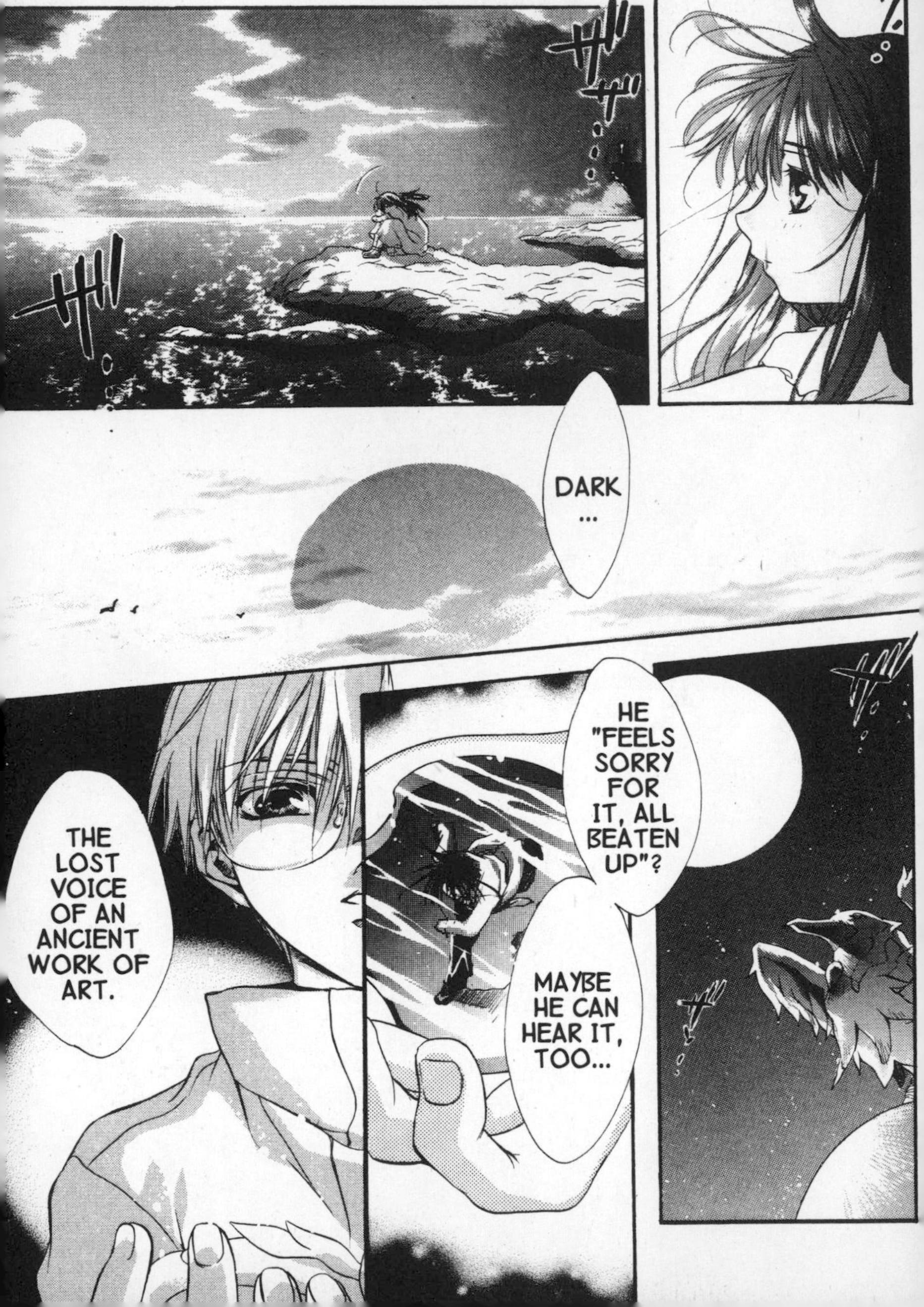
DARK ...
HE "FEELS SORRY FOR IT, ALL BEATEN UP"?
MAYBE HE CAN HEAR IT, TOO...
THE LOST VOICE OF AN ANCIENT WORK OF ART.

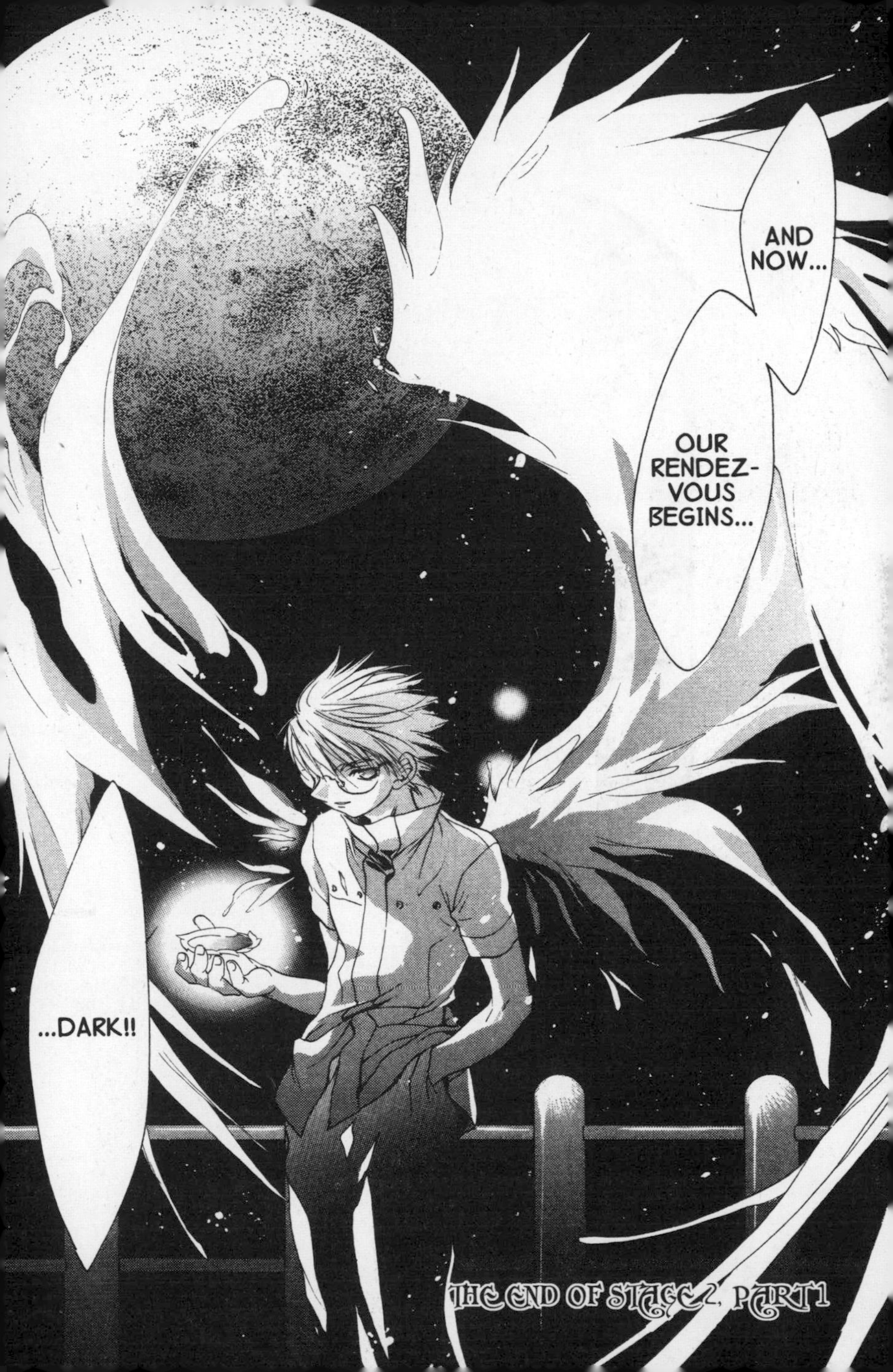
AND NOW...
OUR RENDEZ-VOUS BEGINS...
...DARK!!
THE END OF STAGE 2, PART 1

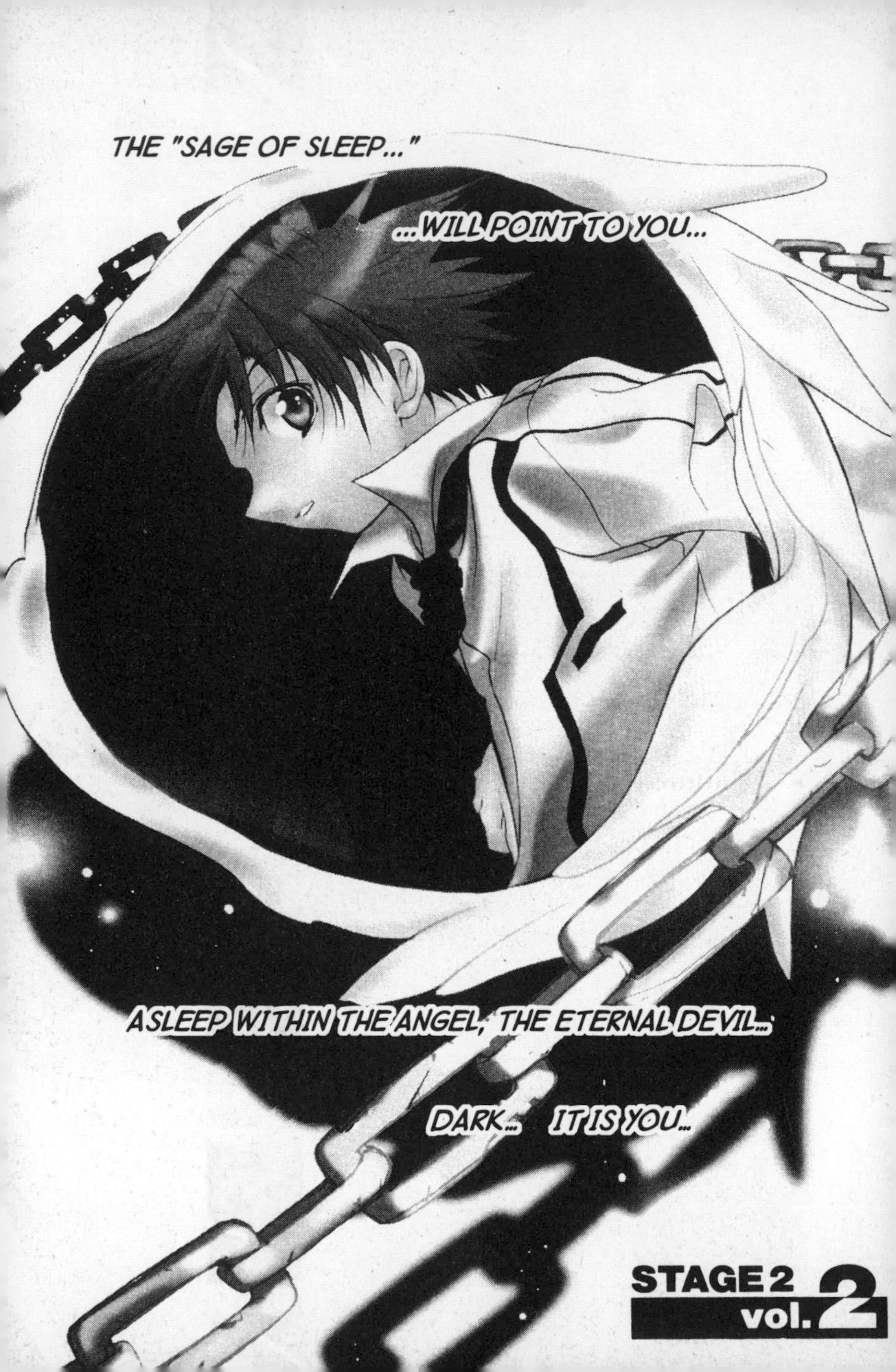
THE "SAGE OF SLEEP..."
...WILL POINT TO YOU...
ASLEEP WITHIN THE ANGEL, THE ETERNAL DEVIL...
DARK... IT IS YOU...
STAGE 2
vol. 2

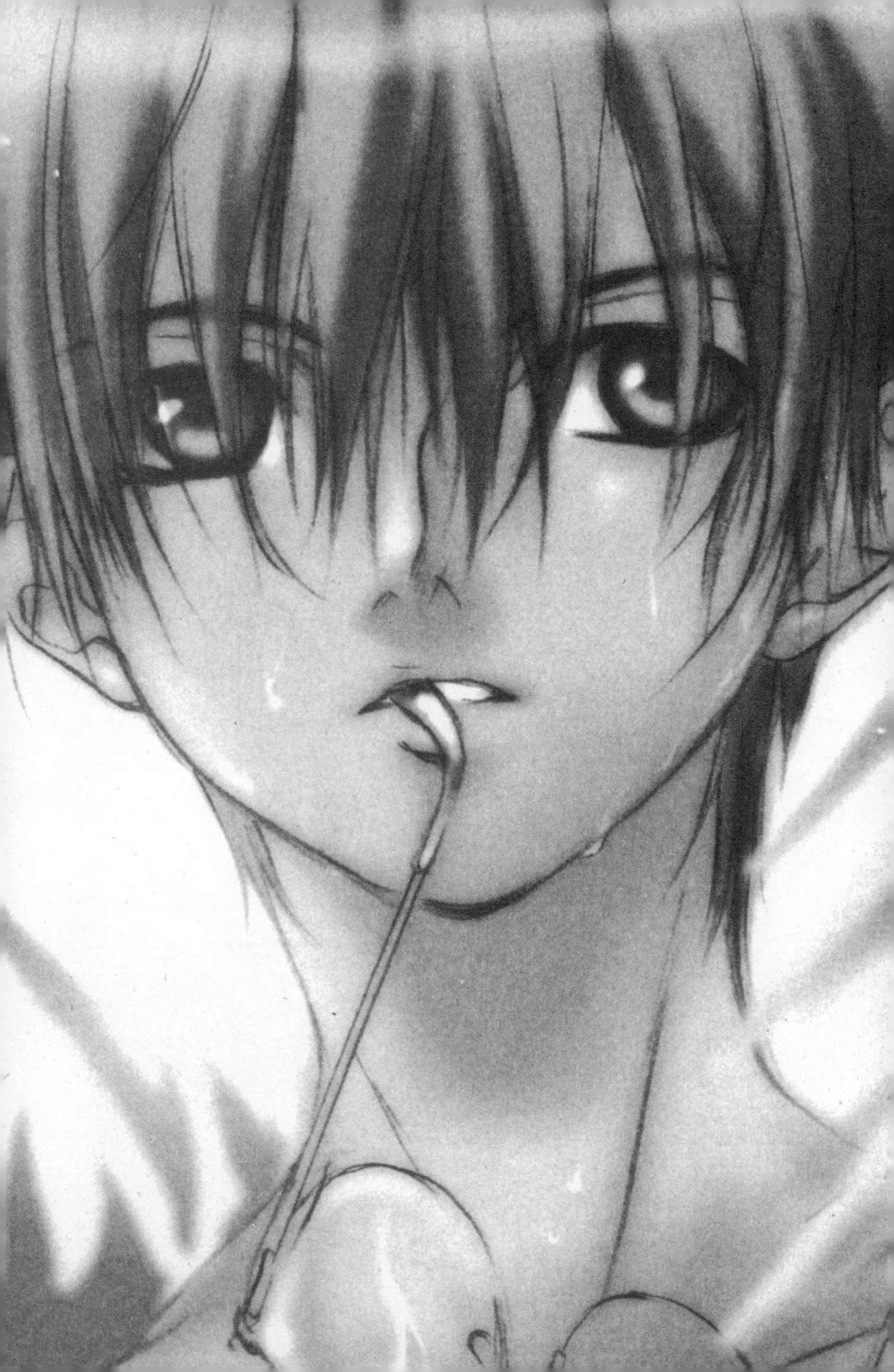

STAGE 2 vol. 2

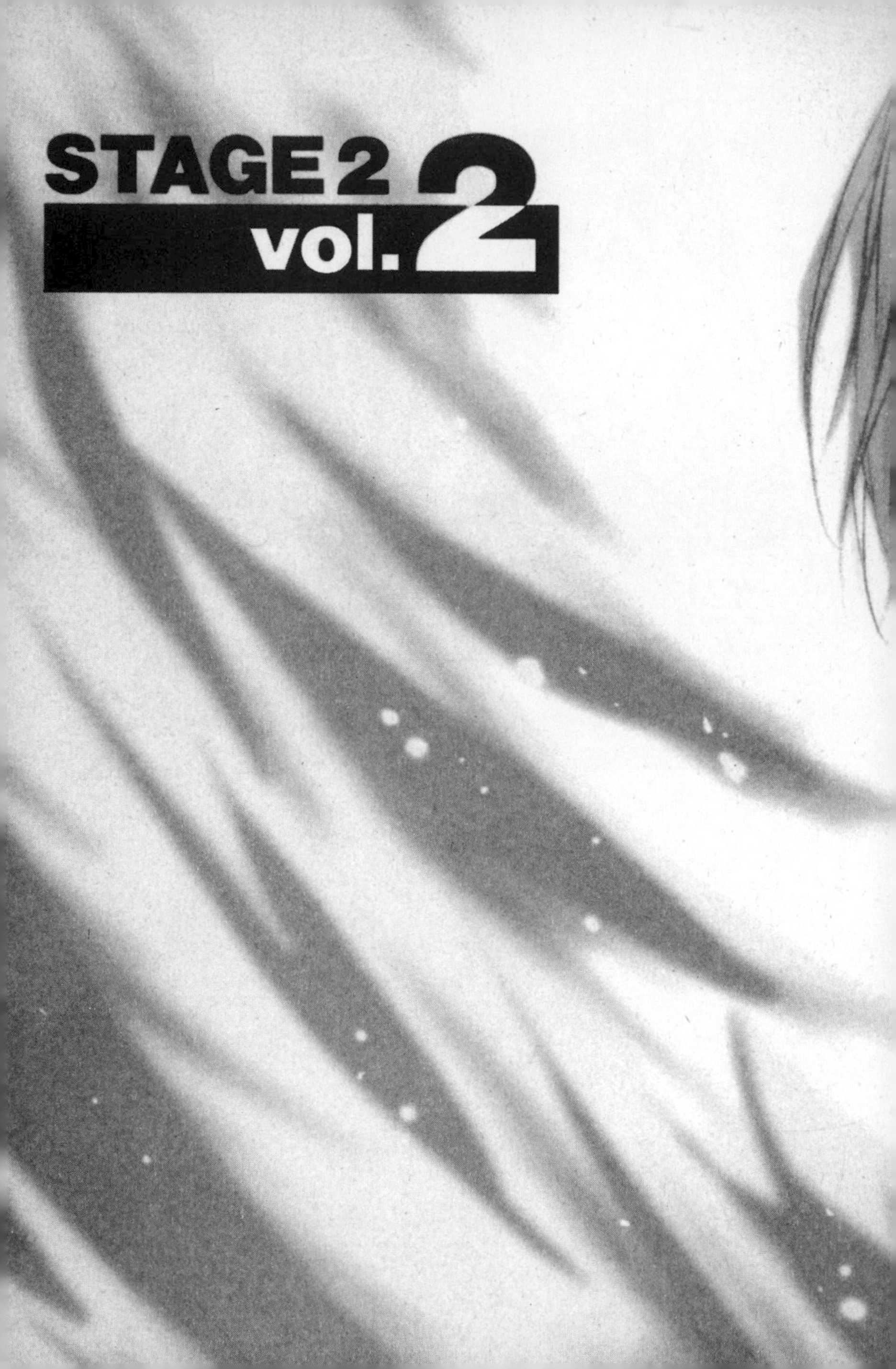

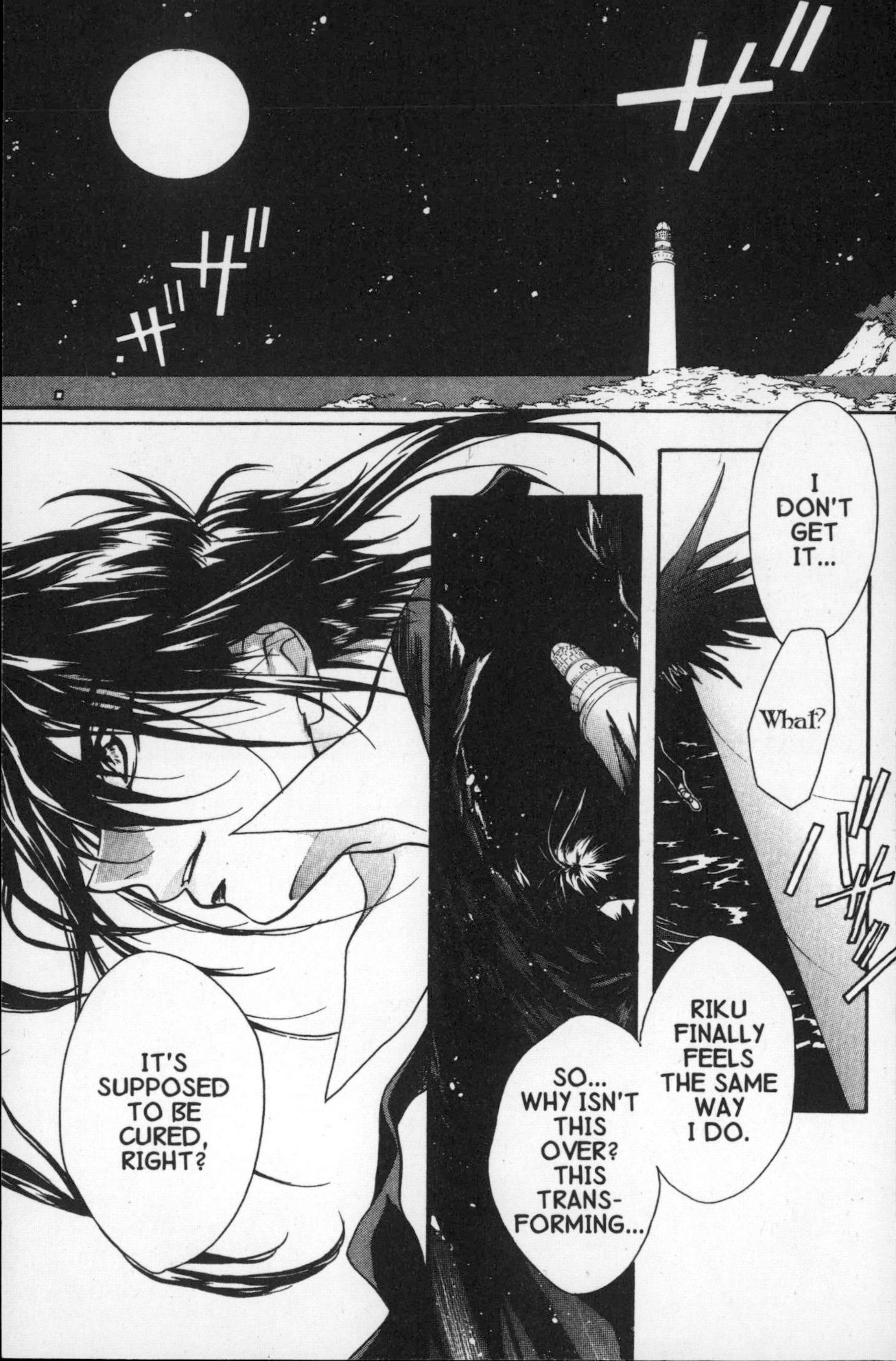
I DON'T GET IT...
What?
RIKU FINALLY FEELS THE SAME WAY I DO.
SO... WHY ISN'T THIS OVER? THIS TRANS-FORMING...
IT'S SUPPOSED TO BE CURED, RIGHT?

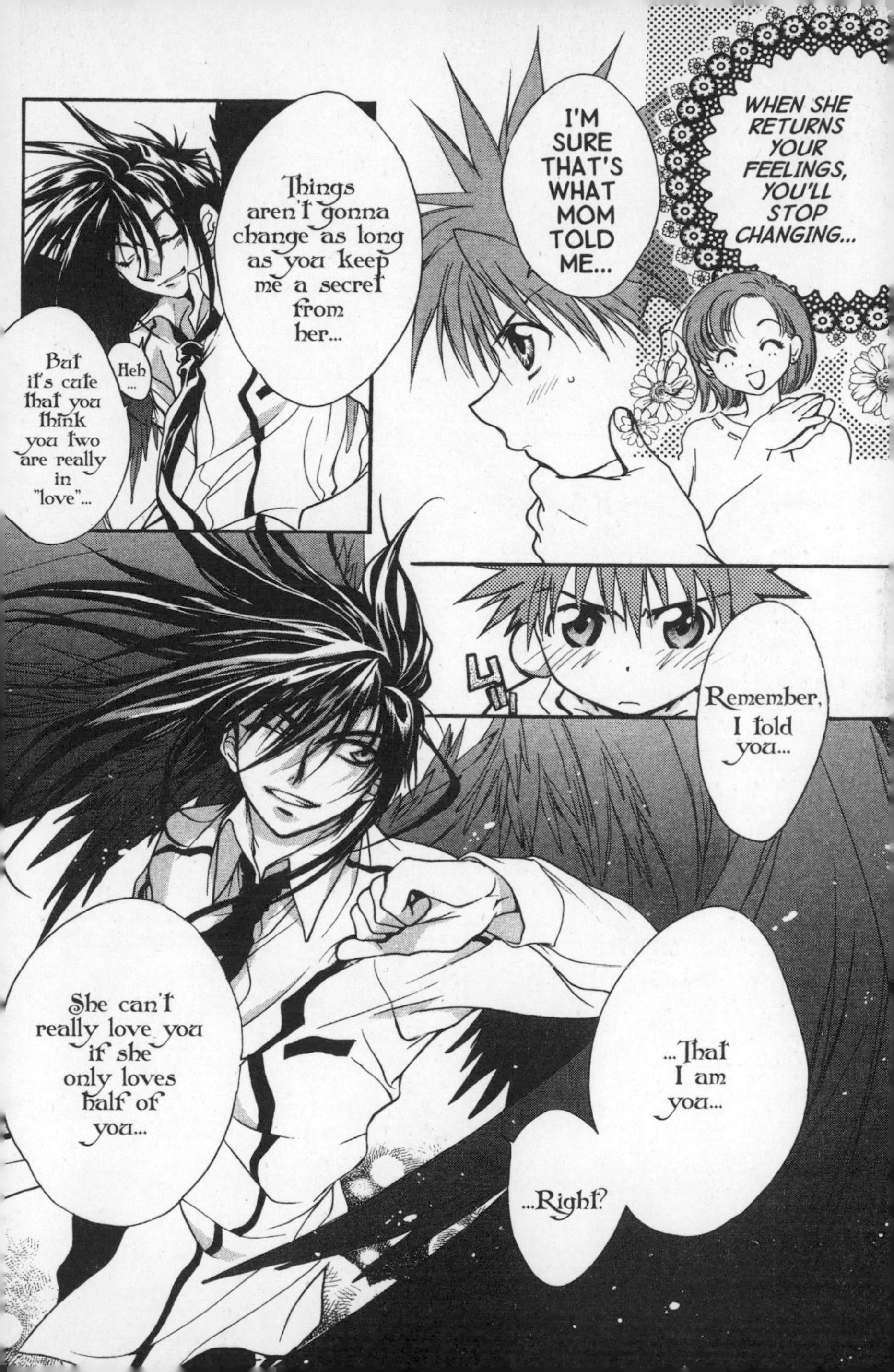
WHEN SHE RETURNS YOUR FEELINGS, YOU'LL STOP CHANGING...
I'M SURE THAT'S WHAT MOM TOLD ME...
Things aren't gonna change as long as you keep me a secret from her...
Heh...
But it's cute that you think you two are really in "love"...
Remember, I told you...
...That I am you...
...Right?
She can't really love you if she only loves half of you...

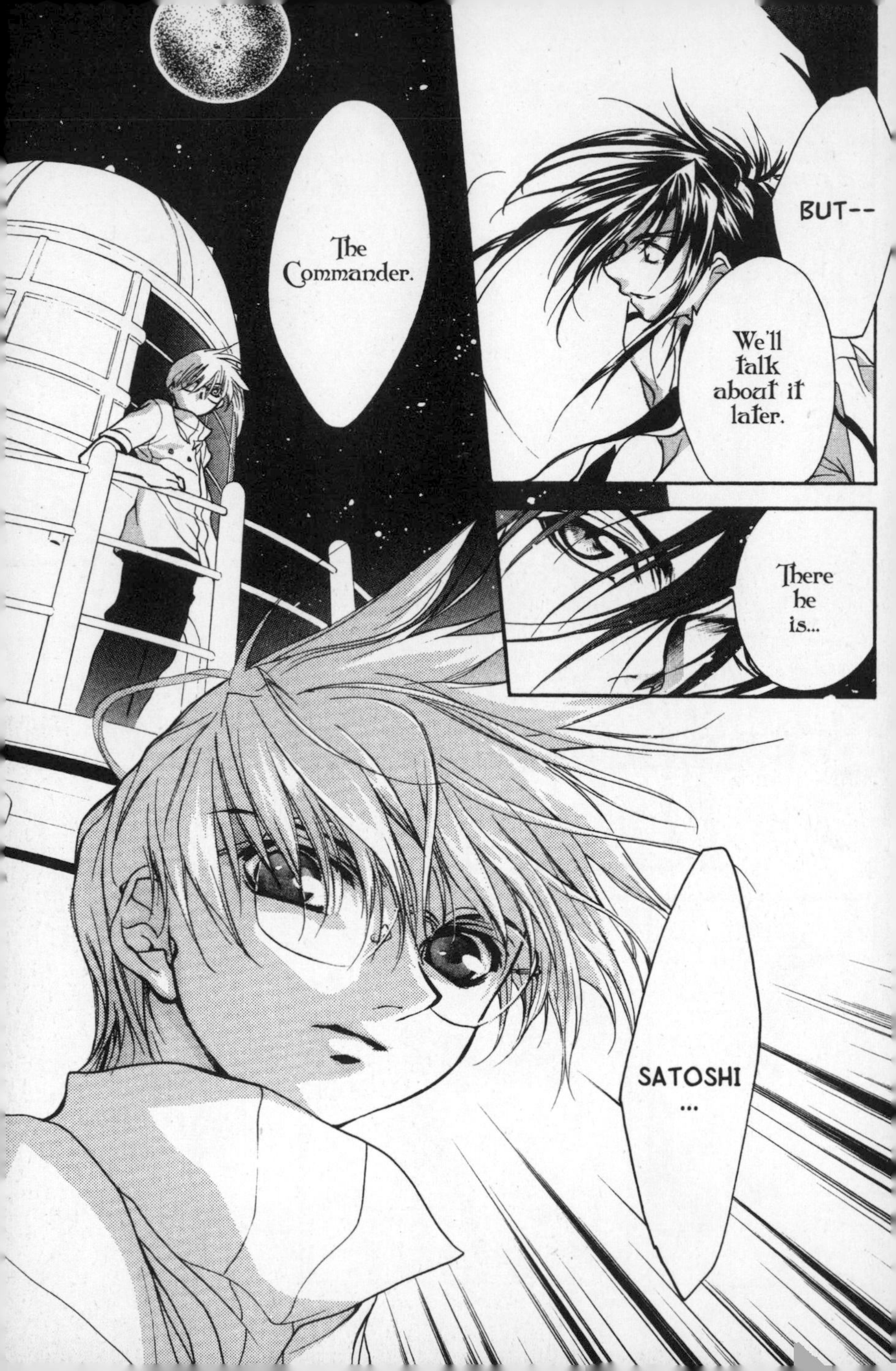
BUT--
We'll talk about it later.
There he is...
The Commander.
SATOSHI ...

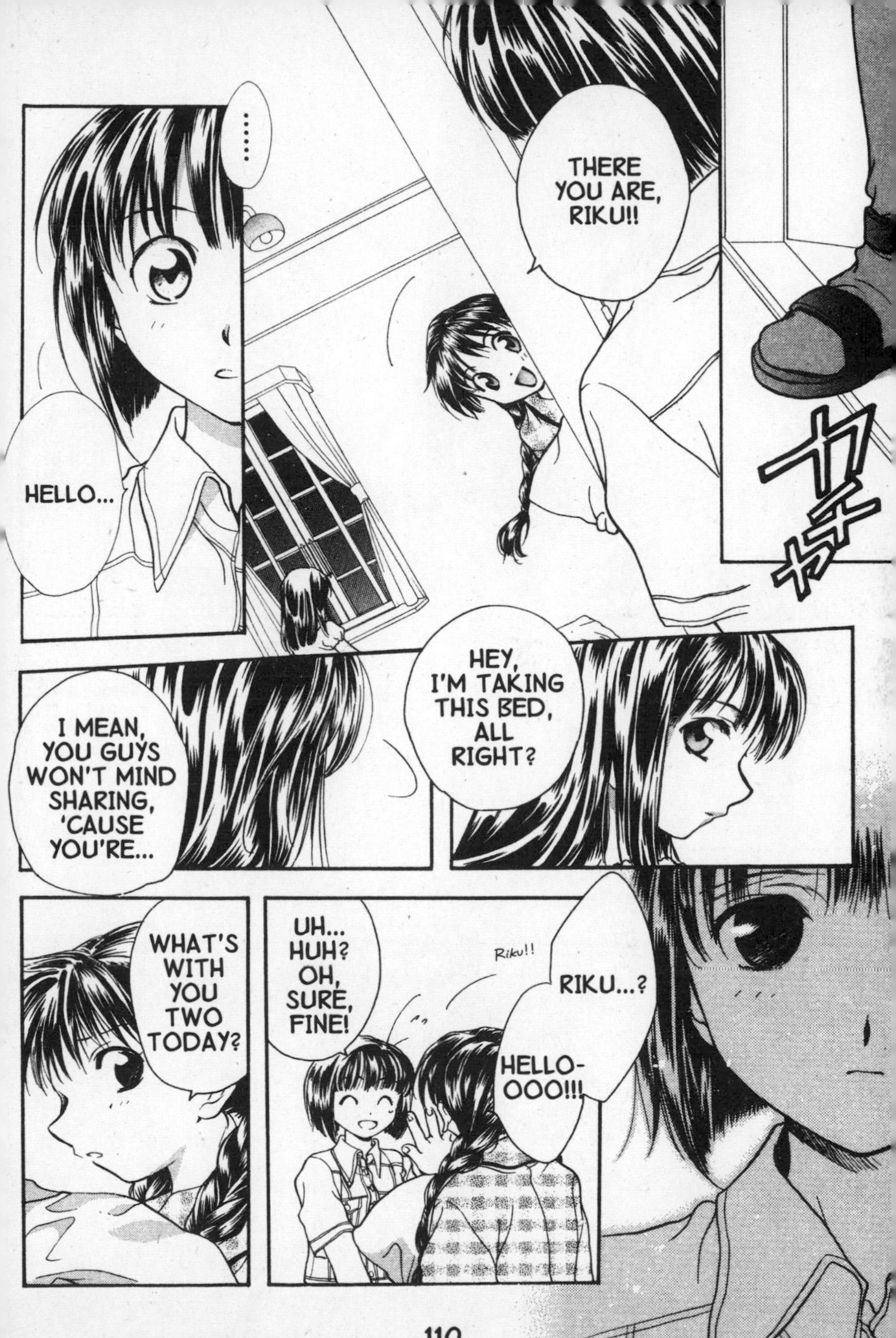

THERE YOU ARE, RIKU!!
......
HELLO...
HEY, I'M TAKING THIS BED, ALL RIGHT?
I MEAN, YOU GUYS WON'T MIND SHARING, 'CAUSE YOU'RE...
RIKU...?
Riku!!
HELLO-OOO!!!
UH... HUH? OH, SURE, FINE!
WHAT'S WITH YOU TWO TODAY?

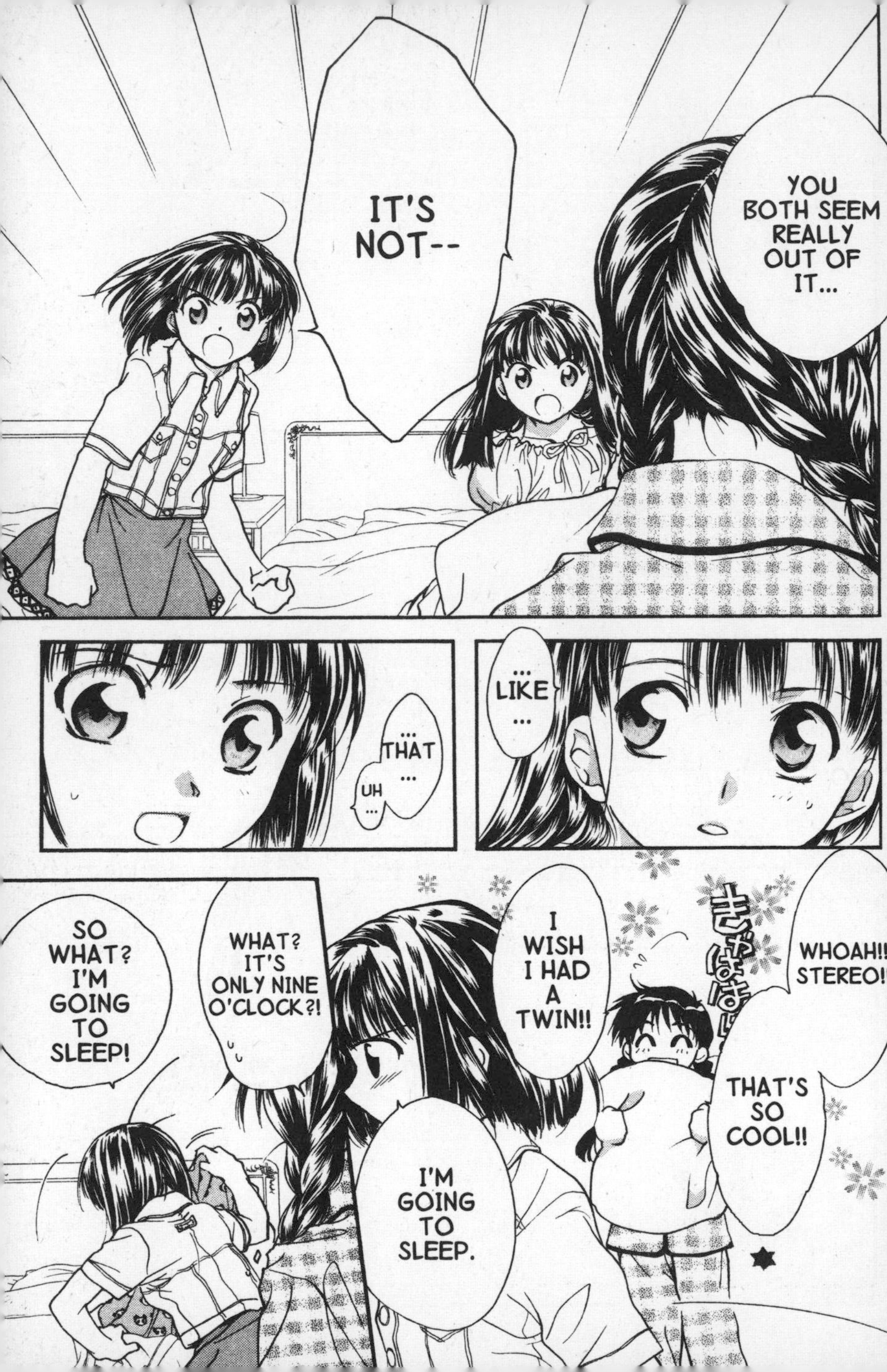
YOU BOTH SEEM REALLY OUT OF IT...
IT'S NOT--
...LIKE...
...THAT...
UH...
WHOAH!! STEREO!!
THAT'S SO COOL!!
I WISH I HAD A TWIN!!
I'M GOING TO SLEEP.
WHAT? IT'S ONLY NINE O'CLOCK?!
SO WHAT? I'M GOING TO SLEEP!

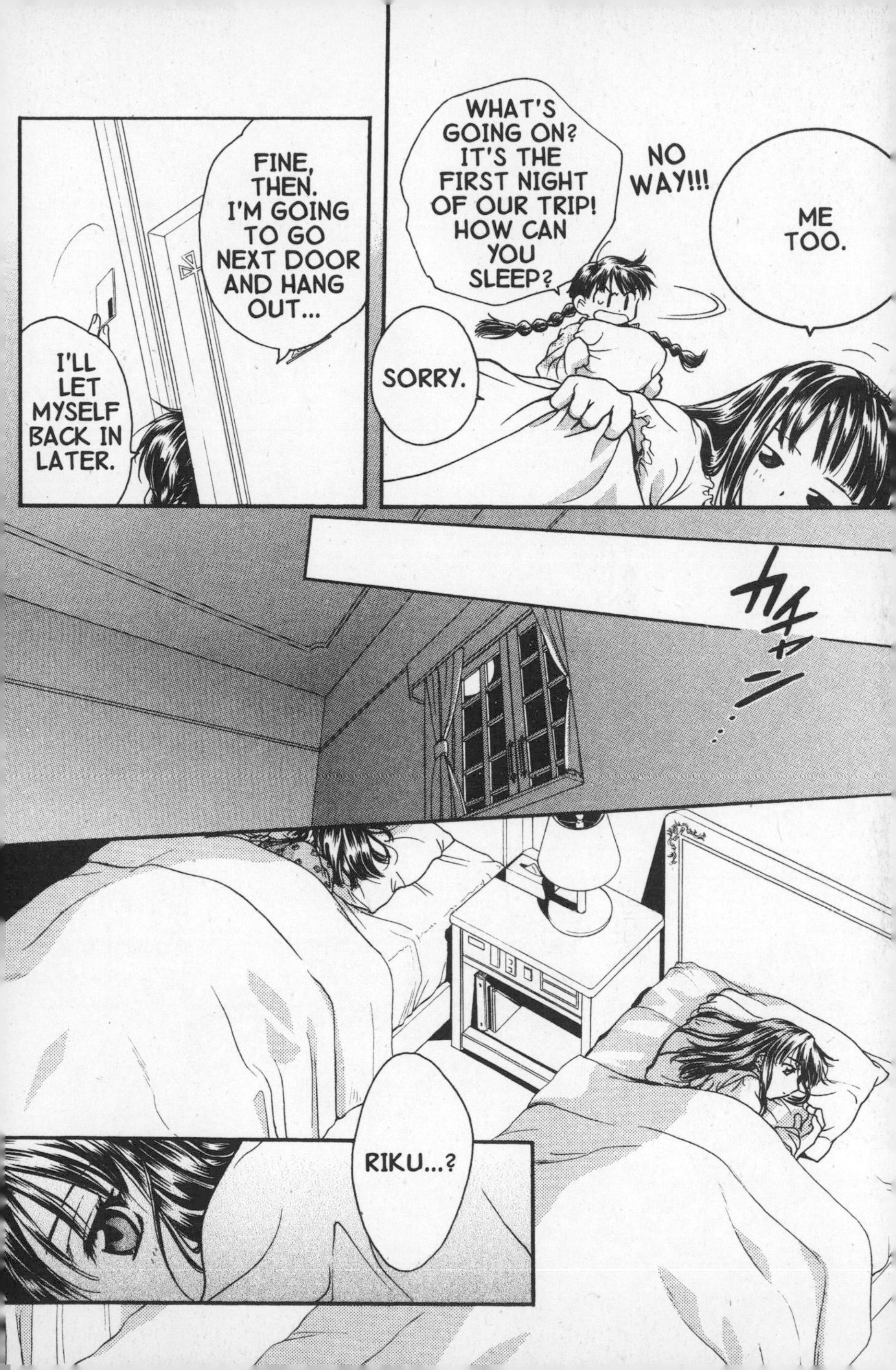
ME TOO.
NO WAY!!!
WHAT'S GOING ON? IT'S THE FIRST NIGHT OF OUR TRIP! HOW CAN YOU SLEEP?
SORRY.
FINE, THEN. I'M GOING TO GO NEXT DOOR AND HANG OUT...
I'LL LET MYSELF BACK IN LATER.
RIKU...?

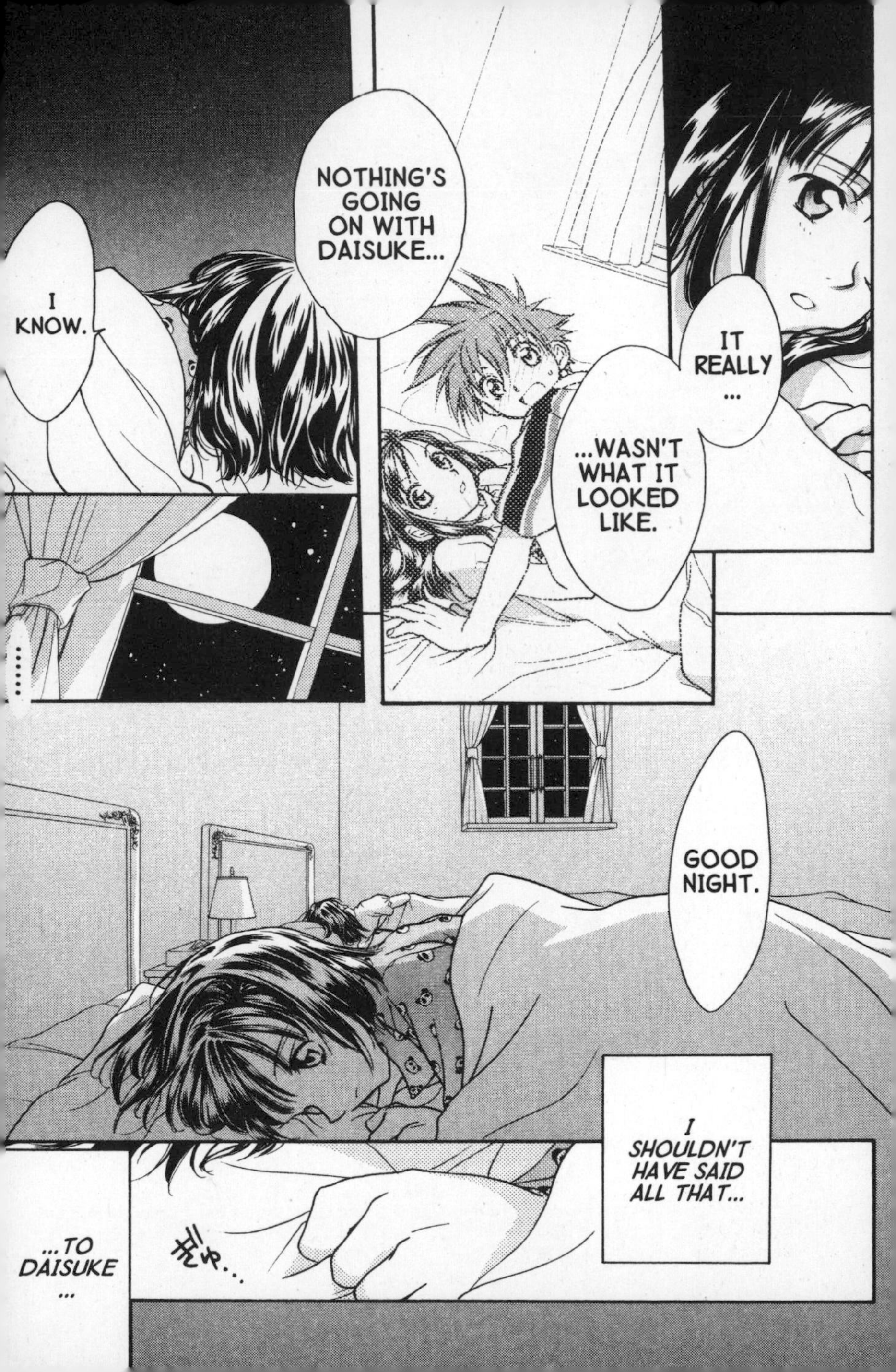
IT REALLY ...
...WASN'T WHAT IT LOOKED LIKE.
NOTHING'S GOING ON WITH DAISUKE...
I KNOW.
......
GOOD NIGHT.
I SHOULDN'T HAVE SAID ALL THAT...
ぎゅ...
...TO DAISUKE ...

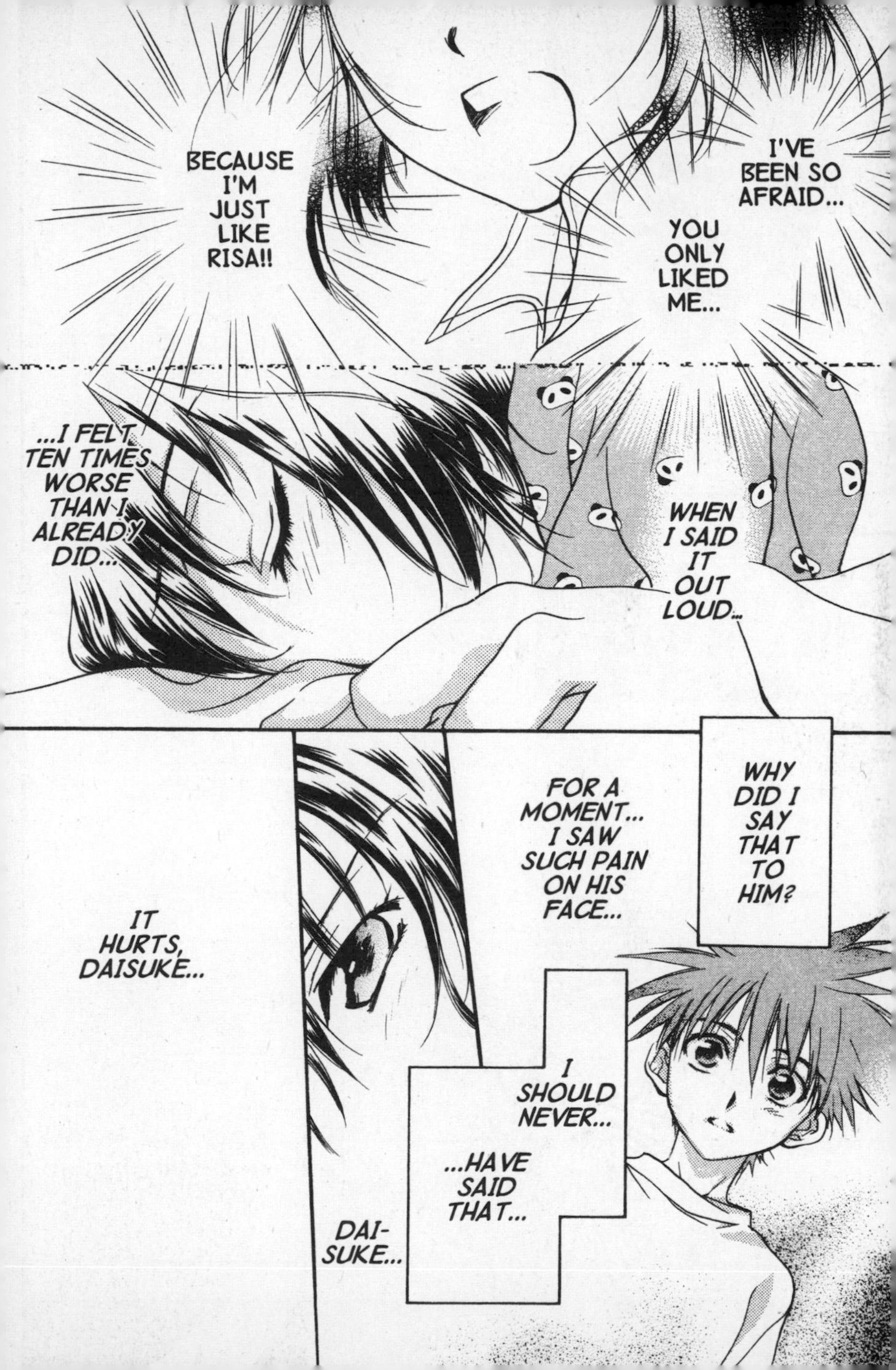
I'VE BEEN SO AFRAID...
YOU ONLY LIKED ME...
BECAUSE I'M JUST LIKE RISA!!
WHEN I SAID IT OUT LOUD...
...I FELT TEN TIMES WORSE THAN I ALREADY DID...
WHY DID I SAY THAT TO HIM?
FOR A MOMENT... I SAW SUCH PAIN ON HIS FACE...
I SHOULD NEVER...
...HAVE SAID THAT...
DAI-SUKE...
IT HURTS, DAISUKE...

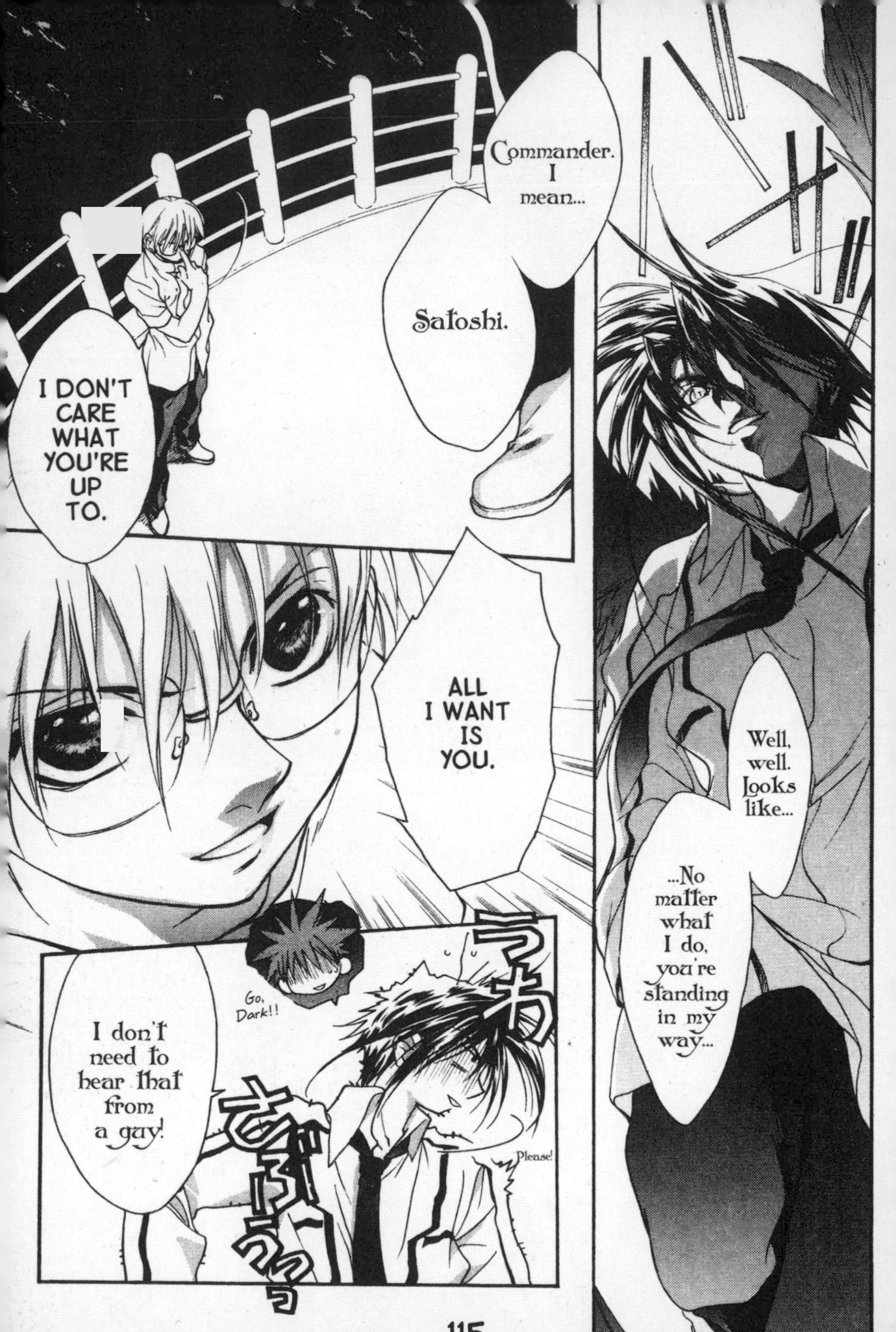
Well, well. Looks like...
...No matter what I do, you're standing in my way...
Commander. I mean...
Satoshi.
I DON'T CARE WHAT YOU'RE UP TO.
ALL I WANT IS YOU.
Go, Dark!!
Please!
I don't need to hear that from a guy!

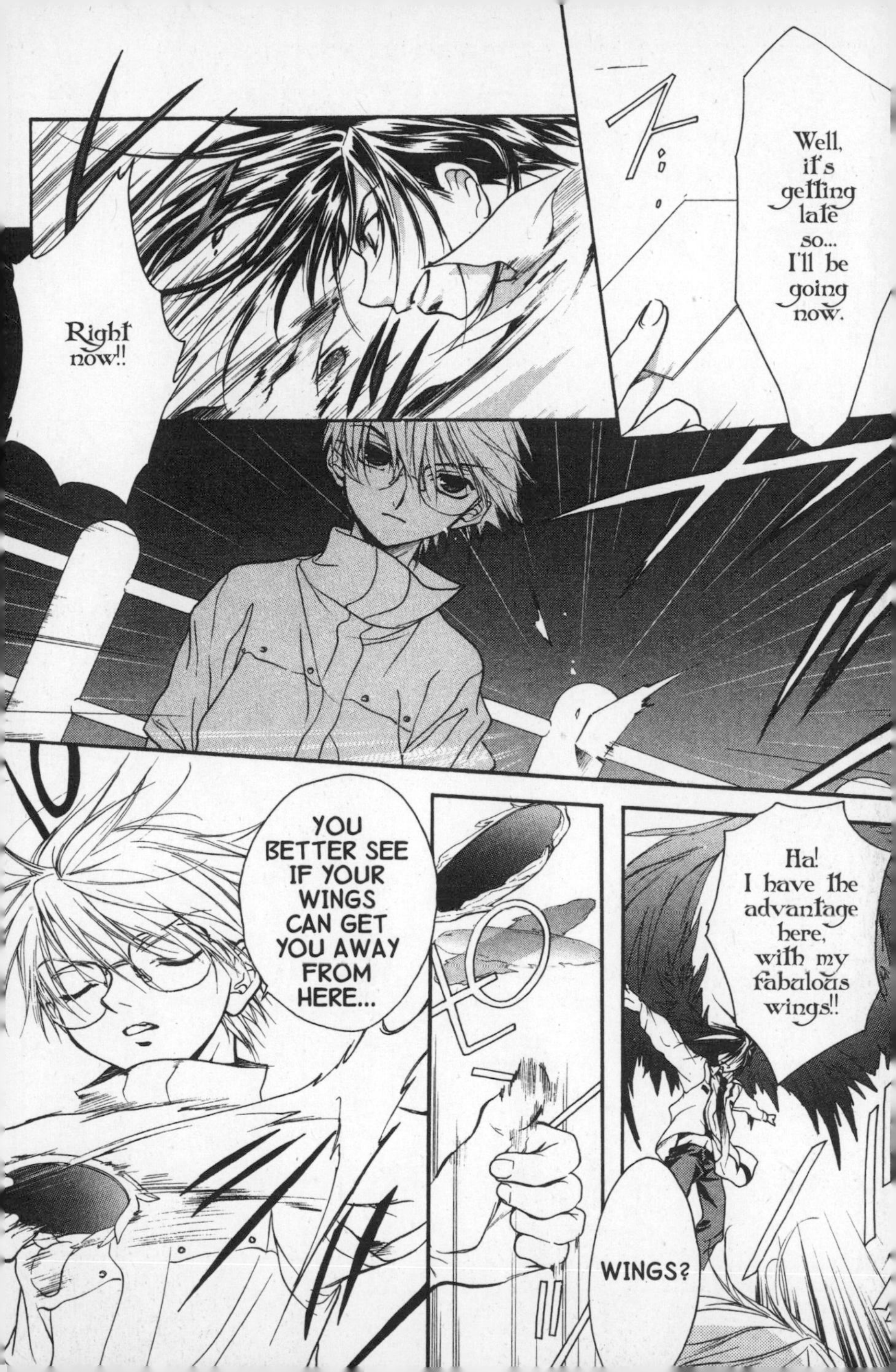
Well, it's getting late so... I'll be going now.
Right now!!
Ha! I have the advantage here, with my fabulous wings!!
WINGS?
YOU BETTER SEE IF YOUR WINGS CAN GET YOU AWAY FROM HERE...

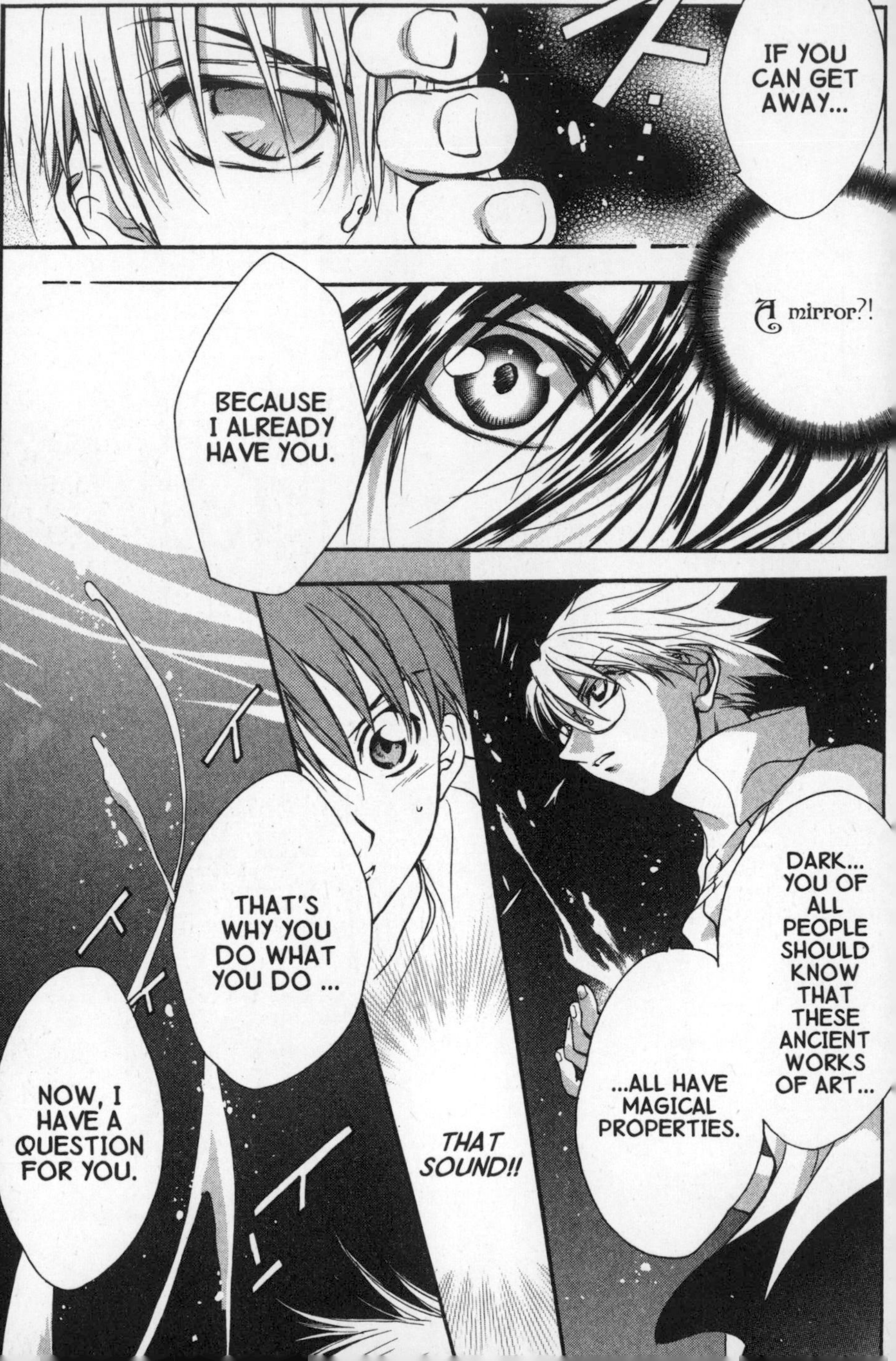
IF YOU CAN GET AWAY...
A mirror?!
BECAUSE I ALREADY HAVE YOU.
DARK... YOU OF ALL PEOPLE SHOULD KNOW THAT THESE ANCIENT WORKS OF ART...
...ALL HAVE MAGICAL PROPERTIES.
THAT SOUND!!
THAT'S WHY YOU DO WHAT YOU DO ...
NOW, I HAVE A QUESTION FOR YOU.

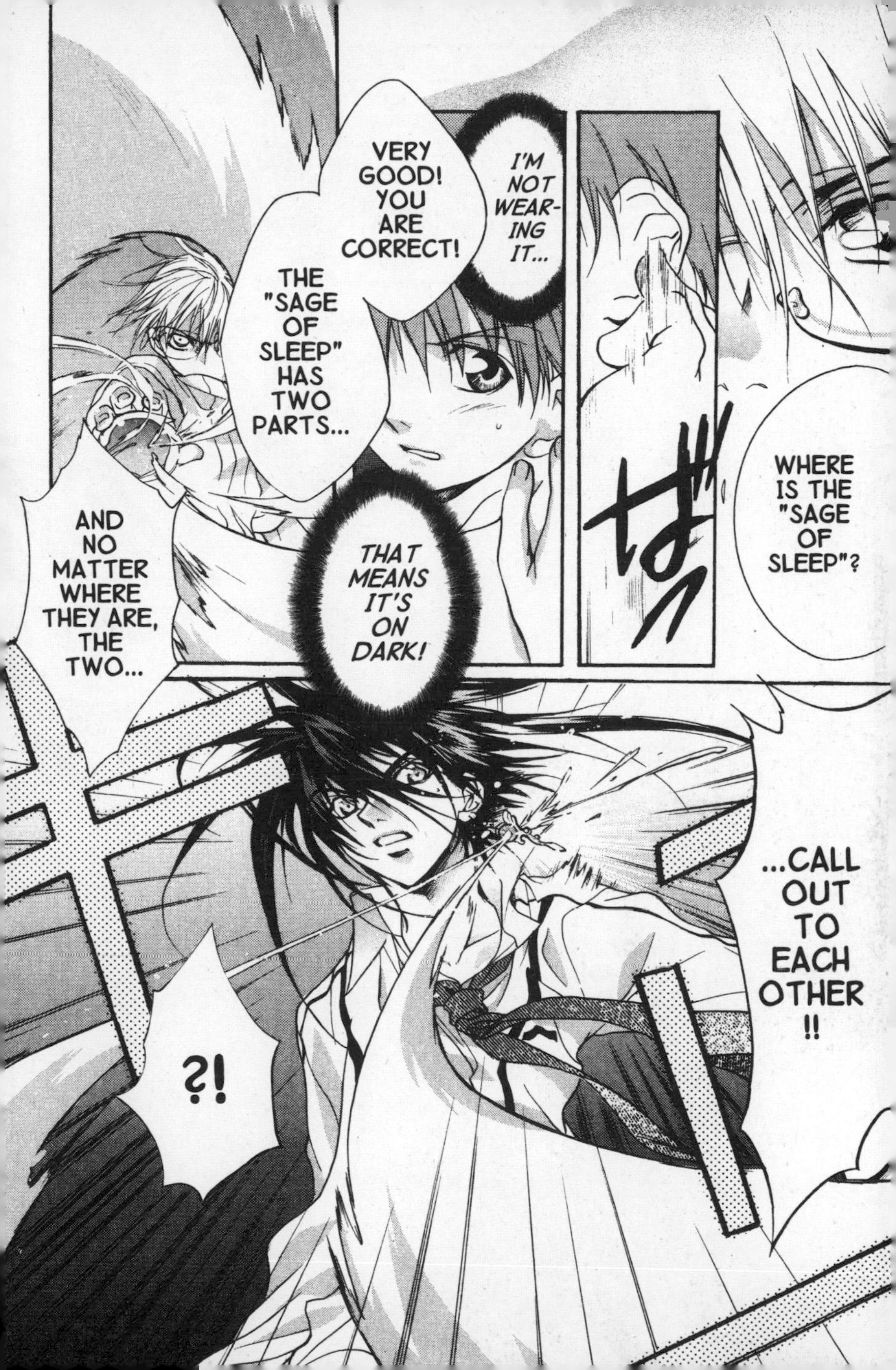
WHERE IS THE "SAGE OF SLEEP"?
I'M NOT WEARING IT...
VERY GOOD! YOU ARE CORRECT!
THE "SAGE OF SLEEP" HAS TWO PARTS...
THAT MEANS IT'S ON DARK!
AND NO MATTER WHERE THEY ARE, THE TWO...
...CALL OUT TO EACH OTHER!!
?!

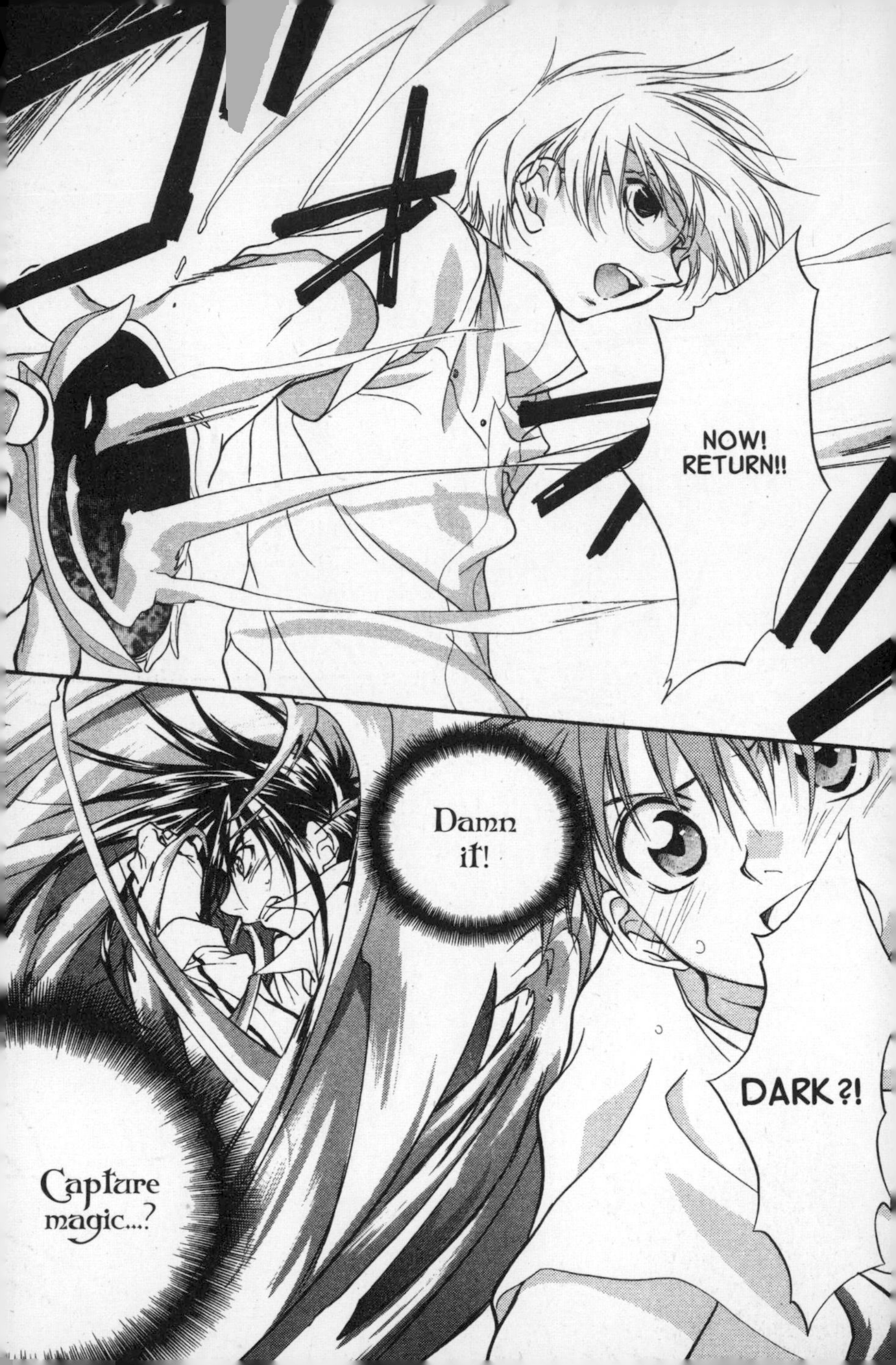
NOW! RETURN!!
Damn it!
DARK?!
Capture magic...?

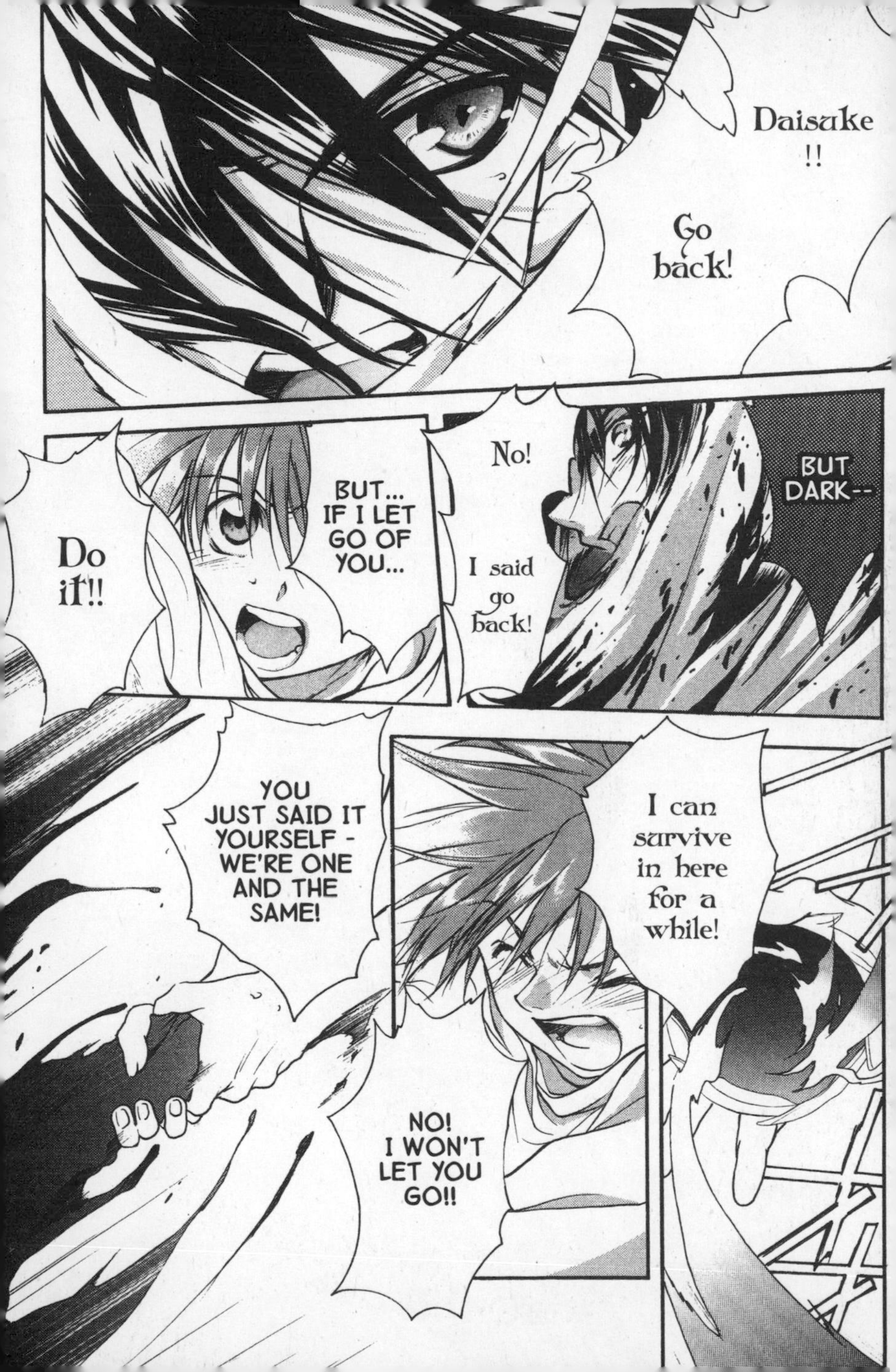
Daisuke !!
Go back!
BUT DARK--
No!
I said go back!
BUT... IF I LET GO OF YOU...
Do it!!
I can survive in here for a while!
YOU JUST SAID IT YOURSELF - WE'RE ONE AND THE SAME!
NO! I WON'T LET YOU GO!!

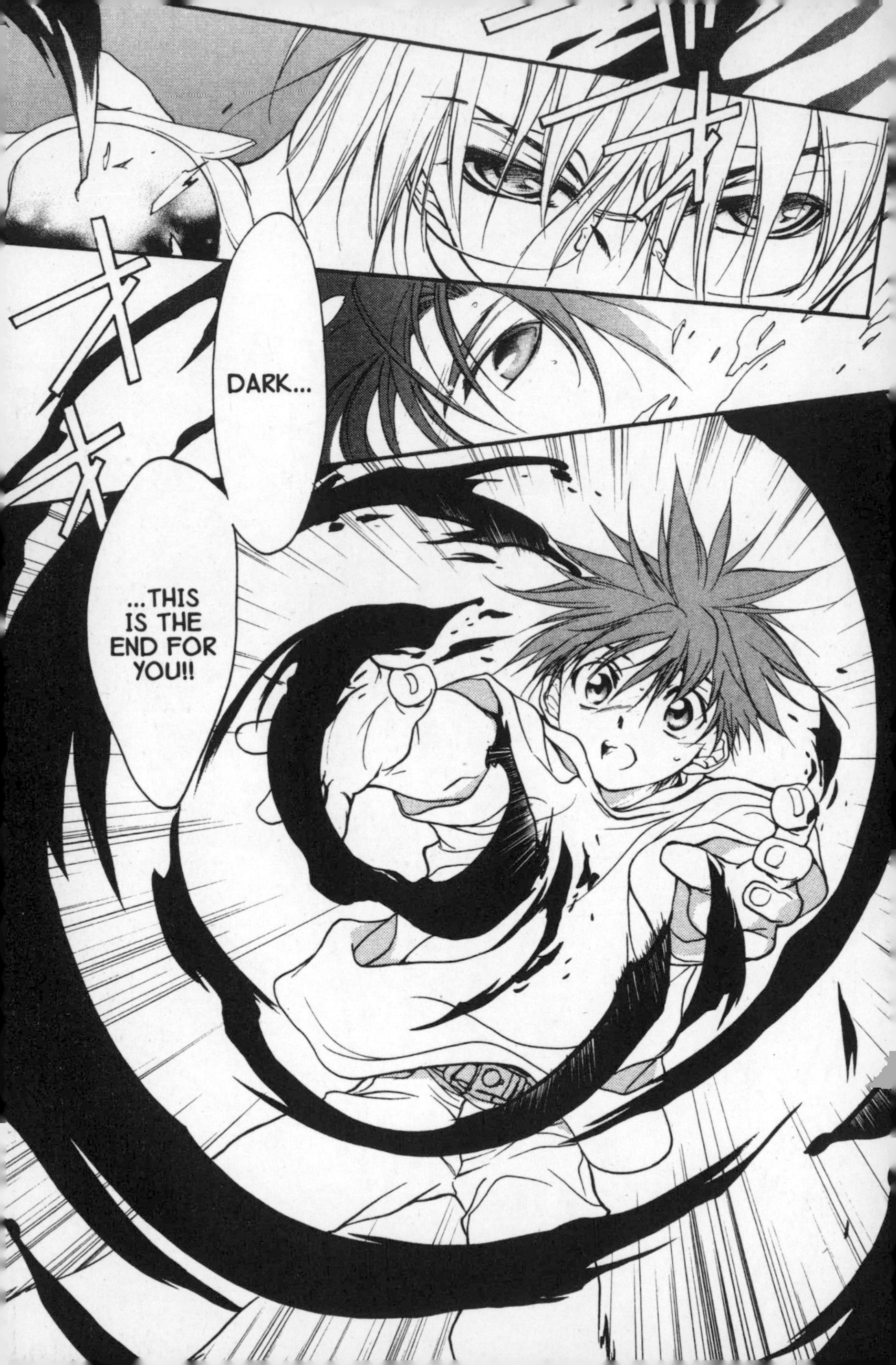
DARK...
...THIS IS THE END FOR YOU!!

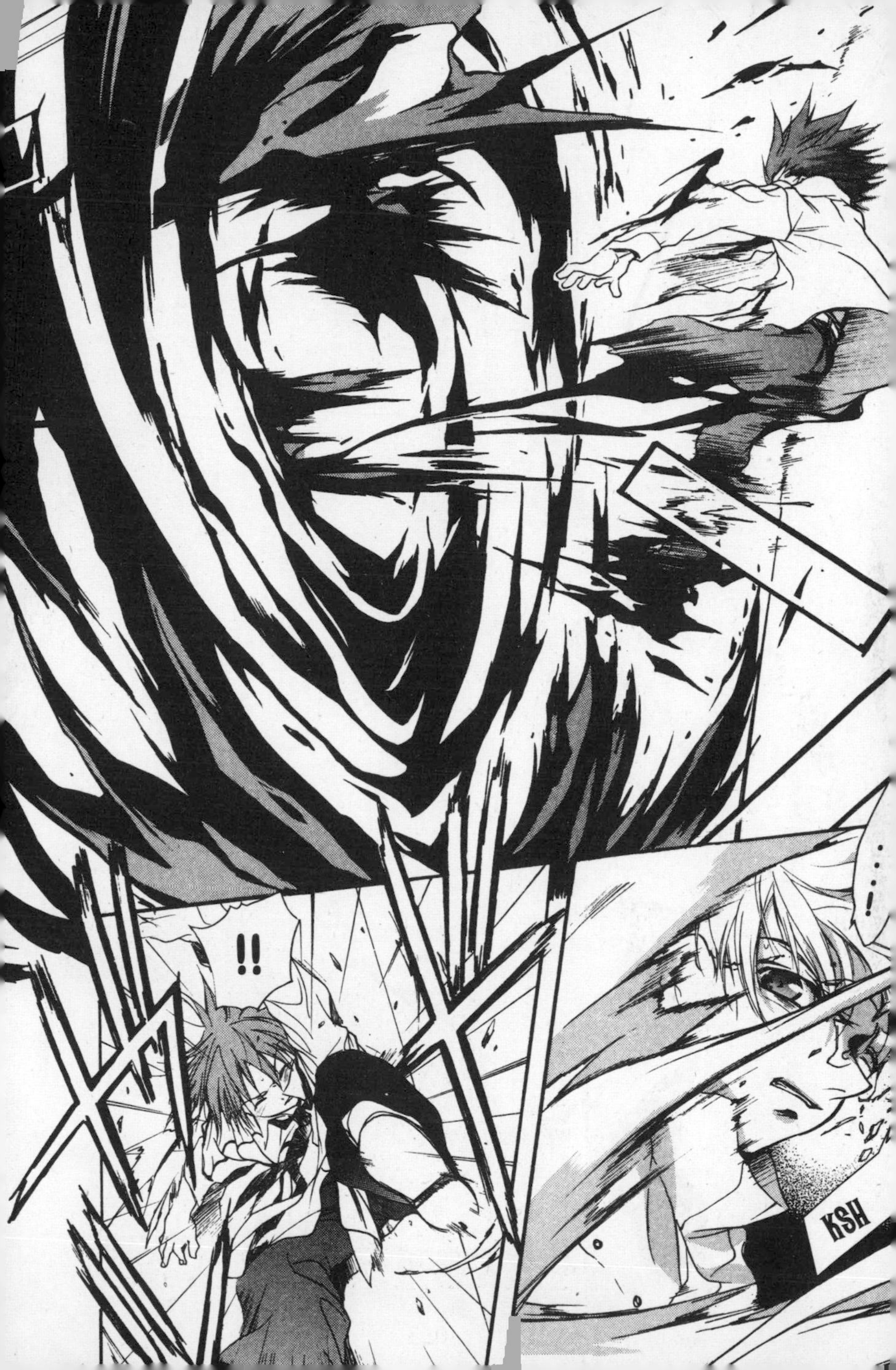
...!
KSH
!!

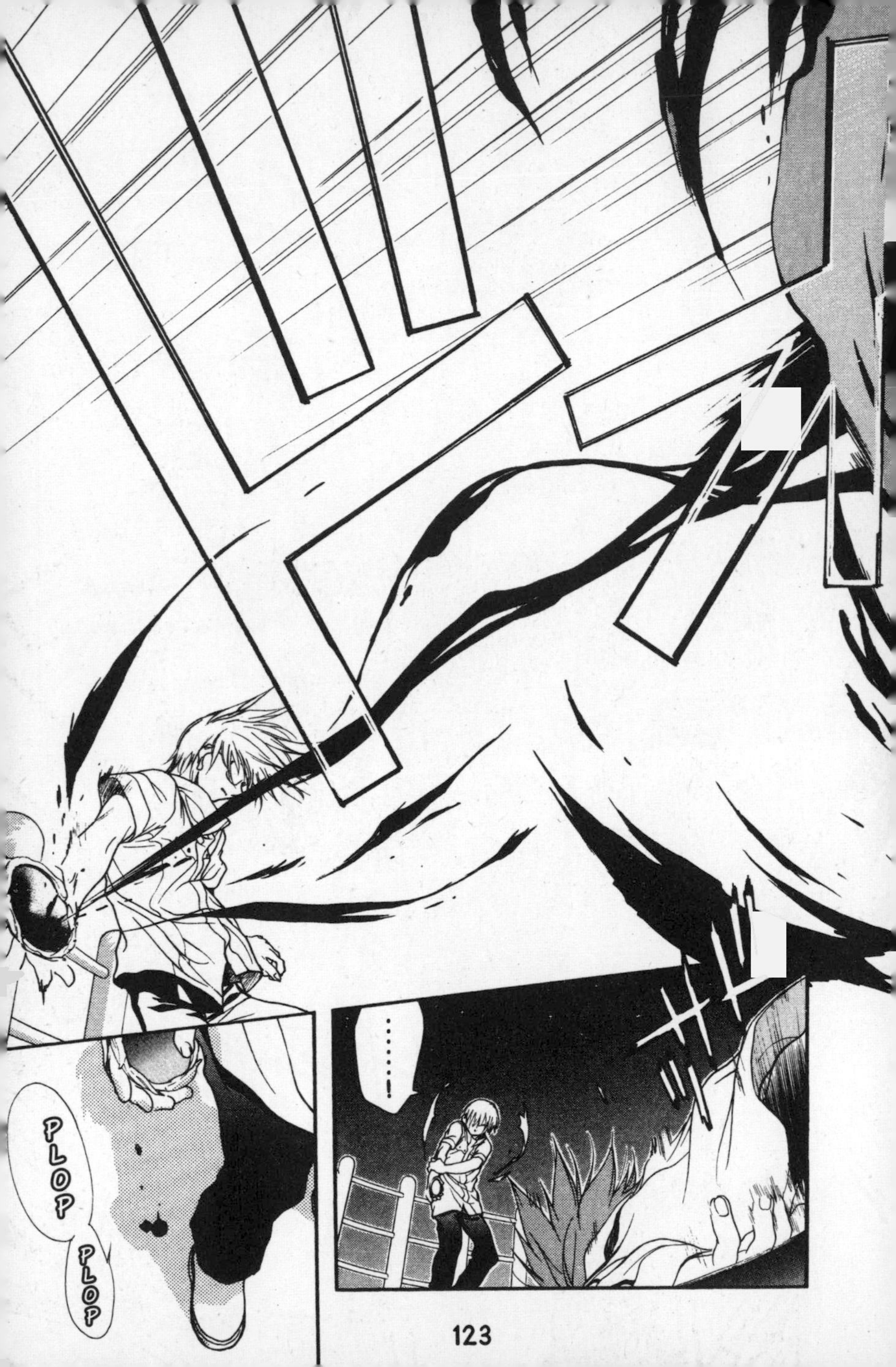
......!
PLOP
PLOP

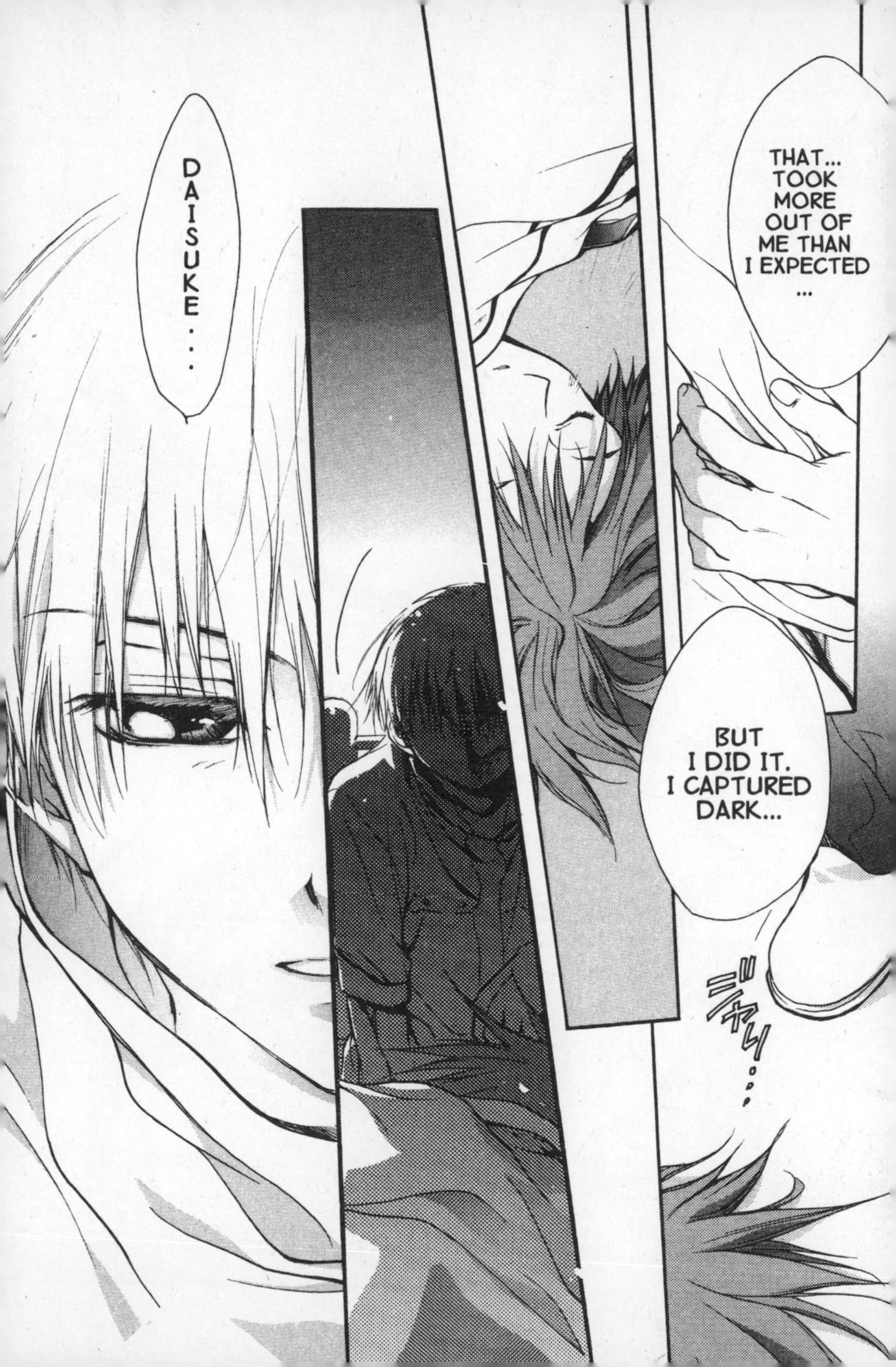
THAT... TOOK MORE OUT OF ME THAN I EXPECTED ...
BUT I DID IT. I CAPTURED DARK...
DAISUKE...

vol.2

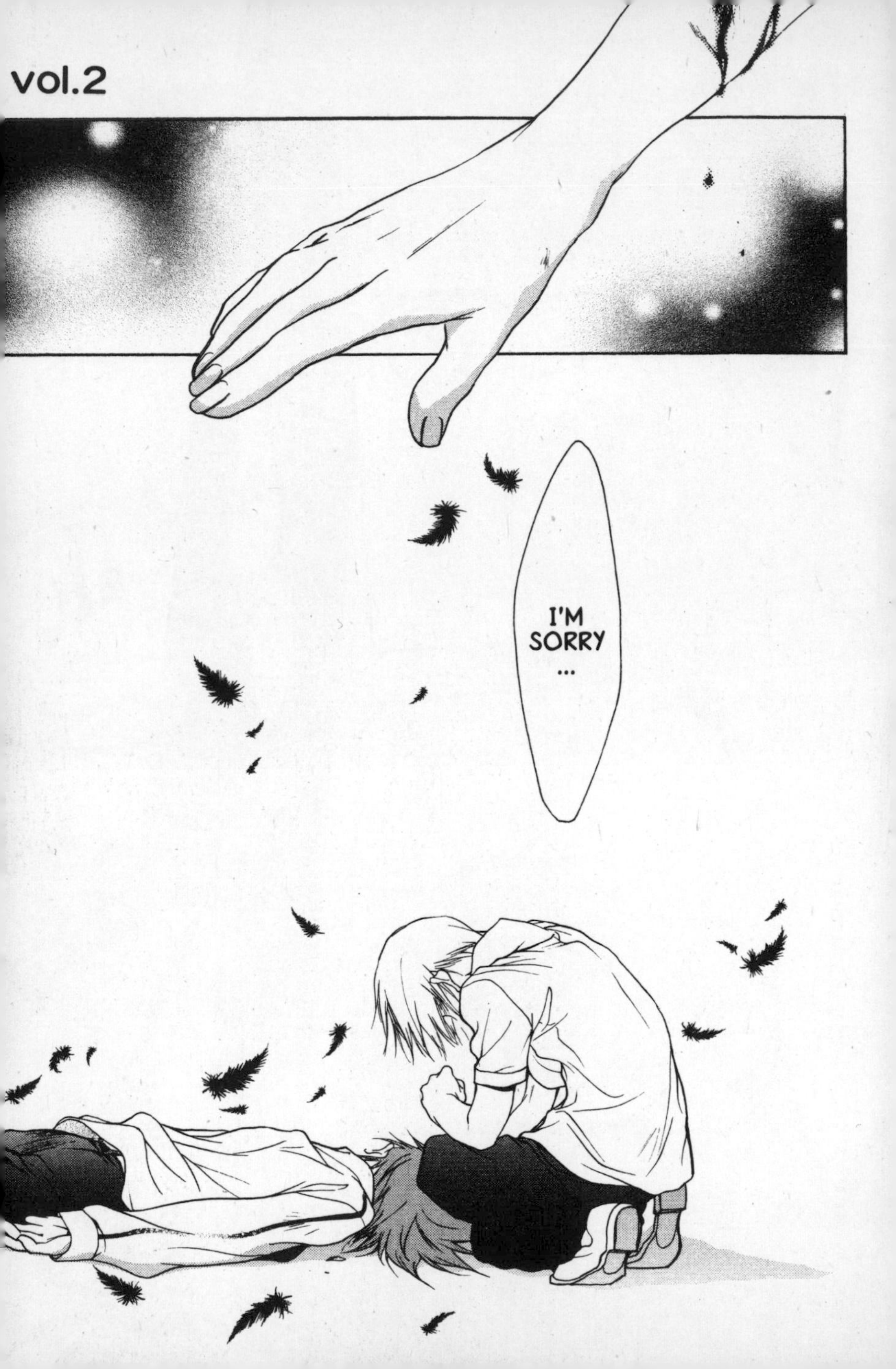
I'M SORRY ...

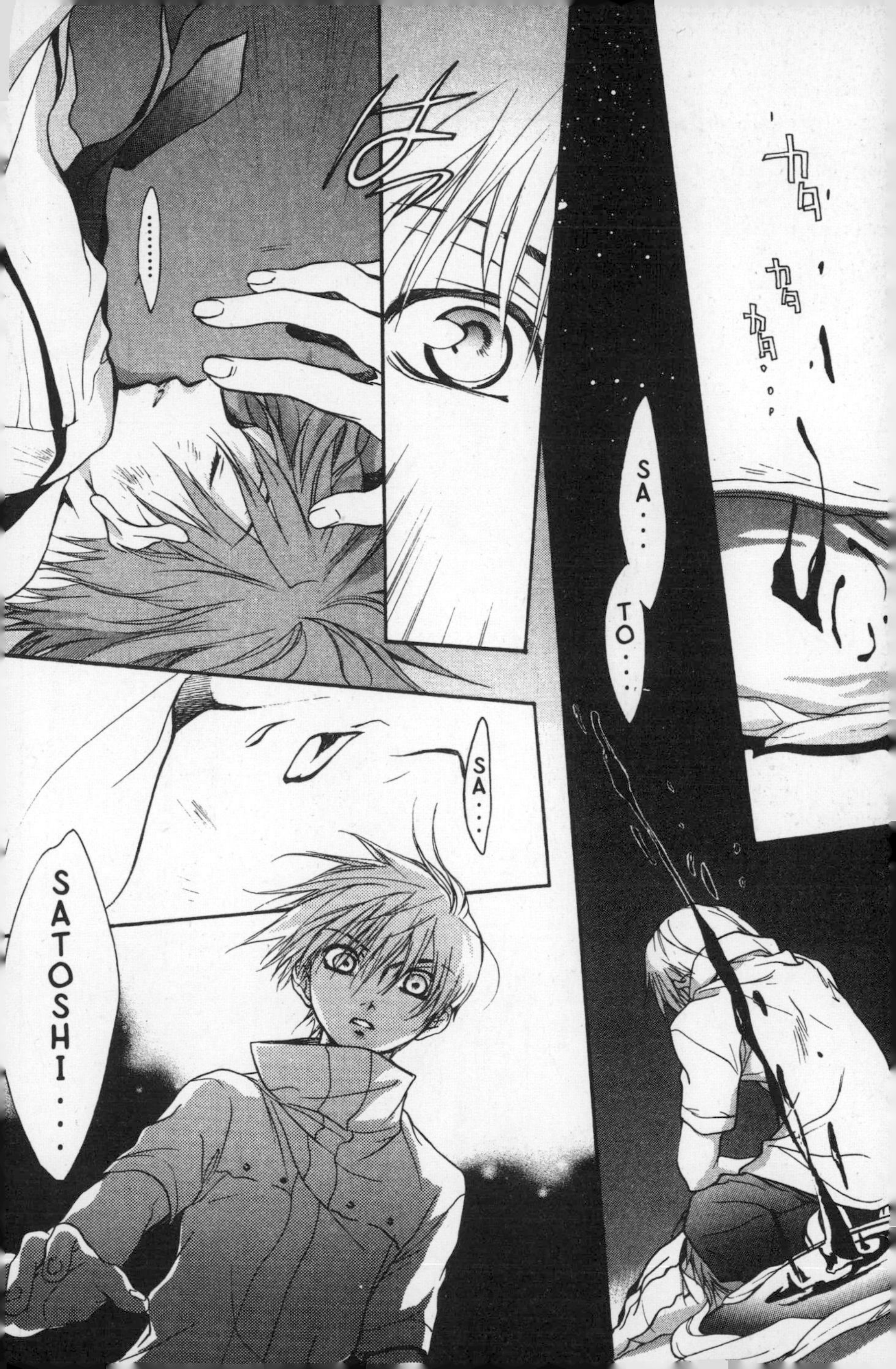

カタ
カタ
カタ。。。
SA... TO...
はっ
......
SA... SA...
SATOSHI...

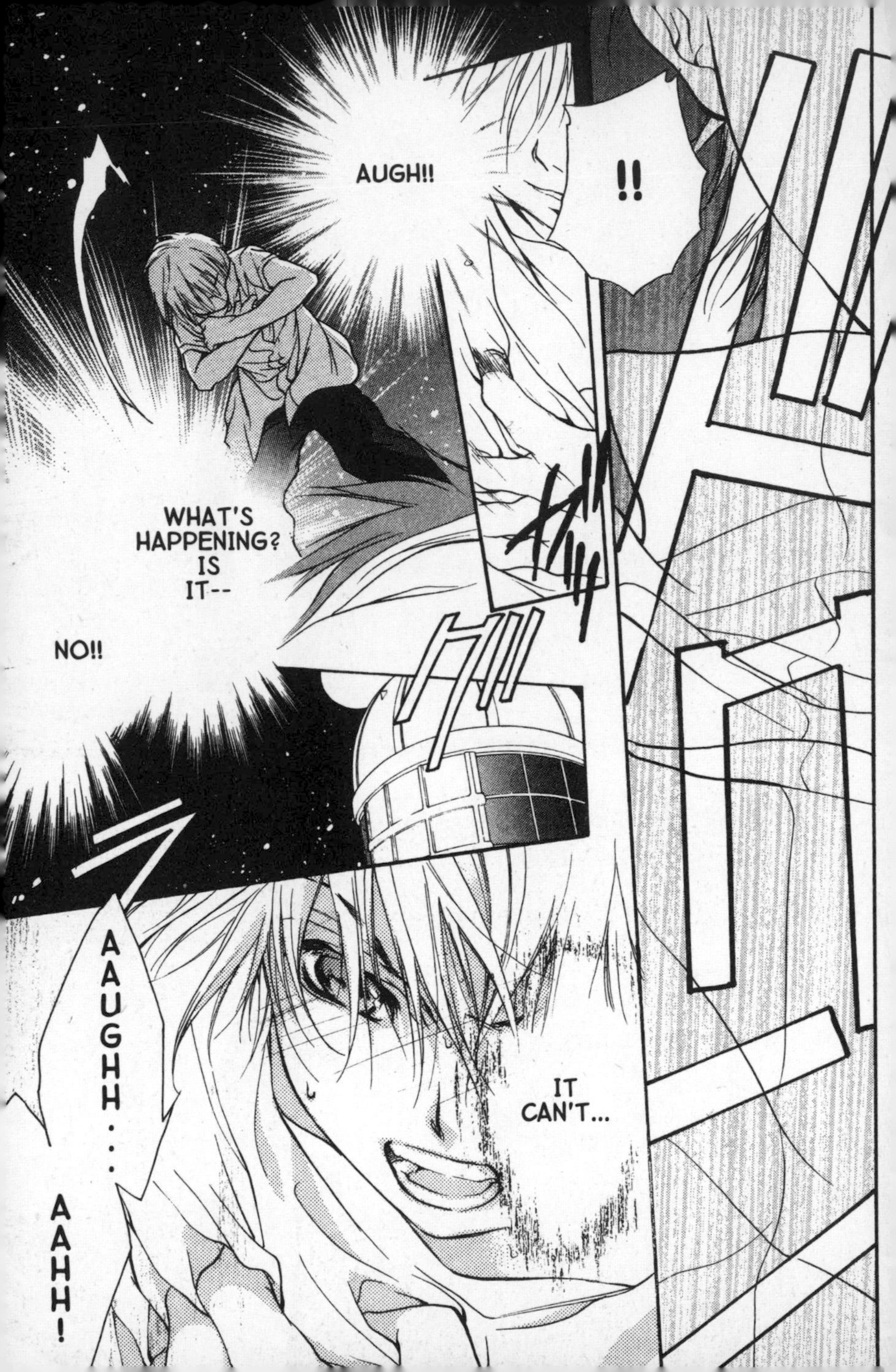
!!
AUGH!!
WHAT'S HAPPENING? IS IT--
NO!!
IT CAN'T...
AAUGHH... AAHH!

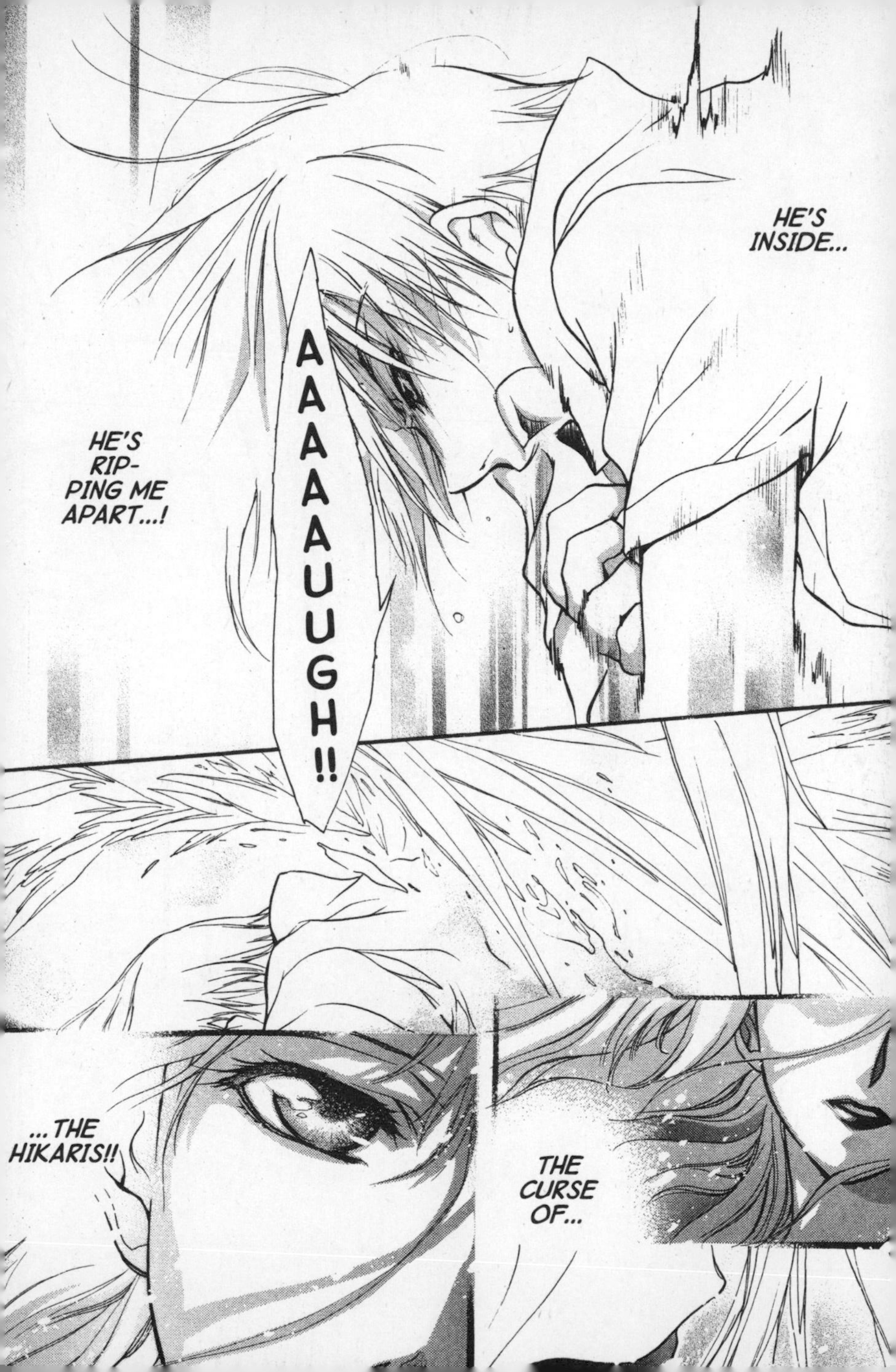
HE'S INSIDE...
AAAAAUUGH!!
HE'S RIPPING ME APART...!
THE CURSE OF...
...THE HIKARIS!!

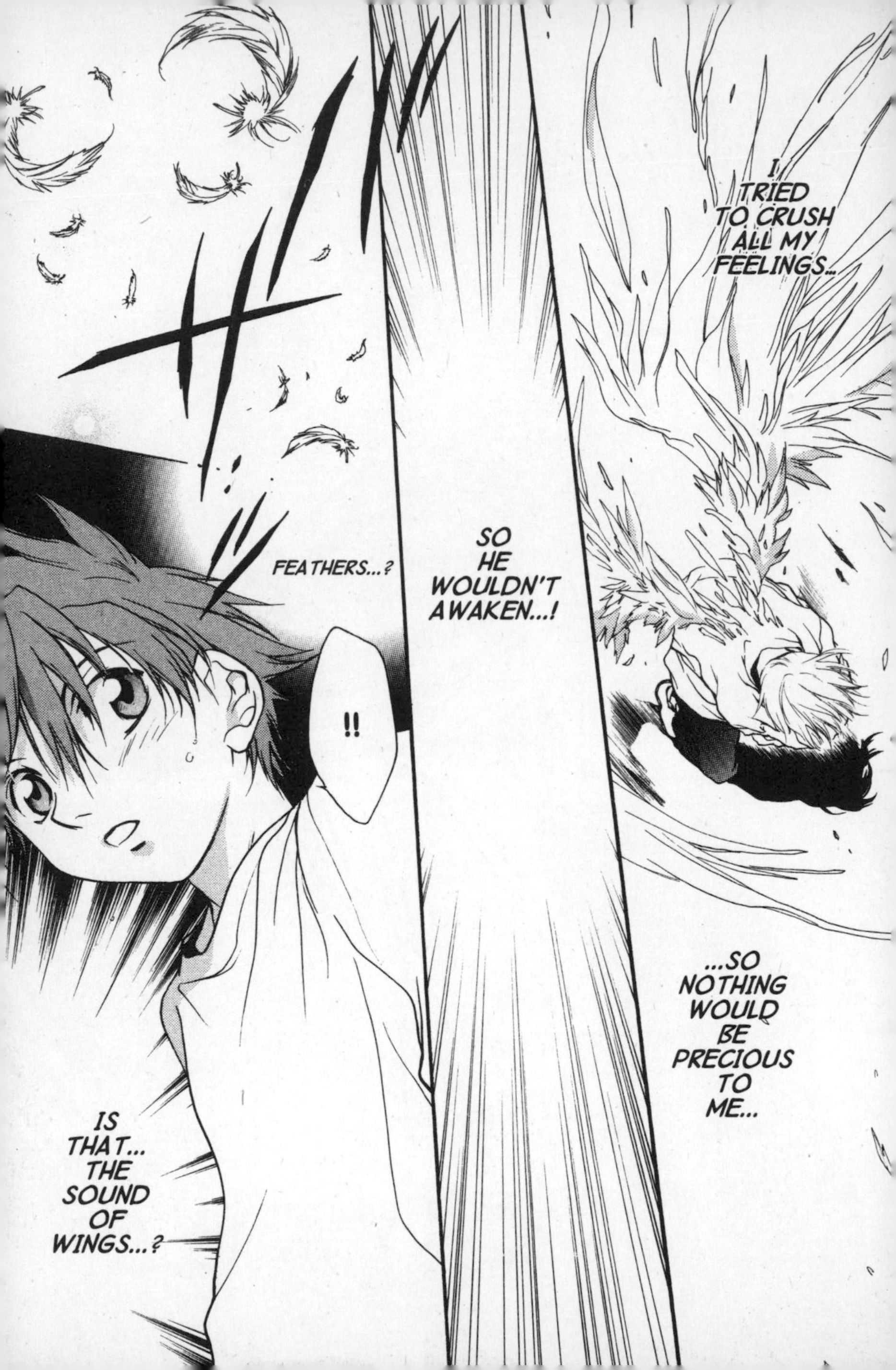
I TRIED TO CRUSH ALL MY FEELINGS...
...SO NOTHING WOULD BE PRECIOUS TO ME...
SO HE WOULDN'T AWAKEN...!
FEATHERS...?
!!
IS THAT... THE SOUND OF WINGS...?

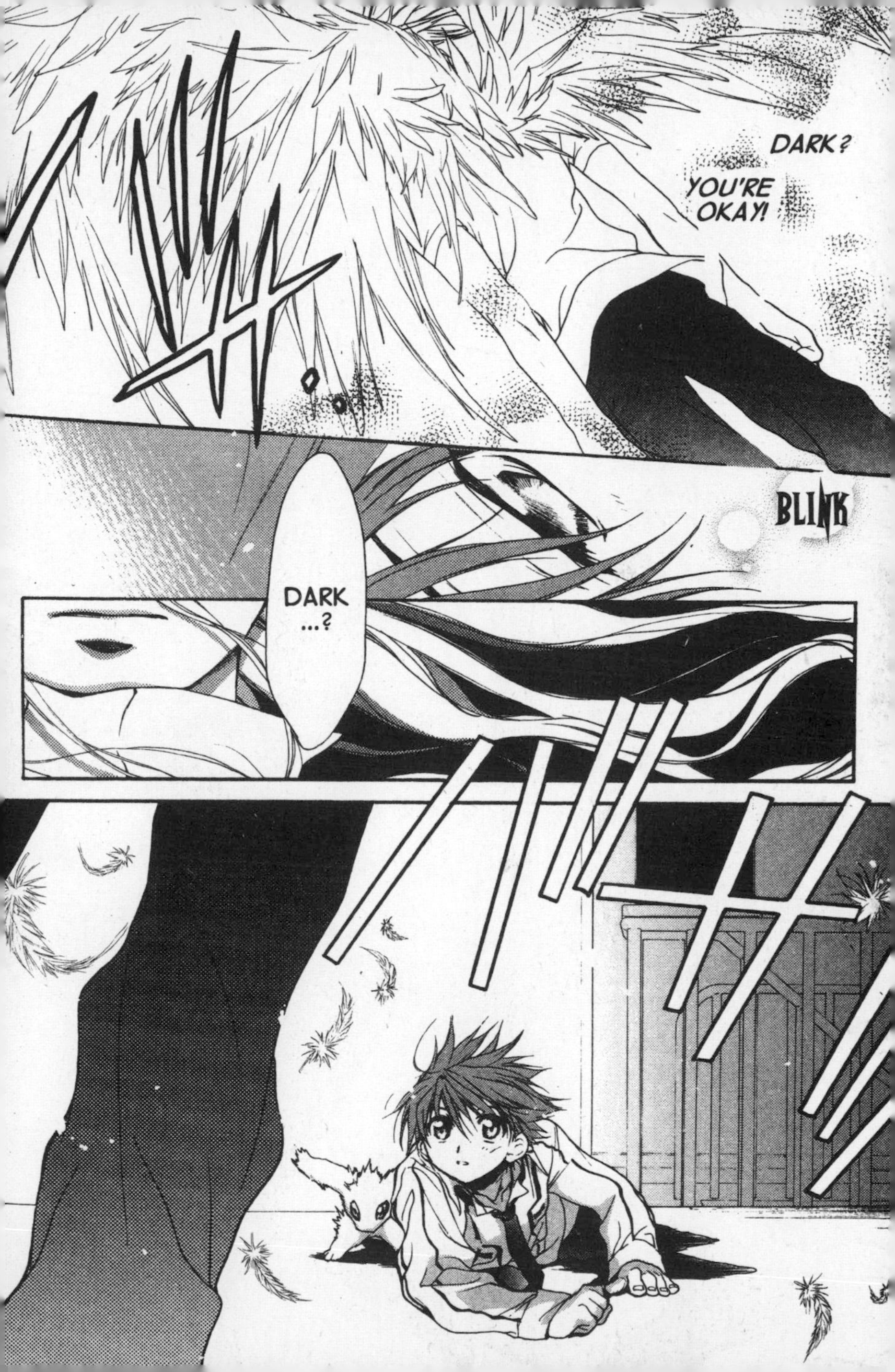
DARK?
YOU'RE OKAY!
BLINK
DARK ...?

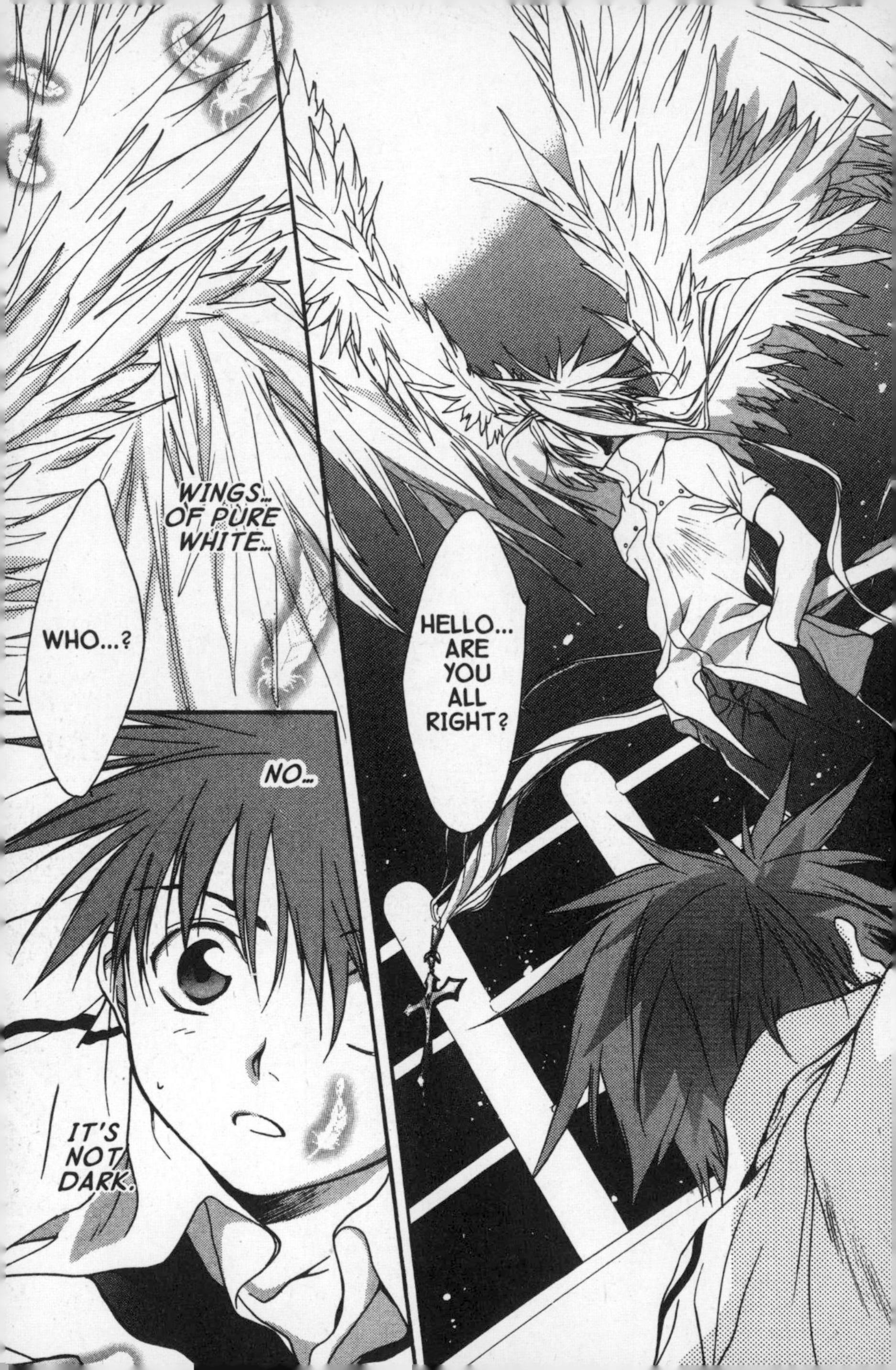
HELLO... ARE YOU ALL RIGHT?
WINGS... OF PURE WHITE...
WHO...?
NO...
IT'S NOT DARK.

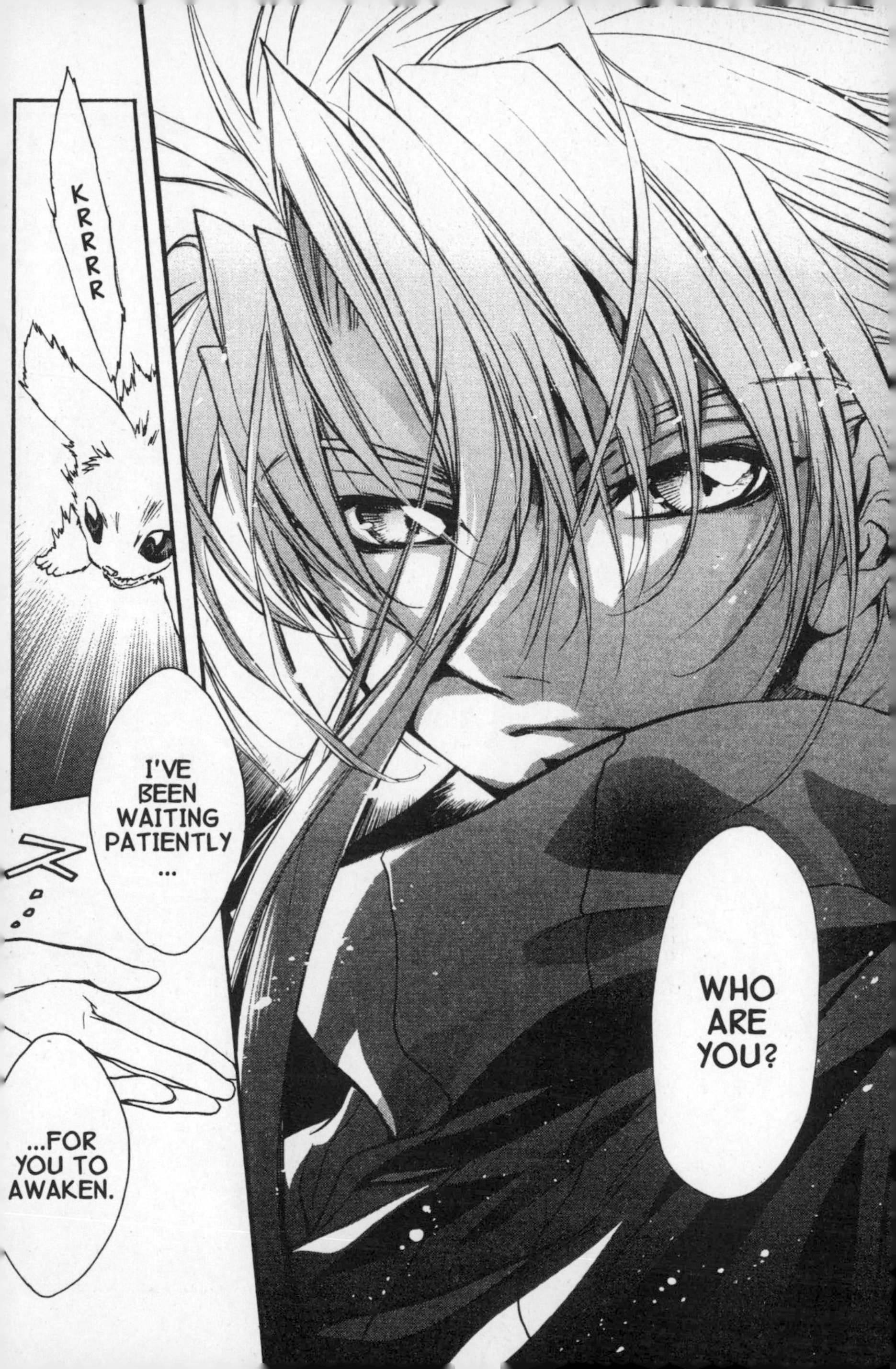
KRRRR
I'VE BEEN WAITING PATIENTLY ...
ス
...FOR YOU TO AWAKEN.
WHO ARE YOU?

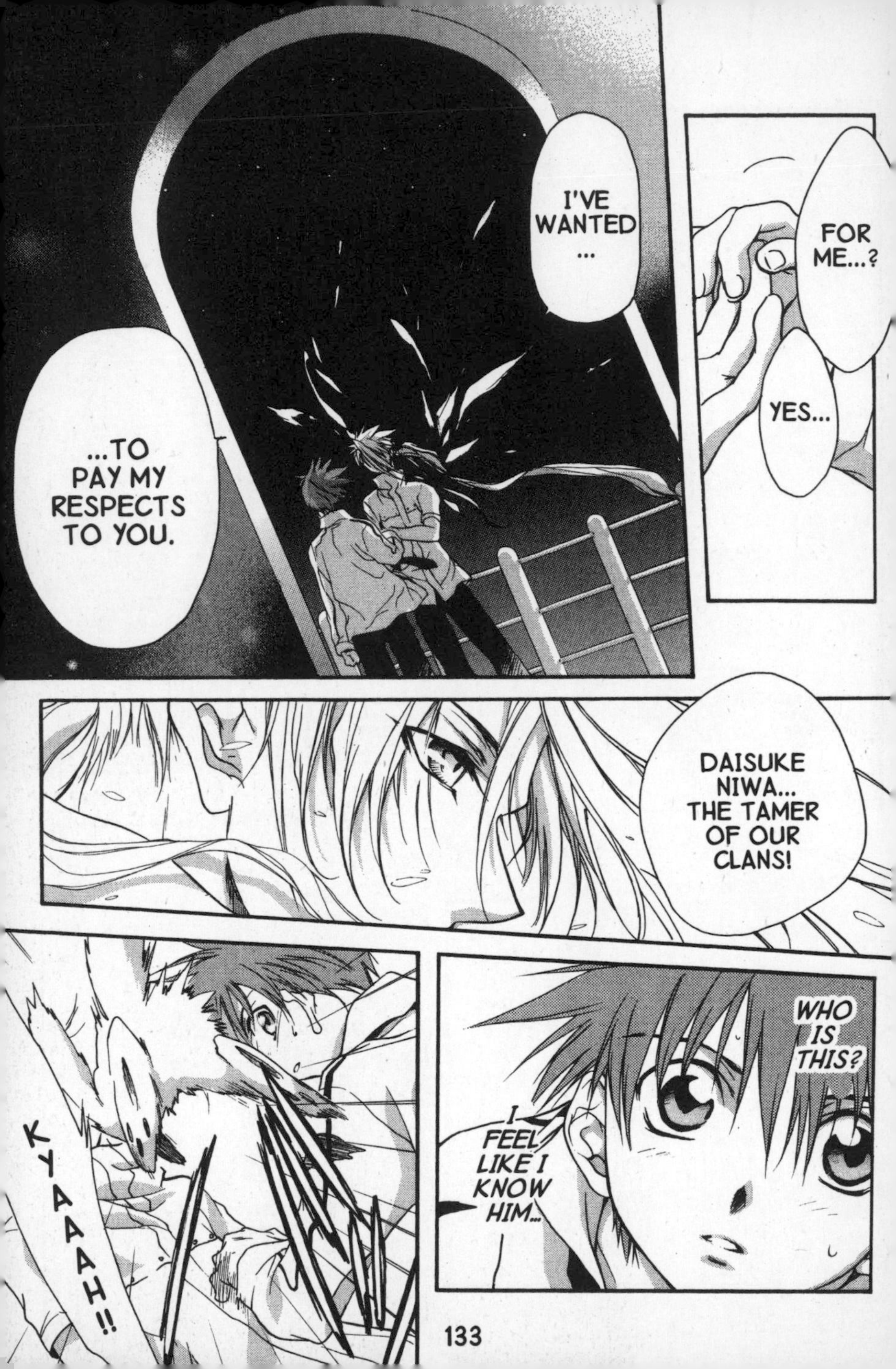
FOR ME...?
YES...
I'VE WANTED ...
...TO PAY MY RESPECTS TO YOU.
DAISUKE NIWA... THE TAMER OF OUR CLANS!
WHO IS THIS?
I FEEL LIKE I KNOW HIM...
KYAAAH!!

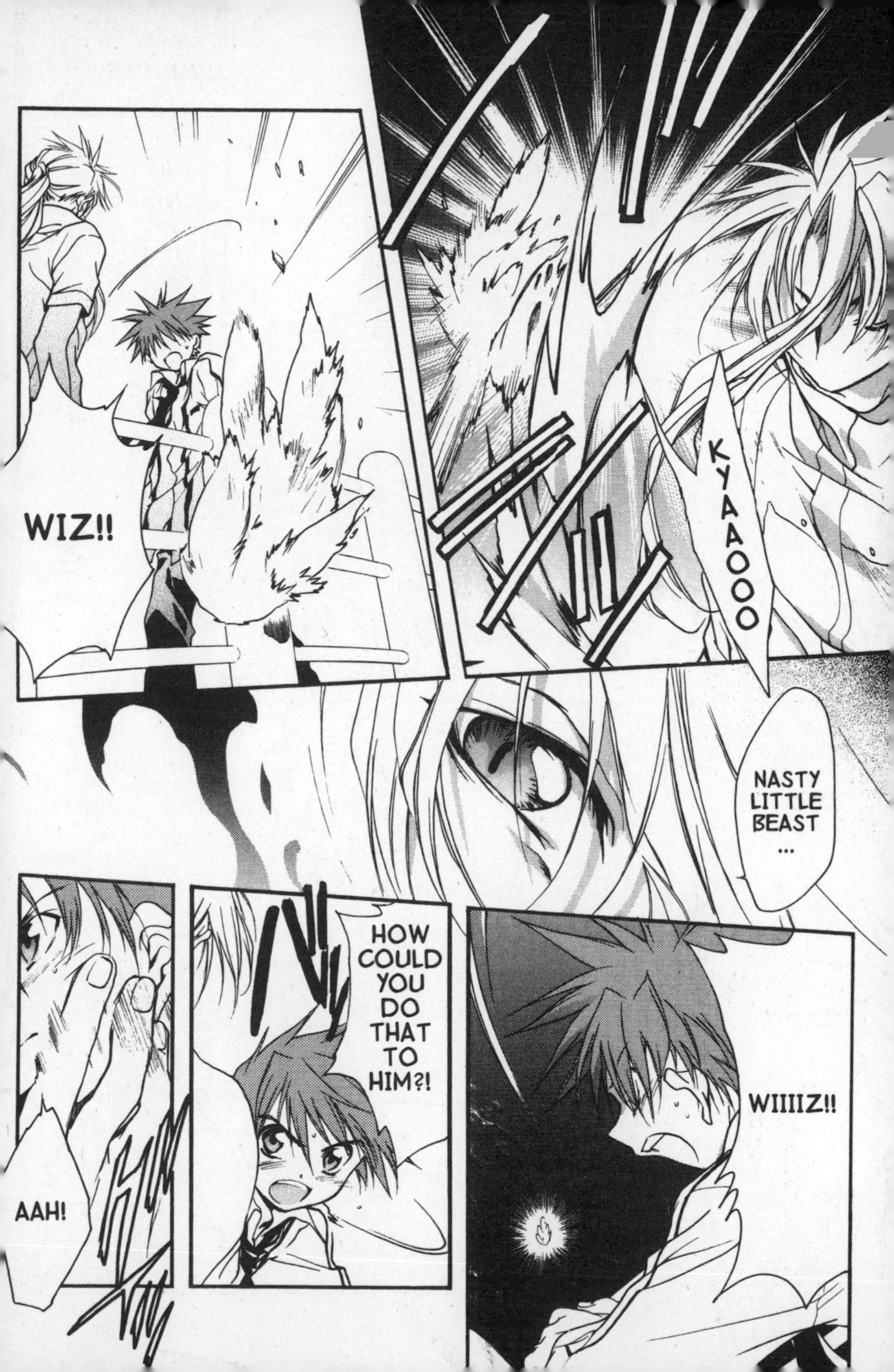
KYAAOOO
WIZ!!
NASTY LITTLE BEAST ...
WIIIIZ!!
HOW COULD YOU DO THAT TO HIM?!
AAH!

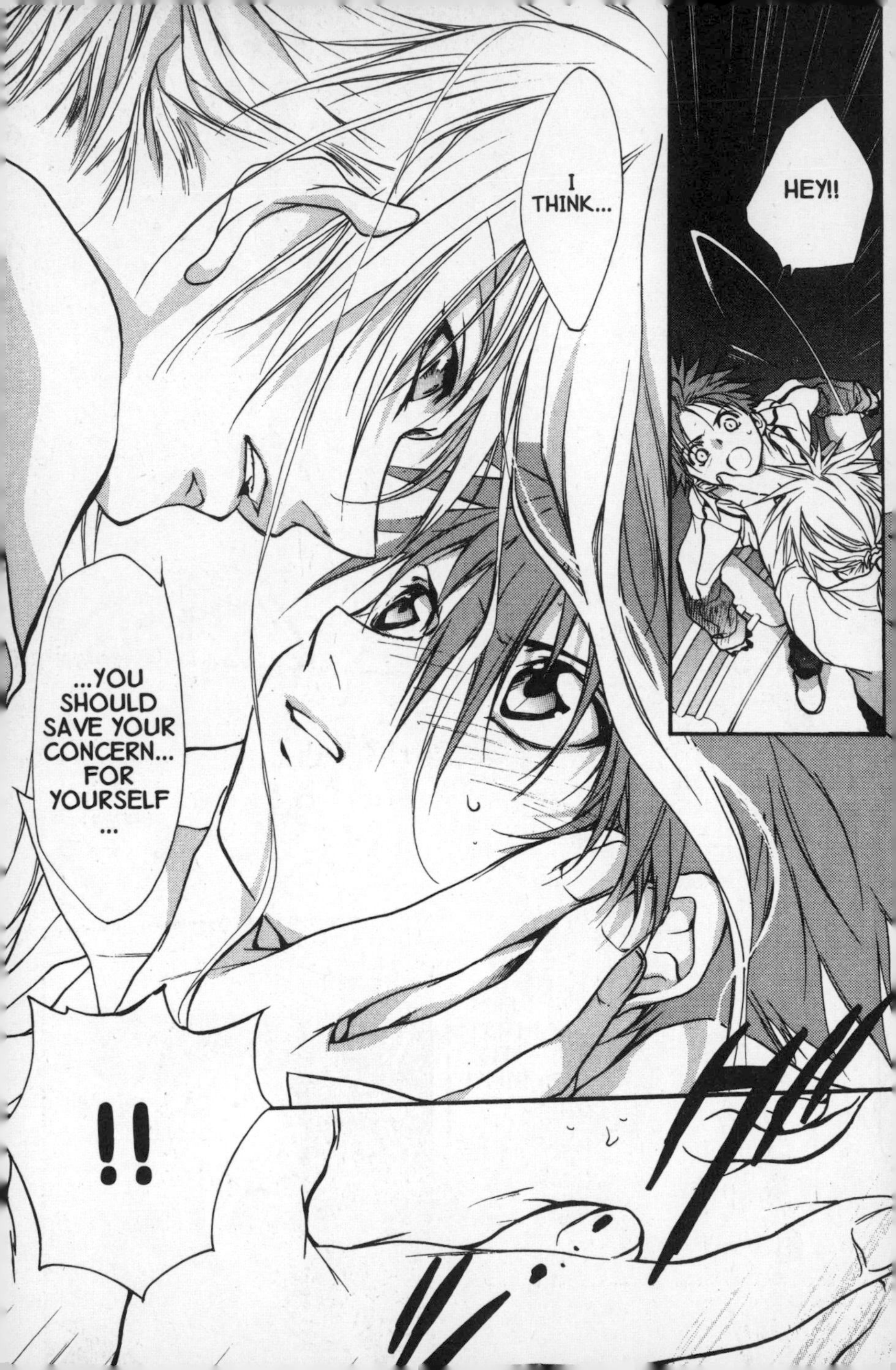
HEY!!
I THINK...
...YOU SHOULD SAVE YOUR CONCERN... FOR YOURSELF ...
!!

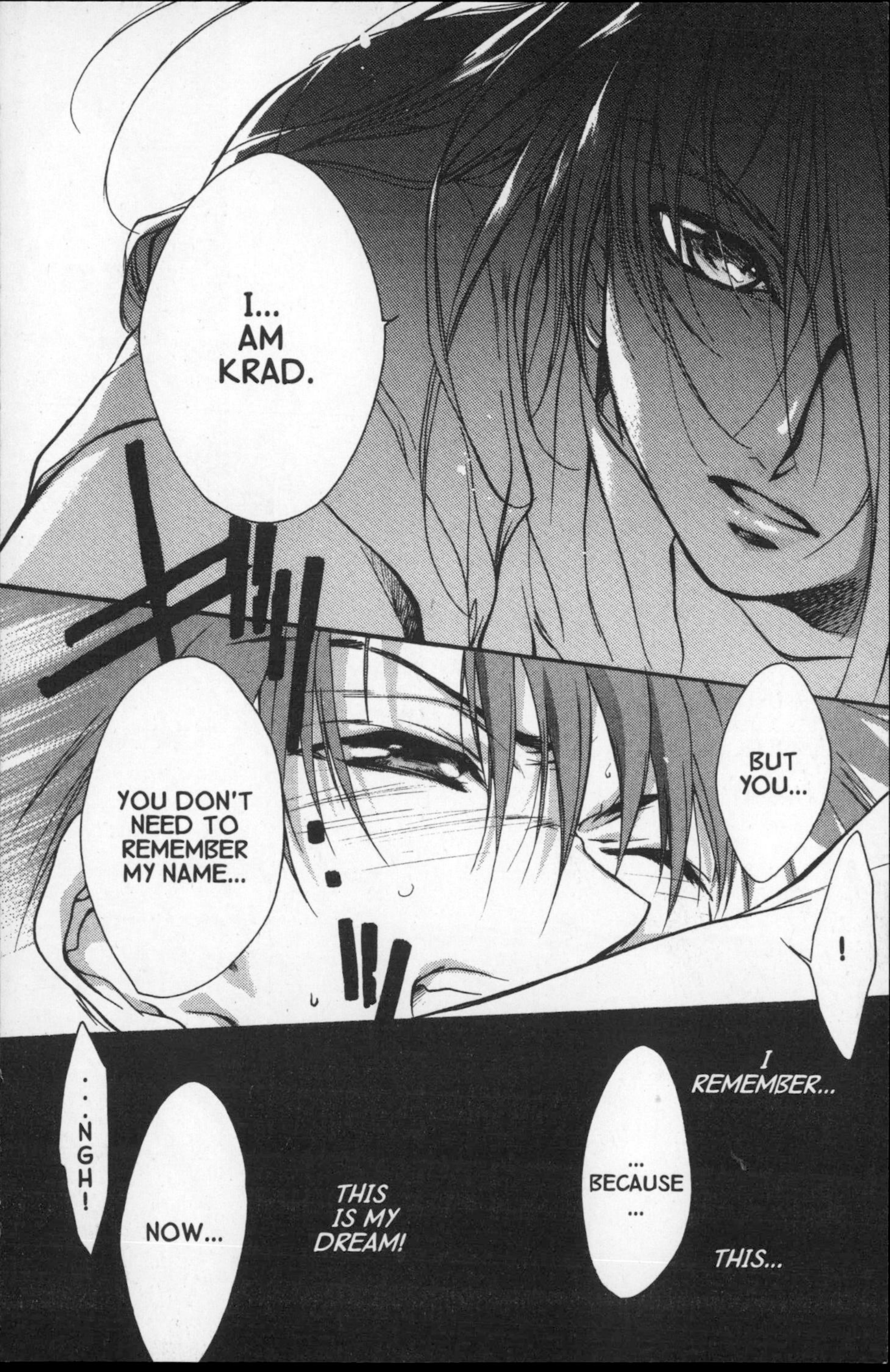
I... AM KRAD.
BUT YOU...
YOU DON'T NEED TO REMEMBER MY NAME...
!
I REMEMBER...
... BECAUSE ...
THIS...
THIS IS MY DREAM!
NOW...
...NGH!

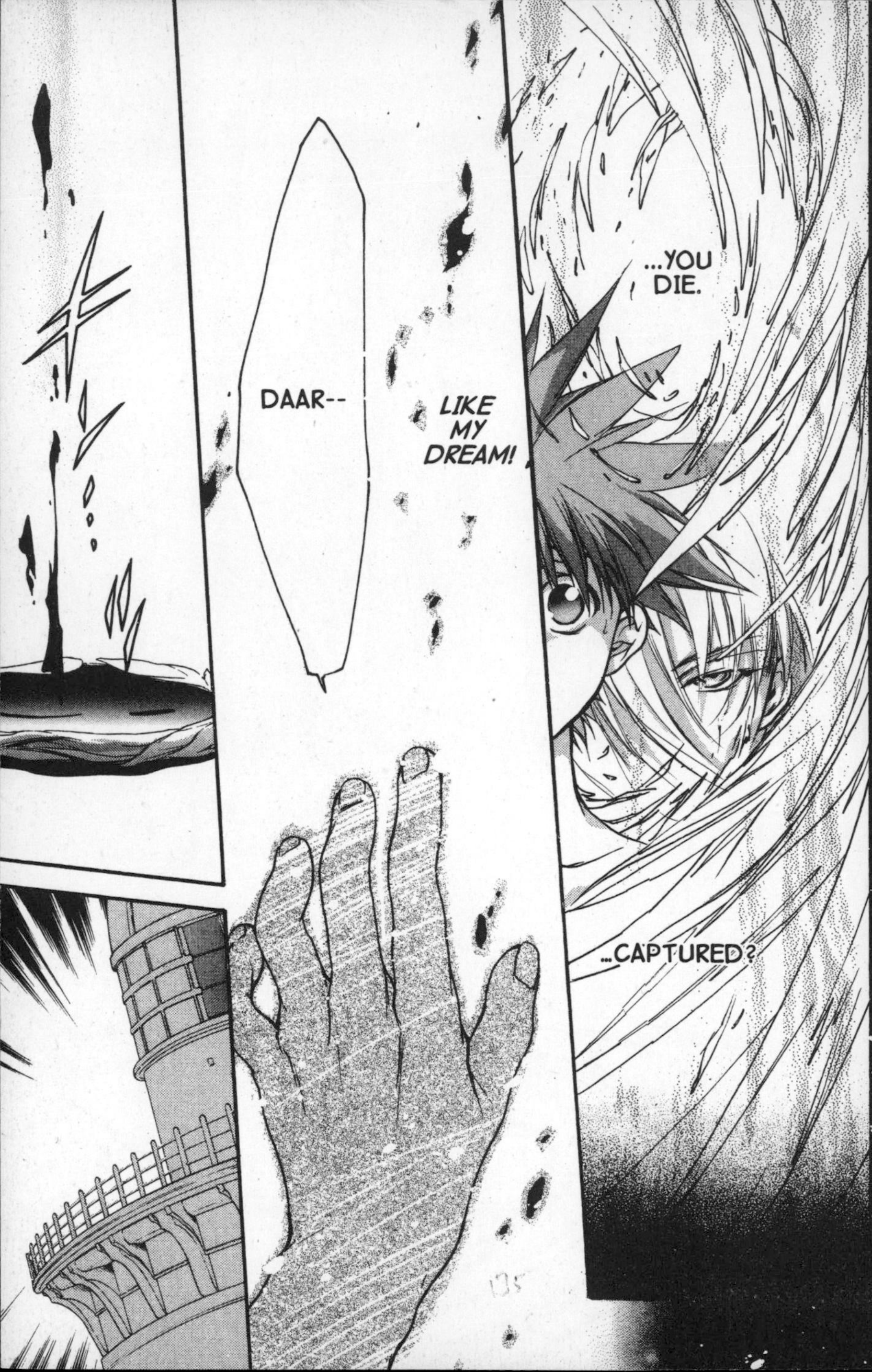
...YOU DIE.
...CAPTURED?
LIKE MY DREAM!
DAAR--

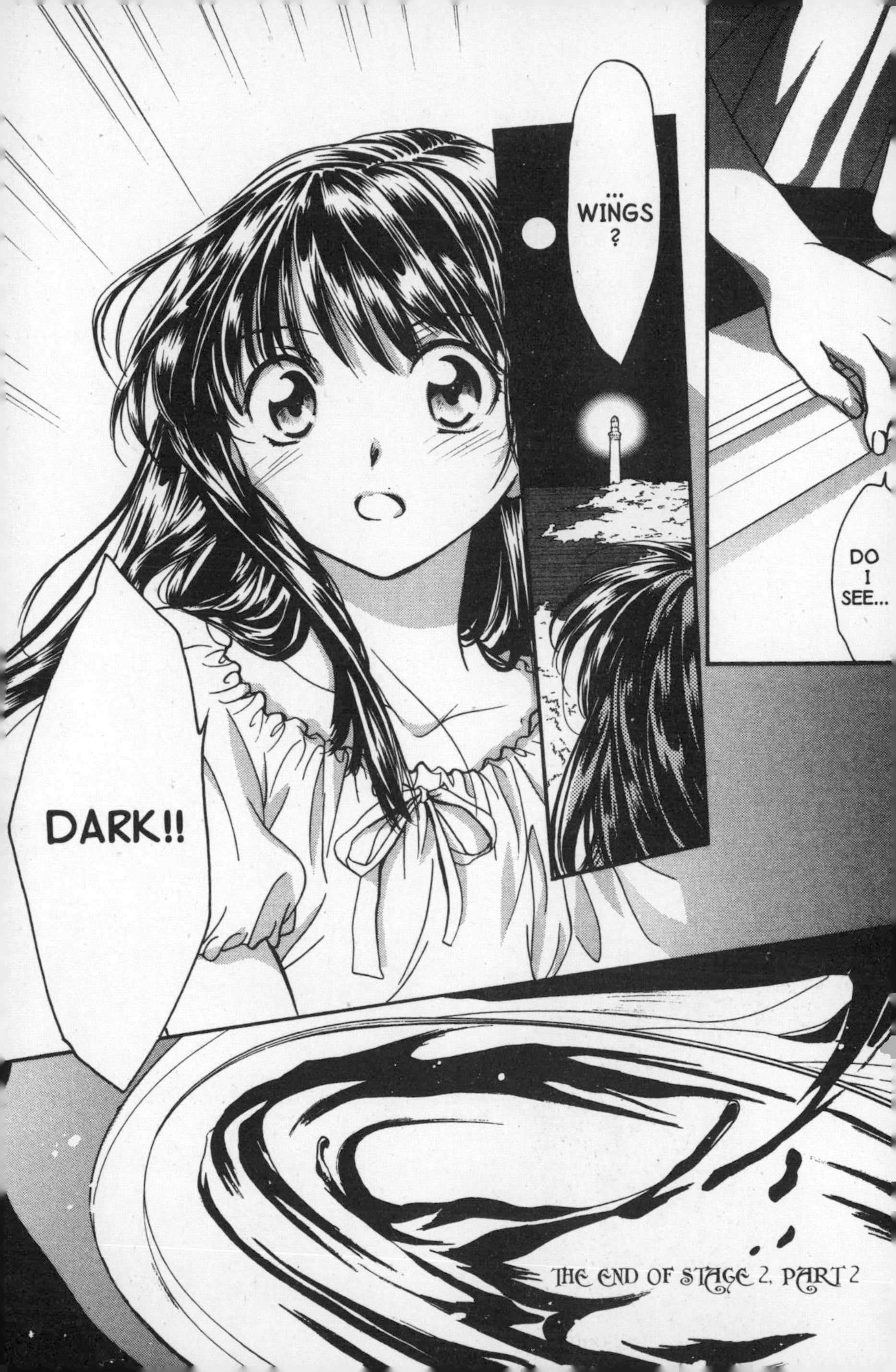
DO I SEE...
...WINGS?
DARK!!
THE END OF STAGE 2, PART 2

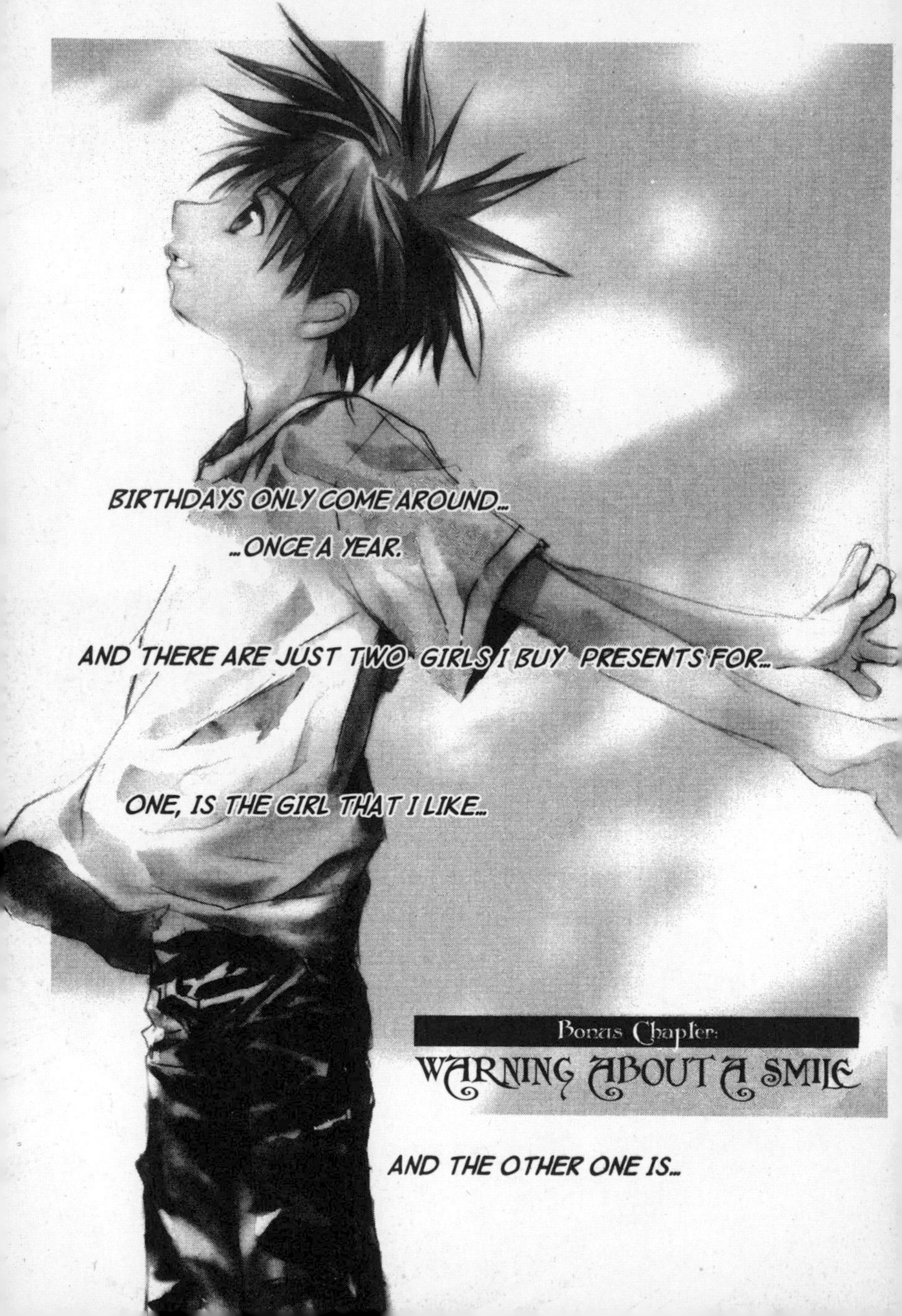
BIRTHDAYS ONLY COME AROUND...
...ONCE A YEAR.
AND THERE ARE JUST TWO GIRLS I BUY PRESENTS FOR...
ONE, IS THE GIRL THAT I LIKE...
Bonus Chapter:
WARNING ABOUT A SMILE
AND THE OTHER ONE IS...

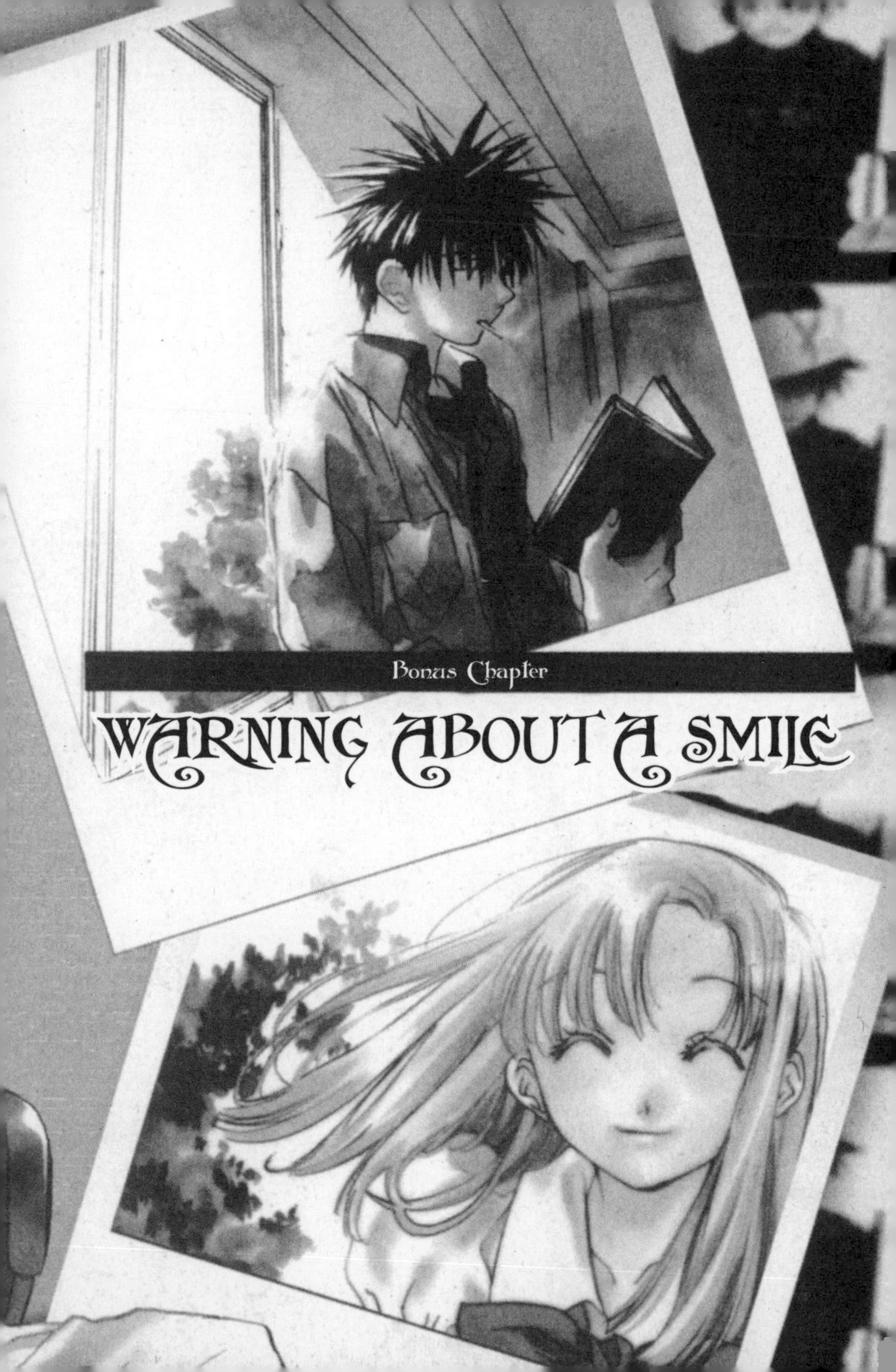
Bonus Chapter
WARNING ABOUT A SMILE

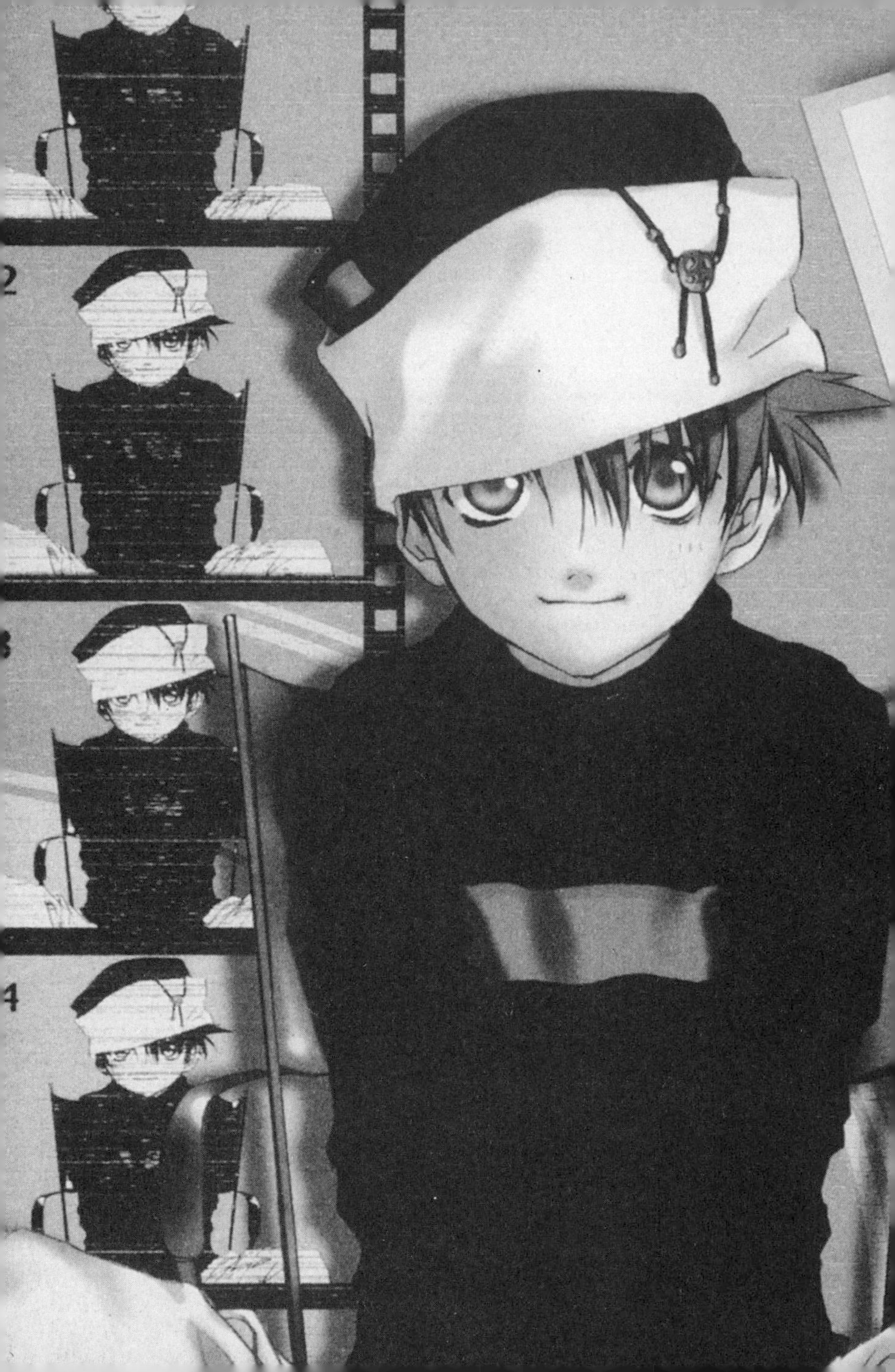

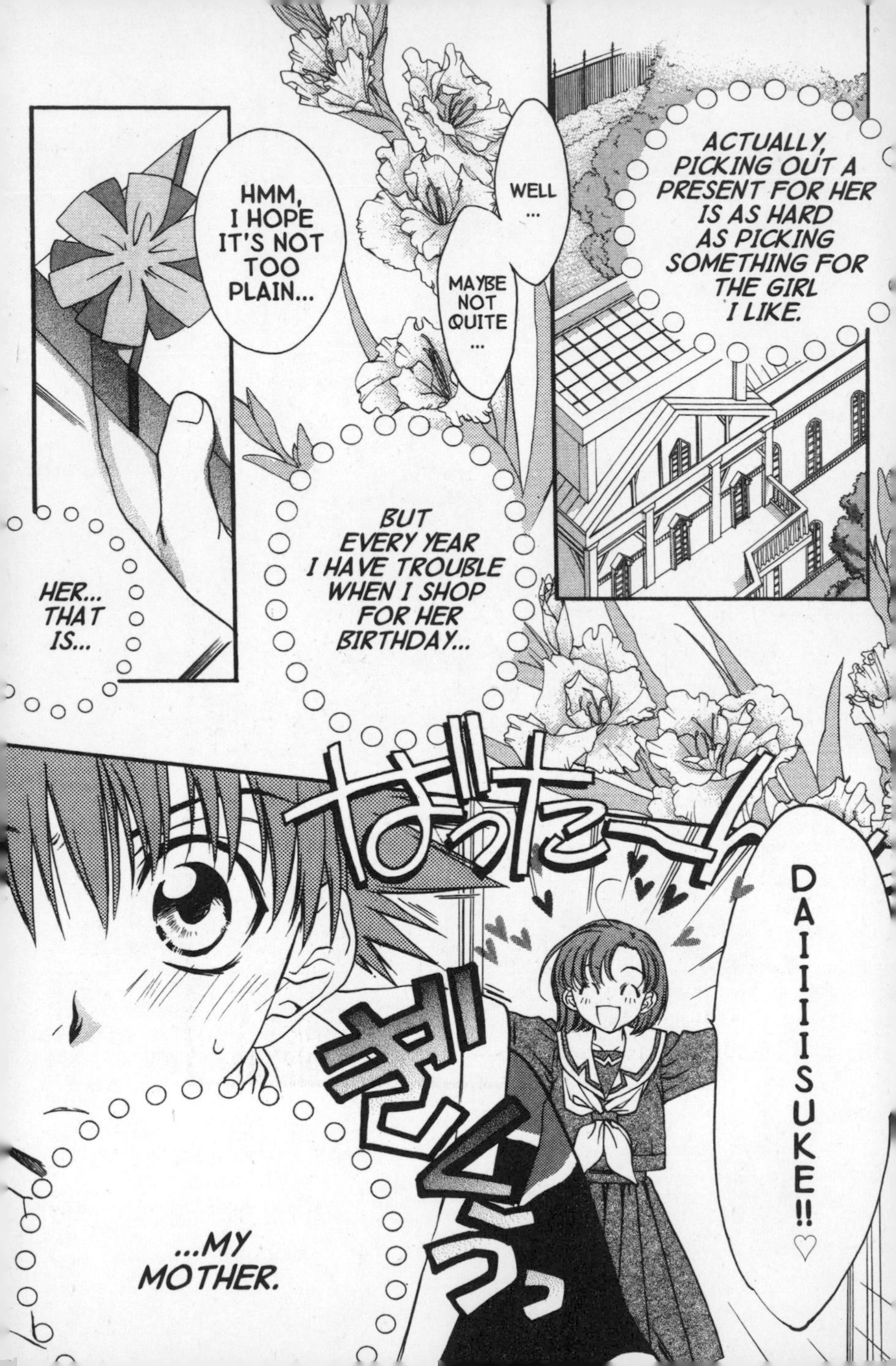

ACTUALLY, PICKING OUT A PRESENT FOR HER IS AS HARD AS PICKING SOMETHING FOR THE GIRL I LIKE.
WELL...
MAYBE NOT QUITE...
HMM, I HOPE IT'S NOT TOO PLAIN...
BUT EVERY YEAR I HAVE TROUBLE WHEN I SHOP FOR HER BIRTHDAY...
HER... THAT IS...
ずばったーん
DAIIIISUKE!! ♡
ぎゅうっ
...MY MOTHER.

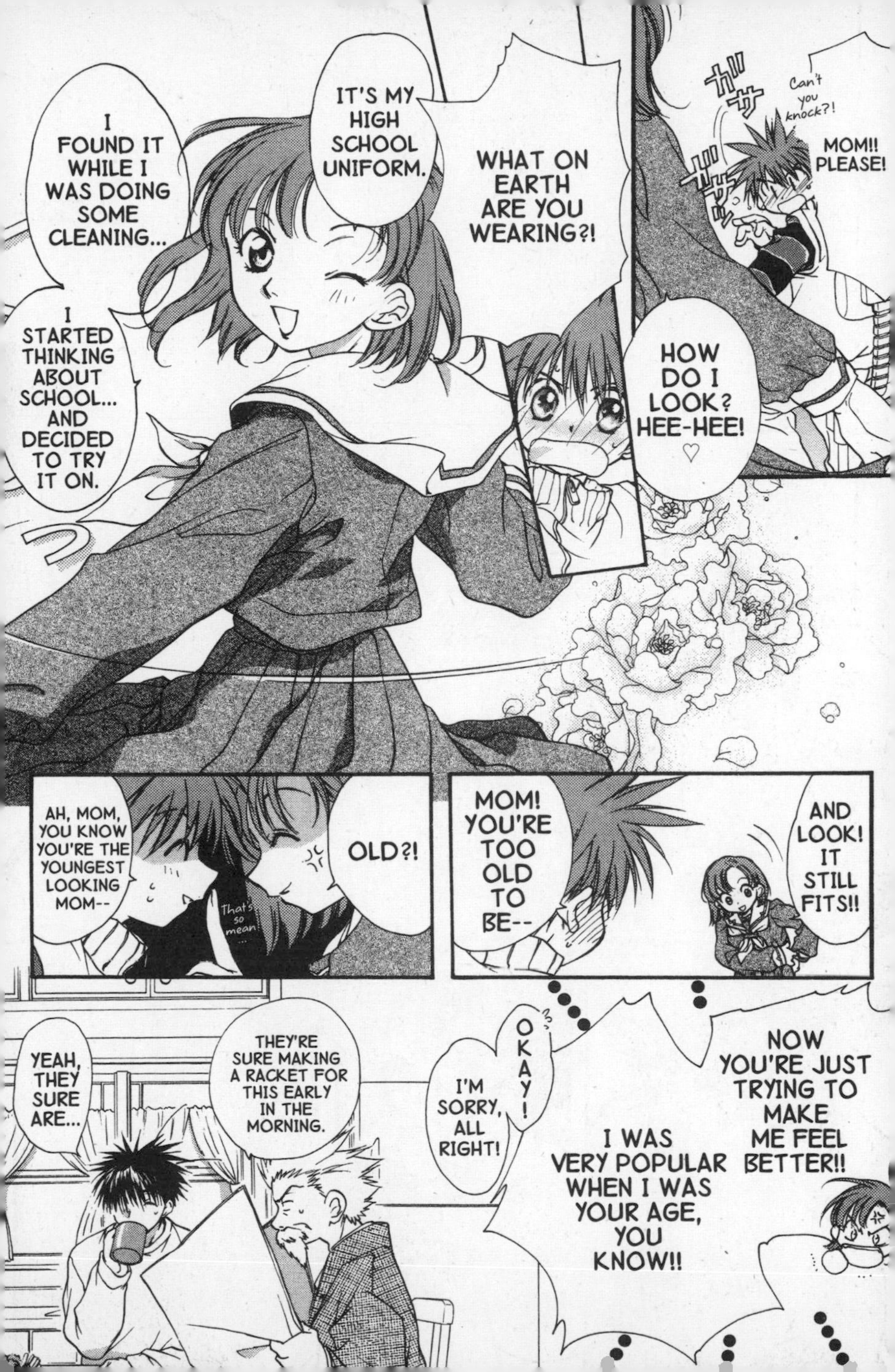
ガサ
ガサ
Can't you knock?!
MOM!! PLEASE!
WHAT ON EARTH ARE YOU WEARING?!
IT'S MY HIGH SCHOOL UNIFORM.
I FOUND IT WHILE I WAS DOING SOME CLEANING...
I STARTED THINKING ABOUT SCHOOL... AND DECIDED TO TRY IT ON.
HOW DO I LOOK? HEE-HEE! ♡
AND LOOK! IT STILL FITS!!
MOM! YOU'RE TOO OLD TO BE--
OLD?!
That's so mean...
AH, MOM, YOU KNOW YOU'RE THE YOUNGEST LOOKING MOM--
NOW YOU'RE JUST TRYING TO MAKE ME FEEL BETTER!!
I WAS VERY POPULAR WHEN I WAS YOUR AGE, YOU KNOW!!
OKAY!
I'M SORRY, ALL RIGHT!
THEY'RE SURE MAKING A RACKET FOR THIS EARLY IN THE MORNING.
YEAH, THEY SURE ARE...

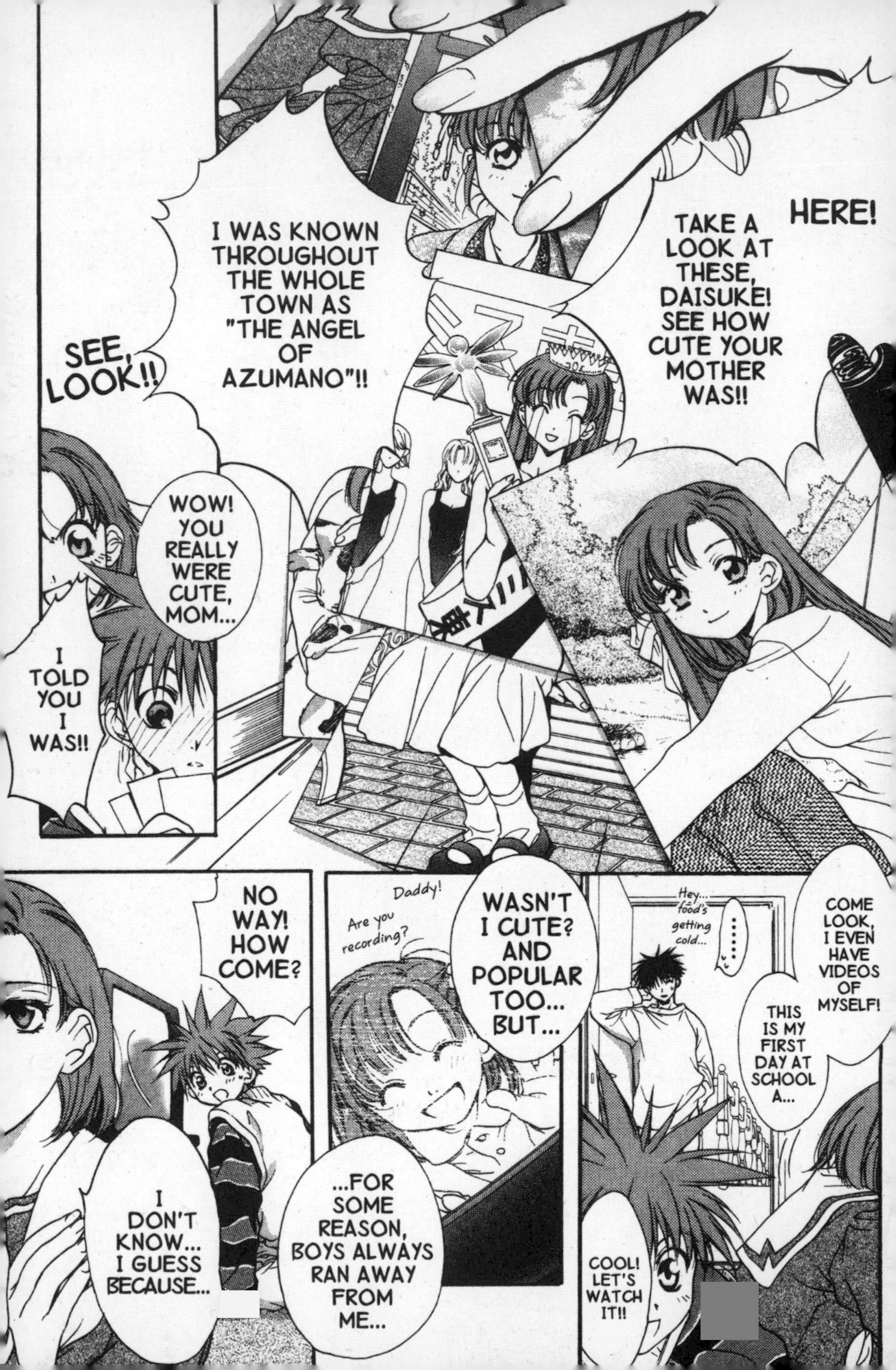
HERE!
TAKE A LOOK AT THESE, DAISUKE! SEE HOW CUTE YOUR MOTHER WAS!!
I WAS KNOWN THROUGHOUT THE WHOLE TOWN AS "THE ANGEL OF AZUMANO"!!
SEE, LOOK!!
WOW! YOU REALLY WERE CUTE, MOM...
I TOLD YOU I WAS!!
COME LOOK, I EVEN HAVE VIDEOS OF MYSELF!
THIS IS MY FIRST DAY AT SCHOOL A...
Hey... food's getting cold...
......
COOL! LET'S WATCH IT!!
Daddy!
Are you recording?
WASN'T I CUTE? AND POPULAR TOO... BUT...
...FOR SOME REASON, BOYS ALWAYS RAN AWAY FROM ME...
NO WAY! HOW COME?
I DON'T KNOW... I GUESS BECAUSE...

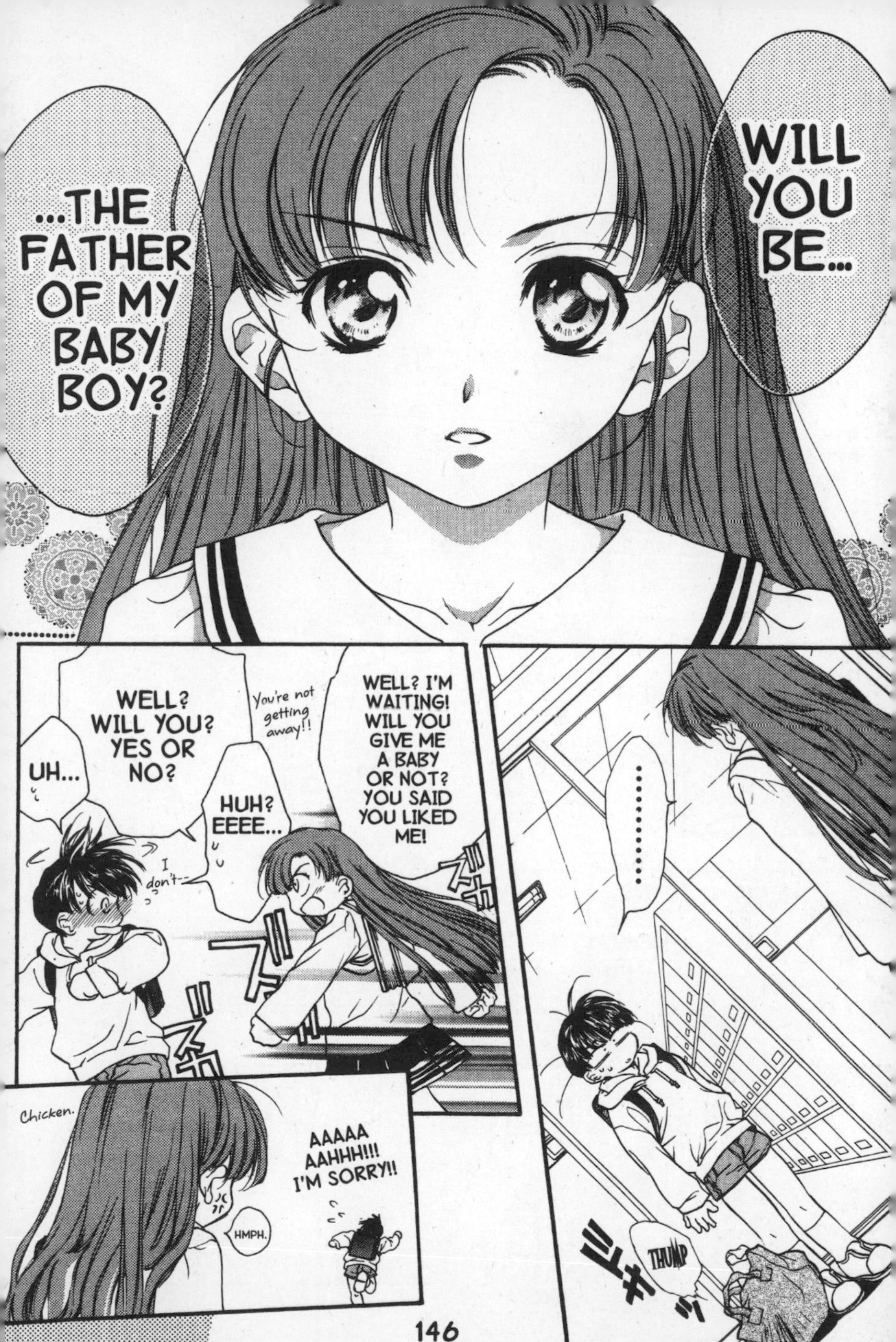
WILL YOU BE...
...THE FATHER OF MY BABY BOY?
......
THUMP
WELL? I'M WAITING! WILL YOU GIVE ME A BABY OR NOT? YOU SAID YOU LIKED ME!
You're not getting away!!
WELL? WILL YOU? YES OR NO?
HUH? EEEE...
UH...
I don't-
AAAAA AAHHH!!! I'M SORRY!!
HMPH.
Chicken.

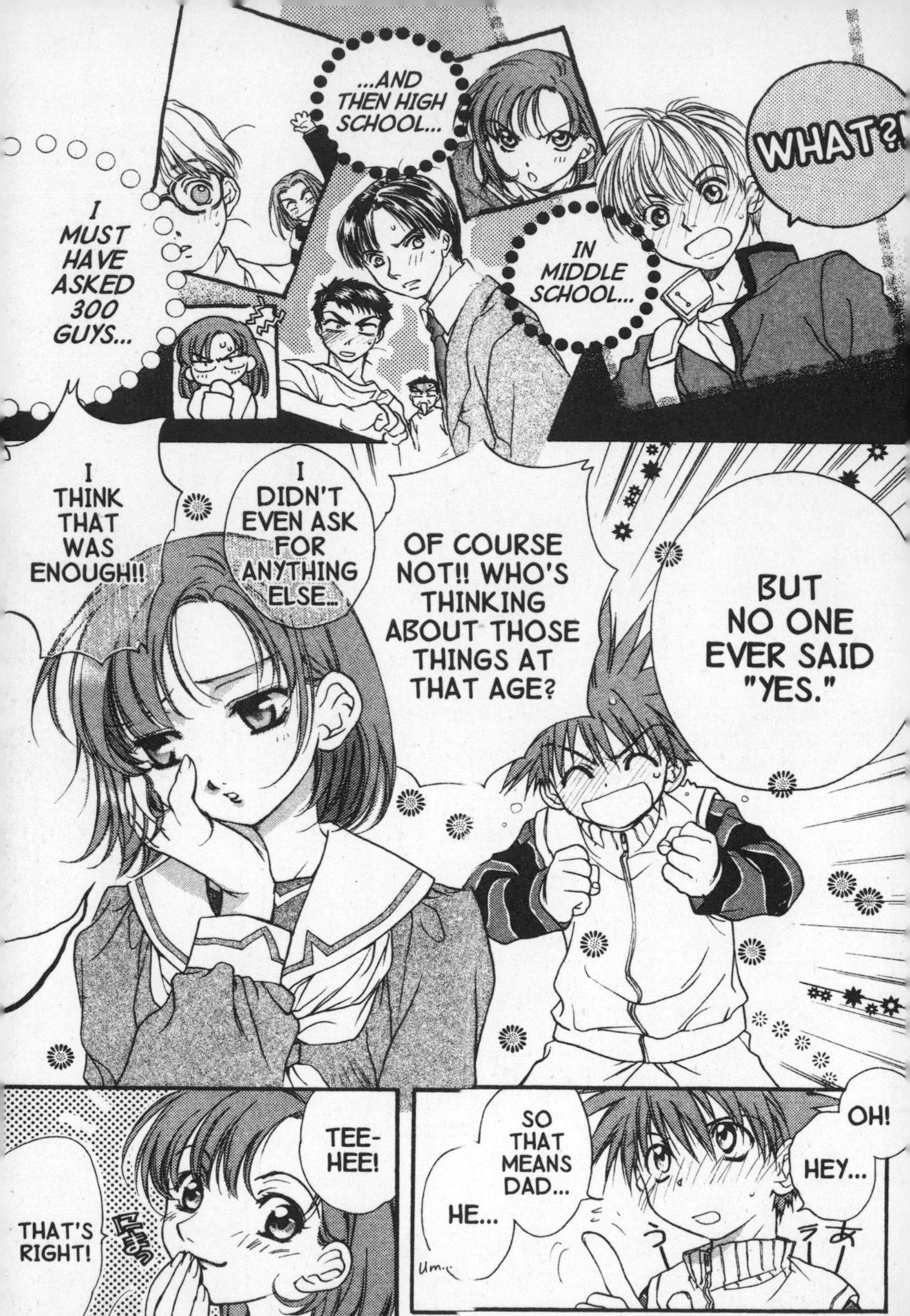
IN MIDDLE SCHOOL...
...AND THEN HIGH SCHOOL...
I MUST HAVE ASKED 300 GUYS...
WHAT?!
BUT NO ONE EVER SAID "YES."
OF COURSE NOT!! WHO'S THINKING ABOUT THOSE THINGS AT THAT AGE?
I DIDN'T EVEN ASK FOR ANYTHING ELSE...
I THINK THAT WAS ENOUGH!!
OH!
HEY...
SO THAT MEANS DAD...
HE...
Um...
TEE-HEE!
THAT'S RIGHT!

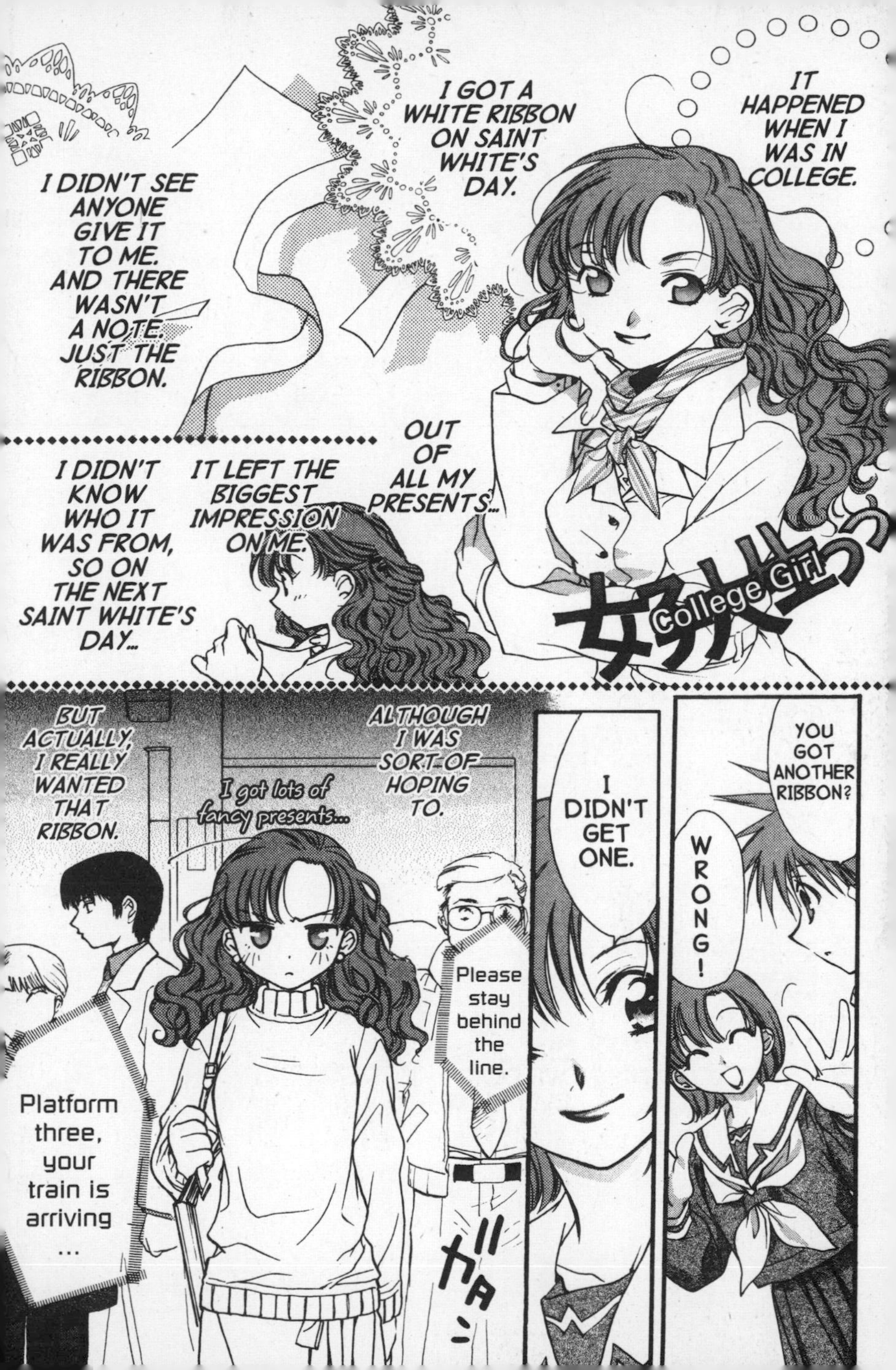
IT HAPPENED WHEN I WAS IN COLLEGE.
I GOT A WHITE RIBBON ON SAINT WHITE'S DAY.
OUT OF ALL MY PRESENTS...
College Girl
I DIDN'T SEE ANYONE GIVE IT TO ME. AND THERE WASN'T A NOTE. JUST THE RIBBON.
IT LEFT THE BIGGEST IMPRESSION ON ME.
I DIDN'T KNOW WHO IT WAS FROM, SO ON THE NEXT SAINT WHITE'S DAY...
YOU GOT ANOTHER RIBBON?
WRONG!
I DIDN'T GET ONE.
ALTHOUGH I WAS SORT OF HOPING TO.
I got lots of fancy presents...
BUT ACTUALLY, I REALLY WANTED THAT RIBBON.
Please stay behind the line.
Platform three, your train is arriving ...

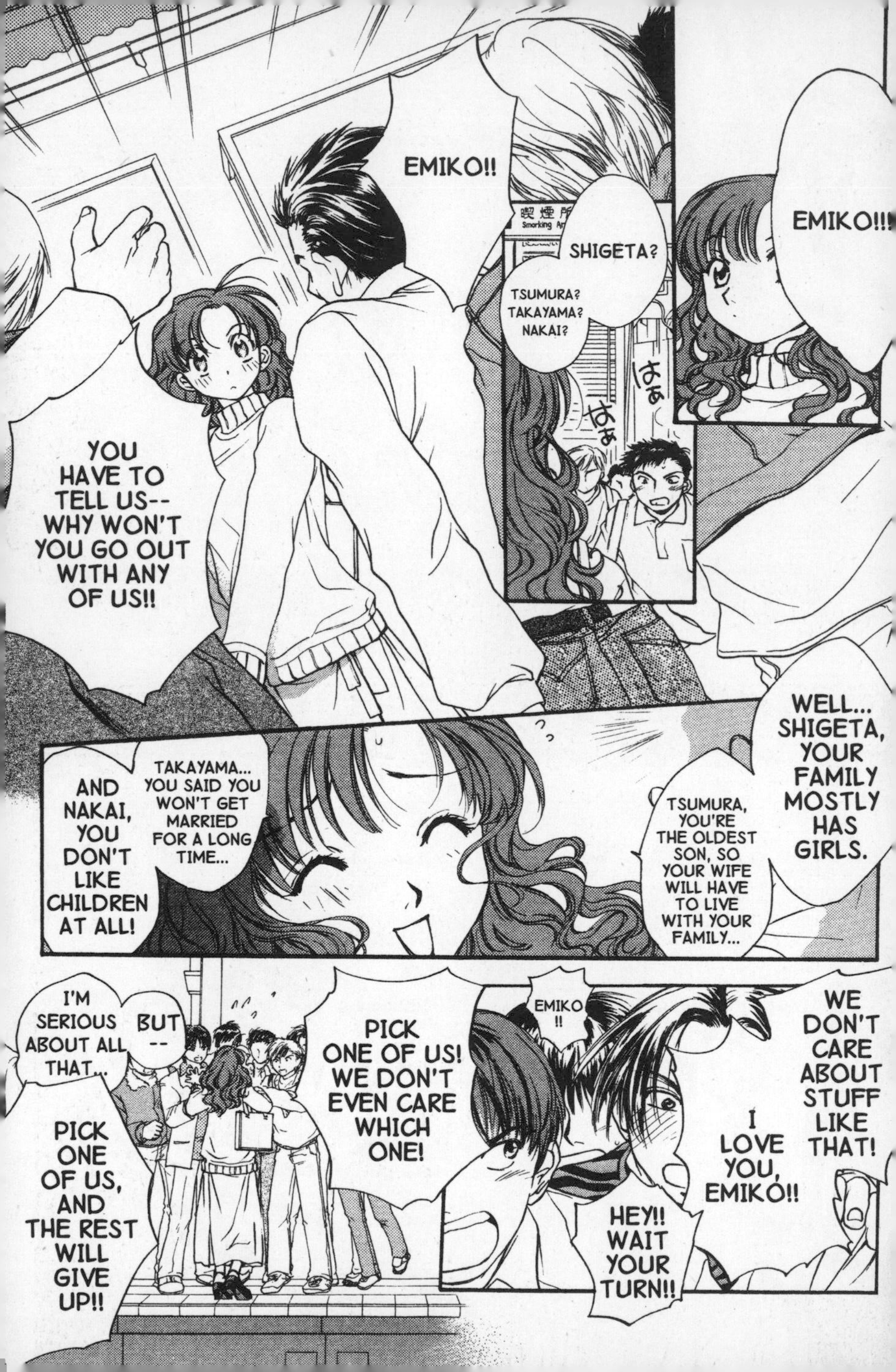
EMIKO!!!
SHIGETA?
TSUMURA? TAKAYAMA? NAKAI?
はぁ
はぁ
喫煙所
EMIKO!!
YOU HAVE TO TELL US-- WHY WON'T YOU GO OUT WITH ANY OF US!!
WELL... SHIGETA, YOUR FAMILY MOSTLY HAS GIRLS.
TSUMURA, YOU'RE THE OLDEST SON, SO YOUR WIFE WILL HAVE TO LIVE WITH YOUR FAMILY...
TAKAYAMA... YOU SAID YOU WON'T GET MARRIED FOR A LONG TIME...
AND NAKAI, YOU DON'T LIKE CHILDREN AT ALL!
WE DON'T CARE ABOUT STUFF LIKE THAT!
I LOVE YOU, EMIKO!!
EMIKO !!
HEY!! WAIT YOUR TURN!!
PICK ONE OF US! WE DON'T EVEN CARE WHICH ONE!
BUT --
I'M SERIOUS ABOUT ALL THAT...
PICK ONE OF US, AND THE REST WILL GIVE UP!!

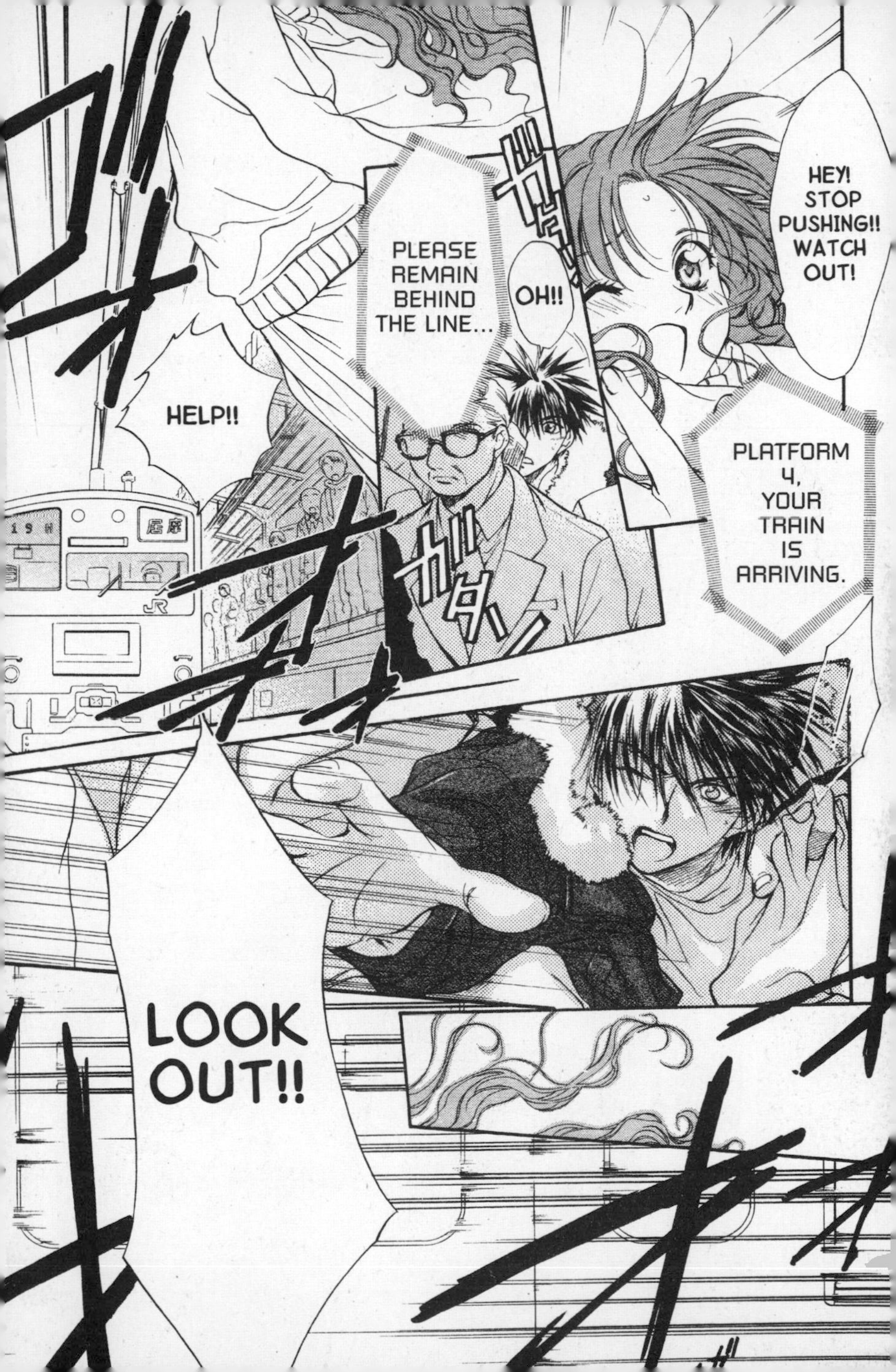
HEY! STOP PUSHING!! WATCH OUT!
OH!!
PLEASE REMAIN BEHIND THE LINE...
PLATFORM 4, YOUR TRAIN IS ARRIVING.
HELP!!
LOOK OUT!!

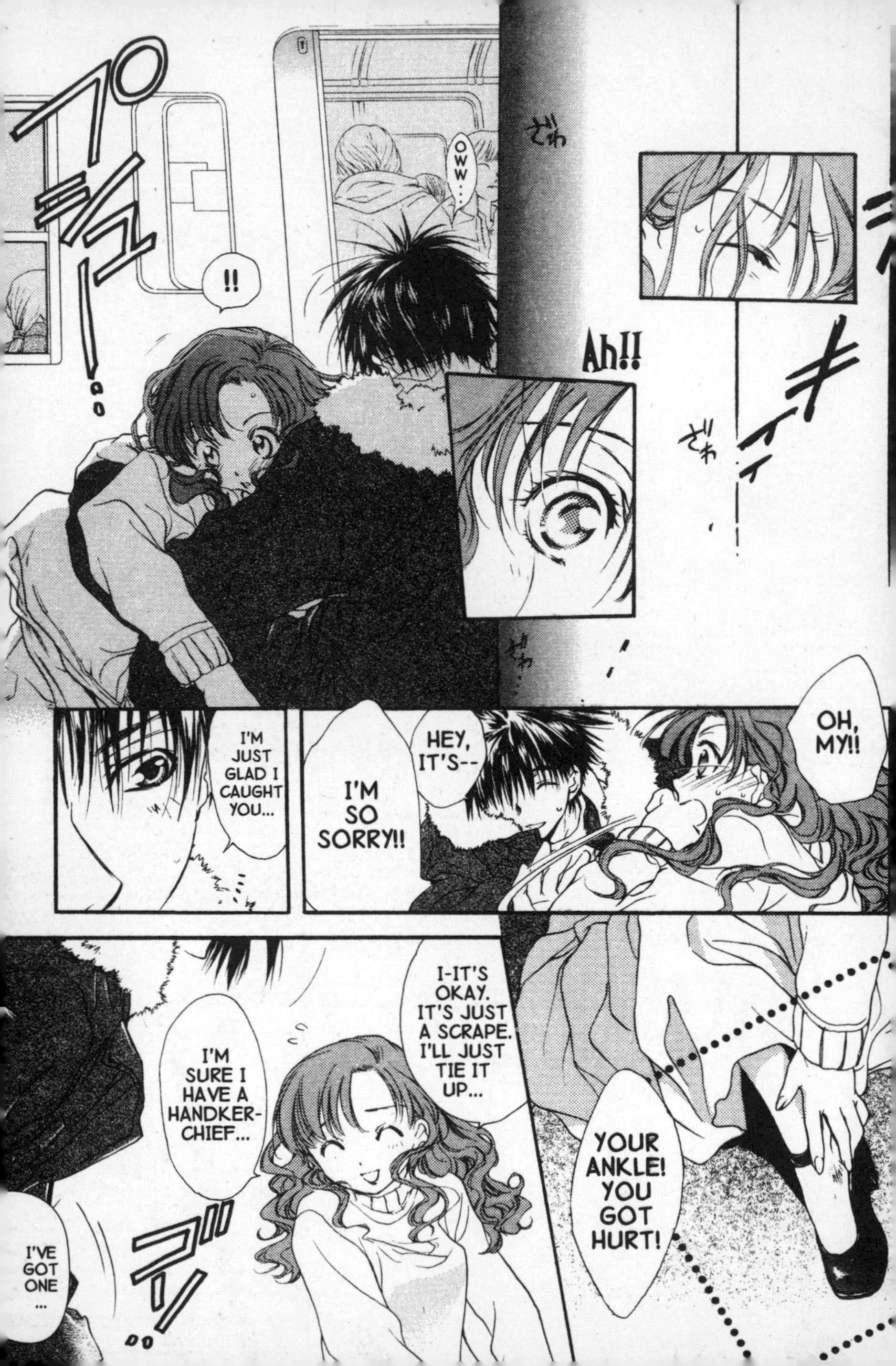
ざわ
Ah!!
キィィ
ざわ
ざわ
プシュー
OWW...
!!
OH, MY!!
HEY, IT'S--
I'M SO SORRY!!
I'M JUST GLAD I CAUGHT YOU...
YOUR ANKLE! YOU GOT HURT!
I-IT'S OKAY. IT'S JUST A SCRAPE. I'LL JUST TIE IT UP...
I'M SURE I HAVE A HANDKERCHIEF...
I'VE GOT ONE ...

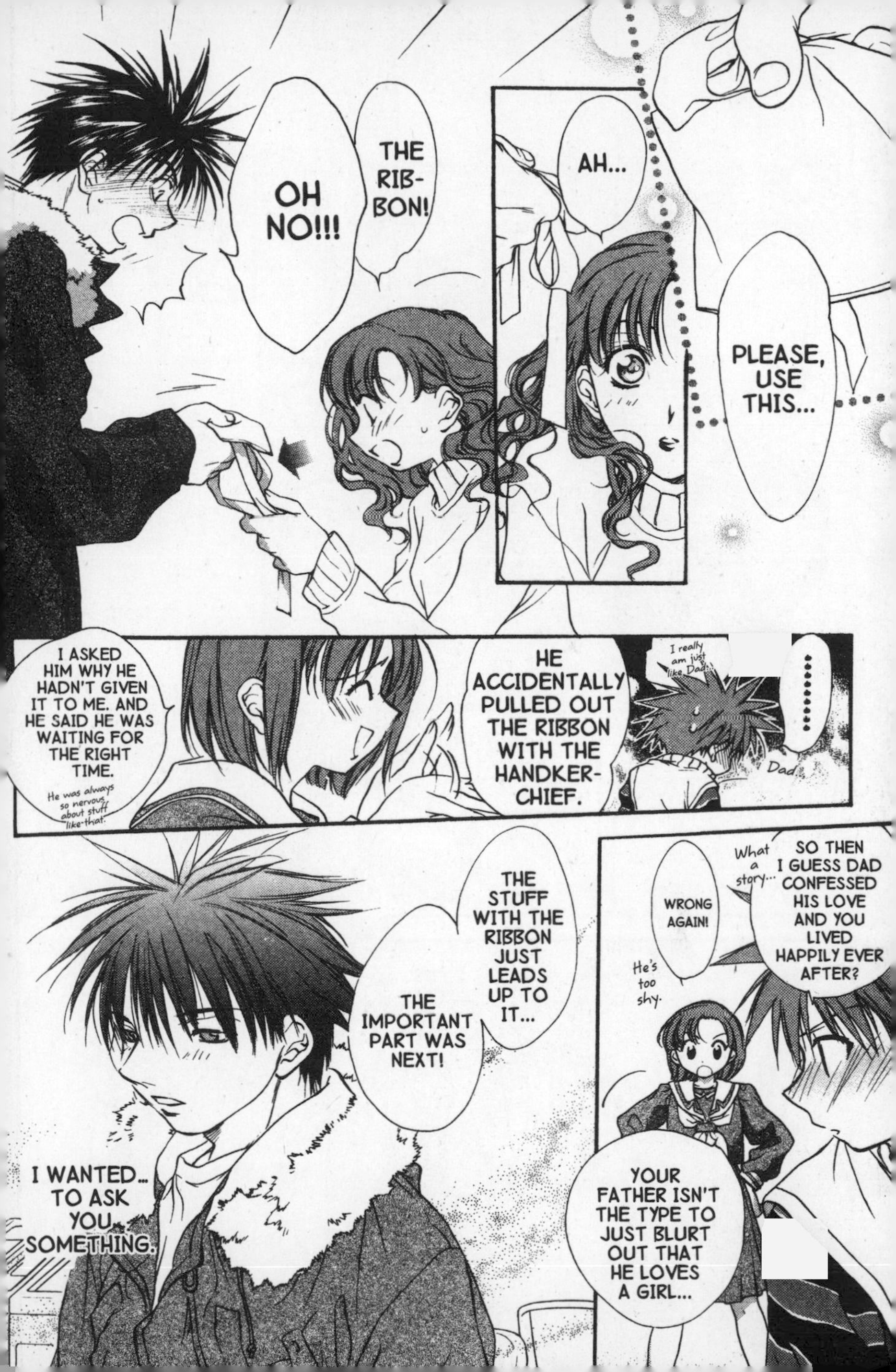
PLEASE, USE THIS...
AH...
THE RIBBON!
OH NO!!!
......
I really am just like Dad..!
Dad...
HE ACCIDENTALLY PULLED OUT THE RIBBON WITH THE HANDKERCHIEF.
I ASKED HIM WHY HE HADN'T GIVEN IT TO ME. AND HE SAID HE WAS WAITING FOR THE RIGHT TIME.
He was always so nervous about stuff like that.
SO THEN I GUESS DAD CONFESSED HIS LOVE AND YOU LIVED HAPPILY EVER AFTER?
What a story...
WRONG AGAIN!
He's too shy.
YOUR FATHER ISN'T THE TYPE TO JUST BLURT OUT THAT HE LOVES A GIRL...
THE STUFF WITH THE RIBBON JUST LEADS UP TO IT...
THE IMPORTANT PART WAS NEXT!
I WANTED... TO ASK YOU SOMETHING.

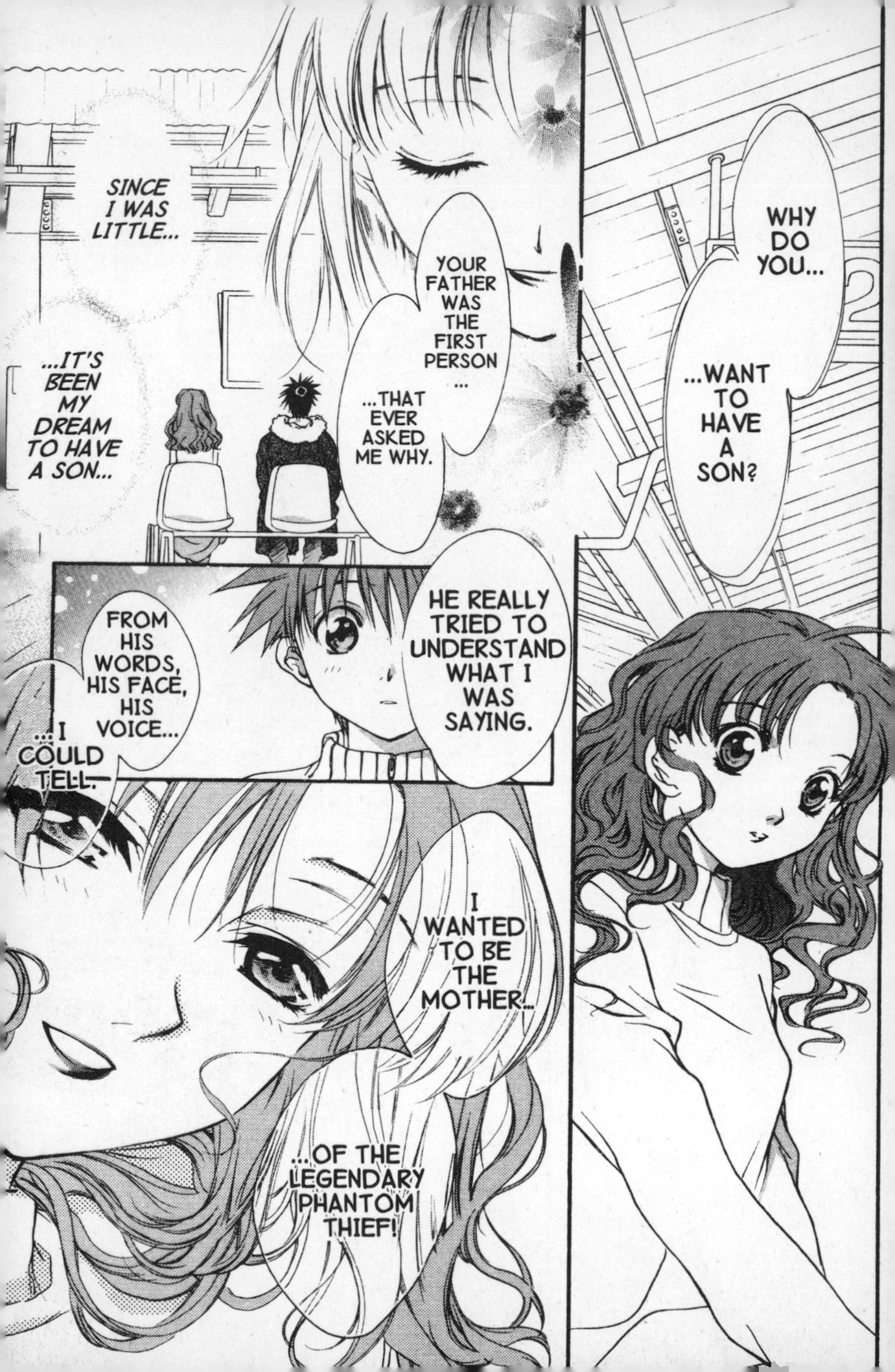

WHY DO YOU...
...WANT TO HAVE A SON?
SINCE I WAS LITTLE...
...IT'S BEEN MY DREAM TO HAVE A SON...
YOUR FATHER WAS THE FIRST PERSON...
...THAT EVER ASKED ME WHY.
HE REALLY TRIED TO UNDERSTAND WHAT I WAS SAYING.
FROM HIS WORDS, HIS FACE, HIS VOICE...
...I COULD TELL.
I WANTED TO BE THE MOTHER...
...OF THE LEGENDARY PHANTOM THIEF!

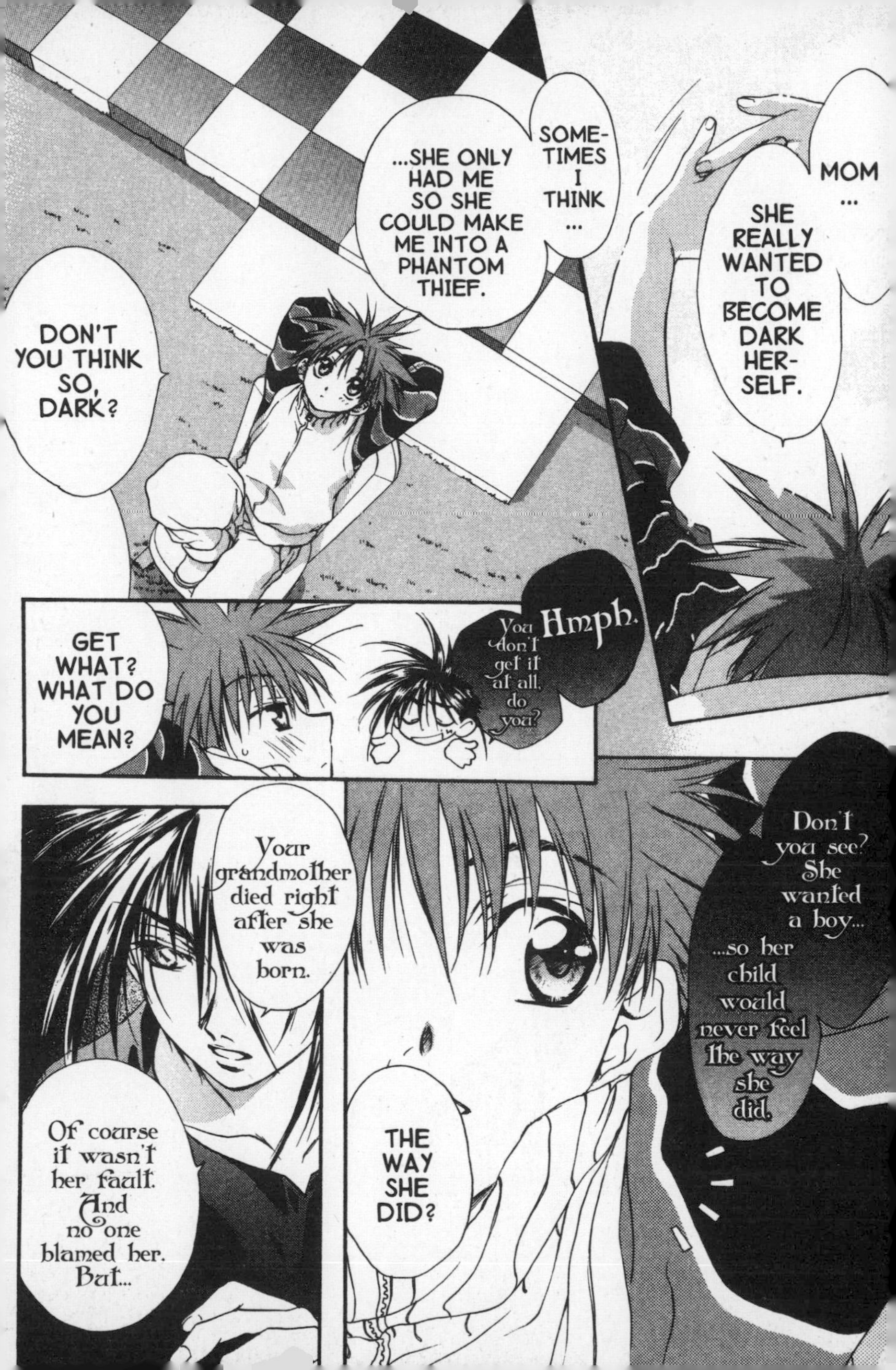
MOM... SHE REALLY WANTED TO BECOME DARK HER-SELF.
SOME-TIMES I THINK...
...SHE ONLY HAD ME SO SHE COULD MAKE ME INTO A PHANTOM THIEF.
DON'T YOU THINK SO, DARK?
Hmph.
You don't get it at all, do you?
GET WHAT? WHAT DO YOU MEAN?
Don't you see? She wanted a boy...
...so her child would never feel the way she did.
THE WAY SHE DID?
Your grandmother died right after she was born.
Of course it wasn't her fault. And no one blamed her. But...

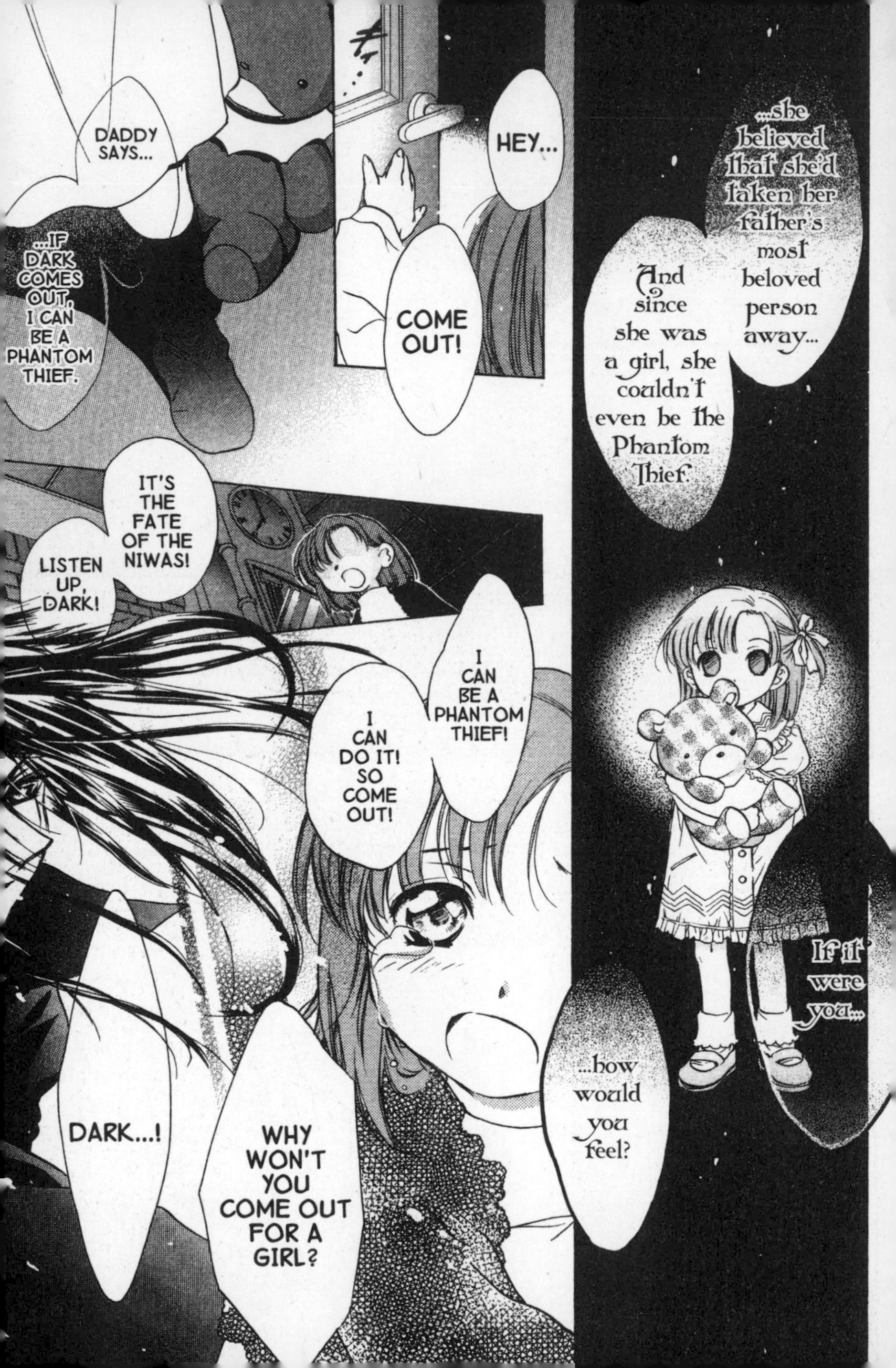
...she believed that she'd taken her father's most beloved person away...
And since she was a girl, she couldn't even be the Phantom Thief.
If it were you...
...how would you feel?
HEY...
COME OUT!
DADDY SAYS...
...IF DARK COMES OUT, I CAN BE A PHANTOM THIEF.
IT'S THE FATE OF THE NIWAS!
LISTEN UP, DARK!
I CAN BE A PHANTOM THIEF!
I CAN DO IT! SO COME OUT!
WHY WON'T YOU COME OUT FOR A GIRL?
DARK...!

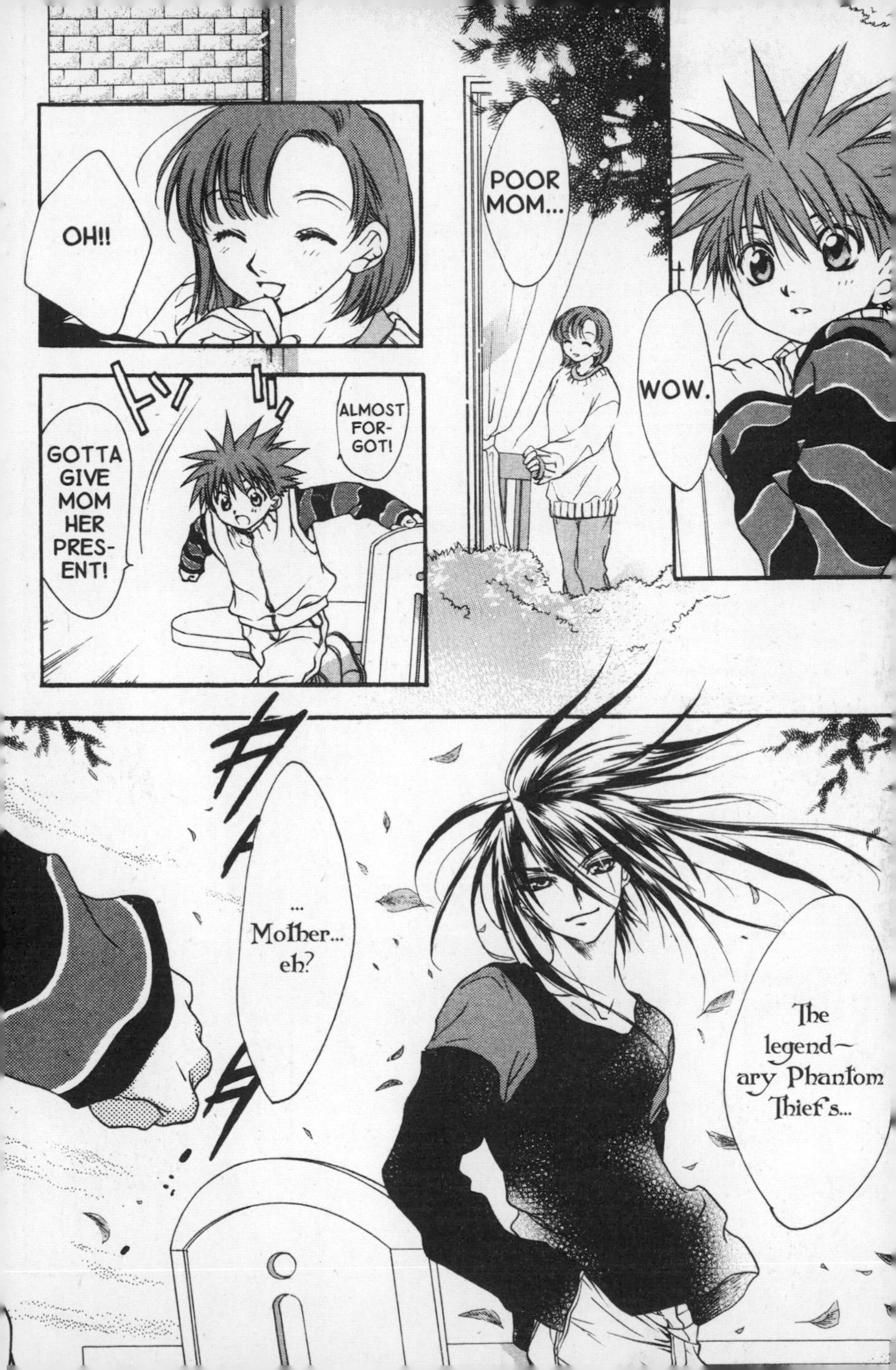
WOW.
POOR MOM...
OH!!
ALMOST FOR-GOT!
GOTTA GIVE MOM HER PRES-ENT!
The legend-ary Phantom Thief's...
... Mother... eh?

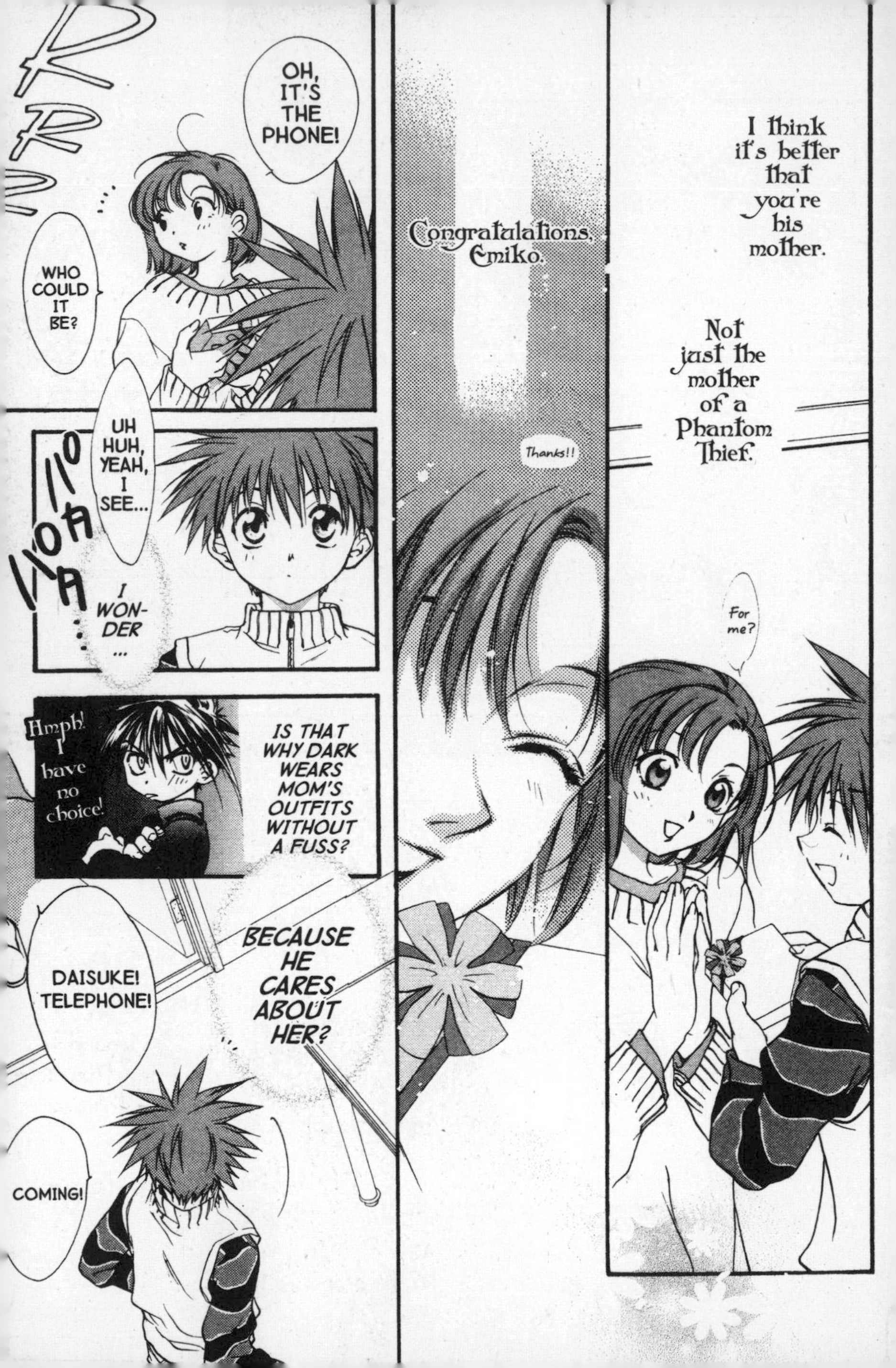

I think it's better that you're his mother.
Not just the mother of a Phantom Thief.
For me?
Congratulations, Emiko.
Thanks!!
OH, IT'S THE PHONE!
RRR
...
WHO COULD IT BE?
UH HUH, YEAH, I SEE...
I WONDER...
...
IS THAT WHY DARK WEARS MOM'S OUTFITS WITHOUT A FUSS?
Hmph! I have no choice!
BECAUSE HE CARES ABOUT HER?
...
DAISUKE! TELEPHONE!
COMING!

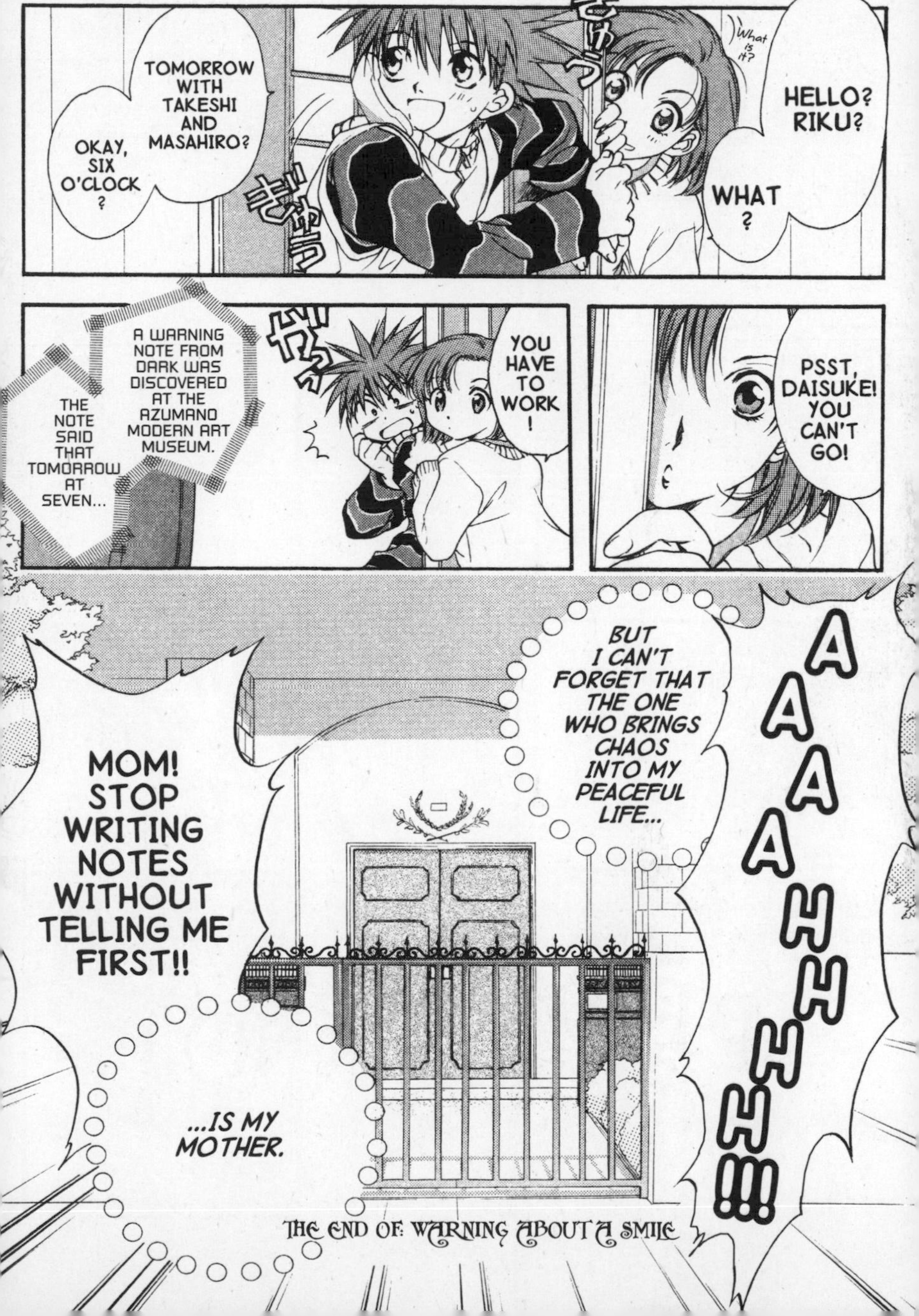
ぎゅう
What is it?
HELLO? RIKU?
WHAT?
TOMORROW WITH TAKESHI AND MASAHIRO?
OKAY, SIX O'CLOCK?
ぎゅう
PSST, DAISUKE! YOU CAN'T GO!
YOU HAVE TO WORK!
A WARNING NOTE FROM DARK WAS DISCOVERED AT THE AZUMANO MODERN ART MUSEUM.
THE NOTE SAID THAT TOMORROW AT SEVEN...
AAAAHHHH!!!
BUT I CAN'T FORGET THAT THE ONE WHO BRINGS CHAOS INTO MY PEACEFUL LIFE...
MOM! STOP WRITING NOTES WITHOUT TELLING ME FIRST!!
...IS MY MOTHER.

THE END OF: WARNING ABOUT A SMILE

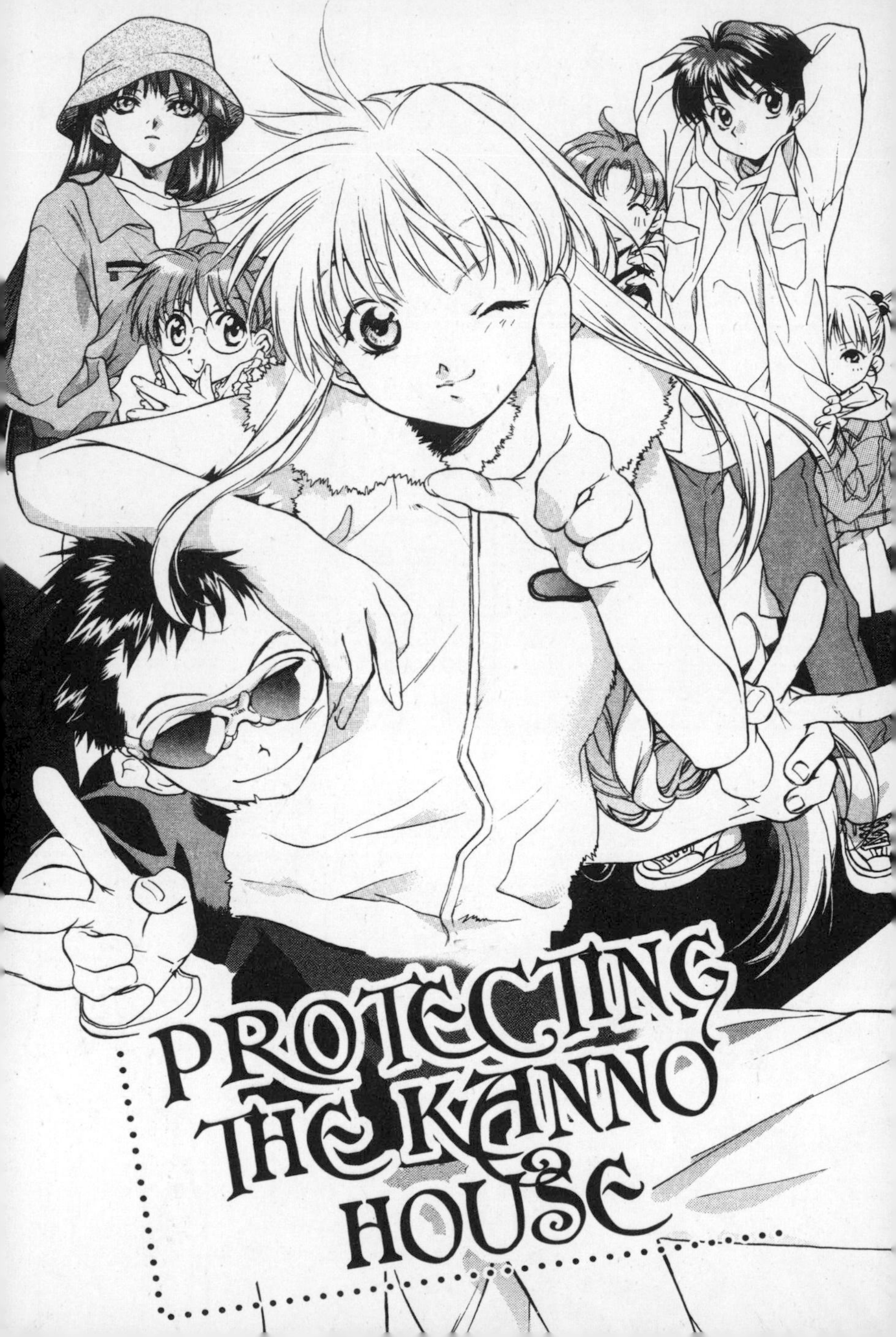
PROTECTING
THE KANNO
HOUSE

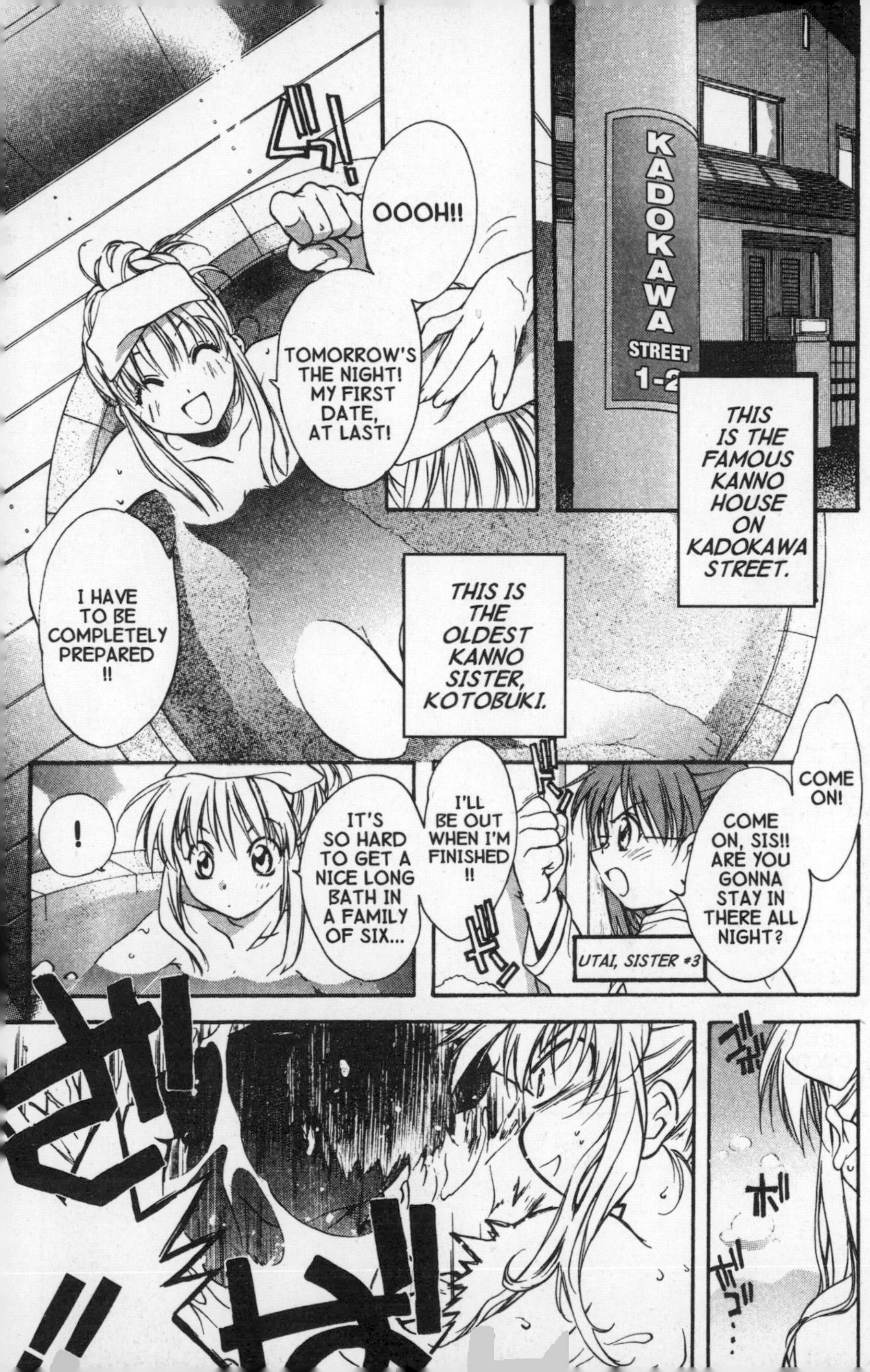
KADOKAWA
STREET
1-2
THIS IS THE FAMOUS KANNO HOUSE ON KADOKAWA STREET.
OOOH!!
TOMORROW'S THE NIGHT! MY FIRST DATE, AT LAST!
THIS IS THE OLDEST KANNO SISTER, KOTOBUKI.
I HAVE TO BE COMPLETELY PREPARED!!
COME ON!
COME ON, SIS!! ARE YOU GONNA STAY IN THERE ALL NIGHT?
UTAI, SISTER #3
I'LL BE OUT WHEN I'M FINISHED!!
IT'S SO HARD TO GET A NICE LONG BATH IN A FAMILY OF SIX...
!

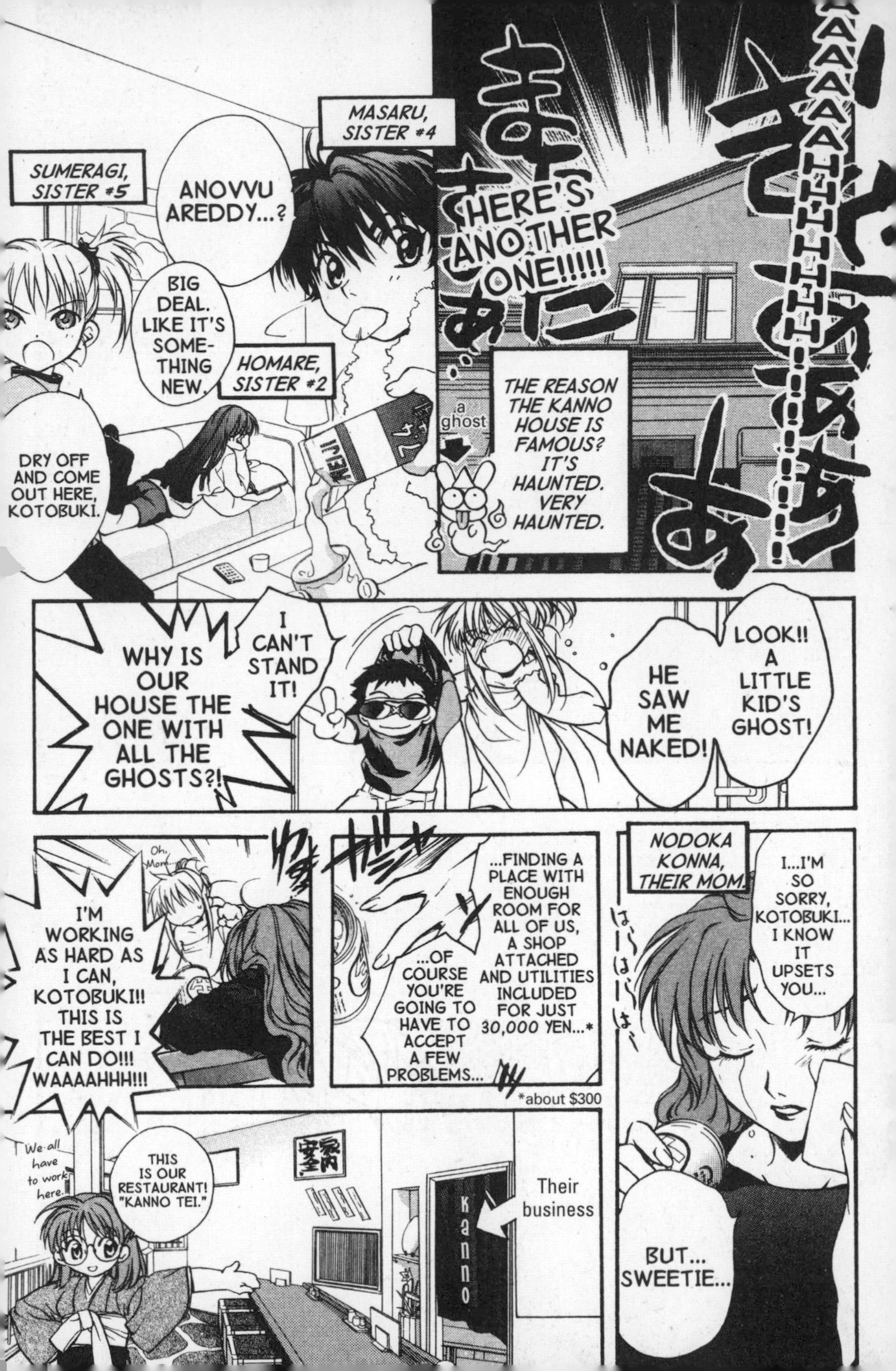
AAAAAAHHHHHHH!!!!!!!
HERE'S ANOTHER ONE!!!!!
a ghost
THE REASON THE KANNO HOUSE IS FAMOUS? IT'S HAUNTED. VERY HAUNTED.
MASARU, SISTER #4
ANOVVU AREDDY...?
SUMERAGI, SISTER #5
BIG DEAL. LIKE IT'S SOME-THING NEW.
HOMARE, SISTER #2
DRY OFF AND COME OUT HERE, KOTOBUKI.
LOOK!! A LITTLE KID'S GHOST!
HE SAW ME NAKED!
I CAN'T STAND IT!
WHY IS OUR HOUSE THE ONE WITH ALL THE GHOSTS?!
NODOKA KONNA, THEIR MOM.
I...I'M SO SORRY, KOTOBUKI... I KNOW IT UPSETS YOU...
BUT... SWEETIE...
...FINDING A PLACE WITH ENOUGH ROOM FOR ALL OF US, A SHOP ATTACHED AND UTILITIES INCLUDED FOR JUST 30,000 YEN...*
...OF COURSE YOU'RE GOING TO HAVE TO ACCEPT A FEW PROBLEMS...
*about $300
Oh, Mom...
I'M WORKING AS HARD AS I CAN, KOTOBUKI!! THIS IS THE BEST I CAN DO!!! WAAAAHHH!!!
Their business
THIS IS OUR RESTAURANT! "KANNO TEI."
We all have to work here.

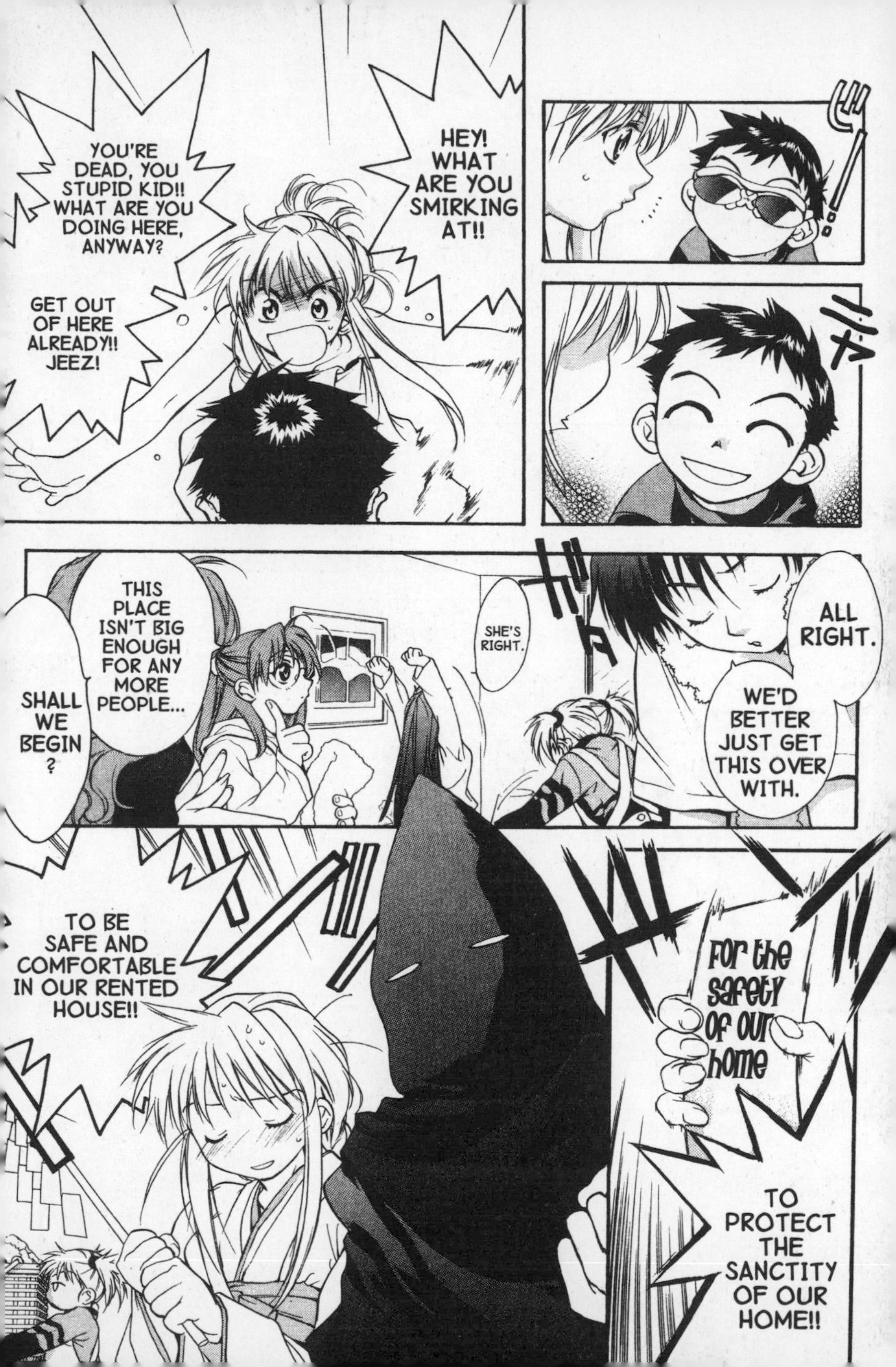
HEY! WHAT ARE YOU SMIRKING AT!!
YOU'RE DEAD, YOU STUPID KID!! WHAT ARE YOU DOING HERE, ANYWAY?
GET OUT OF HERE ALREADY!! JEEZ!
ALL RIGHT.
WE'D BETTER JUST GET THIS OVER WITH.
SHE'S RIGHT.
THIS PLACE ISN'T BIG ENOUGH FOR ANY MORE PEOPLE...
SHALL WE BEGIN?
For the safety of our home
TO PROTECT THE SANCTITY OF OUR HOME!!
TO BE SAFE AND COMFORTABLE IN OUR RENTED HOUSE!!

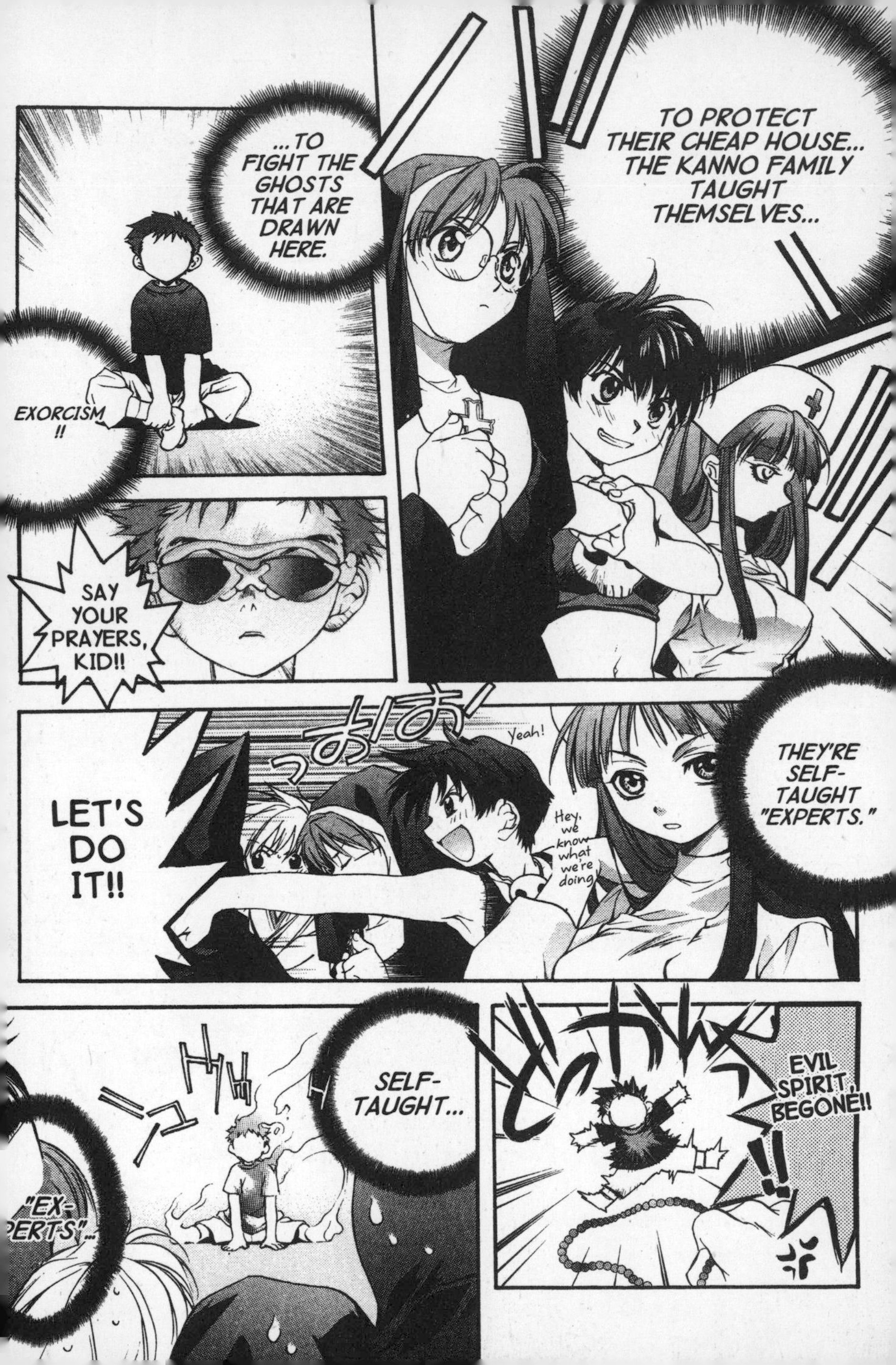
TO PROTECT THEIR CHEAP HOUSE... THE KANNO FAMILY TAUGHT THEMSELVES...
...TO FIGHT THE GHOSTS THAT ARE DRAWN HERE.
EXORCISM!!
SAY YOUR PRAYERS, KID!!
THEY'RE SELF-TAUGHT "EXPERTS."
Yeah!
Hey, we know what we're doing
LET'S DO IT!!
EVIL SPIRIT, BEGONE!!
SELF-TAUGHT...
"EX-PERTS"...

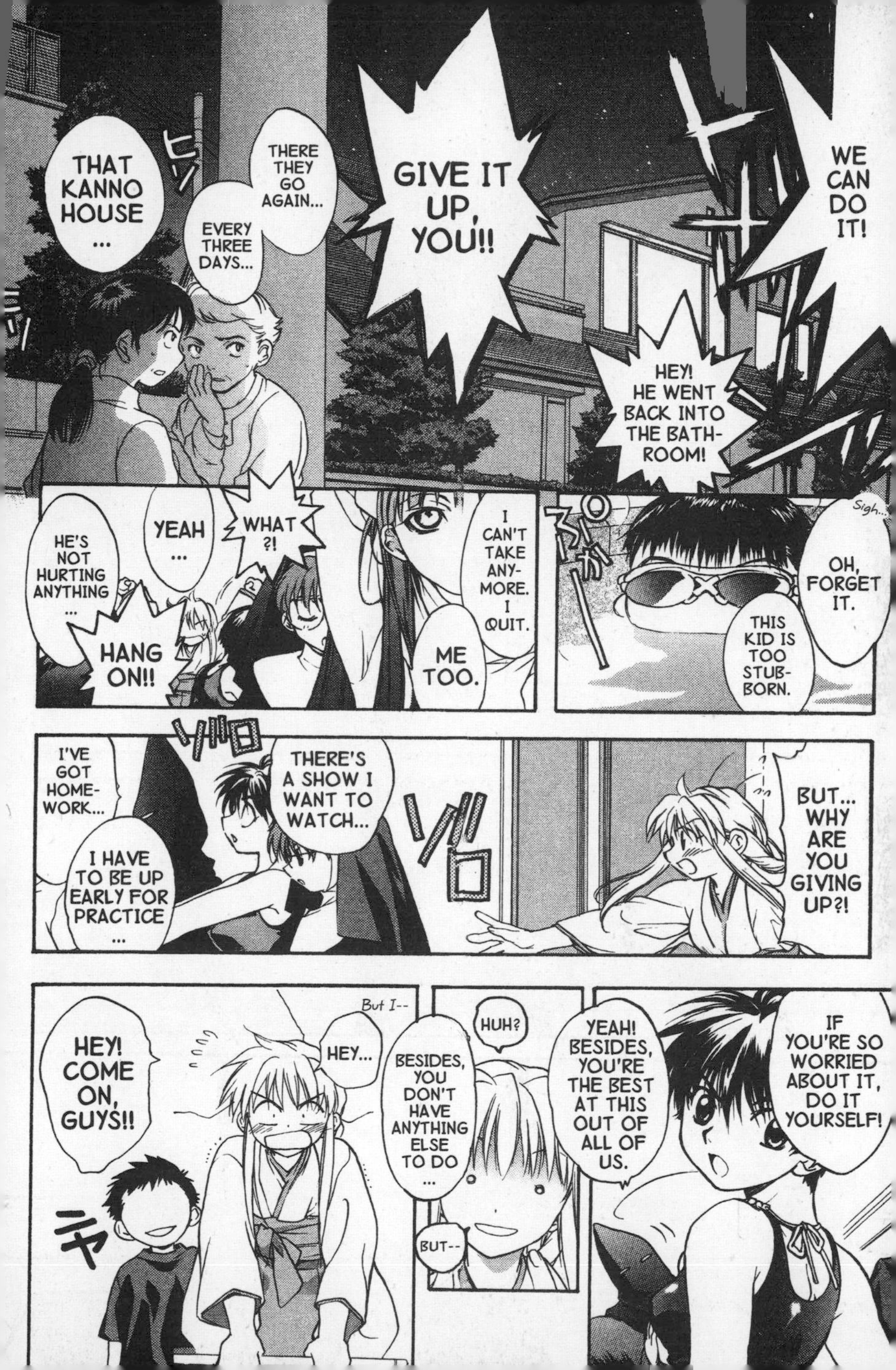
WE CAN DO IT!
HEY! HE WENT BACK INTO THE BATH-ROOM!
GIVE IT UP, YOU!!
THERE THEY GO AGAIN...
EVERY THREE DAYS...
THAT KANNO HOUSE ...
Sigh...
OH, FORGET IT.
THIS KID IS TOO STUB-BORN.
I CAN'T TAKE ANY-MORE. I QUIT.
ME TOO.
WHAT ?!
YEAH ...
HE'S NOT HURTING ANYTHING ...
HANG ON!!
BUT... WHY ARE YOU GIVING UP?!
THERE'S A SHOW I WANT TO WATCH...
I'VE GOT HOME-WORK...
I HAVE TO BE UP EARLY FOR PRACTICE ...
IF YOU'RE SO WORRIED ABOUT IT, DO IT YOURSELF!
YEAH! BESIDES, YOU'RE THE BEST AT THIS OUT OF ALL OF US.
HUH?
BESIDES, YOU DON'T HAVE ANYTHING ELSE TO DO ...
BUT--
But I--
HEY...
HEY! COME ON, GUYS!!
ニヤ

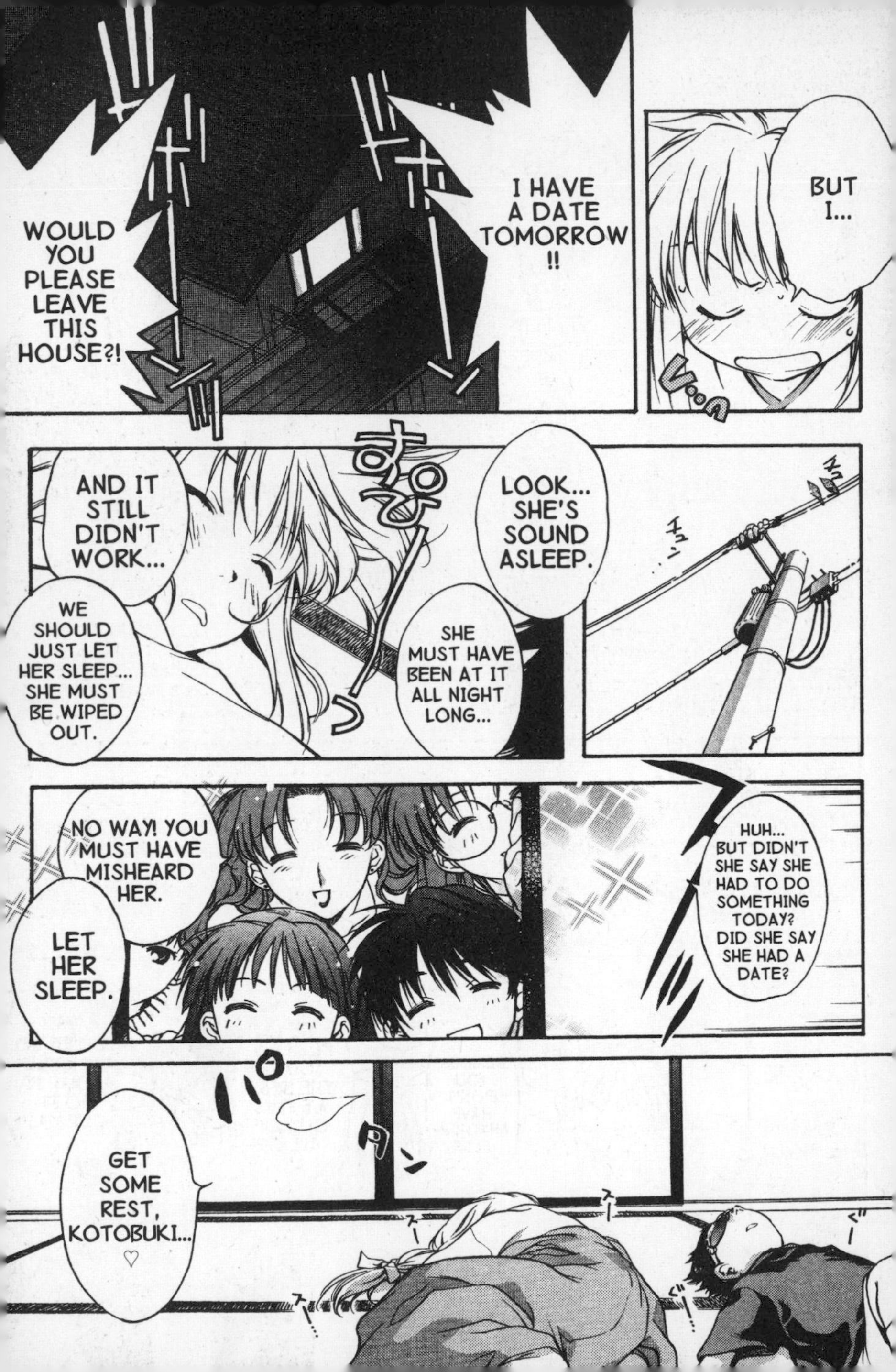
BUT I...
I HAVE A DATE TOMORROW !!
WOULD YOU PLEASE LEAVE THIS HOUSE?!
LOOK... SHE'S SOUND ASLEEP.
SHE MUST HAVE BEEN AT IT ALL NIGHT LONG...
AND IT STILL DIDN'T WORK...
WE SHOULD JUST LET HER SLEEP... SHE MUST BE WIPED OUT.
HUH... BUT DIDN'T SHE SAY SHE HAD TO DO SOMETHING TODAY? DID SHE SAY SHE HAD A DATE?
NO WAY! YOU MUST HAVE MISHEARD HER.
LET HER SLEEP.
GET SOME REST, KOTOBUKI... ♡

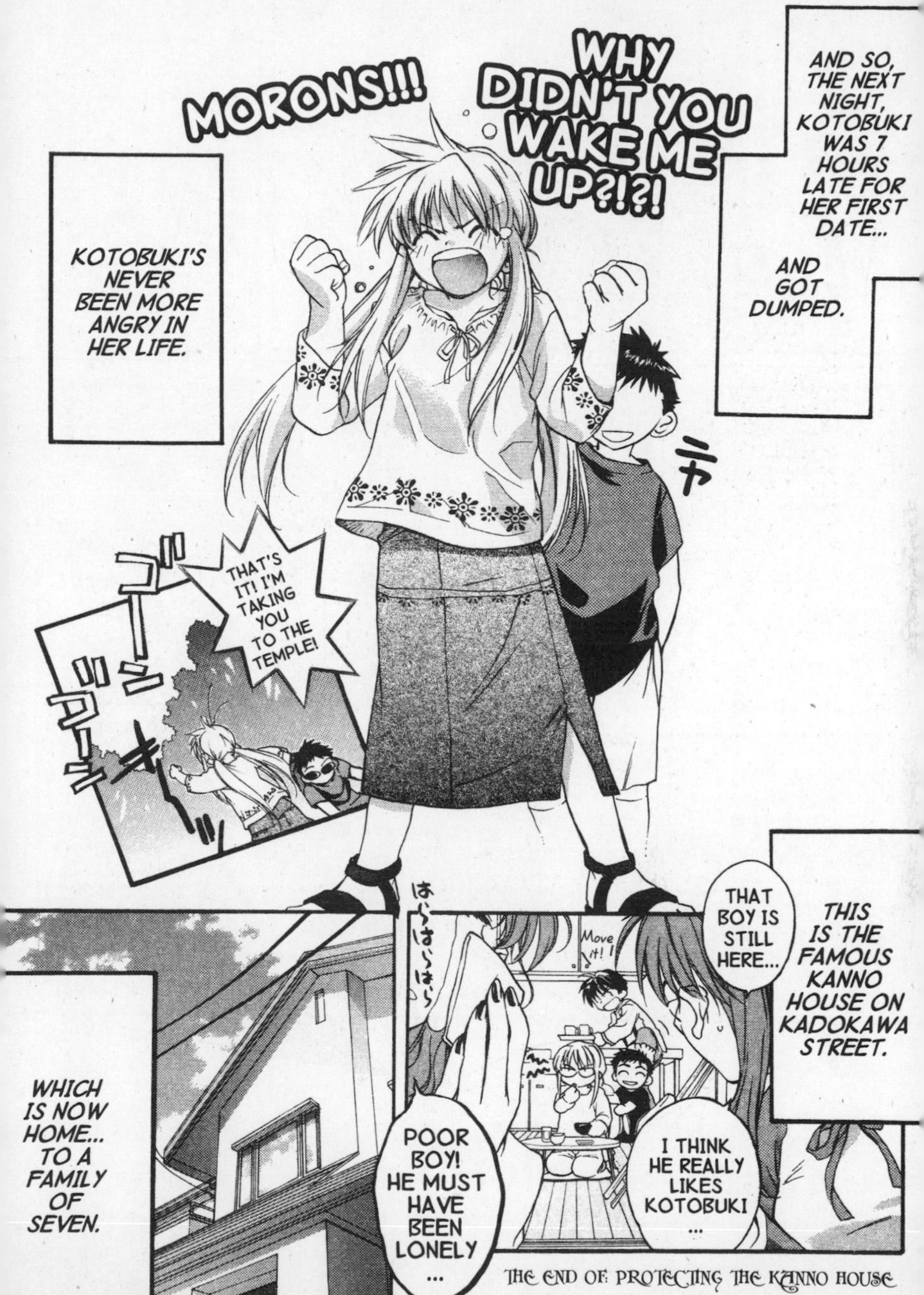
AND SO, THE NEXT NIGHT, KOTOBUKI WAS 7 HOURS LATE FOR HER FIRST DATE...
AND GOT DUMPED.
WHY DIDN'T YOU WAKE ME UP?!?!
MORONS!!!
KOTOBUKI'S NEVER BEEN MORE ANGRY IN HER LIFE.
ニヤ
THAT'S IT! I'M TAKING YOU TO THE TEMPLE!
THIS IS THE FAMOUS KANNO HOUSE ON KADOKAWA STREET.
THAT BOY IS STILL HERE...
Move it!
I THINK HE REALLY LIKES KOTOBUKI ...
はらはらはら
POOR BOY! HE MUST HAVE BEEN LONELY ...
WHICH IS NOW HOME... TO A FAMILY OF SEVEN.

THE END OF: PROTECTING THE KANNO HOUSE

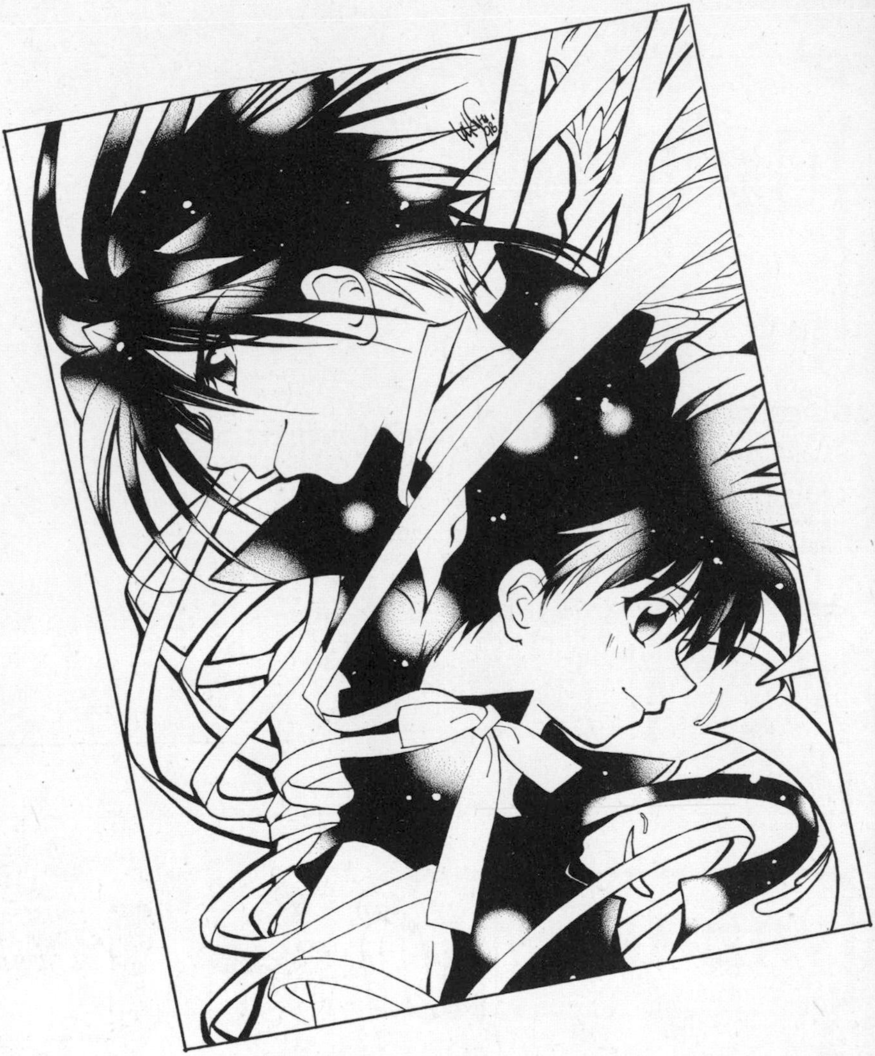

YUKIRU SUGISAKI

D·N·ANGEL VOL.4

One Night Magic

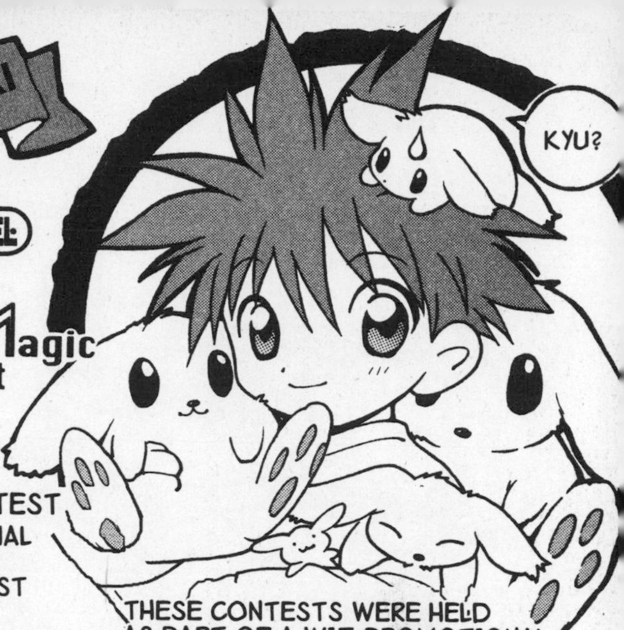
KYU?

THE WIZ TWIN CONTEST
1) WIZ STUFFED ANIMAL CONTEST
2) GIRLFRIEND CONTEST

THESE CONTESTS WERE HELD AS PART OF A WIZ PROMOTIONAL CAMPAIGN. HERE ARE THE WINNERS!♡

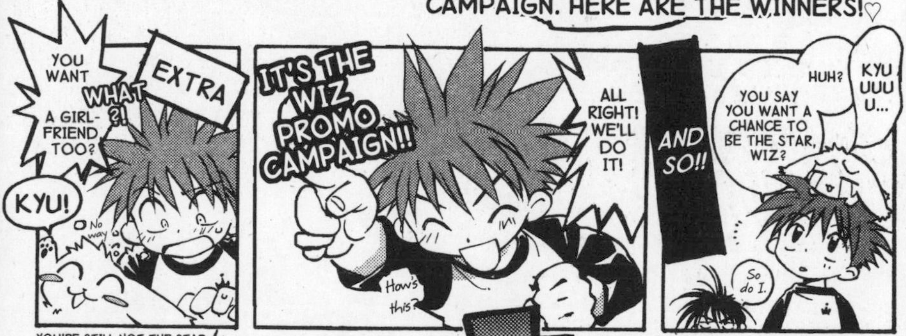
HUH?
KYU UUU U...
YOU SAY YOU WANT A CHANCE TO BE THE STAR, WIZ?
So do I.
AND SO!!
ALL RIGHT! WE'LL DO IT!
IT'S THE WIZ PROMO CAMPAIGN!!
How's this?
EXTRA
YOU WANT WHAT?! A GIRL-FRIEND TOO?
KYU!
No way
YOU'RE STILL NOT THE STAR

WIZ ANALYSIS

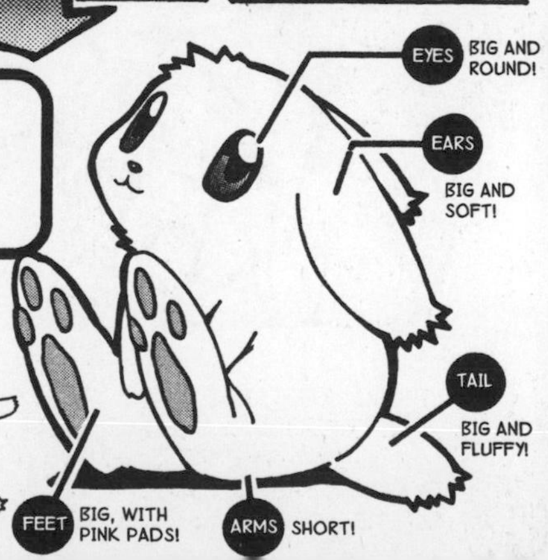
EYES BIG AND ROUND!
EARS BIG AND SOFT!
TAIL BIG AND FLUFFY!
FEET BIG, WITH PINK PADS!
ARMS SHORT!

HE'S SO SOFT!!

(AND SO FLUFFY)

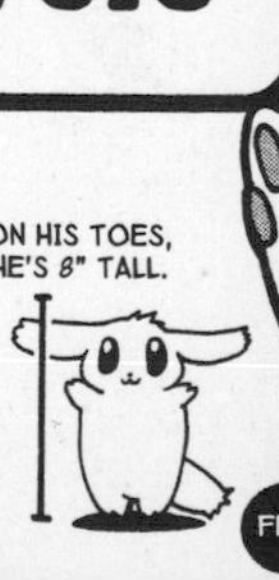
ON HIS TOES, HE'S 8" TALL.

HE LOVES:

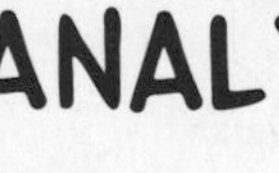
That's so sweet!

STRAWBERRIES, DAISUKE.

HE HATES:

WATER, LEARNING WORDS, HOLDING STILL.

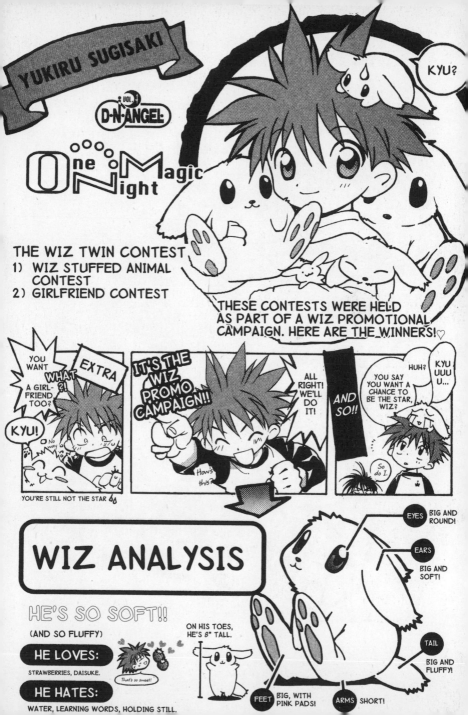

1 WIZ STUFFED ANIMAL CONTEST

AND THE WINNERS!

▼ MADE BY RUKA, FROM OKAYAMA.
"I THINK HE CAME OUT A LITTLE GOOFY IN A FEW PLACES. BUT IT'S THE CUTEST WIZ I COULD MAKE! SO I'M SATISFIED."

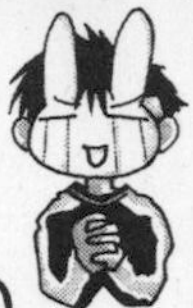

THE PROPORTIONS ARE FINE, AND IT'S SOOO ADORABLE! IT LOOKS LIKE IT WOULD BE AS SOFT AS THE REAL WIZ. I WANT TO HUG IT AND HUG IT! ♥

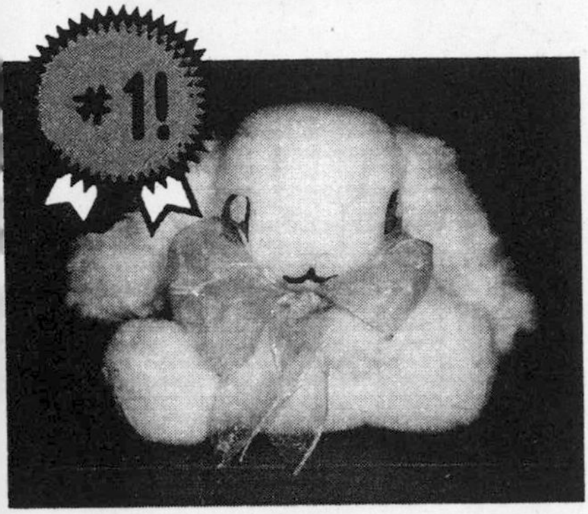
#1!

FINAL VERSION

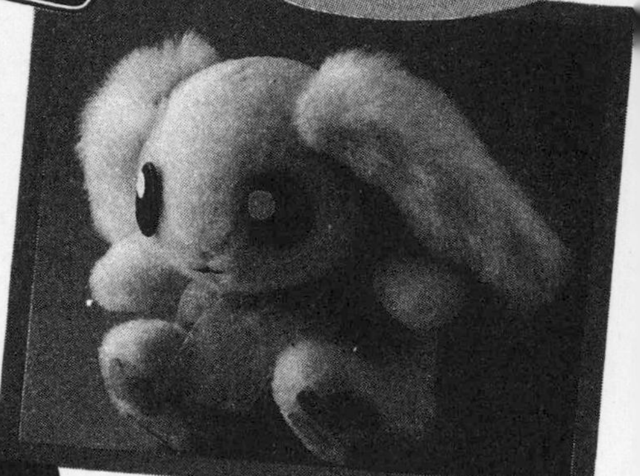

AND THIS IS THE OFFICIAL WIZ DOLL BEING PRODUCED, BASED ON RUKA'S WINNING DESIGN!!!

2 WIZ'S GIRLFRIEND CONTEST

AND THE WINNER IS: MARRON! ♥

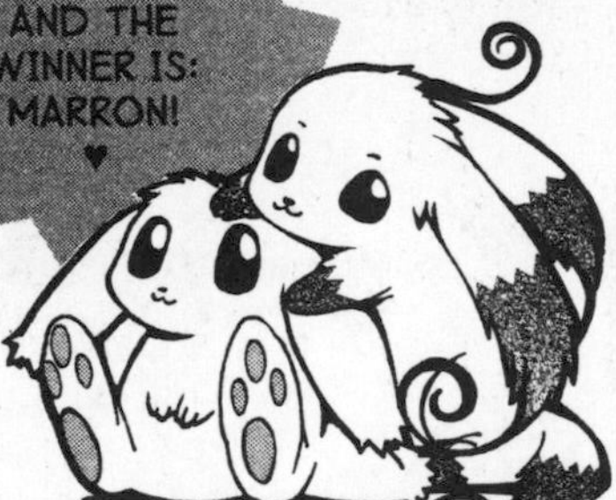

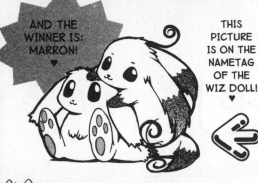

THIS PICTURE IS ON THE NAMETAG OF THE WIZ DOLL! ♥

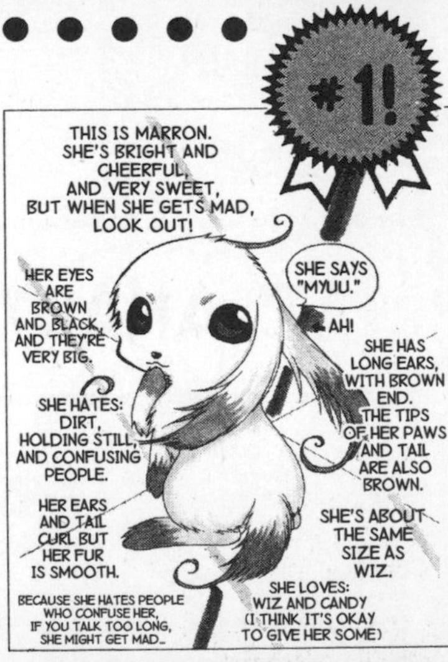
#1!
THIS IS MARRON. SHE'S BRIGHT AND CHEERFUL, AND VERY SWEET, BUT WHEN SHE GETS MAD, LOOK OUT!
HER EYES ARE BROWN AND BLACK, AND THEY'RE VERY BIG.
SHE SAYS "MYUU."
AH!
SHE HAS LONG EARS, WITH BROWN END. THE TIPS OF HER PAWS AND TAIL ARE ALSO BROWN.
SHE HATES: DIRT, HOLDING STILL, AND CONFUSING PEOPLE.
HER EARS AND TAIL CURL BUT HER FUR IS SMOOTH.
SHE'S ABOUT THE SAME SIZE AS WIZ.
BECAUSE SHE HATES PEOPLE WHO CONFUSE HER, IF YOU TALK TOO LONG, SHE MIGHT GET MAD...
SHE LOVES: WIZ AND CANDY (I THINK IT'S OKAY TO GIVE HER SOME)

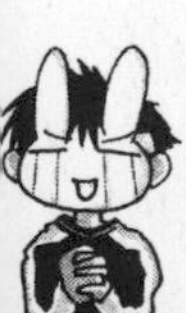

IT'S SO CUTE THAT HER EARS AND TAIL HAVE CURLS!! AND SHE'S BEAUTIFUL, TOO! WIZ IS SO HAPPY, HE'LL STAY WITH HER FOREVER! BUT HE MAKES A LOT OF NOISE SO SHE MIGHT GET MAD AT HIM...

BY EMIKO UEBAYASHI, FROM HYOUGO

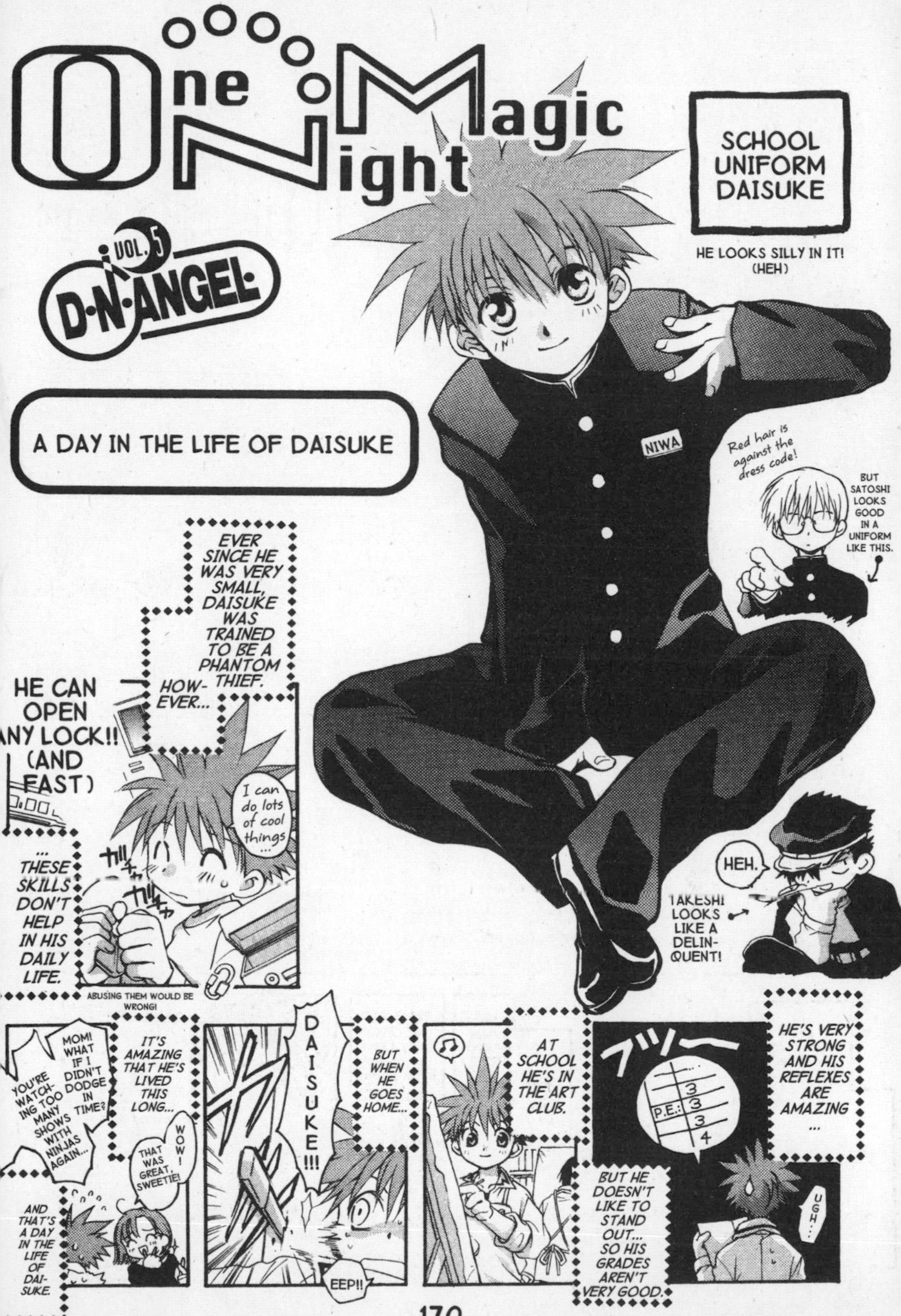
One Magic Night
VOL. 5
D·N·ANGEL
SCHOOL UNIFORM DAISUKE
HE LOOKS SILLY IN IT! (HEH)
NIWA
A DAY IN THE LIFE OF DAISUKE
Red hair is against the dress code!
BUT SATOSHI LOOKS GOOD IN A UNIFORM LIKE THIS.
HEH.
TAKESHI LOOKS LIKE A DELINQUENT!
EVER SINCE HE WAS VERY SMALL, DAISUKE WAS TRAINED TO BE A PHANTOM THIEF.
HOWEVER...
HE CAN OPEN ANY LOCK!! (AND FAST)
I can do lots of cool things...
...THESE SKILLS DON'T HELP IN HIS DAILY LIFE.
ABUSING THEM WOULD BE WRONG!
HE'S VERY STRONG AND HIS REFLEXES ARE AMAZING...
P.E.: 3 3 3 4
UGH...
BUT HE DOESN'T LIKE TO STAND OUT... SO HIS GRADES AREN'T VERY GOOD.
AT SCHOOL HE'S IN THE ART CLUB.
BUT WHEN HE GOES HOME...
DAISUKE!!!
EEP!!
IT'S AMAZING THAT HE'S LIVED THIS LONG...
WOW! THAT WAS GREAT, SWEETIE!
MOM! WHAT IF I DIDN'T DODGE IN TIME?
YOU'RE WATCHING TOO MANY SHOWS WITH NINJAS AGAIN...
AND THAT'S A DAY IN THE LIFE OF DAISUKE.

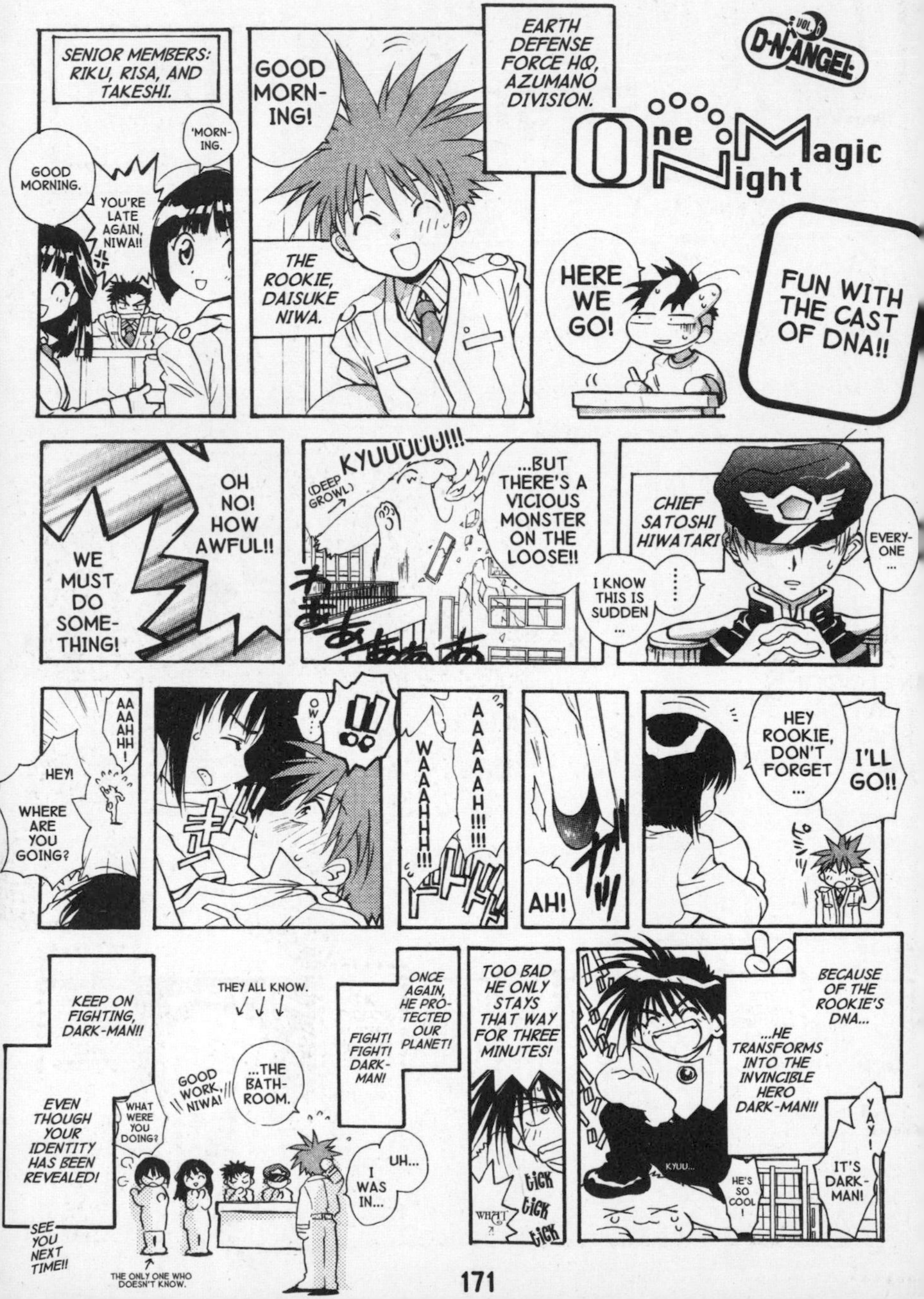
D·N·ANGEL VOL. 6
One Magic Night
HERE WE GO!
FUN WITH THE CAST OF DNA!!
EARTH DEFENSE FORCE HQ, AZUMANO DIVISION.
GOOD MORNING!
THE ROOKIE, DAISUKE NIWA.
SENIOR MEMBERS: RIKU, RISA, AND TAKESHI.
'MORNING.
GOOD MORNING.
YOU'RE LATE AGAIN, NIWA!!
CHIEF SATOSHI HIWATARI
EVERYONE...
......
I KNOW THIS IS SUDDEN...
...BUT THERE'S A VICIOUS MONSTER ON THE LOOSE!!
KYUUUUUU!!!
(DEEP GROWL)
OH NO! HOW AWFUL!!
WE MUST DO SOMETHING!
HEY ROOKIE, DON'T FORGET...
I'LL GO!!
AH!
AAAAAAH!!!!!!
WAAAAHHH!!!
OW...
!!
AAAAAHH!
HEY!
WHERE ARE YOU GOING?
BECAUSE OF THE ROOKIE'S DNA...
...HE TRANSFORMS INTO THE INVINCIBLE HERO DARK-MAN!!
YAY!
IT'S DARK-MAN!
HE'S SO COOL!
KYUU...
TOO BAD HE ONLY STAYS THAT WAY FOR THREE MINUTES!
tick
tick
tick
WHAT
ONCE AGAIN, HE PROTECTED OUR PLANET!
FIGHT! FIGHT! DARK-MAN!
THEY ALL KNOW.
...THE BATHROOM.
GOOD WORK, NIWA!
WHAT WERE YOU DOING?
UH...
I WAS IN...
KEEP ON FIGHTING, DARK-MAN!!
EVEN THOUGH YOUR IDENTITY HAS BEEN REVEALED!
SEE YOU NEXT TIME!!
THE ONLY ONE WHO DOESN'T KNOW.

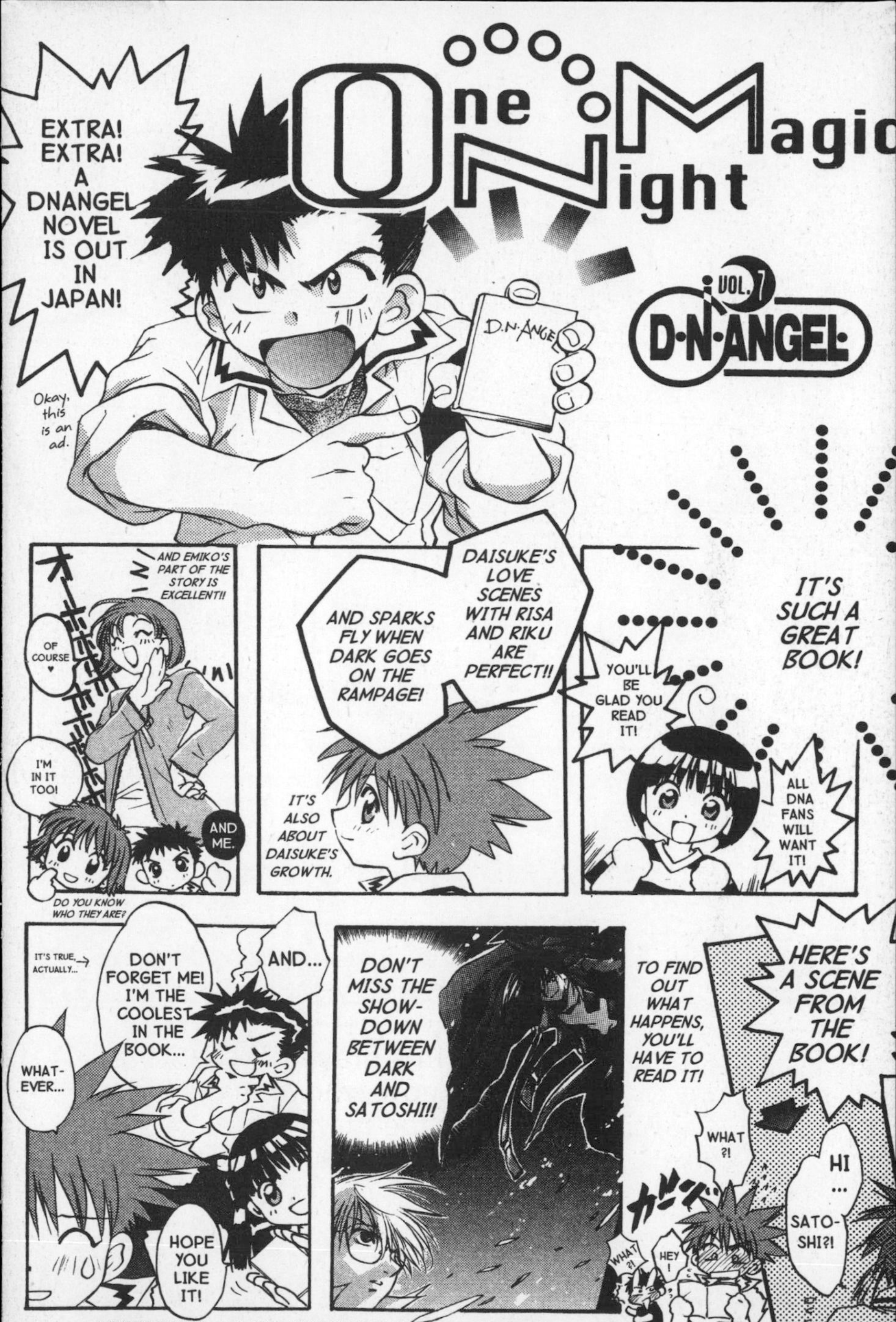
One Magic Night
VOL.7
D·N·ANGEL
EXTRA! EXTRA! A DNANGEL NOVEL IS OUT IN JAPAN!
D.N.ANGEL
Okay, this is an ad.
IT'S SUCH A GREAT BOOK!
YOU'LL BE GLAD YOU READ IT!
ALL DNA FANS WILL WANT IT!
DAISUKE'S LOVE SCENES WITH RISA AND RIKU ARE PERFECT!!
AND SPARKS FLY WHEN DARK GOES ON THE RAMPAGE!
IT'S ALSO ABOUT DAISUKE'S GROWTH.
AND EMIKO'S PART OF THE STORY IS EXCELLENT!!
OF COURSE ♥
I'M IN IT TOO!
AND ME.
DO YOU KNOW WHO THEY ARE?
HERE'S A SCENE FROM THE BOOK!
WHAT?!
HI ... SATO-SHI?!
HEY!
WHAT?!
TO FIND OUT WHAT HAPPENS, YOU'LL HAVE TO READ IT!
DON'T MISS THE SHOW-DOWN BETWEEN DARK AND SATOSHI!!
AND...
DON'T FORGET ME! I'M THE COOLEST IN THE BOOK...
IT'S TRUE, ACTUALLY...
WHAT-EVER...
HOPE YOU LIKE IT!

PUBLISHED IN JAPAN -- D.N. ANGEL: MERMAID'S TEAR, AND D.N.ANGEL: SNOW QUEEN.
WRITTEN BY JUNKO OKAZAKI. ORIGINAL STORY AND ILLUSTRATIONS BY YUKIRU SUGISAKI.

D·N·ANGEL

THINGS TO COME...

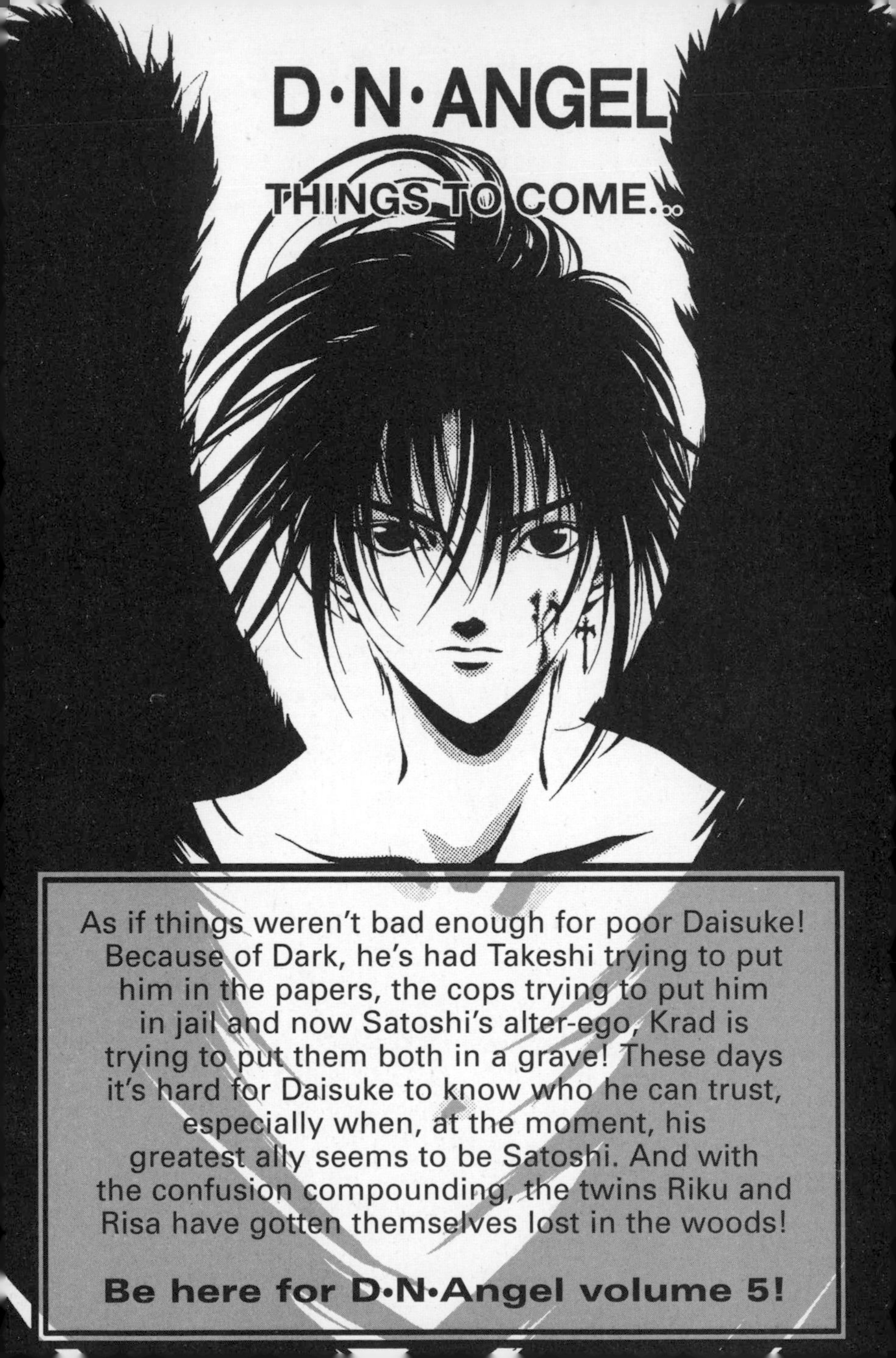

As if things weren't bad enough for poor Daisuke! Because of Dark, he's had Takeshi trying to put him in the papers, the cops trying to put him in jail and now Satoshi's alter-ego, Krad is trying to put them both in a grave! These days it's hard for Daisuke to know who he can trust, especially when, at the moment, his greatest ally seems to be Satoshi. And with the confusion compounding, the twins Riku and Risa have gotten themselves lost in the woods!

Be here for D·N·Angel volume 5!

ALSO AVAILABLE FROM ☺TOKYOPOP®

ALSO AVAILABLE FROM ☺TOKYOPOP®

MANGA

.HACK//LEGEND OF THE TWILIGHT
@LARGE
ABENOBASHI: MAGICAL SHOPPING ARCADE
A.I. LOVE YOU
AI YORI AOSHI
ANGELIC LAYER
ARM OF KANNON
BABY BIRTH
BATTLE ROYALE
BATTLE VIXENS
BOYS BE...
BRAIN POWERED
BRIGADOON
B'TX
CANDIDATE FOR GODDESS, THE
CARDCAPTOR SAKURA
CARDCAPTOR SAKURA - MASTER OF THE CLOW
CHOBITS
CHRONICLES OF THE CURSED SWORD
CLAMP SCHOOL DETECTIVES
CLOVER
COMIC PARTY
CONFIDENTIAL CONFESSIONS
CORRECTOR YUI
COWBOY BEBOP
COWBOY BEBOP: SHOOTING STAR
CRAZY LOVE STORY
CRESCENT MOON
CROSS
CULDCEPT
CYBORG 009
D•N•ANGEL
DEMON DIARY
DEMON ORORON, THE
DEUS VITAE
DIABOLO
DIGIMON
DIGIMON TAMERS
DIGIMON ZERO TWO
DOLL
DRAGON HUNTER
DRAGON KNIGHTS
DRAGON VOICE
DREAM SAGA
DUKLYON: CLAMP SCHOOL DEFENDERS
EERIE QUEERIE!
ERICA SAKURAZAWA: COLLECTED WORKS
ET CETERA
ETERNITY
EVIL'S RETURN
FAERIES' LANDING
FAKE
FLCL
FLOWER OF THE DEEP SLEEP, THE
FORBIDDEN DANCE
FRUITS BASKET

G GUNDAM
GATEKEEPERS
GETBACKERS
GIRL GOT GAME
GRAVITATION
GTO
GUNDAM SEED ASTRAY
GUNDAM WING
GUNDAM WING: BATTLEFIELD OF PACIFISTS
GUNDAM WING: ENDLESS WALTZ
GUNDAM WING: THE LAST OUTPOST (G-UNIT)
HANDS OFF!
HAPPY MANIA
HARLEM BEAT
HYPER RUNE
I.N.V.U.
IMMORTAL RAIN
INITIAL D
INSTANT TEEN: JUST ADD NUTS
ISLAND
JING: KING OF BANDITS
JING: KING OF BANDITS - TWILIGHT TALES
JULINE
KARE KANO
KILL ME, KISS ME
KINDAICHI CASE FILES, THE
KING OF HELL
KODOCHA: SANA'S STAGE
LAMENT OF THE LAMB
LEGAL DRUG
LEGEND OF CHUN HYANG, THE
LES BIJOUX
LOVE HINA
LOVE OR MONEY
LUPIN III
LUPIN III: WORLD'S MOST WANTED
MAGIC KNIGHT RAYEARTH I
MAGIC KNIGHT RAYEARTH II
MAHOROMATIC: AUTOMATIC MAIDEN
MAN OF MANY FACES
MARMALADE BOY
MARS
MARS: HORSE WITH NO NAME
MINK
MIRACLE GIRLS
MIYUKI-CHAN IN WONDERLAND
MODEL
MOURYOU KIDEN: LEGEND OF THE NYMPHS
NECK AND NECK
ONE
ONE I LOVE, THE
PARADISE KISS
PARASYTE
PASSION FRUIT
PEACH GIRL
PEACH GIRL: CHANGE OF HEART
PET SHOP OF HORRORS
PITA-TEN

07.15.04T

PITA-TEN™

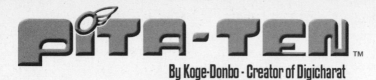

By Koge-Donbo - Creator of Digicharat

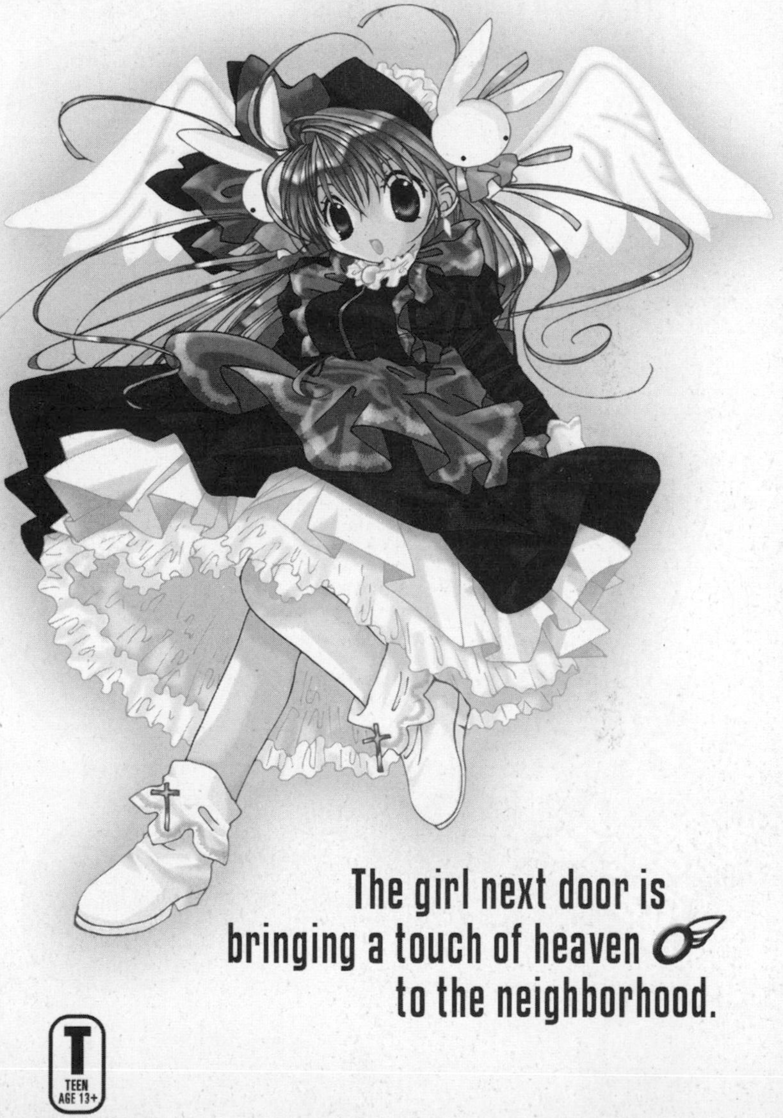

The girl next door is
bringing a touch of heaven
to the neighborhood.

T
TEEN
AGE 13+

LEGAL DRUG™

When no ordinary prescription will do...

FROM CLAMP
CREATORS OF
❃CHOBITS
❃TOKYO BABYLON

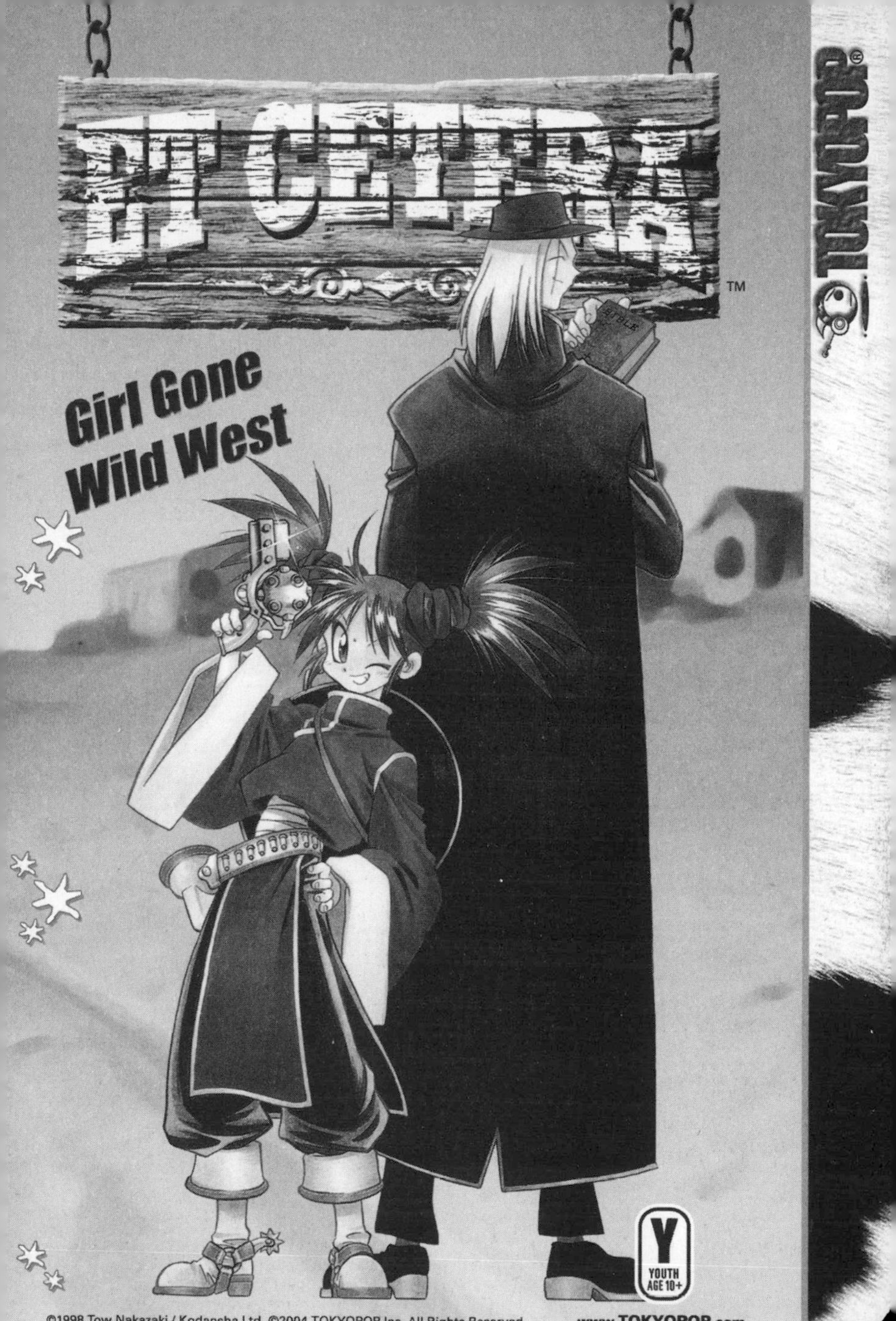
ET CETERA™
Girl Gone
Wild West
BIBLE
Y
YOUTH
AGE 10+
TOKYOPOP®

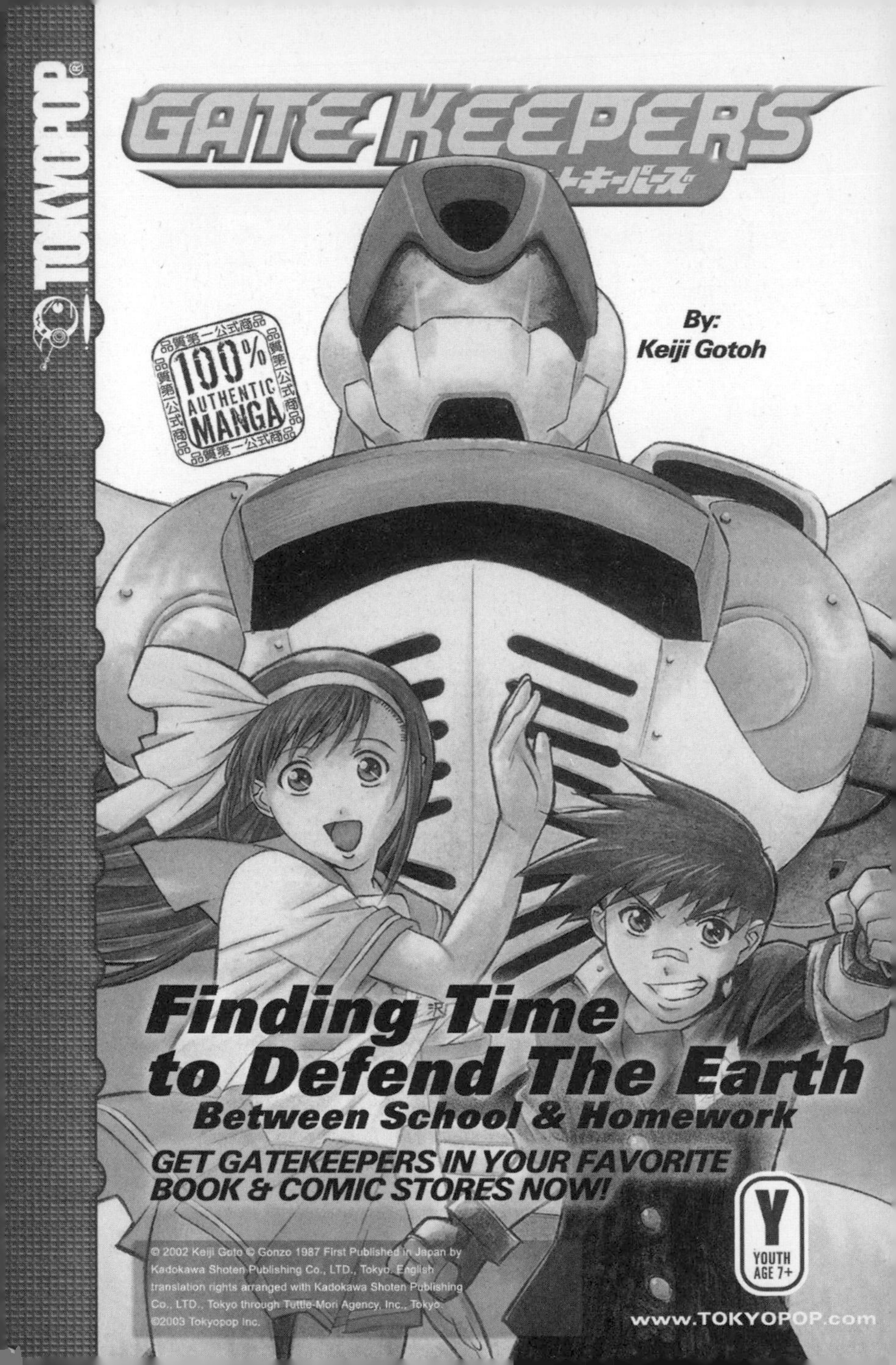
TOKYOPOP®
GATE KEEPERS
By:
Keiji Gotoh
100% AUTHENTIC MANGA
Finding Time
to Defend The Earth
Between School & Homework
GET GATEKEEPERS IN YOUR FAVORITE
BOOK & COMIC STORES NOW!
Y
YOUTH
AGE 7+
© 2002 Keiji Goto © Gonzo 1987 First Published in Japan by Kadokawa Shoten Publishing Co., LTD., Tokyo. English translation rights arranged with Kadokawa Shoten Publishing Co., LTD., Tokyo through Tuttle-Mori Agency, Inc., Tokyo. ©2003 Tokyopop Inc.
www.TOKYOPOP.com

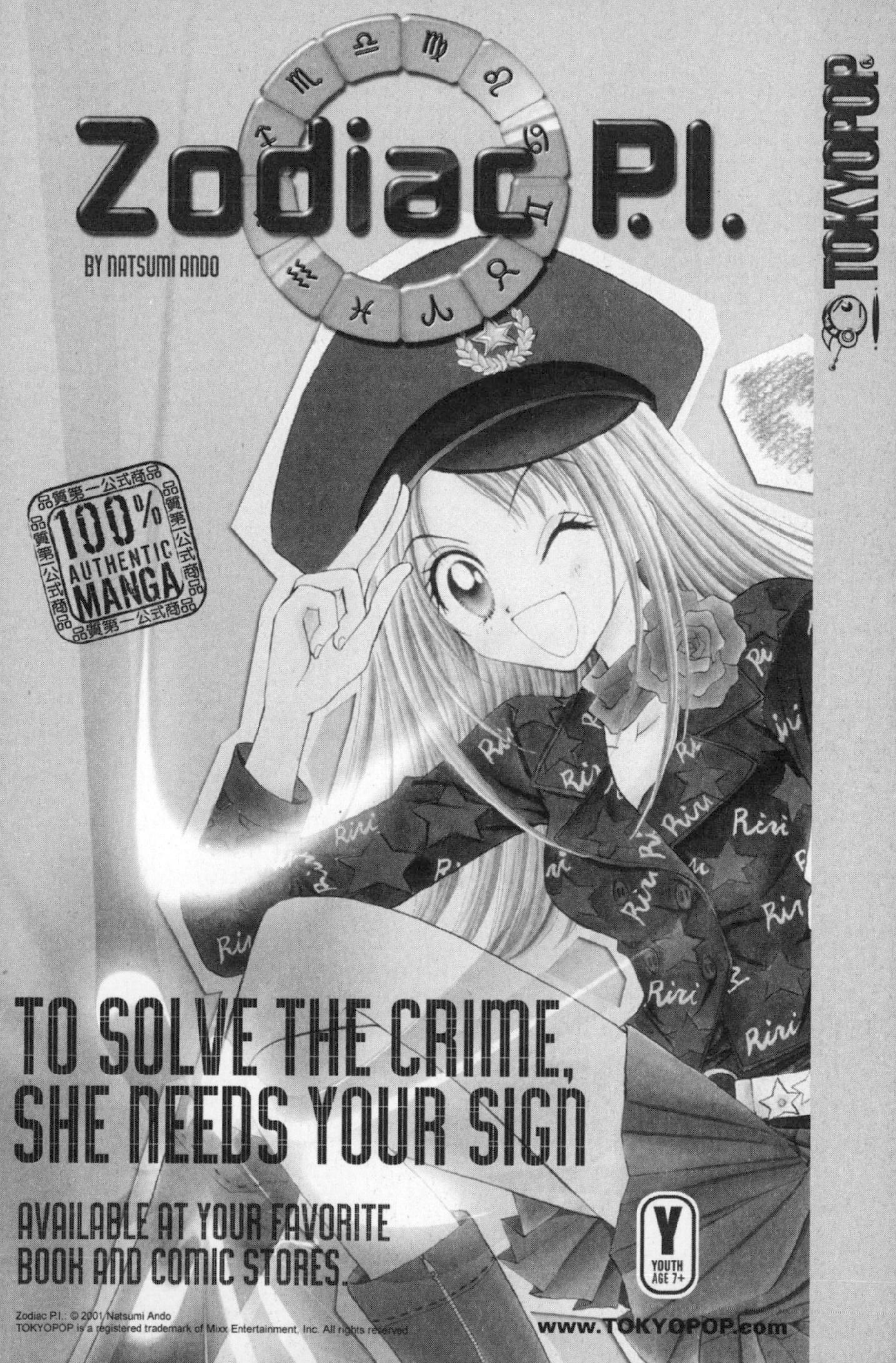
Zodiac P.I.
BY NATSUMI ANDO
TOKYOPOP
100% AUTHENTIC MANGA
品質第一公式商品
TO SOLVE THE CRIME, SHE NEEDS YOUR SIGN
AVAILABLE AT YOUR FAVORITE BOOK AND COMIC STORES.
Y YOUTH AGE 7+
Zodiac P.I.: © 2001 Natsumi Ando
TOKYOPOP is a registered trademark of Mixx Entertainment, Inc. All rights reserved
www.TOKYOPOP.com

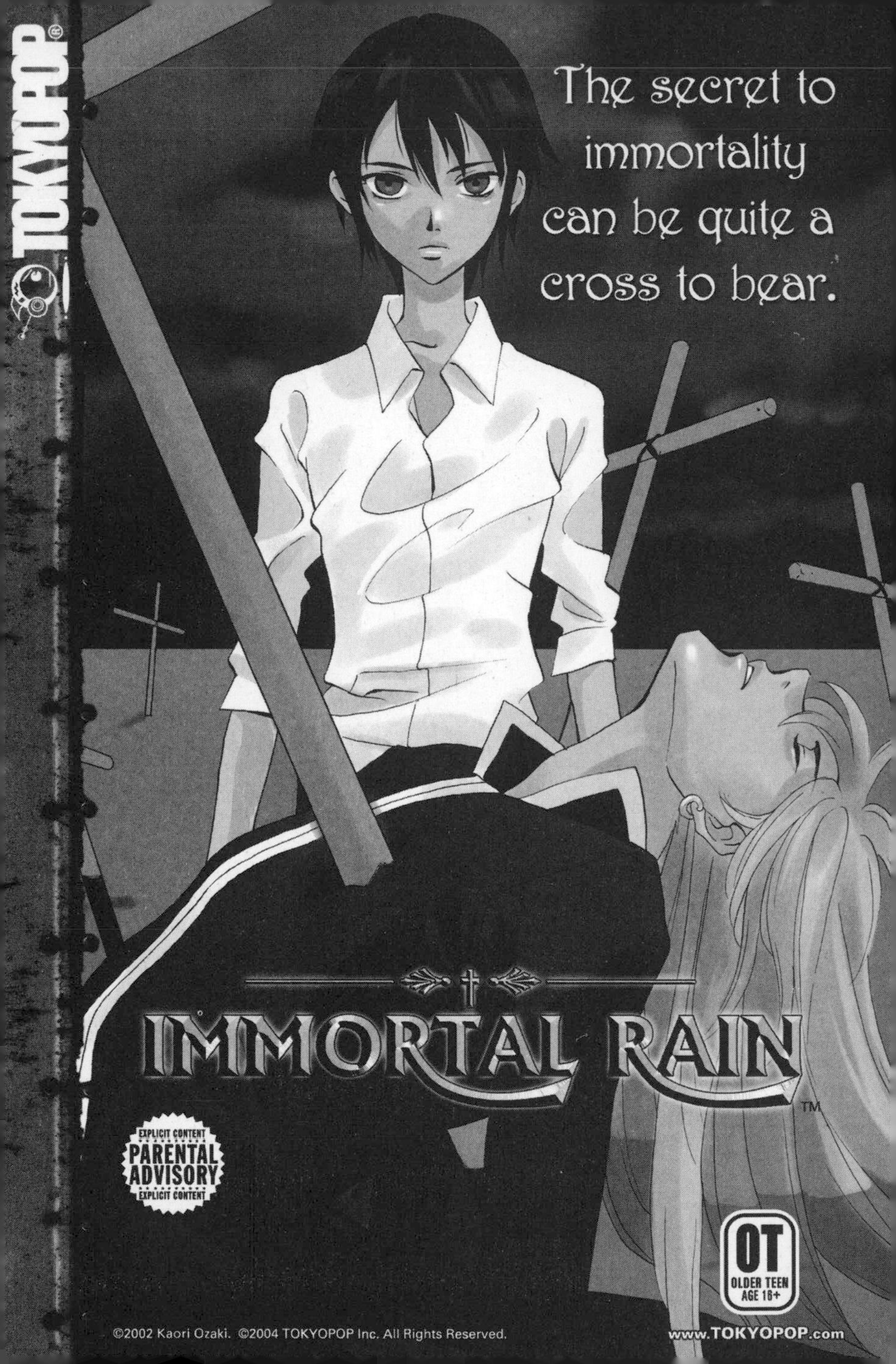
TOKYOPOP
The secret to immortality can be quite a cross to bear.
IMMORTAL RAIN™
EXPLICIT CONTENT
PARENTAL ADVISORY
EXPLICIT CONTENT
OT
OLDER TEEN
AGE 16+
©2002 Kaori Ozaki. ©2004 TOKYOPOP Inc. All Rights Reserved.
www.TOKYOPOP.com

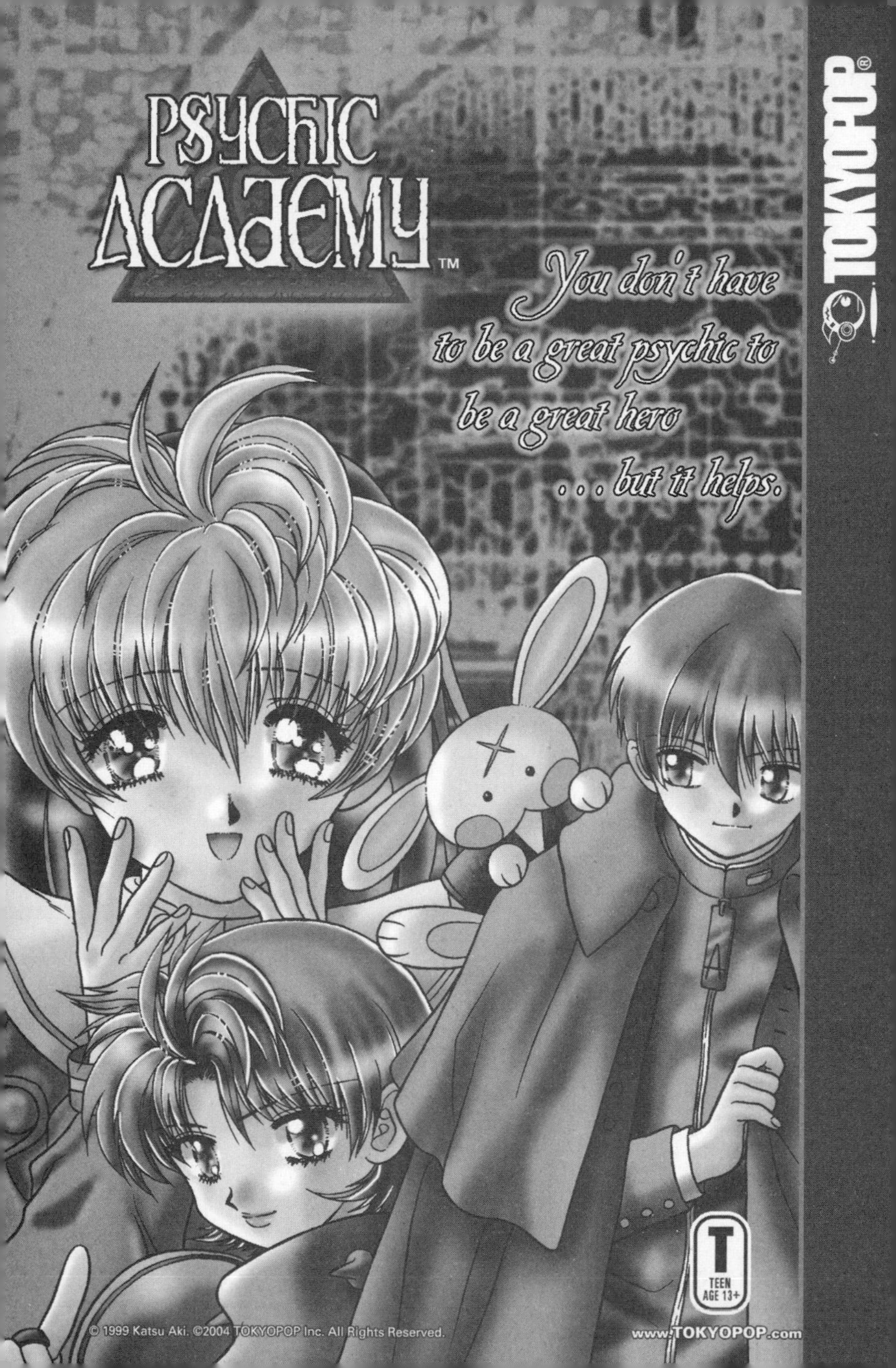
PSYCHIC ACADEMY™
You don't have to be a great psychic to be a great hero
. . . but it helps.
TOKYOPOP
T TEEN AGE 13+
© 1999 Katsu Aki. ©2004 TOKYOPOP Inc. All Rights Reserved.
www.TOKYOPOP.com

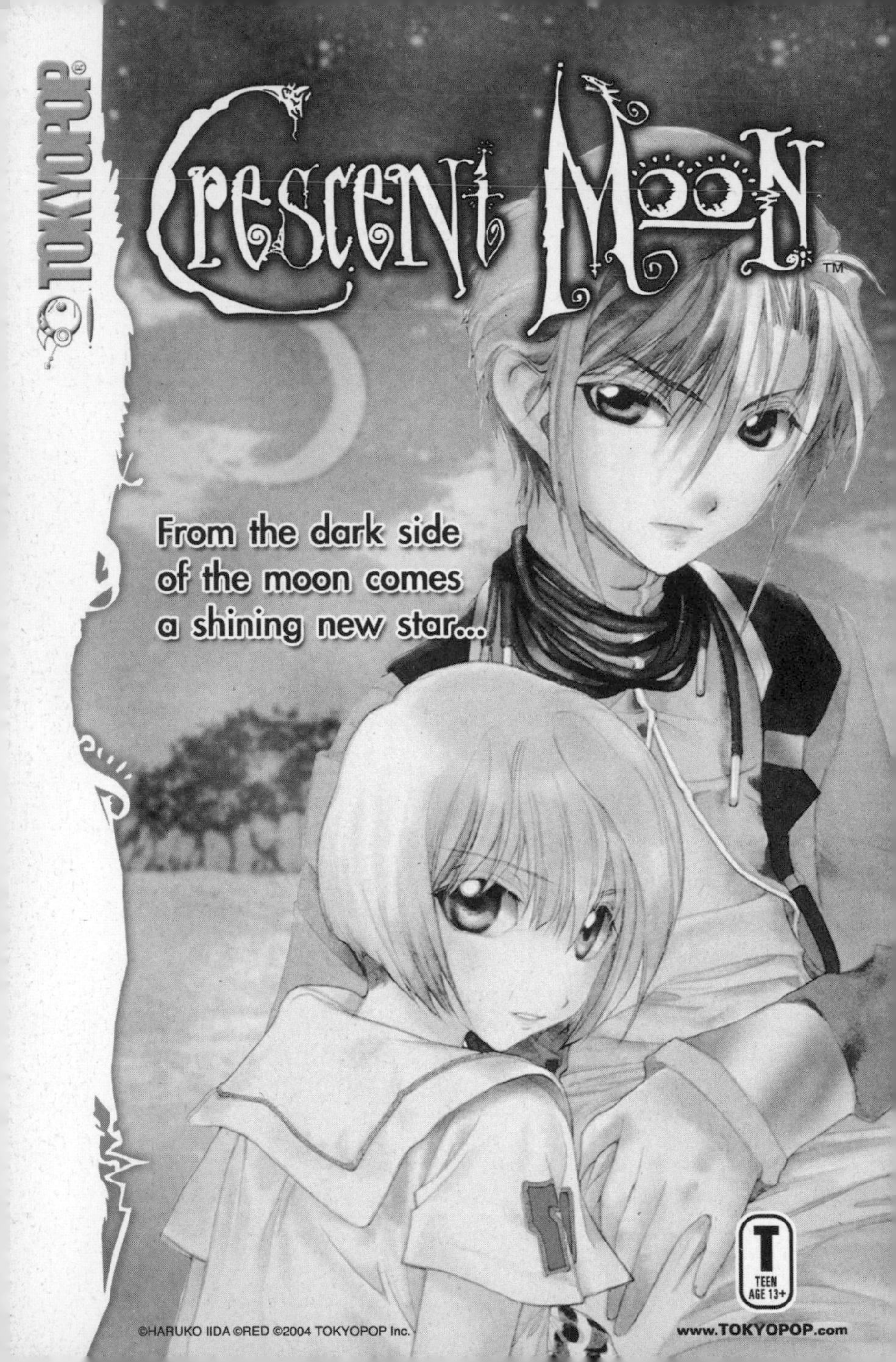
TOKYOPOP
Crescent Moon™
From the dark side of the moon comes a shining new star...
T
TEEN AGE 13+
©HARUKO IIDA ©RED ©2004 TOKYOPOP Inc.
www.TOKYOPOP.com

STOP!

This is the back of the book.
You wouldn't want to spoil a great ending!

This book is printed "manga-style," in the authentic Japanese right-to-left format. Since none of the artwork has been flipped or altered, readers get to experience the story just as the creator intended. You've been asking for it, so TOKYOPOP® delivered: authentic, hot-off-the-press, and far more fun!

DIRECTIONS

If this is your first time reading manga-style, here's a quick guide to help you understand how it works.

It's easy... just start in the top right panel and follow the numbers. Have fun, and look for more 100% authentic manga from TOKYOPOP®!